Breaking the Chains
Labour in South Africa in the 1970s and 1980s

Breaking the Chains

Labour in South Africa in the 1970s and 1980s

Gerald Kraak

WITHDRAWN

Pluto Press
LONDON • BOULDER, COLORADO

First published 1993 by Pluto Press
345 Archway Road, London N6 5AA
and 5500 Central Avenue
Boulder, Colorado 80301, USA

Copyright © 1993 Gerald Kraak

The right of Gerald Kraak to be identified as the author of this work has been asserted by him in accordance with the Copyright, Designs and Patents Act 1988.

British Library Cataloguing in Publication Data
A catalogue record for this book is available from the British Library

ISBN   0-7453-0705-1 hbk
        0-7453-0706-X pbk

Library of Congress Cataloging in Publication Data
Kraak, Gerald.
    Breaking the chains : labour in South Africa in the 1970s and 1980s / Gerald Kraak.
        p. cm.
    Includes bibliographical referneces and index.
    ISBN 0-7453-0705-1   0-7453-0706-X pbk.
    1. Labor movement–South Africa–History–20th century. 2. Trade-unions–South Africa–History–20th century. 3. Working class--South Africa–Political activity–History–20th century.
    4. Apartheid–South Africa–History.   I. Title.
    HD8801.K73 1993
    331.88'0968'09047–dc20   93-27896
                                                                       CIP

Designed and Produced for Pluto Press by
Chase Production Services, Chipping Norton
Typeset from author's disks by
Stanford DTP Services, Milton Keynes
Printed in the EC by TJ Press, Padstow

Contents

Maps, tables and charts   vii
Acknowledgements   ix
Acronyms and abbreviations   x
Preface   xvi

Historical introduction   xxv
   Legacy of oppression

Part I
1 The labour market
      Influx control   3
      Impact of controls   12
      Restructuring   13

Part II
2 In the countryside
      Tied to the land – workers on the farms   29
      In the bantustans   41
      Rural resistance   45

3 In the towns and cities
      Housing   51
      Getting to work   59
      Wages, cost of living and unemployment   63
      Shopfloor relations and working conditions   77

4 At the mines
      Basic conditions   91
      Accommodation   100
      Struggles at the mines   102

Part III
5 Industrial law
- Restructuring — 113
- Bantustans — 125

6 The struggle for the right to organise
- Chronological overview — 127
- Struggles over registration and recognition — 136
- Struggles against official bargaining machinery — 148
- Rolling back employer and government controls — 158
- New tactics, new trends — 166

7 Trade unions
- The established trade union movement — 174
- Rise of the independent unions — 180
- Unions formed between 1973 and 1976 — 183
- Unions formed after 1976 — 190
- The quest for unity — 194

Part IV
8 Resistance to apartheid
- Workplace and community — 209
- Union responses — 219
- New tactics under the state of emergency — 227
- Political struggle — 240
- Conclusion — 247

Postscript — 249
Appendix Growth of Membership of trade unions affiliated to COSATU and NACTU, 1980–1986 — 252
Notes and references — 260
Bibliography — 281
Index — 297

Maps, tables and graphs

Maps

Map 1.1:	Provinces, major towns and bantustans	20
Map 1.2:	Decentralisation strategy	22

Tables

Table 0.1(a):	Employment of the economically active population by sector and group, 1985	xx
Table 0.1(b):	Employment of the black economically active population in the 'independent' bantustans, 1980	xxi
Table 0.2:	Employment of whites, Coloureds and Africans by sex and industrial branch, 1985	xxii
Table 1.1:	The distribution of the African population of South Africa by region, 1960–1980	7
Table 1.2(a):	The impact of population controls on the economically active black workforce, 1980	8
Table 1.2(b):	The number of contract workers and commuters employed in the South African workforce, 1985	9
Table 2.1:	Farm wages in cash and kind, per region, 1980	37
Table 3.1:	Average monthly earnings by group in the main sectors of the economy, 1974–1984 (in rands)	75
Table 3.2:	Reduction in employment for selected economic sectors, 1981–1985	75
Table 3.3:	Occupational breakdown of the economically active population by race and sex, 1985	80
Table 3.4:	Maximum work hours in Wage Determinations and Industrial Council agreements current in 1984	86
Table 6.1:	Number of strikes and stoppages per year, 1970–1987	129
Table 6.2:	Reasons for strikes, 1980–1986	130
Table 7.1:	Profile of the independent trade union movement, post mergers, 1988	202
Table 8.1:	Responses to calls for stay-aways and on-site stoppages, 1982–1987	232

Graphs

Graph 3.1: Hourly wages (rands) set by Industrial Councils for labourers in selected sectors and regions current in June 1986, compared to regional Household Supplemented Living Levels (HSLLs)   66

Graph 3.2: Hourly wages (rands) set by Wage Boards for labourers in selected sectors and regions current in June 1986, compared to the average Household Supplemented Living Level (HSLL) of R1.96   68

Acknowledgements

This book could not have been published without a generous subsidy from the International Labour Organisation in Geneva, Switzerland.

Anita Campbell, Iris Crane, Avis Hart and Tanya Joseph spent many hours typing and retyping drafts of the manuscript. My special thanks to them for their effort, warmth and humour.

I am indebted to Jane Barrett for her detailed comments and encouragement.

Thanks are also due to Adrian Harper for his help in producing the tables, to the staff of the Research Department at the International Defence and Aid Fund (IDAF) for their assistance with research and to Ian Kerkhof, Auret van Heerden, Norman Levy, and Elaine Unterhalter for their help, encouragement and advice.

All maps in this publication are reproduced with the permission of IDAF.

Finally, my gratitude to Giulietta Fafak for producing the graphs.

Acronyms and abbreviations

ACTWUSA	Amalgamated Clothing and Textile Workers Union of South Africa
AFCWU	African Food and Canning Workers Union
AFRA	Association for Rural Advancement
AGRICOR	Agricultural Development Corporation (Bophuthatswana)
AMWU	African Mine Workers Union
ANC	African National Congress
AZACTU	Azanian Congress of Trade Unions
AZAPO	Azanian People's Organisation
AZASO	Azanian Students' Organisation
BAMCWU	Black Allied Mining and Construction Workers Union
BAMTWU	Black Allied Mining and Tunnel Workers Union
BAWU	Black Allied Workers Union
BCAWU	Building, Construction and Allied Workers Union
BLAGWU	Black Allied and General Workers Union
BMWU	Black Municipal Workers' Union
BRICKAWU	Brick and Allied Workers Union
BTR	British Tyre and Rubber
CAHAC	Cape Housing Action Committee
CAWU	Construction and Allied Workers Union
CCAWUSA	Commercial Catering and Allied Workers Union
CGWU	Chemical and General Workers Union
CLOWU	Clothing Workers Union
CNETU	Council of Non-European Trade Unions
CNIP	Ciskei National Independence Party
COSAS	Congress of South African Students
COSATU	Congress of South African Trade Unions
CSIR	Council for Scientific and Industrial Research

Acronyms and Abbreviations

CTC	Ciskei Transport Corporation
CTMWA	Cape Town Municipal Workers Association
CUSA	Council of Unions of South Africa
CWIU	Chemical Workers Industrial Union
DET	Department of Education and Training
DHAC	Durban Housing Action Committee
DWA	Domestic Workers Association
DWEP	Domestic Workers Education Project
EAWTU	Electrical and Allied Workers Trade Union
EPSF&AWU	Eastern Province Sweet, Food and Allied Workers Union
ERAPO	East Rand People's Organisation
FAWU	Food and Allied Workers Union
FBWU	Food and Beverage Workers Union
FCWU	Food and Canning Workers Union
FEDCRAW	Federal Council of Retail and Allied Workers
FEDSAW	Federation of South African Women
FOSATU	Federation of South African Trade Unions
GAWU	Garment and Allied Workers Union *or* General and Allied Workers Union *or* Glass and Allied Workers Union
GDP	Gross Domestic Product
GM	General Motors
GWIU	Garment Workers Industrial Union
GWU	General Workers Union
GWUSA	General Workers Union of South Africa
HARWU	Hotel and Restaurant Workers Union
HSL	Household Subsistence Level
HSLL	Household Supplemented Living Level
IAWUSA	Insurance and Allied Workers Union of South Africa
ICU	Industrial and Commercial Workers Union
IMF	International Metal Federation
ISCOR	Iron and Steel Corporation

LRAA	Labour Relations Amendment Act
MACWUSA	Motor Assembly and Components Workers Union of South Africa
MAWU	Metal and Allied Workers Union
MGWUSA	Municipal and General Workers Union of South Africa
MICWU	Motor Industries Combined Workers Union
MWASA	Media Workers Association of South Africa
MWU	Mine Workers Union
MWUSA	Municipal Workers Union of South Africa
NAAWU	National Automobile and Allied Workers Union
NACTU	National Council of Trade Unions
NAFCOC	National African Federated Chamber of Commerce
NECC	National Education Crisis Committee
NEHAWU	National Education, Health and Allied Workers Union
NICISEMI	National Industrial Council for the Iron, Steel, Engineering and Metallurgical Industry
NUDAW	National Union of Distributive and Allied Workers
NUFW	National Union of Furniture Workers
NUM	National Union of Mineworkers
NUMARWOSA	National Union of Motor Assembly and Rubber Workers of South Africa
NUMSA	National Union of Metalworkers of South Africa
NUTW	National Union of Textile Workers
OVGWU	Orange Vaal General Workers Union
PEBCO	Port Elizabeth Black Civic Organisation
PEYCO	Port Elizabeth Youth Congress
POTWA	Post and Telecommunications Workers Association
PPAWU	Paper, Printing and Allied Workers Union
PUTCO	Public Utility Transport Corporation
PWAWU	Paper, Wood and Allied Workers Union
PWV	Pretoria-Witwatersrand-Vaal

RAWU	Retail and Allied Workers Union
RSC	Regional Service Council
SAAWU	South African Allied Workers Union
SABMAWU	South African Black Municipal and Allied Workers Union
SABS	South African Boilermakers' Society
SACC	South African Council of Churches
SACLA	South African Confederation of Labour
SACOS	South African Council of Sport
SACTU	South African Congress of Trade Unions
SACWU	South African Chemical Workers Union
SADF	South African Defence Force
SADWA	South African Domestic Workers Association
SADWU	South African Domestic Workers Union
SAISWA	South African Iron and Steel Workers Association
SALDRU	South African Labour and Development Research Unit
SAMWU	South African Mine Workers Union *or* South African Municipal Workers Union
SARHWU	South African Railway and Harbour Workers Union
SASOL	South African Coal, Oil and Gas Corporation
SAT & LC	South African Trades and Labour Council
SATAWU	South African Textile and Allied Workers Union
SATS	South African Transport Services
SATV	South African Television
SCA	Soweto Civic Association
SEIFSA	Steel and Engineering Industries Federation of South Africa
SFAWU	Sweet, Food and Allied Workers Union
TAWU	Textile and Allied Workers Union *or* Transport and Allied Workers Union
TBVC	Transkei, Bophuthatswana, Venda and Ciskei
TEBA	Employment Bureau of Africa
TGWU	Transport and General Workers Union
TTT	Trans-Tugela Transport company
TUACC	Trade Union Advisory and Coordinating Council
TUCSA	Trade Unions Council of South Africa
TWIU	Textile Workers Industrial Union

UAW	Union of Automobile Workers
UBCO	Uitenhage Black Civic Organisation
UDF	United Democratic Front
UIF	Unemployment Insurance Fund
UMMAWUSA	United Metal, Mining and Allied Workers Union of South Africa
UWUSA	United Workers Union of South Africa
WCACC	Western Cape African Chamber of Commerce
WCC	Workmen's Compensation Commissioner
WCTA	Western Cape Traders Association
WPGWU	Western Province General Workers Union
WPMAWU	Western Province Motor Assembly Workers Union

Our people spend their lives in the dark pits of the mines, the inside of factories and working long hours in the sun on the farms. We made South Africa rich. We built the roads, the cars, the clothes we wear, the shops, houses, factories and food we eat.

But in South Africa millions of workers and their families live in poverty, hunger and starvation. Our lives and families are broken by the pass laws and migrant labour, we live in matchbox houses with no families. Our children are given a slave education which condemns them to the factories and mines, while a minority live in wealth so great that they are amongst the richest in the world. Their wealth is made through the blood, sweat and toil of the working class.

... [W]e must challenge this domination. Our demands are clear. We want our freedom from apartheid and the cheap wage system. We must mobilise and build organisations everywhere in the factories, farms, mines, schools, townships and rural areas.

... [T]he working class must play a leading role in the struggle for freedom. We must involve ourselves in all spheres of struggle.

... [W]e urge all worker leaders ... and all patriots in South Africa to work together, plan and co-ordinate our actions to win our freedom and break the chains of poverty and cheap labour which bind the majority of people in South Africa today.

(May Day Message, 1986
Elijah Barayi, president of the Congress
of South African Trade Unions)

Preface

This book is intended as a text book on labour in South Africa in the 1970s and 1980s. It is not the first to deal with recent labour history. Steven Friedman's *Building Tomorrow Today: African Workers in Trade Unions 1970–1984*, (Ravan, 1987) and Jeremy Baskin's *Striking Back: A History of COSATU* (Ravan, 1991), are vivid and detailed union histories written from committed points of view. There is also a wealth of material in journals and related publications. The object of this study is modest: to draw together for the first time the data dispersed among several contemporary publications and studies into a single text. In particular it situates recent trade union history within an analysis of the prevailing legal, social and economic conditions, largely absent from other texts. It also tries to provide a dispassionate account of the relationship between the unions and the political organisations which opposed the apartheid state in the second half of the 1980s. It is hoped that this work will serve as a prior reference for students of Southern African studies, social history and related disciplines.

The research and writing of this book was completed before the momentous reforms of 1990 which brought into prospect a negotiated end to apartheid. Most of the work was done while I was employed as a researcher at the International Defence and Aid Fund (IDAF) and its purpose – in keeping with the aims of IDAF – was to inform and raise support for the international campaign against apartheid. It is therefore an unashamedly partisan account written from a position of broad sympathy with the liberation movement. It gives primacy to resistance as the major factor forcing the state to concede reform. It also reflects the concerns of the international anti-apartheid campaign in the period in which it was written. These were firstly to convey the conditions of the 1970s and 1980s, and how they were shaped by apartheid's social engineering, and secondly to analyse the period in terms of its domination by the polarities of repression and resistance.

The reforms of 1990 have inevitably altered the perspectives of historians. Students writing today would attempt to relate the events of the 1970s and 1980s more closely to the reforms of the 1990s; to seek in them the seeds of the changes which have now occurred. They would appraise the strategies of the state, business, political organisations and the trade union movement, and the complex interplay between them in bringing about reform. They would also seek, with the prospect of a majority government in view and in the context of the emerging debate about the autonomy of the trade union movement, to subject the past relationships between unions and the liberation movement to much more critical scrutiny than occurs here. A conclusive account of the period remains to be written. It is hoped that the empirical data collected here will usefully inform future work.

In the 1970s and 1980s trade unionism and political resistance to white minority rule revived after almost two decades of quiescence in which the policy of apartheid was consolidated. The challenge to employers and the state from the shopfloor and the streets of the townships was a primary factor forcing the government to abandon repression and concede the principle of majority rule in the early 1990s.

Rising industrial and political militancy in the 1970s, a shortage of white skilled labour, and international disinvestment campaigns, forced the state to lift many restrictions on the rights of African workers to organise on the shopfloor.

The reforms were partial. Excluded from their scope were the million and a half workers on farms, those employed as domestic servants and the millions working in the bantustans. However, workers in manufacturing, and later those in mining, took advantage of the changes to revive the trade union movement. Increasingly confident, they struck out in a wave of industrial militancy in the early 1980s to win higher wages, improve shopfloor conditions and build trade unions in South Africa's mines and industries. Black workers pushed back state and employer controls in the workplace, which had kept them in conditions of near servitude since the beginning of industrialisation.

Changes in the labour relations structure were not matched by political reforms. Although the regime restructured the constitution, bringing sections of the Coloured and Indian communities into a segregated tricameral parliament, the African majority continued to be excluded from political structures above the level of local councils or bantustans.

The government's attempts to impose this political system coincided with mass mobilisation over rising rents, conditions in schools and other issues arising out of the impact of apartheid on the lives of black people. In September 1984 demonstrations and protests turned into a sustained and widespread uprising against the apartheid system. Scarcely any town, village or rural area was left untouched. Only the occupation of townships by troops and the imposition of emergency rule allowed the government to retain control. In the years which followed thousands died, were detained or were forced underground.

The trade union movement was deeply affected by these developments, moving from the shopfloor to take its organised strength beyond the factory gates into campaigns such as worker stay-aways, consumer and rent boycotts, initially in alliance with political organisations. But as political activists were detained, murdered by right-wing vigilantes and hit-squads, or forced underground, and as the activities of political organisations were restricted under the State of Emergency, the trade union movement took up their fight.

By 1987 the state had begun to take measures against the trade union movement itself – before this, because of its place in the labour relations structure, it had enjoyed some protection from the more wide-ranging repression meted out to the national political organisations. New legislation modified the bargaining machinery in order to claim back much that the unions had won on the shopfloor. In February 1988, when 17 anti-apartheid organisations were effectively banned under State of Emergency regulations, the largest trade union federation representing black workers, the Congress of South African Trade Unions (COSATU), was prohibited from carrying out any political activity.

As the 1980s ended the trade unions stood, as they had at the beginning of the decade, at a crossroads. Then the unions faced the challenge of building and uniting isolated and scattered factory committees into a national movement able to confront employers (and, more challenging still, the state). At the end of the decade, with a presence in every major sector, the unions faced the equally awesome challenge of defending their hard-won gains, consolidating their strength and taking forward the struggle they had helped to shape.

Notes
Structure of the book
The first part of this book explains how the policies of apartheid were used to direct and allocate labour in ways that worked to the benefit of employers and against the interest of black workers, particularly African workers. The process of the restructuring of controls in the 1980s, examined in detail, is placed in the historical context of controls which created three distinct sets of conditions for workers: in agriculture, in mining and in the rest of the urban-based economy. Part II describes

Preface

the conditions in these three sectors, showing in each case how the apartheid system as a whole conditioned the relations between worker and employer. Part III focuses on workers' organisation and the action of workers to change their conditions of work, while Part IV deals with the role of workers in the struggle to bring an end to apartheid.

Time-frame
Events moved rapidly in South Africa at the end of the 1980s and the shift to a post-apartheid dispensation (made concrete with the reforms of 2 February 1990) was already discernable as the decade closed. Some of the legislation which shaped the structure of the labour force in the previous 42 years was already being dismantled and this process accelerated in the early 1990s. This transition and the revised strategy of the state adopted in the 1990s is not the subject of this book, as has already been pointed out. In providing for a cohesive account true to the conditions and climate of the pre-transition era, the cut-off point used in this book is 1988 except where accuracy and context demand dealing with later developments.

Note on the distribution of the workforce
Accurate discussion of the distribution of the South African workforce is complicated by the way in which the country has been divided by apartheid. The central government conducts a population census every five years but this excludes those bantustans deemed to be 'independent' (Transkei, Bophuthatswana, Ciskei and Venda). In each of these areas the authorities collect separate statistics, at different times. Obtaining comparable statistics for the workforce nationally is therefore difficult. The analysis below, based on the 1985 census, excludes the relatively small number of workers formally employed in the four 'independent' bantustans which are generally too impoverished to sustain independent economic activity aside from limited subsistence agriculture. (For a detailed breakdown of employment in Transkei, Bophuthatswana, Venda and Ciskei, see Table 0.1(b).)

Most South African workers are black. In 1985 white workers made up just over a fifth of the labour force. Through their privileged access to political power and the job market they have come to constitute the managerial, supervisory and skilled strata of the workforce (see Table 0.1(a)). Africans, the majority of black workers, made up just under two-thirds of the economically active workforce outside the 'independent' bantustans. Most are employed in the industrial conurbation of Pretoria, Witwatersrand and the Vaal Triangle (PWV) (see Tables 0.1(a) and 1.2(a)).

Table 0.1(a) Employment of the economically active population by sector and group, 1985

Economic sector	White	Coloured	Asian	African	Total
Agriculture/Forestry	88,656	177,631	5,608	907,695	1,179,590
Mining/Quarrying	87,905	11,569	1,658	641,933	743,065
Manufacture	361,604	249,911	96,625	671,378	1,379,518
Electricity/Gas/Water	32,887	7,573	570	51,690	92,720
Construction	104,519	107,266	13,659	330,895	556,339
Commerce/Catering/Accommodation	303,796	129,005	70,148	438,927	941,876
Transport/Communications	181,962	41,898	13,734	180,562	418,156
Finance/Insurance/Real estate	240,126	24,292	12,938	61,848	339,204
Community, social and personal services	506,642	235,364	39,246	1,183,788	1,965,040
Not classifiable	64,681	137,484	38,488	836,202	1,076,855
Totals	1,972,778	1,121,993	292,674	5,304,918	8,692,363

Note: excludes the independent bantustans.
Source: South Africa 1987, Table 21.

In this study the black working population is taken to include Coloured and Indian workers; they are only referred to as separate groups where this is necessary in order to describe the apartheid system.

Coloured and Indian workers constitute 16 per cent of the workforce. In two urban areas they form large proportions of the working class population. In Cape Town Coloured workers make up three-quarters of black workers and in the Durban area Indian workers constitute just over a third (see Table 1.2(a)). The situation of Coloured and Indian workers in the 1970s and 1980s, like that of African workers, was determined by a continuing history of political oppression. Although not subject to the same controls on movement as Africans, the Coloured and Indian communities were forced to live and trade in segregated residential areas, had only highly restricted access to agricultural land and were also subjected to the discriminatory practices of apartheid. Some had access to skilled jobs vacated by whites, but most still worked in unskilled and semi-skilled jobs (see Table 3.3). Their living standards, wages and working conditions were not very different to those of African workers outside the bantustans.

Table 0.1(b) Employment of the black economically active population in the 'independent' bantustans, 1980

	Transkei	Bophuthatswana	Venda	Ciskei
Industrial group				
Agriculture	420,238	157,121	50,480	11,540
Mining	20,974	32,878	216	1,480
Manufacturing	7,824	20,055	578	28,040
Electricity	1,043	1,165	50	580
Construction	15,198	21,825	1,315	4,640
Commerce	11,355	22,612	1,289	14,040
Transport	3,579	7,439	568	4,900
Financing	1,076	1,234	32	900
Services	49,016	52,295	3,813	31,760
Unspecified and unemployed	23,486	16,576	1,209	38,340
Total economically active	553,789	333,200	59,550	136,220

Source: BENSO 1983, Part II, Table 7.

The principal sectors of the South African economy are agriculture, mining and manufacturing. Agriculture, with the lowest wages and worst working conditions, involved more workers than either mining or manufacture, even though mechanisation dramatically reduced its labour force in the late 1970s and 1980s. Subsistence agriculture continued in the bantustans where conditions allowed. There was little commercial farming in these areas – only about 10 per cent of agricultural production was marketed.[1] Commercial farming and forestry dominated agriculture outside the bantustans, employing 14 per cent of workers in 1985, three-quarters of whom were African (see Table 0.1(a)). During harvesting, seasonal labour recruited in the bantustans boosted these figures. Most African agricultural workers were women, who received very low wages, which contributed to the profits generated by the agricultural sector of the economy.[2]

The mines employed 9 per cent of all workers outside the bantustans, 86 per cent of whom were Africans (see Table 0.1(a)). The mines relied almost solely on contract labour – workers employed on temporary contracts of nine months to a year, who returned to the bantustans, or

Table 0.2 Employment of whites, Coloureds, Indians and Africans by sex and industrial branch, 1985

Economic sector	White Male	White Female	Coloured Male	Coloured Female
Fisheries	348	86	2,121	166
Gold mines	46,901	2,666	1,108	51
Coal mines	11,621	1,171	147	22
Other mines	13,016	1,751	7,277	341
Building/Construction	48,513	7,540	59,013	1,020
Food	18,612	6,936	14,215	14,219
Beverages/Tobacco	7,160	2,727	4,705	1,700
Textiles	7,406	2,652	7,821	14,335
Clothing	3,217	3,095	5,726	40,393
Wood	4,468	1,232	8,281	2,706
Furniture	3,561	1,565	8,029	2,360
Paper	6,177	1,364	4,654	1,756
Printing	13,464	6,806	9,089	2,500
Chemicals	8,759	3,459	2,716	1,506
Petro-chemicals	18,308	4,807	6,384	516
Rubber	6,747	2,133	4,612	2,194
Leather	388	103	2,191	516
Shoes	1,029	674	4,749	5,442
Non-metalliferous mineral products	10,933	3,113	7,527	1,990
Basic metals	40,338	4,844	1,907	205
Metal products	25,541	5,510	10,436	2,493
Machinery	21,776	4,293	5,307	813
Electrical machinery	16,971	5,372	3,946	9,771
Miscellaneous manufacture	3,967	1,746	3,187	2,500
Transport equipment	27,827	4,564	15,030	3,464
Commerce	107,063	124,584	34,601	39,574
Motor trade	33,177	10,899	11,436	2,411
Financial institutions	48,085	69,827	5,841	8,508
Transport and communications	18,897	9,811	13,736	1,226
Local authorities	38,347	14,227	23,152	3,047
Electricity/Gas/Water	30,488	5,085	6,998	151
Personal services	20,059	25,665	6,473	13,997
Sport and entertainment	9,819	7,558	2,416	960
Professional, medical and other	68,965	72,648	6,799	11,793
Government and provincial admin.	143,899	131,398	44,625	44,669
Non-'independent' bantustans	910	265	1	0
SA Transport Services	91,767	10,545	15,900	170
Postal services	30,418	18,284	9,605	449
Totals	1,008,942	581,005	381,761	239,934

Source: South Africa 1985, p.5.

	Asian		African		Total
	Male	Female	Male	Female	
	18	0	792	38	3,569
	58	3	463,394	3,771	517,952
	345	31	83,144	1,005	97,486
	259	11	84,795	1,541	108,991
	7,822	269	277,843	2,194	404,214
	8,956	1,142	86,513	20,071	170,664
	567	27	25,468	1,245	43,599
	5,614	2,321	34,954	31,003	106,106
	6,499	19,410	4,766	27,946	111,052
	574	48	34,195	10,549	62,053
	3,458	122	12,458	1,034	32,587
	3,667	115	16,968	447	35,148
	2,903	203	12,252	534	47,751
	1,173	129	20,491	825	39,058
	2,053	140	31,672	626	64,506
	2,095	215	20,827	1,575	40,398
	806	188	3,508	1,501	9,201
	4,823	2,281	2,792	2,714	24,504
	1,129	53	57,731	6,056	88,532
	1,578	17	60,114	665	109,668
	3,191	101	74,671	4,111	126,054
	2,967	144	31,631	765	67,696
	1,959	1,150	25,085	6,283	70,537
	636	375	7,953	3,300	23,664
	2,911	302	47,373	1,028	102,499
	22,873	13,918	203,654	76,853	623,120
	4,997	542	44,516	5,816	113,794
	2,603	3,206	17,025	4,301	159,396
	6,048	554	94,358	3,018	147,648
	4,983	577	105,915	8,299	198,547
	359	40	48,402	600	92,123
	5,495	2,746	68,090	76,222	218,747
	2,770	872	11,916	3,242	39,553
	3,788	2,280	36,005	38,839	241,117
	12,475	8,513	122,058	92,213	599,850
	12	2	57,170	55,741	114,101
	1,883	22	98,704	668	219,659
	1,849	32	26,661	1346	88,644
	136,196	62,101	2,455,864	497,985	5,363,788

to neighbouring countries, at the end of each contract. The reluctance of South African workers to work at the mines resulted in the employment of a large complement of mine workers from neighbouring states (35 per cent of the mine labour force in 1986).[3]

Fifteen per cent of workers (almost half of them African) were employed in manufacture, which (see Table 0.1(a)) relied heavily on African workers living permanently outside the bantustans. Contract workers and commuters from bantustan townships also constituted a significant proportion of the industrial workforce. Manufacture was heavily concentrated in the so-called metropolitan areas, namely the Port Elizabeth–Uitenhage complex in the Eastern Cape, the Durban–Pinetown complex in Natal, the PWV area in the Transvaal and the Western Cape. In manufacturing most workers were employed in metal, steel and related heavy industries, sectors which included a high proportion of contract workers. Metal and steel industries were mainly based in the East Rand area of the PWV. The motor and components industry, concentrated in the Eastern Cape cities of Port Elizabeth and Uitenhage with smaller plants around Pretoria and in Cape Town, employed a large complement of more skilled labour and consequently a high ratio of Coloured and Indian workers, as well as African workers with permanent residence rights (see Table 0.2). Light manufacturing industries like canning, packaging and transport were major employers in the Western Cape.[4]

In the construction sector most Africans were employed on contract in unskilled occupations, with Coloured and Indian workers as artisans and skilled workers. Both African and Coloured women predominated in the clothing, textile and shoe-making industries (see Table 0.2). African women were only able to move into these sectors as white women, and then African men, moved up the skills ladder. There was relatively little movement of women into other branches of manufacture, except in the bantustans and in decentralised industries, where wages were lower. The services sector (which includes catering, cleaning jobs and domestic service) employed almost 40 per cent of black women in the labour force, the majority in domestic service.[5]

The state sector (government, civil service, local authorities, etc.) and parastatals (water, electricity, telecommunications, state-owned industrial enterprises, etc.), although overlapping with manufacture in terms of the statistics used here, were significant employers. They employed 34 per cent of whites and 14 per cent of blacks in the 1980s, but by the end of the decade government policies of privatisation and deregulation were set to reduce these figures.[6]

Historical introduction

Legacy of oppression
The system against which workers in South Africa struggled was built on conquest. Workers in many countries are oppressed, face violence and are deprived of their rights; only in South Africa, however, were the majority of the population denied the most fundamental rights of labour solely on the grounds that they were black. Restrictions on their freedom of movement, employment and organisation as workers were bound up with the national oppression of the black majority by the white minority.

The indigenous people of the country were dispossessed of their land by Europeans who, armed with superior firepower, defeated African armies in a series of colonial wars from the middle of the seventeenth century. By the end of the nineteenth century much of the African population had been displaced or forced to become labourers or tenants on white-owned land in all areas except a number of small scattered 'reserves'. These were later made the basis of today's 'bantustans', areas which comprise 13 per cent of the country, outside of which the African majority was denied the right to own land except for limited residential purposes.

There was little significant economic development in these areas and they served as labour reservoirs for the farms and industries owned by whites. Many who had farmed the land were forced into a search for jobs on white settlers' farms. Movement out of the 'reserve' areas was further stimulated by the growth of the mining industry. Diamonds were discovered in 1867, and then gold, creating within a predominantly agricultural society the nucleus of an industrial economy. As the demand for labour grew, colonial governments applied additional coercion in the form of hut and poll taxes and restrictions on land ownership to force people off the land and into wage labour. Agricultural production in the 'reserves' progressively collapsed, ravaged by declining resources, population pressure and land hunger.

Manufacturing industry developed later, its roots in small industries which sprang up to serve the mines. It burgeoned during the Second

World War as a source of goods and armaments for the Allies, and again in the 1960s, when large-scale foreign investment provided the stimulus.

The periods of industrial expansion resulted in the movement of Africans into the urban centres in large numbers. An urban African working-class population living permanently outside the 'reserves' took root. By the 1960s it was in its third generation. However, the process set contradictory forces in motion. The white ruling group was composed of different interest groups representing agriculture, mining and manufacture, which sometimes competed for labour. They placed pressure on the governments of the day to use population controls to direct labour to different sectors of the economy. At the same time the growth of the African urban population posed a political threat.

Controls on the movement of Africans and on their rights to live outside the bantustans have shifted and changed in response to these factors. Their application reflected the conflicting interests and policy objectives in play within the government's overall strategy for managing the political implications of a growing urban African population. The controls, backed by a vast administrative and repressive machinery, have at different times affected every aspect of the lives of the African majority – employment, trade union rights, family life, housing and education. They have also determined the structure of the workforce in crucial ways. Repeatedly, and each time with more effectiveness, trade unions and political organisations have arisen to lead resistance in the country's industrial heartland.

PART I

1 The Labour Market

The relationship between worker and employer in South Africa, and the structure of the labour force, was in the period under review determined by an all-embracing system for the control of the black population which has included measures to direct the flow of labour. The principal instruments for this, backed up by a massive use of force, have been restrictions on the freedom of Africans to seek work of their choice, to live where there was work and to have their families live with them. Although the controls changed as the economy developed, the objectives remained the same – to cater for the labour needs of the white minority while ensuring control of the black labour force both in the workplace and politically.

This chapter outlines the system as it was modified in the 1960s, and the restructuring which began in the 1980s. It explains how the measures have served to maintain white minority control by segmenting and stratifying the black working population, creating separate labour markets for different economic sectors and dividing workers by gender, into 'insiders' and 'outsiders' and into settled workers and migrants.

Influx control

In the 1940s, after a major expansion of manufacturing industry had induced rapid growth in the urban black working population, and in a climate of rising political militancy, a new phase of control was initiated. The object was not merely to limit the growth of the black population in urban concentrations of economic activity, but to reverse the movement of labour overall. During the 1950s and early 1960s, the ground was prepared with the establishment of bantustan administrations and tighter segregation and control of urban black residential areas, the enforcement of which resulted in increased political repression.

Contract labour
From 1952 all African adults, including, for the first time, women, were required to carry 'reference books'. At the same time controls were

tightened: only certain categories of Africans had the right to remain in urban areas – usually those with long and proven evidence of residence outside the reserve areas; other workers could usually only remain on short-term contracts. Police and other officials monitored the status of Africans in the industrial centres, carrying out spot checks on the reference books, in which permission to be in an area was shown. Those who could not produce a valid 'stamp' were arrested.

In the late 1960s controls were tightened even further to entrench contract labour as the main form of labour supply to the areas outside the bantustans. In 1968 the Bantu Labour Regulations (Government Notice 74 of 1968) were issued. These set up a system of 'Tribal Labour Bureaux', charged with registering all workseekers in the bantustans and regulating their employment. Employers had to requisition labour through the bureaux. Workers from the bantustans were no longer free to go to the towns and cities in search of work but were instead allocated to employers on temporary contracts of six to nine months' duration. They had to return to the bantustans at the end of each contract to register for a new term of employment.

The labour bureaux granted licences to recruitment agencies which requisitioned hundreds of workers at a time for employers in the cities. The bureaux placed workseekers in one of 17 categories of employment. They were channelled into the least skilled, worst paid and most arduous categories of work: farming, mining, construction, forestry and, in the case of women, particularly domestic service. In theory workers could choose their category, but labour officers could refuse them if that category was oversubscribed. The bureaux could also route workers to sectors where shortages of labour had arisen. In 1974 the system was described in these words:

> Migrant workers from the Bantustans are processed through labour bureaux which are more like cattle markets than anything else. Men register there as workseekers then stand around to wait recruitment. They wait for days, weeks, months. Then comes the great day. The recruiting agent arrives. Two hundred and fifty men line up. He wants one hundred and eighty-four labour units for the company he represents. He walks along the line and beckons to those he chooses. This one looks wrong, this one looks young and teachable, this one is too old, this one looks too thin. This one says he doesn't want to work at eight rand per week, because he was paid eleven rand in his last job. He must be too cheeky. Those who are not picked must wait weeks, maybe months, until the next recruiting agent comes.[1]

The implementation of the new system reduced competition for labour between the low-wage sectors of mining and farming on the one hand and the more highly paid posts in manufacture on the other: workers were forced into sectors they had previously avoided.

An embargo was placed on the further employment of women outside the bantustans except as domestic servants. They were confined to what subsistence farming was possible in the bantustans, or were channelled into seasonal work on white farms. Male bantustan workers went away on contract each year, without their wives and children.

New patterns of employment arose, particularly as the economy entered into recession. In the late 1970s workers in the KwaZulu bantustan, for example, began accepting work in sectors they had previously rejected as unemployment increased and job options were further limited by the 1968 regulations. They had previously spurned underground jobs at mines and only took on posts as clerks, mine policemen or 'bossboys'. By 1978, however, they were accepting other categories of work to the extent that the mine-recruiting agency was turning applicants away. Similarly, the recruiting agency for sugar plantations in Natal, which used to requisition from the Transkei bantustan, ceased operation as local workseekers were arriving at the plantations of their own accord.[2]

In times of recession bantustan bureaux were often closed and, short of going to the cities illegally, workers in the affected areas had no further prospect of work. The availability of unemployed workers trapped in the bantustans blunted the impact of worker organisation; striking contract workers could be dismissed en masse and replaced by fresh recruits from the bantustans.

Decentralisation of economic growth
Another aspect of the attempt to reduce the African population outside the bantustans during the 1960s was a programme to divert economic growth from the four main industrial regions to areas in or near the bantustans. Financial incentives, as well as exemptions from taxes and from regulations stipulating minimum wages and conditions, were offered to industrialists willing to invest in new industries in or near the bantustans. The Physical Planning Act of 1967 barred employers in some industries outside the bantustans from employing additional African labour without ministerial consent.

Wages in the new industries were appallingly low and workers avoided them. Ultimately it was mainly women workers trapped in the bantustans who came to be employed in these industries, such as food manufacturing, textiles, leather and the manufacture of household goods.[3]

Creation of a commuter workforce
The government reduced housing stock in townships outside the bantustans and concentrated new building programmes inside them. Africans could not own houses in the townships and lived there as tenants of the state. New urban settlements were established inside the bantustans, many close to their boundaries. As the contract labour system was applied and as the housing shortage outside the bantustans increased, more workers were forced to live in the new settlements and 'commute' daily or weekly across bantustan boundaries to work.

Several African townships adjacent to cities were incorporated into nearby bantustans simply by shifting bantustan boundaries a few kilometres to include them. Their residents became subject, overnight, to the 1968 regulations, commuting daily as contract workers to their workplace and back. During the 1960s and 1970s Mdantsane, near East London, became part of the Ciskei bantustan; Umlazi and KwaMashu, near Durban, were incorporated into the KwaZulu bantustan and several African townships near Pretoria were absorbed into the Bophuthatswana bantustan. By the 1980s only 41,000 of the original one million Africans resident in Durban, for example, still lived in areas falling outside KwaZulu.[4]

These actions significantly increased the population under the control of the bantustans (see Table 1.1). The number of commuters rose steadily from 290,000 in 1970 to 470,600 in 1982 (see also Table 1.2(b)).[5] In 1960 there were only three officially designated towns in the bantustans, with a total population of 33,468. By 1978 there were 1.5 million people living in such towns.[6]

Coloured labour preference policy
In the Western Cape, which has the largest concentration of South Africa's Coloured population, additional restrictions on Africans were introduced. In 1955 the Western Cape was made a 'Coloured Labour Preference Area'. Employers who wanted to employ Africans needed a certificate from the Department of Labour showing that no suitably qualified Coloured worker was available. In the four years preceding 1981, 10,000 Africans were refused employment on these grounds.[7]

Controls were stepped up to squeeze out 'illegal' Africans, with the government undertaking to reduce the African population of Cape Town by 5 per cent annually from 1966 onwards.[8]

Table 1.1 The distribution of the African population of South Africa by region, 1960–1980

Year/Sex	1960	1970	1980
Metropolitan areas	2,396,037	2,996,210	3,416,971
Male	1,319,010	1,699,398	1,924,531
Female	1,077,027	1,296,812	1,492,440
Percentage	19.98	19.19	16.29
Other urban areas	1,088,663	1,400,208	1,903,447
Male	602,503	799,576	1,071,853
Female	486,160	600,632	831,594
Percentage	9.08	8.97	9.07
Rural areas	3,767,410	3,829,232	4,323,545
Male	1,890,900	2,014,135	2,290,236
Female	1,876,510	1,815,097	2,033,309
Percentage	31.42	24.53	20.61
Bantustans	4,739,855	7,385,954	11,338,308
Male	2,110,668	3,270,366	5,210,469
Female	2,629,187	4,115,588	6,127,839
Percentage	39.53	47.31	54.04
Total	11,991,965	15,611,604	20,982,271
Male	5,923,081	7,783,475	10,497,089
Female	6,068,884	7,828,129	10,485,182

Note: Metropolitan areas are the major industrial areas of the country, outside the bantustans (Cape Town, East London, Kimberley, Port Elizabeth, Durban, Pietermaritzburg, the East Rand, Vanderbijl Park, Sasolburg, Bloemfontein and the Orange Free State Gold Fields).
Source: Simkins, 1981, pp.19–21.

Controls outside the bantustans

These policies were matched by the growth of repressive regulations and practices aimed at seeking out and then expelling workers without permission to be in urban areas.

The key control law was the Black (Urban Areas) Consolidation Act (No. 25 of 1945). Section 10(1) of the Act placed an embargo on all

Table 1.2(a) The impact of population controls on the economically active black workforce, 1980 (increase/decrease in 000s)

Area	Coloured	Indian	Total	African Contract workers	Commuters	Other	Total
PWV	69	33	102	240	115	793	1,148
Port Elizabeth/ Uitenhage	58	2	60	23	38	118	179
Cape Peninsula	382	6	388	42	0	73	115
Durban/Pinetown	19	155	174	31	161	61	253
Other areas	398	58	456	336	215	1,562	2,096
Total	926	254	1,180	677	529	2,607	4,528
Bantustans							
Bophuthatswana	#	#		-197	161	#	
Ciskei	1		1	-56	38	98	
Gazankulu	0	0	0	-50	9	40	
KwaZulu	1	2	3	-261	364	262	
Lebowa	0	0	0	-175	66	163	
Qwaqwa	0	0	0	-43	7	11	
Kangwane	0	0	0	-48	36	3	
KwaNdebele	0	0	0	-44	9	13	
Transkei	#	#	0	-308	9	#	
Venda	#	#	0	-35	5	#	
Total	928	256	1,184	1,217	704	#	

Sources: South Africa 1984, p.351; BENSO 1983, Tables 10 and 12.
Note: # - Not known.

Africans coming into the areas outside the bantustans for longer than 72 hours unless they complied with one of four sub-clauses:

(a) they were born in the area;
(b) they had worked continuously for the same employer for ten years or several employers for 15 years;
(c) they were the wives or dependants (under 18 years of age) of the above;
(d) they had special permission to remain there (usually on contract).

Table 1.2(b) The number of contract workers and commuters employed in the South African workforce, 1985

Areas of origin:	Contract workers	Commuters
INDEPENDENT BANTUSTANS		
Transkei	372,127	3,286
Bophuthatswana	275,485	123,766
Venda	58,362	5,958
Ciskei	65,423	48,001
Total	771,397	181,011
NON-INDEPENDENT BANTUSTANS		
KwaZulu	484,637	277,452
Qwaqwa	72,694	2,830
Lebowa	258,572	70,663
Gazankulu	97,315	7,439
Kangwane	70,591	46,953
KwaNdebele	78,430	23,225
Development Trust and other areas	8,598	12,988
Total	1,070,837	441,550
Total for all bantustans	1,842,234	622,561

Source: South Africa 1985.

The tenuous privilege of being 'an insider', of living and working permanently outside the bantustans and free from the restrictions of contract labour, hinged around qualifying under clauses (a), (b), or (c) of Section 10(1).

The areas outside the bantustans were divided into 'prescribed' and 'non-prescribed areas'. 'Prescribed areas' included the large urban concentrations and some smaller industrial towns; white farms and rural towns made up the 'non-prescribed' areas. People living in non-prescribed areas were generally refused work in towns or cities and channelled into farm labour. Workers in prescribed areas were also restricted. They could not transfer their Section 10(1) rights from one prescribed area to another – for example, workers qualified to work in Johannesburg could not work in Pretoria or Cape Town without jeopardising their status.

The 1968 regulations prevented most workers from the bantustans from obtaining rights under clauses (a) or (b), because the compulsion to return to the bantustans at the end of each contract prevented them fulfilling the conditions of continuous residence and employment.

After 1968, preference for jobs outside the bantustans was given to workers recruited on contract. The mobility of bantustan workers, who came to the cities without a contract, was limited by the 72-hour clause – they would only be registered for work for which no contract labour was available. Local housing regulations were tightened to restrict their mobility further. They had to show that they lived in officially approved accommodation, which was severely limited by cut-backs in housing. Aside from single-sex barracks or hostels, built specifically to house contract labour, the only other approved accommodation was for registered lodgers of tenants in family housing.

Controls on women
Women experienced even greater difficulty than men in obtaining permission to remain outside the bantustans, especially because of the embargo on their employment in any categories of work other than domestic service. Other work could only be filled by women from the bantustans if local men or women were not available.

The only other way that a woman from a bantustan could live and work outside the bantustans was as the wife of a legally qualified male worker. Both parties had to have access to 'suitable accommodation', which was taken in the case of married couples to mean family housing.

Curfews
In some areas outside the bantustans African workers were also subject to curfews. Section 31 of the Black (Urban Areas) Consolidation Act allowed local authorities to introduce curfews, barring Africans without permits from the streets at night, except in black townships. Although in the second half of the 1970s curfews were suspended in many areas, as late as 1982 they were still being strictly enforced in Krugersdorp, Westonaria and Randfontein. Some 200,000 Africans were prosecuted for transgressing these regulations between 1976 and 1985.[9]

Trespass Act
The Trespass Act provided for the removal of Africans living without consent on white-owned premises or land. Between 1983 and 1985,

for example, 282,717 Africans were arrested on charges of trespass, many of them the husbands or friends of domestic servants housed in rooms in the back yards of their employers' property, or on the roofs of blocks of flats.[10]

The enforcement of controls
Until the late 1980s this system of controls was enforced through checks on 'passes'. These documents listed a person's status: permanent resident, contract worker, commuter or dependant. They had to be carried at all times and produced on demand to police or officers of the Administration Boards which ran the African townships. Passes showed at a glance whether the bearers were legally in the area, the nature of their employment and at which labour bureau and for what categories of work they were registered.

Africans could be summonsed at any time (in the street, in a bus queue, at their places of work), or roused from their beds to produce their passes. Failure to do so was an offence carrying penalties of up to R100 in fines or three months' imprisonment. Workers illegally in an area faced various penalties (fines and imprisonment) and could be removed to the bantustans. Millions of ordinary working people were criminalised. In the early 1980s, for example, over 500 people were arrested every day for pass-law offences.[11]

Since 1916 an estimated 17 million people have been arrested under various laws restricting the movement of Africans.[12] In the late 1970s and early 1980s an average of 40 per cent of South Africa's daily prison population were pass-law offenders.[13]

The actual number of prosecutions was disguised after 1972 when special 'Aid Centres' were established to deal with pass offenders. Africans arrested for pass-law offences were referred to these centres for screening. Between 1972 and 1981 an average of 160,000 people were referred each year.[14] The proclaimed functions of the centres were to try 'to legalise the position of people referred to them, find employment where possible and provide advice'.[15] In practice, however, they served a largely repressive function. They were extensions of the courts and routinely prepared and investigated cases against people, and ordered illegal workers out of prescribed areas or placed them in farm labour. During the latter half of the 1970s an average of 20,000 workers per year were directed to employment, principally farm labour, through Aid Centres. Around 40,000 per year were sent back to bantustans, while over 170,000 were passed on to the courts for prosecution.[16]

People prosecuted under the pass laws were also routinely channelled into farm labour under a special 'parole' system in prisons (see Chapter 2 below). In the late 1970s between 80,000 and 100,000 prisoners were being paroled to farmers and other employers as labourers each year.[17]

Offenders were tried in special Commissioners' Courts falling under the Department of Co-operation and Development, which was charged with all aspects of the administration of Africans living outside the bantustans. These courts were presided over by functionaries of the Department who had no formal judicial training. A government commission found in 1983 that 'the standard of justice dispensed in the Commissioners' Courts was unacceptably low' and that the high number of pass-law offenders jailed resulted from simple abuses of legal procedure. The vast majority of people prosecuted were unrepresented, resulting in a system of 'conveyor-belt' justice with the accused shunted through the courts at the rate of one a minute. Bail was also systematically refused to defendants.[18]

Impact of Controls

These controls structured the working population in crucial ways. By 1980 one-third of Africans working outside the bantustans were contract workers. The redrawing of bantustan boundaries had reduced a further 17 per cent to the status of commuters (see Tables 1.2(a) and (b)). The proportion of the African population living within bantustan borders increased from 40 per cent to 54 per cent between 1960 and 1980 (see Table 1.1).

Over two decades the controls stratified the workforce into two distinct groups: a smaller urban population qualified to live and work permanently outside the bantustans and a larger group of contract workers and commuters allowed there only for the duration of their contracts or for the length of the working day. The comparatively stable position of the permanent residents, and their easier access to opportunities for training, favoured them in the search for jobs and housing. They filtered into skilled and semi-skilled occupations in industry. Contract workers were forced into the manual, unskilled and more dangerous jobs, most markedly in the Western Cape, affected as it was by the Coloured Labour Preference Policy.

The lives of ordinary working people were dominated by the insecurities of their status. Contract workers lived lonely lives in township hostels, away from their families. Permanent residents were subject to the constant and unpredictable compulsion to produce passes. Illegal workers ran a daily gauntlet of controls, haunted by the certainty of greater hardships if they were sent back to the bantustans.

In the late 1970s and 1980s the controls were overhauled in response to changing economic and political forces. These changes, which strengthened the position of the permanent residents and increased their numbers, are described in greater detail below. The main aim of government policy, however, remained that of reducing the growth of this sector of the workforce by a 'deconcentration' policy, restrictions on 'citizens' of 'independent' bantustans and the enforcement of housing regulations.

The modified policy had the potential to promote divisions within the workforce. It benefited workers already working outside the bantustans, even if illegally. They had first choice of new employment and legal housing, while new workseekers from the bantustans were obstructed by a shortage of approved accommodation, by action against illegal squatting and by a scarcity of jobs caused by recession. Those from 'independent' bantustans were subject to immigration controls, and hindered by their place in the hierarchy of labour created by the old controls – 'illegals' in the cities had the edge over the bantustan unemployed, commuters over new workseekers, miners over farm workers, and men over women.

Restructuring

In the second half of the 1970s the state began to restructure the controls in response to changing economic and political conditions. Defiance of the regulations on a wide scale and the rising level of resistance to apartheid, particularly in the main urban centres, had led also to a search for more effective ways of policing and expelling illegal workers. International condemnation of the brutal repression of the Soweto uprising of 1976 brought increased pressures for disinvestment. The government appointed two commissions, the Riekert Commission and the Wiehahn Commission, to investigate aspects of the labour relations system and to recommend ways of streamlining it.

Up to this point, when stabilising the workforce had become an urgent priority, workers had resisted controls as a matter of survival. In 1979, at the tail-end of a recession, academic research showed the economic advantages of defying influx control, even if it meant time in prison. The income of a worker from the Ciskei bantustan who worked illegally in Pietermaritzburg for nine months and spent three in prison, would be eight times greater than if he were to remain in the bantustan.

Similarly a worker from Bophuthatswana who worked illegally in Pretoria for three months and spent nine months in jail, would still earn more than in the bantustan.[19]

In addition, although it was ruthlessly applied, legislation had failed to stem the growth of a vast illegal population outside the bantustans. For example, an estimated 42 per cent of the African population in the Western Cape lived there illegally. In other parts of the country there were 2.5 million people living in squatter camps, most of them illegally.[20]

The decentralisation policy had been only partially successful. Under the scheme 68,500 jobs were created for Africans in the 1960s and a further 34,900 jobs between 1970 and 1978 – roughly 3,878 a year. However, in the same period an average of 20,000 new workers were registered as workseekers each year in the bantustans.[21]

Pressures on the system also manifested themselves in marginal changes in the laws and regulations. In the second half of the 1970s curfews were suspended in many areas, and in the early 1980s some slight changes followed challenges in the courts.

In 1981 came the first of two legal challenges to the 1968 regulations. In September of that year a contract labourer, Mehlolo Rhikoto, challenged the authorities to accept that he qualified to live in Germiston because he met the terms of Section 10(1)(b). He had worked for one employer under ten different contracts. In an historic ruling the Rand Supreme Court found that the continuity of his employment was not broken by the temporary absences caused by the legal compulsion to return to the bantustan to renew his contract. The court found that he and his employer 'had a common and continuing intention that he remain in employment. At most what was created was a semblance of breaks.'[22] Some 130,000 workers (9 per cent of the 1.4 million contract labour force) and a potential 145,000 of their dependants stood to benefit from the Rhikoto judgement.[23]

Also in 1981 Nonceba Komani petitioned the Bloemfontein Appeal Court to allow her to join her husband in Cape Town, in spite of the shortage of family housing there, on the grounds that he was registered as a lodger. The court ruled in her favour and opened the way for women in similar circumstances to qualify too. By 1984, 24,688 people had been allowed into the urban centres because of this judgement.[24]

After September 1984 there were some changes in the way pass-law offenders were prosecuted. Following an investigation by the Hoexter Commission, prosecutions were moved from the special Commissioners' Courts to the regular magistrates courts, and there was a sharp drop in the number of prosecutions.[25]

Labour zoning

By the mid-1970s other anomalies in the existing controls had crystallised. As the states of Southern Africa became independent and their economies developed, the mining sector suffered a cut-back in the supply of labour from South Africa's neighbouring states. The urgency of the mines' position became apparent when, in spite of wage increases and a high level of internal unemployment between 1974 and 1979, they still failed to attract sufficient labour from the bantustans. Only 4,000 workers volunteered in 1974 to replace the 100,000 withdrawn by Malawi (see Chapter 4 below) and a shortfall of some 58,000 workers was experienced throughout the mining industry.[26]

Restructuring of the labour supply to the mines took several forms. Individual labour bureaux in the bantustans were increasingly 'zoned' exclusively for mine labour. As a result 'reservoirs' of workers skilled in mining occupations developed in certain areas. Mining employers also introduced a bonus-card system which involved the registration of miners in a centralised computer system detailing skills, experience and work record.

The agricultural labour pool contracted in similar ways to mining. In 1970 farmers recruited 45,000 workers from outside South Africa, but by 1977 this had fallen to only 16,000.[27] During the late 1960s mechanisation had led to the displacement of what had been the predominant forms of labour supply – labour tenancy and sharecropping (see Chapter 2 below). Farmers came to rely increasingly on smaller groups of more skilled permanently resident farm workers supplemented by casual or seasonal workers drawn from neighbouring bantustans. As in the case of mining, there was a trend towards the zoning of specific bantustan areas for these forms of farm labour. Farmers were encouraged to register their workers, contributing to the centralisation of information. Workers straying out of their allocated work categories were sent back to the bantustans.

The report of the Riekert Commission (see below) was followed by a further streamlining of the system of bantustan labour bureaux. Bureaux in remote bantustan districts were replaced by 'assembly centres' closer to the boundaries of the bantustans and nearer the major mining, farming and industrial areas. Workseekers now had to travel from distant areas to the assembly points, to await recruitment.

A study of Johannesburg municipal contract workers in 1980 concluded that the new measures had led to:

the effective denial to large portions of the bantustan population of the opportunity of being recruited as contract workers. This has been felt at two levels: (1) The tendency to exclude categories of individuals such as those over the age of 45 – being too weak; those under the age of 25 – being too dangerous, too political; the inexperienced; the unhealthy; those with 'bad records'; and the women ... For reasons of political and economic expediency, the tendency has been to rationalise recruitment of labour in such a way that the bantustan areas nearest the major industrial centres are drawn on first when contract workers are required, while areas furthest away are drawn on last. In general, workers in the bantustans may only get what are known as 'contract workers' jobs' i.e. the dregs, the jobs that city workers refuse. However the people in the most remote areas do not even have access to the full range of contract worker jobs as do those in the less remote areas. They are on the bottom of the scrapheap of the industrial reserve army of labour.[28]

As in the case of agriculture and mining, anomalies also occurred in the supply of labour to manufacturing. During the 1960s and early 1970s the need to compete in the international economy fostered mechanisation and the use of more capital-intensive technology. This created demands for a settled technologically skilled labour force, and at the same time the technological changes displaced a section of the existing manufacturing labour force, increasing the number of unemployed. Economic recessions, from 1974 to 1979, and from 1981 onwards, further increased the number of unemployed workers in the cities. Existing methods of control were not always successful in removing this 'superfluous' labour to the bantustans. Vast numbers of workers continued to live illegally outside the bantustans.

The Riekert Commission and manufacture
The restructuring of the supply of labour to manufacture reflected the above concerns. It incorporated many of the recommendations of the Riekert Commission, the main import of which was to increase the mobility of Africans who had acquired Section 10 rights. The report argued that Africans living outside the bantustans should no longer be regarded as 'temporary sojourners' and that their position should be stabilised through the removal of restrictions on the use of their labour. Relaxation of controls, stability in terms of family life and increased access to training would help provide a permanent skilled labour force. On the other hand the permanent residents would be protected from com-

petition for jobs by still tighter restrictions on the employment of workers from the bantustans. According to the Commission:

> Owing to the potential extent and the nature of the migration of Blacks from rural areas to urban areas, serious social and sociological welfare problems will arise in urban areas in South Africa for both the established populations in urban areas, White, Coloured, Asian and Black, and the new entrants, if the migration process is left uncontrolled ... it will give rise to large scale unemployment in urban areas, lower wages and a threat to the interests of established inhabitants ... Control over the rate of urbanisation is, in the light of circumstances in South Africa, an absolutely essential social security measure.[29]

The Commission recommended that people should be allowed to leave the bantustans in search of work without going through the labour bureaux, but that permission to remain outside the bantustans should depend on proof of employment, availability of suitable accommodation and the absence of local qualified labour. Their families should be allowed to join them if accommodation was available. But at the same time, stricter provision should be made to remove those who did not meet these criteria. The onus should be on employers rather than police and pass officials to enforce the new criteria.

Most of the Commission's recommendations were never formulated into comprehensive legislation and they remained a source of controversy within ruling circles. However, some were implemented in the form of *ad hoc* regulations, on a piecemeal and often temporary basis. Initial steps were taken to lift some Section 10 restrictions, but recession and political unrest in the urban areas caused a retreat.

In accordance with Riekert's proposals, a moratorium on the prosecution of illegal workers was declared between July and October of 1979, and such workers were invited to register their employment. However, while some 84,379 people benefited from this measure it also exposed a previously hidden section of the workforce and many were endorsed out because they did not have suitable accommodation or approved work. Illegal workers who lost their jobs after the moratorium expired were refused re-registration for new employment.[30]

From June 1980 new regulations allowed movement from one prescribed area to another without loss of rights. The previous restrictions had created a shortage of skilled labour in some prescribed areas while surpluses built up in others. The change allowed for far more efficient use of the existing labour pool and reduced recruitment from the bantustans. Initially these changes did not apply in the Western Cape, where the Coloured Labour Preference Policy continued to be applied until 1985, even though it had failed to prevent the growth of an illegal workforce in the region.[31]

In 1980 two bills were published which incorporated the repressive aspects of the Riekert recommendations, but failed to recognise the permanence of the African population outside the bantustans. Both were dropped following widespread opposition, including representations from employers in manufacture. In May 1981 a new bill was published, the Orderly Movement and Settlement of Black Persons Bill. It was even more restrictive than the existing controls. Again, the bill was widely opposed and dropped. The question of reforming the controls was then referred to the President's Council, a central government advisory body. Between 1979, when Riekert reported, and 1985, when the Council's findings were published, there was no substantial change in the existing controls.

Restrictions on workers from the bantustans were generally tightened from 1980 onwards. Certain categories of work were closed to them. Workseekers already resident outside the bantustans were forced to take up jobs which they had previously shunned. In July 1979 an amendment to the Black Urban Areas Consolidation Act was gazetted, increasing the penalty for employing illegal labour to a R500 fine or three months' imprisonment or both. This shifted the frontline of control on movement from police towards employers. Pass raids were now concentrated on places where workers worked, as well as on their homes as previously.

A downturn in the economy from 1981 brought the imposition of the most severe controls since the early 1970s. The position of contract workers who had jobs was adversely affected in November 1982, when the West Rand Administration Board reimposed regulations preventing contract workers in the area under its control who became unemployed from seeking new jobs without first returning to the bantustans and re-registering with labour bureaux. During 1983 the Steel and Engineering Industries Federation of South Africa (SEIFSA), after consultation with the Department of Labour, dispensed with 12-month contracts and from then on workers were hired on one month's probation and thereafter could be dismissed at a single day's notice. Local regulations were introduced on the West Rand in January 1983 to counter the 'Komani' ruling. They stated that contract workers would lose their jobs if they were joined by their families. In July this became national policy when the Laws on Co-operation and Development Amendment Act was passed.[32] As a consequence fewer than 20 per cent of the 120,000 workers who tried to leave the bantustans each year between 1980 and 1983 managed to find employment.[33]

The authorities also began expelling foreign workers from South Africa. When the Zimbabwean government decided in 1981 not to renew a contract with a South African mine-labour recruiting agency, Pretoria used this as a pretext to deport Zimbabwean workers – in 1981 it expelled 4,000 and announced its intention to expel another 16,000.[34]

The bantustan programme: new controls
The bantustans were a crucial element in the restructuring of controls. Prior to 1979 even Africans enjoying Section 10 rights were regarded as 'temporary sojourners' whose political aspirations would be met in the bantustans. Under the Bantu Homelands Citizenship Act of 1970 every African was assigned to a bantustan (even if born, or continuously resident, outside them), principally on the basis of language.

From 1979 various commissions, including the Riekert Commission, recommended the acceptance of a permanent African population outside the bantustans and the creation of structures to accommodate them politically which were not necessarily linked to bantustans. But measures to limit and reduce this part of the population continued: the continuing expansion of a commuting workforce was one index of this, as was the imposition of 'independence' on bantustans.

With the imposition of 'independence' on the Transkei (1976), Bophuthatswana (1977), Venda (1979) and the Ciskei (1981), people assigned to these bantustans lost their claim to South African citizenship and were regarded as bantustan 'nationals' (see Map 1.1). Under the acts conferring 'independence' on these territories, the Section 10 rights of those who already had them were preserved. However, any children born after the date of 'independence' would have no such rights and would only be allowed to remain outside the bantustans with special permission. By 1981, 9 million people had lost their claim to South African citizenship in this way. In the long term, the government intended that within a generation of the accession of the last bantustan to 'independence', no African would qualify for Section 10 rights.[35]

As 'foreigners', workers from 'independent' bantustans now became subject to immigration controls. The Admissions of Persons to the Republic Act (No. 59 of 1972) and other legislation on immigration became part of the battery of influx-control measures. The act, which provided for immigration control of people entering South Africa from anywhere in the world, gave passport officials powers to arrest and deport, without reference to the courts. Between August 1981 and December

Map 1.1: Provinces, Major Towns and Bantustans

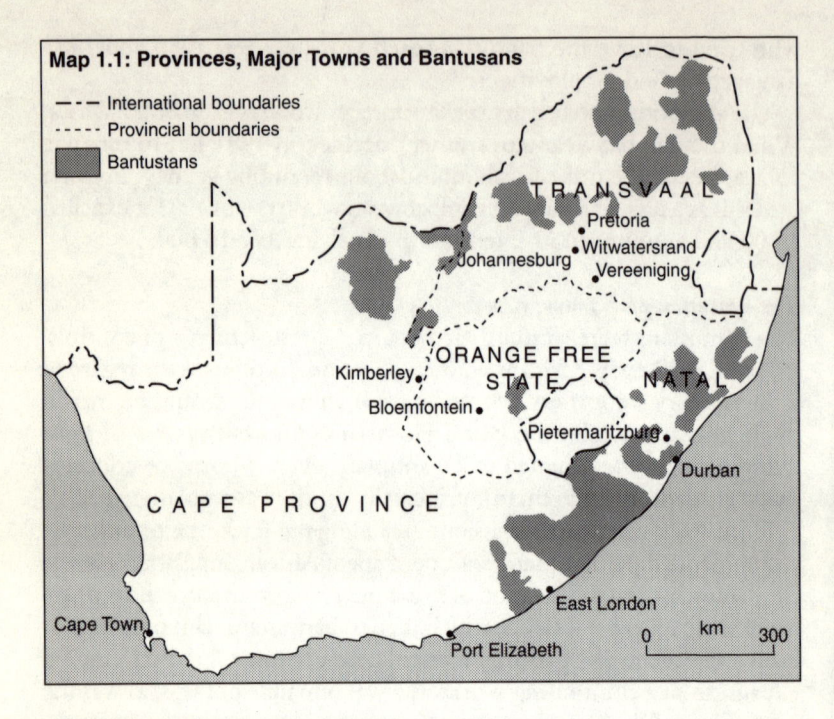

– – – International boundaries
- - - - Provincial boundaries
▓ Bantustans

1982, for example, 4,000 people were evicted from Cape Town to the Transkei bantustan in this way.[36]

Immigration legislation was further modified to facilitate its use as a means of control of movement. Members of the South African Police and officials of the Department of Co-operation and Development were designated as agents empowered to 'deport' people under the Admissions of Persons Act. A new law, the Aliens and Immigration Laws Amendment Act of 1984, contained provisions corresponding very closely to existing influx-control regulations. 'Aliens' (including residents of independent bantustans) entering the country as workseekers required permits. Employers taking on 'aliens' had to register them and faced a R5,000 fine or two years' imprisonment for employing those without permits. 'Aliens' entering illegally could be jailed or fined and were subject to deportation not only by passport control officers but also by police and officials of the Department of Co-operation and Development.

1986: new directions
In September 1985 the President's Council's review of influx control was finally published, as *An Urbanisation Strategy for South Africa*. Its findings

were accepted in a government White Paper, which appeared in 1986. The review built on the Riekert recommendations, but was also shaped by economic and political developments which had taken place in the intervening years. Not least of these was the failure of the decentralisation programme to generate employment in the bantustans and the developing interests of the manufacturing sector. According to a government official commenting in 1983: 'We had not succeeded in getting the economic base necessary to keep the Blacks living in their own areas ... the previous methods had not succeeded and ... we had to use new instruments to reach the goal.'[37]

In the same period government spokespersons also expressed their concern at the continued defiance of controls on urban population growth and the flow of labour away from the bantustans. They drew particular attention to the flow into the PWV area which was 'threatening to become a single vortex of the entire process of black urbanisation and the integration of the periphery on the core of the South African economy'.[38]

Mounting and increasingly effective resistance spurred government attempts to accommodate the permanent urban population politically and reduce its size. Attempts to deflect economic and population growth away from the main urban centres were intensified in economic planning from the early 1980s. A new policy of 'economic deconcentration' emerged, in which the country was divided into nine development regions (see Map 1.2). Within each region, industrial growth points were identified and industrialists encouraged to locate new investment through financial incentives and tax exemptions.

Whereas the decentralisation policy of the 1960s aimed to create new industry in and near the bantustans, the new regions encircled and in some cases cut across the bantustan boundaries. Where feasible the growth points were located close to bantustans to make them accessible to commuters.[39] However, the aim was to disperse labour from the major urban centres to satellites further afield, not necessarily in the bantustans. New housing for Africans was to be located in or close to the new growth points.

The redirection of labour to new growth points was reinforced by moves towards regional labour zoning. In the areas of Natal falling under the Drakensberg and Port Natal Administration Boards, for example, there was after 1981 a cut-back in recruitment from other bantustans and a greater reliance on workers from KwaZulu.[40]

Control over the provision of housing was also used to relocate workers. House-building in Pretoria was frozen, for example, and

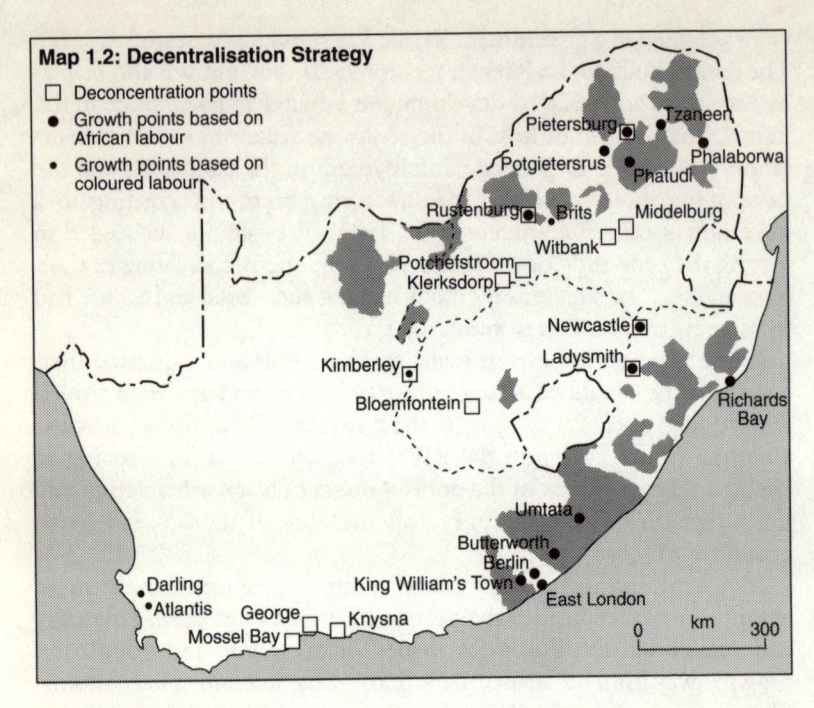

Map 1.2: Decentralisation Strategy
- ☐ Deconcentration points
- ● Growth points based on African labour
- ● Growth points based on coloured labour

workers encouraged to move to Soshanguve, north of Pretoria, where housing was available.[41] In 1983 the population of Bloemfontein's main township, Mangaung, was frozen at a maximum of 100,000 people and new workseekers were directed to Botshabelo, the principal industrial deconcentration point in the Orange Free State, some 70 kilometres from Bloemfontein (see Map 1.2).[42]

The interests of the manufacturing sector featured strongly in the President's Council report when it was published in 1985. Manufacturers had continued to lobby for the removal of restrictions on the free movement of labour to allow for the growth of a skilled industrial workforce. Agricultural interests played a less prominent role in shaping controls than in the past, reflecting the decline of its economic and hence political importance. Between 1950 and 1984 its contribution to GDP had declined from 14.5 to 6.7 per cent, whereas that of manufacture had increased from 16.5 per cent to 24.3 per cent.[43] The nature of agriculture had also changed, making it less dependent on previous forms of labour supply. Continued mechanisation and the further decline of small-scale, labour-intensive farming through drought and recession in the 1980s rendered the controls obsolete as a primary means of securing agricultural workers. Modern farming methods required a small, relatively skilled labour force, settled on the farms, supplemented by casual labour from bantustans during harvesting. As recession set in after 1981, and trade union organisation raised wage levels at the mines, the mining sector no longer experienced shortages of labour. The President's Council report was thus mostly geared towards securing labour for manufacturing industry.

It recommended that the Black Urban Areas (Consolidation) Act be scrapped as the primary instrument of population control. Contract labour, passes, curfews, Aid Centres and other restrictions should fall away. Workers from the bantustans should be allowed to proceed freely to any urban area, as long as they had access to 'approved housing'. No other restriction would apply. A policy of 'orderly urbanisation' would encourage people to settle in areas where housing and employment were available. Although not explicitly stated, the policy was partly aimed at facilitating the movement of population to the deconcentration points.

From the government's White Paper, it appeared also that the concept of approved housing would be widened to include officially approved squatter communities and designated site-and-service schemes. Official standards of housing would be adjusted to facilitate more rapid construction.

The 1986 policy appeared to break new ground in several other respects. It envisaged a larger group of permanently settled Africans in the major urban areas and the incorporation of those already illegally resident in these areas, which previous controls had failed to dislodge. It also changed the nature of the controls, which would be used to deflect further population growth away from the major urban areas. The monitoring of passes and the eviction of offenders were replaced with more comprehensive controls over squatting.

Clauses in the Abolition of Influx Control Act, introduced in the wake of the White Paper, tightened up the Prevention of Illegal Squatting Act of 1951 and the Slums Act of 1979. The new clauses gave wide discretionary powers to magistrates and local authorities to demolish illegal squatter camps and to transfer their residents to 'site-and-service' resettlement camps. Landowners or lessees could be compelled to remove squatters from land deemed unsuitable for residential occupation, and those landowners who allowed squatters to erect structures without official approval faced a R2,000 fine or 12 months in jail.[44] They would also face penalties if they allowed illegal squatting on their property or took on tenants in contravention of housing regulations.

They had to notify the central Population Register of all tenants living on their property.

In February 1989 controls on illegal squatting were tightened even further when the Prevention of Illegal Squatting Act was amended to remove from the courts powers to issue interdicts halting the demolition of squatter camps, and to increase penalties on landowners who allowed squatters to settle illegally.

Key elements of government policy on the direction and control of African labour thus remained in place after the 1986 reforms. By the end of 1989, however, there were few clear pointers as to how national policy would evolve in the 1990s. Authorities in different parts of the country adopted differing tactics.

In the year following the Act 95,384 people were arrested under the Trespass Act for occupying property without the permission of the lawful owner. This was a dramatic increase over 1985, when 21,035 people were arrested.[45] Squatter communities were demolished and removed in the Eastern and Western Cape, while in the PWV as many as 10,000 shack-dwellers faced eviction and removal in mid-1987. By the end of the year some 4,600 structures had already been demolished in the region and over 1,000 squatters arrested and charged. This represented a substantial escalation of action against squatters.[46]

Evictions of squatters continued in 1987, 1988 and 1989, concentrated on the East Rand (where in October 1989 more than 10,000 people were made homeless by the demolition of illegal shacks), the Eastern Cape and parts of the border region. Overall, however, there was a relative decline in the level of evictions.[47]

In other parts of the country local authorities adopted policies tolerating the growth of squatter settlements. The Cape Provincial Administration, for example, made land available for the settlement of squatters in the Southern Cape Peninsula.[48] Similar policies were pursued in parts of the PWV.

This differentiated approach led the South African Institute of Race Relations to speculate that it had become government policy to allow the growth of 'internal' (squatter) settlements as part of its wider aim of 'orderly urbanisation', but once the ceiling of such growth was reached the restrictive aspects of the Prevention of Illegal Squatting Act could once again be applied.[49]

The 1986 Abolition of Influx Control Act abolished the 1968 regulations which had institutionalised the contract labour system, although it remained the preferred system of labour recruitment at the mines. But severe restrictions on the movement of people from 'independent' bantustans remained. In 1985, the government had announced that common citizenship would be restored to people who had lost it when the bantustans to which they had been assigned became independent. However, when the promised Restoration of South African Citizenship Act was passed in 1986 it was very limited in scope. The Act restored common citizenship only to three narrowly defined categories of people who had been assigned to a bantustan which had been made 'independent'. Under the legislation only an estimated 1,750,000 of the 9 million people affected by bantustan 'independence' stood to regain their citizenship.[50]

In law, citizens of the 'independent' bantustans to whom common citizenship was not restored were still required to seek visas to work outside the borders of the bantustans to which they were assigned, in terms of the Aliens and Immigration Laws Amendment Act. In practice, 'citizens' of the TBVC territories (Transkei, Bophuthatswana, Venda and Ciskei) were administratively exempted from obtaining visas to work outside these territories. However, in terms of a circular issued by the Department of Home Affairs in July 1986, employers wishing 'to recruit foreign Black Labour should first obtain a "no objection to recruiting" recommendation from the nearest Divisional Inspector of the Department of Manpower'. The same circular also stipulated that TBVC residents should register their employment with the nearest Department of Home Affairs office if they did not 'enter South Africa through a port of entry'.[51]

In practice there were few prosecutions of people deemed to be citizens of independent bantustans under the Aliens Act and similar 'immigration' legislation. In 1988 (the latest figures available) only 166 people (85 of them TBVC residents) were deported under the legislation.[52] Decades of the application of influx-control laws had by the close of the decade shaped the labour force and economy in such a way that migrant labour remained a structural part of the economy. High unemployment in the rural areas, scarcity of jobs in the industrial centres, the drastic shortage of housing in the official townships and the uncertain overcrowded status of squatter settlements were all factors keeping millions of workseekers permanently moving around the country in a desperate search for work and a place to live.

PART II

2 In the Countryside

In the 1970s and 1980s much of the African population was confined to the rural areas by controls on movement and economic forces. Thirteen per cent of African workers lived and worked on white farms. Of the 14 million Africans in the bantustans, just over two-thirds lived in rural areas.[1] However, some 41 per cent of these lived in 'closer settlements' – urban-type settlements created by forced removals, without access to land.[2]

Restrictions on movement, unemployment in industrial centres and limited access to education and training tied agricultural workers to the white-owned farms. Those forced by the migrant labour system to stay in the bantustans survived on what subsistence agriculture remained possible, the proceeds of informal employment and money sent home by contract workers.

Tied to the land – workers on the farms

Workers on farms owned by whites were excluded from the reforms of the early 1980s which lifted restrictions on worker organisation in manufacture and mining. White farmers, a powerful political interest group, effectively opposed reform of labour relations in the agricultural sector, which they saw as threatening their supply of cheap labour and their protection from the more competitive wages and conditions in industry and mining. Farm workers were still denied the right to organise and excluded from most of the legislation specifying working conditions, minimum wages and standards of health and safety.

In 1982 the National Manpower Commission, a government body which monitors and formulates labour relations policy, began an investigation into the employment of farm and domestic workers, with a view to bringing their conditions into line with manufacture and mining. But by the close of the decade no findings had been published.

The agricultural sector is diverse, comprising grain, fruit and wine farming, cattle and sheep ranching and forestry. Working conditions vary in each. The modernisation of agriculture in the early 1970s involved radical changes in farming methods. Large mechanised conglomerates with smaller, more skilled labour forces swiftly absorbed and replaced smaller farms which had been run by individual farmers along almost feudal lines. In 1964 there were 100,000 white farm units, declining to some 50,000 in 1984.

Although mechanisation radically reduced the size of the workforce, agriculture remained the largest employer of labour. In 1983 it was estimated that there were between 600,000 and 800,000 permanently employed farm workers, mostly working and living on 50,000 white-owned farms. A further half a million people lived on farms as their direct dependants.[3] Another 112,000 people were employed as seasonal workers during planting and harvesting periods. The figures exclude an estimated 150,000 workers on farms in the Eastern Transvaal who had entered the country illegally from Mozambique. Most farm workers in 1983 were African, except for some 150,000 Coloured workers in the Western Cape.[4]

Historically, white farming developed at the expense of African peasant agriculture. Deprived of land by colonial conquest, African peasants leasing plots from the new white landowners produced much of the country's marketed production at the turn of the century. Various types of sharecropping relationships developed between landowners and their African tenants. Many white farmers were poor and indebted, lacking labour and oxen to plough their land. They allowed tenants to occupy land in exchange for their labour and resources. But as they became wealthier, white farmers subjected their tenants to increasingly exploitative relationships, forcing them to work longer hours in exchange for rights of occupation and cultivation.[5]

In the 'reserve' areas and on freehold land still owned by Africans, however, independent African peasant farmers continued to compete with their white counterparts. After 1907 the state intervened to strengthen the position of white farmers. In 1913 the Land Act gave whites exclusive rights over 87 per cent of the country. African farmers could only purchase freehold land in the remaining 13 per cent, the 'reserves', and many more had to squat on white farms or became labour tenants. The Act outlawed the payment of rent by labour tenants in forms other than labour, undermining sharecropping relationships. The provisions of the Masters and Servants Act, which contained heavy penalties for desertion from employment, were extended to cover labour tenants, tying them to the land. Illegal sharecropping relationships persisted, however, particularly in Natal and the Transvaal, where absentee landlords leased large tracts of land to African families.

For almost a century white farming was based on various types of sharecropping and tenancy. In the late 1960s mechanisation of agriculture resulted in larger-scale farming and allowed farmers to absorb their tenants' plots, particularly on maize and wine farms and to a lesser extent on sugar plantations. Labour-intensive activities such as picking, harvesting, watering and weeding were replaced by combine harvesting, mass irrigation schemes and use of herbicides. Many tenants were made redundant. In a corresponding development, small farmers were often absorbed into wealthier conglomerates and the tenants on these farms were forced off the land.

After 1960 the state embarked on a policy of modernising agriculture. A phased elimination of labour tenancy was initiated in 1969: 30 September 1980 was fixed as the date by which it was to end. New regulations restricted the tenant labour force on each farm to a maximum of five families. Additional labour had to be recruited from bantustans on contract or as casual workers. Hundreds of thousands of redundant tenants were forcibly removed. Men were allowed to accept work in the country towns, but their families had to remain behind in bantustan resettlement villages. By the mid-1970s new labour tenant contracts had been prohibited in the whole of the Orange Free State, 41 districts of the Transvaal, three in the Cape and 23 in Natal.[6] Between 1960 and 1980 some 1.25 million people were evicted from white farms to the bantustans – most in the 1970s. Many were forced to leave behind homes and sell off stock at a fraction of its real value.[7] Tenants resisting eviction were arrested and prosecuted, their homes burnt or bulldozed and property confiscated.

The abolition of tenancy resulted in a more coercive system of labour relations. Some farmers used the threat of removal to force tenants to sign contracts to work for them at extremely low rates. In the Weenen area of Natal, where some 20,000 people were evicted, workers found conditions in the bantustans so bad that they returned in desperation to farms to work illegally under highly exploitative conditions.[8]

During the 1970s controls on movement were also systematically tightened to provide seasonal and casual labour for farmers.[9] After 1968 the passes of almost all Africans living in rural areas outside the bantustans were endorsed only for farm labour, as were those of people living in some bantustan areas. Bureaux in certain bantustans were prohibited from recruiting into non-agricultural jobs. Farmers also benefited directly from the creation of resettlement areas into which former tenants were moved, where it was easy to recruit cheap seasonal labour.[10]

These developments had devastating effects on workers in the bantustan areas zoned for farm labour. They had no means of livelihood in seasons when their labour was not required. Research in the Eastern Cape and Transvaal in the late 1970s showed a high correlation between destitution in particular areas and the closing off of non-agricultural labour recruitment. Large groups of workers moved from farm to farm desperately searching for work. A rural commuter workforce came into being – workers travelling long distances from the areas where they lived to farms where there was work.[11]

Mechanisation and the intensified controls also had dramatic effects on the composition of the workforce. Because some heavier tasks were eliminated, children were brought in for both permanent and casual work. Women, traditionally paid lower wages than men, made up a greater proportion of casual and seasonal labour.[12]

Pass-law controls, particularly restrictions on women taking jobs outside the bantustans, reinforced the growing predominance of African women in farm labour. It was estimated that by 1984 half of all economically active African women were involved in seasonal or permanent farm labour.[13]

In the Western Cape, the proportion of women in the Coloured farm-labour force also increased. This was due partly to the Coloured Labour Preference Policy, which meant that Coloured women were employed at the expense of African men.[14]

Prison labour

Forced prison labour has been a significant component of the agricultural labour force. Relatively little is known about the system, as the Prisons Act of 1959 prohibits the publication of information about prisons and prisoners without official permission. The Act was passed partly to counter revelations about the use of prisoners on farms in the 1950s. In this period 200,000 people arrested for pass-law offences were handed over to farmers as labour, without even appearing in court, and subjected to barbarous conditions. Prisoners were housed en masse in barracks, barns and sheds. Many were clothed in sacks. They worked extremely long hours without payment or proper meals, and were subjected to assaults and beatings.

Partly in response to exposés in the 1950s, the use of pass offenders as farm workers was transformed into a 'parole' system. Short-term prisoners were handed over to farmers designated 'special prison warders' under the Prisons Act. 'Parolees' had to be paid market wages for their labour and, in theory, they had the right to leave and return to prison if they chose.[15] The system was wide open to abuse. The concept of market wages was loosely defined and made no provision for overtime, bonuses, length of service and other conditions of fair employment. Surveys showed that parolees were forced to work long hours and there were no effective means of ensuring that those who wanted to leave could do so.[16] During the 1970s approximately 100,000 prisoners were 'paroled' each year. The vast majority were put to work on farms.[17]

'Farm jails' were also set up. A 'farm jail' was defined as a 'prison out-station, administered by the Prison Service, for long-term prisoners'. A farmer or consortium of farmers built prisons at their own expense and convicts were housed in them under the supervision of warders provided by the Prisons Department. They worked in the fields during the day. In 1986 there were 22 such jails housing some 10,000 prisoners. Half were in the Western Cape, largely supplying Coloured prisoners to local wine farmers who drew on labour in proportion to their invested share in the jails.[18]

In 1986 the government announced that it would phase out the prison labour schemes. It was one aspect of the broader changes in the pass laws, but was also partly a response to international pressure: Norway, Sweden and Ireland had imposed bans on the import of South African fruit, and the use of prison-labour weighed heavily in their decisions. The government proposed replacing prison labour schemes with a chain of labour camps. Who would be housed in the camps was not disclosed; nor was it clear whether the changes affected paroled labour as well as farm jails.[19] Very little was subsequently published about changes to prison labour schemes, but in February 1988 reports in the press indicated that farmers could still hire prison labour at a cost of R2.95 per prisoner per day.[20]

Child labour
Child labour has been used on farms in South Africa on a wide scale. Legal controls on the employment of children do not cover many of the situations affecting the children of farm workers. Children under 16 cannot be employed without the written consent of their parents or legal guardians, but farmers have often made it a condition of contract that workers allow their children to be drafted into the workforce, particularly during sowing and harvesting periods. In some areas farm workers have contracted out their children as a way of supplementing their meagre incomes.

In 1982 the London-based Anti-Slavery Society published a report estimating that up to 60,000 children worked in farm labour each year, most of them between 9 and 14 years of age. Some were dependants of permanent workers on farms, others were part of the seasonal casual labour force recruited in the bantustans. Their work included hoeing, picking, reaping, harvesting and other heavy manual tasks. Children of permanently employed workers were generally not paid separately but were regarded as part of the contract offered by their parents.[21]

According to the Anti-Slavery Society report, white farmers recruited children from bantustans on a massive scale. Parental consent was often not obtained and the children were misled as to the nature of the work. Once recruited they were trapped on farms by pass laws and lack of skills:

> Many children try to escape this cycle by leaving for urban areas as soon as they can, but they go there illegally, often cannot find work and end up going back to the farms for work. So, in part, the migration from farms into the urban area is turned back, for many of them, into a cycle from the gutters of the city into the fields and back again. The Eastern Transvaal and Natal are two areas in South Africa where these patterns can be seen in all their aspects. Children under 16 are employed by farmers who simply drive their trucks into bantustans and pick up however much labour they need. Here they live in barns or stone compounds, have their passes removed so that they cannot desert and often do not know how much they are to be paid.[22]

Child labour was also widespread on wine farms in the Western Cape. A University of Cape Town survey of seven farms in 1983 found that four employed children aged 13 to 16 on a full-time basis. Although the government said in 1988 that it would ban the use of children from farm schools for any kind of labour during school hours, there were reports in June 1989 that the practice was still widespread and that there had not been any convictions of offenders.[23]

Employer–worker relations

The Black Labour Regulations Act of 1911, as amended, provides that agricultural officers appointed by the Department of Co-operation and Development should monitor conditions on farms, but the system appears to have fallen into disuse. When the government last released information on the subject in 1981, it said that no officers had been appointed nor inspections made in the previous two years.[24]

Farm workers experience their oppression and exploitation in a particularly direct and intense way:

> The relationship between farmer and farm labourer in practice and in law assumes the colour of a status relationship under contractual subterfuge, closer to the medieval master-servant relationship than the ideal pure contract doctrine upon which the law bases its conception of industrial employment.[25]

Farm workers were dominated by the personal power of their employer,

> upon whom they are dependent for a wide range of welfare provisions such as, access to productive farm land (for personal cultivation or for grazing); provision of meat and maize for the household; access to education in a farm school for their children; permission for the extended family (no longer permanently employed on the farm) to continue to live on the farm etc.[26]

Control over housing has in particular been used to reinforce the exploitative relationship between employers and workers. In the Western Cape, for example:

> The need for housing ... limits members of farm labourers' families to working on the farm. The male head of the family contracts verbally with the farmer for the entire family. The females are on standby – generally on 12 hours call at harvest time. Some farmers allow farming members to work in town if they pay rent for their rooms on the farm. Others do not allow the family members who do not work on the farm to live there.[27]

Permanent workers who lost their jobs also lost their homes and elderly workers tended to keep working in order to retain a place to live – working members of families had to bear in mind that dismissal could lead to the eviction of their dependants.

The humiliating 'tot system' was an abuse peculiar to the wine farms of the Western Cape. Under the original 'system', officially outlawed in 1961, workers were partly paid in daily allowances of reject wine. The 1961 ban did not, however, prohibit the dispensing of alcohol to workers and the system survived on many farms. According to the Black Sash it was:

> essentially a system of institutionalised alcohol addiction – it gives the employer much greater control over his workforce who are dependent

upon the liquor he can choose not to administer ... Withholding 'dop' [the tots] is the most common and effective form of punishment, while the skills required of labourers in the vineyards are too minimal to be seriously affected by the levels of intoxication they are permitted to reach during working hours.[28]

All 18 farms comprising a wine co-operative near Stellenbosch were found in 1982 to be using the system and it was estimated that between 3 and 5 per cent of the entire annual wine crop was consumed in the form of tots. A study published in 1984 found the system still in operation.[29]

Wages

Exploitation of farm workers was most dramatically reflected in low wages. Payment traditionally took the form of a cash wage supplemented by rations or payment in kind. This could include maize-meal, sugar, soap and other produce; housing; the right to cultivate a plot of land; or access to a farm school for children. The quantity and quality of payments in kind varied tremendously. Provisions for inspectors to monitor the quality of rations, as stipulated in the Labour Relations Act, have never been implemented.

Cash earnings were universally low, with one study in 1982 concluding that 'the only limit on how low South African farmworkers' wages can go is physical starvation.'[30] In the 1980s the situation deteriorated still further. The reduction in agricultural employment increased the number of unemployed dependants relying on each farm worker's wage packet, while mechanisation shortened harvesting times in which work was offered. Only 15 per cent of seasonal workers earned enough in the harvesting season to get through the year without hardship.[31]

There have been no systematic national surveys of farm workers' wages in the period under review. Table 2.1 draws on several area surveys, showing the average wages of farmworkers in 1980 in different parts of the country. It demonstrates wide regional variations.[32]

Later evidence confirmed the low level and wide regional variations of agricultural wages. On some farms in the Western Transvaal in 1983, seasonal workers from the bantustans earned no wages but were paid solely in kind. According to the National Committee Against Removals, during 1985 in parts of the Orange Free State, Transvaal, Northern Natal and Northern Cape, cash wages of R1 per day were common.[33]

Research carried out in 1984 in specific districts of the country put the average monthly wage of farm workers at R30–50. However, the government's agricultural census of 1985, based on a survey of 7,000

Table 2.1 Farm wages in cash and kind, per region, 1980

Region	Cash wage	Value in kind
Eastern Orange Free State	R22.60	R31.98
Western Transvaal	R33.56	R34.26
North Western Orange Free State	R33.51	R49.99
Highveld	R26.42	R50.87
Western Cape I	R53.42	R76.35
Western Cape II	R79.08	R67.24

Source: Farm Labour Project 1982, p.4.

farms, showed an average national monthly wage of R87. But even this higher figure meant that farm workers earned only 18 per cent of the average wage of their counterparts in manufacture.[34] Women earned considerably less than men. One survey in 1982 in the Middelburg area of the Eastern Transvaal showed that men earned R60 per month, while women doing the same work earned half as much.[35]

Working conditions

On many farms, hours of work were generally long and conditions unhealthy and dangerous. Farm workers were excluded from the provisions of the Basic Conditions of Employment Act (1983) which stipulates minimum hours of work, conditions of employment, annual leave and sick pay.

It was customary for farm workers to labour from dawn to dusk, with two one-hour breaks for breakfast and lunch. In some areas fields were floodlit at night to allow for work after dark. There were no comprehensive surveys of working hours for the period under review, but in 1980 the Farm Labour Project calculated that the average farm worker spent 60 hours per week in the fields, spread over five and a half days. Within this average there were wide regional variations. Farmers were not legally bound to pay overtime rates.[36]

Assaults and brutality

Violence, humiliation, torture and even murder were recurring features of life for farm workers and their families. The extent of brutality against farm workers was difficult to assess, as only the more sensational cases reached the press. In remote rural areas with their closely meshed white communities, police and farmers consorted, and most cases of assault went unpunished.

An ombudsman appointed by the South African Council of Churches (SACC) carried out a national investigation into the assault and torture of farm labourers between 1979 and 1981. He concluded that some farmers treated their labourers well, but torture and abuse were widespread. Some farmers 'had come to see themselves as a law unto themselves as far as their workers and their families were concerned' and many farm workers were subjected to corporal punishment 'as part of the farm procedure'. His findings indicated a high incidence of labourers 'being beaten naked, having their clothes cut from them before an assault or their sexual organs wounded ...'[37] As a result of his findings he called on the government to ban the use of sjamboks (whips).

The Association for Rural Advancement (AFRA) reported in 1986 that assaults on farm workers were common throughout Natal. It detailed several instances of flogging by farmers 'who viewed these assaults as their paternalistic right.'[38] In the same year the National Committee Against Removals commented: 'We have reports of frequent assaults on farm labourers, even killings. And the workers are too isolated and vulnerable to protect themselves. They need legislative backing.'[39]

Health and safety
Clinics and other medical services were thinly spread in rural areas. Farmers were not legally bound to provide medical checks for labourers and there were manifold abuses of laws providing for sick pay and sick leave.

Mechanisation increased the number of farm labourers working with heavy machinery, often without adequate protection or training. On maize farms, for example, 60 per cent of the permanent labour force and 45 per cent of seasonal workers used machines in 1981.[40] Legislation laying down minimum standards of safety and protection for workers specifically excluded farm workers. This lack of protection was most marked with regard to pesticides: it was common for workers to spray crops without any form of protective clothing.

Prior to 1976, an average of 300 workers died and a further 2,000 were permanently disabled annually in accidents involving machines and chemicals on farms.[41] The subsequent introduction of new chemical weedkillers and pesticides was particularly hazardous. Reports of deaths of this kind in South Africa in 1985 were 20 times higher than in the United States and Europe.[42] Evidence suggests that most cases of pesticide poisoning were not reported, however, even though they are legally notifiable. Figures issued by the Department of Health and Welfare put pesticidal deaths at 52 for the period between 1979 and 1983. However, the Johannesburg Chemical Laboratory recorded 229 deaths in the same period,[43] while the head of the Department of Pharmacology at the University of the Orange Free State stated in 1985 that cases of pesticide poisoning seen at his hospital alone exceeded government figures for the entire country.[44]

Like industrial workers, farm workers were entitled under the Workmen's Compensation Act to compensation for injuries and sickness sustained on the job. But in many cases they could not claim compensation, because the diseases to which they were exposed were not scheduled in the Act or because symptoms only manifested themselves years after contraction. The Act did not allow workers who were injured or contracted diseases at work to sue employers for damages. When compensation was granted it was calculated as a proportion of the very low earnings of farm workers.

Education, skills and training

For most workers, particularly seasonal labourers, lack of skills and training added to the barriers confining them to farms. Regional surveys conducted between 1980 and 1988 revealed an extremely low education level among farm workers. In a survey of the Vryburg area in 1980, just under a third of children living on farms in the area attended school and only 13 per cent of those studied beyond the first seven years.[45] A 1982 survey of eight farms in the Middelburg district of the Transvaal showed that three-quarters of the farm population over 35 years of age had no education at all.[46] A study of maize farms in the Western Transvaal in the same year found that under a third of permanent workers were able to read or write. A 1988 survey found that the literacy level of farm workers was 35 per cent below the national average for the rural African and Coloured population.[47]

In South Africa, farmers traditionally provided for the education of the children of farm workers, but there was no legal obligation to do so. This arrangement was a further expression of the power farmers had over their workers, and of the semi-feudal status of labour relations on farms.

Until 1987 farmers were responsible for half the cost of providing schools on their farms, with an annual grant from the Department of

Education and Training (DET) accounting for the balance. The policy led to a great neglect of rural education. In 1986 there were 5,484 schools for Africans on farms, of which only one was a secondary school, although 407 primary schools offered education up to the third year of secondary schooling. Although the roughly 600,000 African children at farm schools constituted over a quarter of all African school pupils outside the bantustans, only 13.5 per cent of the budget for African primary and secondary education was allocated to farm schools in 1987.[48]

In 1987 the government promised to upgrade farm schools in line with a DET study which recommended removing schools from the sole control of farmers and centralising them under DET control on state land. Where such land was not available, facilities would continue to be leased from farmers; transport would be provided from farms to such schools, and curricula would be improved and more closely geared to vocational training. Teacher training would also be improved. A Farm School Management and Teacher Development Project was launched by the DET in co-operation with the private sector to oversee aspects of the upgrading of rural schools.

Although the changes could lead to an improvement in rural education in the longer term, the accumulated disadvantage suffered by children on farms, the low priority accorded to African education generally and the power of farmers to keep the workers' children away from school mean that low educational and skill levels among farm workers are likely to remain the norm for a considerable time.[49]

Unemployment

The pace of mechanisation and the abolition of labour tenancy caused much higher levels of unemployment among agricultural workers than in other sectors. Workers displaced from farms in the early 1970s could initially find new jobs in mining, manufacture and construction, but recession and the restructuring of influx controls increasingly closed off these avenues.

Total employment in agriculture dropped from 1,350,000 in 1970 to 973,000 in 1980. Regional surveys give some indication of how this took place.[50] A survey in 1983 of Western Transvaal maize farms found that half the permanent labour force employed in harvesting and weeding had been made redundant by the use of machines and chemicals. Of those retrenched, 37 per cent were made redundant by mechanised harvesting techniques, 32 per cent by the use of chemical herbicides, 24 per cent by the technical re-organisation of harvesting and 7 per cent through the introduction of new storage techniques.[51] Similar changes occurred on wine and sugar farms.

The economic recession of the early 1980s was felt more sharply in the agricultural sector because of a serious three-year drought in the same period. In 1983, the drought led to the lay-off of 50,000 workers on maize farms alone.[52]

Agricultural workers were excluded from the provisions of the Unemployment Insurance Fund, which afforded unemployed industrial workers a minimal form of social security.[53]

In the bantustans

It is many decades since the bantustan areas have been able to support their population through subsistence farming. In the 20 years preceding 1990, forced removals and unemployment caused by drought and mechanisation dramatically increased the population of these areas, exacerbating the pressure on land availability and distribution.

In the 1980s most of those who lived in the bantustan rural areas were officially classified as 'not economically active'. About a third had no access to land. In 1980, 67 people occupied each square kilometre of the bantustans, while in the rest of the country rural population density was only 16 per square kilometre. The rest, with the exception of a small minority, engaged in subsistence production which yielded a small part of their needs, or in limited handicraft production. The bulk of their income came from remittances from contract workers outside the bantustans.[54]

Land hunger

Land hunger has its roots in colonial conquest and the Land Acts of 1913 and 1936 which reserved roughly 87 per cent of the country for white occupation and use. The remaining area – the basis of the present day bantustans – was for Africans.

In 1959 the government-appointed Tomlinson Commission calculated that each farmer in the bantustans would need to cultivate 52.5 morgen (roughly 45 hectares) to survive. Half the population *at that time* would have to be uprooted and made to seek employment elsewhere to achieve the necessary redistribution of land.[55]

Subsequent reports on various bantustans have echoed Tomlinson's calculations. The Quail Commission, reporting to the Ciskei bantustan authorities in the early 1980s, found that the average Ciskei resident lived on 1 hectare of land compared with Tomlinson's recommended minimum of 45 hectares two decades before.[56] The Buthelezi Commission found in 1982 that even if productivity increased by 450 to 500 per cent, the land then available for agriculture in the KwaZulu bantustan would still support only 60 per cent of its population.[57] A parastatal development agency established by the Bophuthatswana bantustan, the Agricultural Development Corporation of Bophuthatswana (AGRICOR), calculated in 1983 that a local farmer would have to have an annual income of R5,000 to match what he could earn, even in low-income jobs, in the urban areas. At this level there was only enough arable land in the bantustan to support roughly 17 per cent of the resident population.[58]

Government responses to these pressures on the land took two forms: agricultural 'betterment' schemes and the movement of people into closer settlements. 'Betterment schemes' – allegedly in pursuit of more efficient land use – involved the abolition of communal tenure, where villages were spread over large tracts of land and people possessed plots according to their social and economic status. People were resettled on smaller plots and stock was culled. In the Transkei bantustan, these processes resulted by 1980 in only 3 per cent of people possessing 15 or more head of cattle, the minimum viable number under local conditions.[59]

These changes in land tenure facilitated the growth of 'agri-business'. Parastatal development agencies promoted investment in a small number of highly mechanised agricultural projects to boost productivity, notably in the KwaZulu, Bophuthatswana and Transkei bantustans.

Investment in bantustans, which until 1977 had been legally restricted to bantustan 'citizens', was opened to all investors, including white-owned agricultural consortia. In the bantustans themselves, only the wealthier landowners, usually linked to the authorities, could secure sufficient credit from the parastatal agencies or private consortia to participate in the schemes. Smaller farmers were displaced. These agricultural projects consolidated individual plots into larger estates. Most were capital intensive, creating little new employment. They served largely to promote the growth of a small number of wealthy farmers.[60]

Both betterment schemes and the promotion of agri-business reinforced control by functionaries of the bantustan administrations. Various studies have found evidence of bribery, corruption and political patronage in the distribution of land:

> The establishment of development projects on tribal land is nearly always with the approval and collaboration of the tribal authority. In

most cases the establishment of a 'development project' involves extensive dispossession of people's land rights. The people who are usually most affected are those who are known members of opposition parties, the poor, migrant workers and the small-scale subsistence producer elements.[61]

As more people were impoverished by betterment schemes and displaced by agri-business, and the bantustan populations were swollen by forced removals, the state initiated a parallel programme of settling landless people in 'closer settlements' or resettlement camps:

> By the 1950s and sixties rural planning became more clearly geared to ... separation and the reception of 'surplus people' in the homelands, than to development. The idea of 'economic units' as a basis of planning was dropped ... with the result that the effect of planning was to squeeze more people onto the land. Even so, it was soon recognised, especially after mass removals from 'white' areas began, that by no means all villagers could have land. The concept of rural towns was developed, to which both excess rural dwellers and those removed from elsewhere would be relocated. In this sense rural planning and betterment became an integral part of the mass removals programme.[62]

Rural towns and closer settlements housing people with no access to land grew rapidly. The Qwaqwa bantustan experienced an influx of population on a staggering scale – its population density increased from 54 people per square kilometre in 1970 to 622 by 1983.[63] Onverwacht (Botshabelo), near Thaba Nchu in Bophuthatswana, grew from 100,000 people in 1981 to 200,000 in 1982 and over 400,000 in 1986.[64] Research in the mid-1980s showed that 9 per cent of bantustan residents lived in closer settlements housing 5,000 people or more.[65]

Unemployment and poverty
In 1984 only one in four bantustan workseekers was able to find work locally: jobs created within the bantustans provided for only 6.8 per cent of the growth in the labour force. Most of the employment which was generated was in bantustan bureaucracies and associated agencies.[66]

Two-fifths of Transkei workers continued to seek employment outside its boundaries in 1984 – only 20 per cent were able to survive through agriculture or informal sector activities within the bantustan.[67]

In the Ciskei, local workers (including those in agriculture) brought in only one-third of the Gross Domestic Product (GDP) in 1983. A survey of the Mhlabatini district of the Kwazulu bantustan in the same year found that less than 10 per cent of the local workforce were formally employed.[68]

The picture that emerges of bantustan rural communities is one in which the young men left to seek work elsewhere while women, young children and the elderly – prevented from leaving by controls on movement – lived on remittances from contract workers, the meagre state pensions of the elderly and, where people had access to land, whatever crops the soil would yield.

For example, in 1981 in the Mhlabatini area of the KwaZulu bantustan, 39 per cent of people were dependent for their livelihood on the remittances of migrant workers. A further 15 per cent lived on the monthly pensions of elderly residents.[69] In the Ciskei bantustan 64 per cent of the GDP in 1981 took the form of remittances from contract labour and commuters.[70] In the Amatola Basin area three out of every four men in the community worked away from home as contract workers, as did half the women, while in the Tsweletswele area 60 per cent of adult males were absent on contract. Two-thirds of the remaining residents of Tsweletswele were under the age of 20: the adult population was overwhelmingly made up of women.[71] In 1985, the official census of the Transkei bantustan revealed that 56 per cent of its economically active male population worked outside the bantustan.[72]

Statistics showed an apparent increase in the standard of living of the bantustan population: the proportion of people living below the minimum living level dropped from 99 per cent in 1960 to 81 per cent in 1980. The figures are deceptive, however. Remittances from migrant workers rose with the relative increases in urban wages in the second half of the 1970s; in particular, with the rise in mine workers' wages. Most of the increase in income, however, can be attributed to the growth of the commuter workforce during the 1970s and the creation of highly paid political bureaucracies. At the same time the population of the bantustans increased from 5 million in 1960 to 11 million in 1980. Although the proportion of people living in poverty decreased, the absolute number of people living below the minimum level increased dramatically from 4.95 million people to 8.91 million. The proportion of the bantustan population receiving no income at all increased from 5 per cent in 1960 to 13 per cent in 1980, i.e. 1.43 million people.[73]

Regional surveys revealed conditions of critical poverty. In 1980 the average bantustan resident was dependent on a per capita monthly income of R73, while Africans in the urban areas of South Africa earned on average R189 per month. In some bantustans the situation was much worse. In the Mhlabatini community of Kwazulu, the average household of around eight people subsisted on R114 per month – only R14.18 per person.[74] In other parts of the bantustan per capita monthly income was no more than R45.[75]

Poverty had a severe impact on health in the bantustans. One compelling indication was the extent of malnutrition and high mortality rates among African children. Fifty-five per cent of deaths in the African community were of children under the age of 7, compared to only 7 per cent among whites.[76] In the late 1970s and early 1980s an average of 30,000 African children are estimated to have died of malnutrition each year. Government statistics did not reveal how many of these children died in the bantustans, but local studies showed a desperate situation.[77] A nutritional survey in the Tsweletswele area of the Ciskei bantustan in 1983 found that two out of every five young children showed signs of wasting and were underweight. Most showed signs of stunted growth, while one in every ten was suffering from kwashiorkor. A 1987 survey of the Botshabelo area of the Qwaqwa bantustan found that more than 40 per cent of children under 5 years old showed retarded growth.[78]

Rural resistance

The difficulties of communication and the isolation of rural areas meant that much resistance in these areas was under-reported. Opposition movements were slow to penetrate into isolated and dispersed communities. The high proportion of seasonal workers made farm workers difficult to organise. The trade union movement in the 1980s managed to organise only a fraction of the agricultural labour force, although such workers were seen as a high priority for protection, together with domestic workers, who are also unprotected by existing labour relations legislation.

On the farms
In the late 1950s, the Farm Plantation and Allied Workers Union, an affiliate of the South African Congress of Trade Unions (SACTU), organised several hundred farm workers in the Transvaal. Strikes were almost impossible and the union sought chiefly to expose conditions and mobilise support from the wider opposition movement. In 1959 the Congress Alliance, an ANC-led coalition of which SACTU was a part, organised a national boycott of potatoes in response to the use of prison labour on Bethal (Transvaal) potato farms. The boycott hit sales and helped force the state to revise aspects of the prison-labour system.

In the 1960s and 1970s there were some isolated strikes – swiftly suppressed – and other sporadic acts of resistance such as crop-burning and desertion. There were only a few reports of strikes by workers on farms in the 1980s, mostly on agricultural co-operatives close to urban settlements. In most cases farmers dismissed the entire workforce or called in police to arrest strikers.

In one instance, in April 1980, 15 people were arrested on charges of public violence following a strike over wages by about 700 seasonal workers at the Kromrivier Apple Co-operative in the Western Cape. Police were called in to disperse workers who threw stones in an angry response to the collapse of talks with management.[79] Of the 15 accused three were under 15 years of age. All were subjected to electric shock torture while held by the police. In the wake of the strike 300 workers were dismissed and forcibly evicted from their hostels and 85 strikers who were contract workers were sent back to the Transkei.[80]

In August of the same year 1,500 women seasonal workers on the Zebedelia Citrus Estate in the Transvaal stopped work, demanding higher wages; all were dismissed.[81] In March 1983, the entire workforce at the Eastern Cape Agricultural Co-op Creamery near Queenstown struck for higher wages. They were immediately dismissed and some charged with intimidation. Publicity in the wake of the strike revealed extremely brutal conditions. The creamery foremen carried guns, and several workers had been assaulted. One worker had his jaw broken when assaulted for arriving late at work; another was shot in the leg.[82] During 1986 there was a mass strike by farm workers on 12 farms in the GaModjadi area of the Transvaal over a range of grievances, including the length of the working day and low wages. At least one of the farmers fired most of his workers.[83]

Women, the lowest paid and most vulnerable of farm workers, played the leading role in some of these strikes. At Zebedelia, all the strikers were women and at the Kromrivier Apple Co-op the strike was initiated by a group of 50 women. All except one of these reported strikes were organised by the Food and Canning Workers Union or its sister union the African Food and Canning Workers Union which merged with other independent unions in 1986 to form the Food and Allied Workers Union (FAWU), the only non-racial or black union with a significant rural base. Organising chiefly in food-processing plants, it had by 1990 extended its presence to workers on Western Cape wine and fruit farms, where its ability to reach workers was facilitated by the proximity of farms to towns, the predominance of co-ops and a largely Coloured labour force – unlike African farm workers, Coloured workers could belong to registered trade unions. The Paper, Wood and Allied Union tried with limited success in the 1980s to extend its base among forestry workers to sugar plantation workers in Natal, and in 1982 the Orange and Vaal General Workers Union began organising farm workers on the Soeteveld Farms consortium owned by the Anglo American Corporation.[84]

When the Congress of South African Trade Unions (COSATU) was formed in 1985, it prioritised expansion into the agricultural sector. Some of its affiliates set up projects to organise farm workers – notably FAWU. Outside the federation a number of small, regionally based unions were also set up to organise on farms. There was a slight increase in strikes on farms after 1985 in response to this organisation, but the unionisation of farm workers, especially those involved in sowing, cultivation and harvesting in more remote areas, remained extremely difficult.

In the bantustans

The dispossession of land, compulsory culling of livestock, enforced changes in land usage, resettlement of people on ground already made barren and the imposition of bantustan 'independence' engendered resistance which sometimes led to widespread rural revolts. In the early 1960s Witzieshoek, Zeerust, Mpondoland and Tembuland were the scenes of bitter, often violent, rebellion involving attacks on bantustan officials, traders and others seen to be collaborating with the authorities. For more than nine months in 1960, the Pondo region of the Transkei was rocked by a widespread revolt against the imposition of bantustan authorities. In some areas an alternative political authority developed in the hills, taking over the allocation of land and other functions.[85] The rebellion was broken only by the imposition of a regional State of Emergency, the arrest and trial of thousands of peasants, the torching of homes of known opposition sympathisers and by police opening fire on demonstrators.[86]

Later phases of resistance took many forms, including resistance to removals and armed attacks on bantustan officials. Changes in land usage, and in particular the development of agri-business from the mid-1970s onwards, sparked widespread and bitter opposition. Agri-business projects, which inevitably led to the dispossession of peasants, were a focal point in the outbreaks of rural unrest. One commentator has stated: 'The situation was reached in 1986 where many such projects required the armed protection of the SADF [South African Defence Force].'[87] Such acts of resistance were poorly documented because they occurred away from the main urban centres, but instances of crop-burning by people dispossessed of land were reported by an official commission in the Transkei bantustan and there were organised thefts of crops from new projects in the Bophuthatswana bantustan by dispossessed peasants.[88]

Resistance often spread from towns and cities to nearby bantustans where broader political issues were taken by commuters and unionised contract workers into dormitory towns and more remote areas, especially in the Ciskei and bantustans bordering or close to the PWV.

Resistance in the Ciskei was closely bound up with wider resistance in the Eastern Cape. Residents of Duncan Village in East London fought long and bitter battles against the threat of incorporation into the Ciskei.[89] In 1983 the bantustan commuter settlement of Mdantsane, alongside East London, was the focus of a prolonged bus boycott which led to violent confrontation between residents and the authorities. Sporadic and repeated bus boycotts had occurred earlier in bantustan areas around the PWV (see Chapter 8 below).

In the mid-1980s there was an upsurge of resistance in almost every bantustan and protests reached into the most remote rural areas. The revision of controls on movement in the late 1970s trapped hundreds of thousands of unemployed youths in the bantustans. At the same time, during the 1984–6 uprising many youths involved in school boycotts in the urban centres sought refuge from state violence in the bantustans.[90] Politicised by their experiences, they helped form youth organisations, stimulating the formation in turn of civic, women's and bantustan residents' associations.

In Lebowa – a desperately poor area with a high rate of youth unemployment to which large numbers of retrenched farm workers were forcibly removed in the early 1980s – there was a full scale uprising between 1985 and 1986. Consumer and bus boycotts, and campaigns in schools for Student Representative Councils and a reduction in fees, were organised by nascent youth and community organisations in the Sekhukhuneland region of the bantustan. There was a campaign to ostracise local police, seen as collaborators with the authorities, banning them from shebeens (drinking clubs), shops, churches and sports clubs, and from using taxis.[91]

Resistance penetrated even into remote rural areas. In the Steelpoort farming region of the North Eastern Transvaal, bordering on Lebowa, trucks ferrying workers from the fields back to the bantustan were stoned and set on fire, cattle fences torn down and livestock and crops stolen. Farmers driving into the bantustan to recruit labour were refused entry at makeshift roadblocks and some came under attack. Workers stayed away from the fields to commemorate May Day and attend the funerals of activists killed by police. White farmers called on the SADF to erect an electrified fence along the bantustan border, while armed police escorted the local white school bus.[92]

In Bophuthatswana, major conflicts occurred between the local authorities and the bantustan population. In the Winterveldt squatter camp, there had been a long campaign over grievances which included attempts by the authorities to evict residents who were not Tswana-speaking. On 26 March 1986 bantustan police opened fire on a meeting of 5,000 residents in the settlement, killing 11 and injuring 70; they then arrested 2,500 people. Disaffection was so widespread that local army units attempted a mutiny in February 1988; this was brutally suppressed by the SADF. [93]

In the KwaNdebele bantustan, young militants forged an alliance with local villagers, their parents, civil servants and local chiefs to oppose impending 'independence'. The authorities organised vigilantes to stamp out opposition. Self-defence units were organised to protect residents from attack. There were mass meetings, worker stay-aways and school boycotts; shops and institutions linked to the authorities were destroyed.[94] In 1988, following two years of repression in the area, the central government announced it would still impose independence — but made no evident further move towards doing so.[95]

In July and August 1988 there was a similar upsurge of resistance in the Venda bantustan, where all sections of the community united in opposition to the authorities to protest over the complicity of officials in the murder of residents. There were school boycotts, mass meetings and a widely supported stay-away in which even elements of the bantustan police and local civil service took part.[96]

There was evidence in some bantustans of a rising level of support for and participation in the ANC's armed struggle. [97]

This period saw opposition in the bantustans transformed. From isolated incidents of rural resistance and protests around transport and related issues in commuter settlements, more widespread resistance arose, encompassing all sections of the population.

3   In the Towns and Cities

In the 1970s and 1980s workers in towns and cities were split along apartheid lines and the different groups housed in segregated areas. Coloured, Indian and African workers lived in separate segregated suburbs or townships, removed from white residential and industrial areas. In most African townships contract workers were separated from those with permanent residence rights.

Just under half the African workforce lived in townships outside the bantustans. Over a quarter were contract workers resident in single-sex dormitories, physically separate from the permanent residents of the townships, and another quarter were commuters living in dormitory towns inside bantustan boundaries.[1]

The areas where black workers lived functioned as labour dormitories. The provision of essential services – housing, transport, sewerage, water, electricity and health care – was rudimentary. Both the state and employers tried to reduce the costs of providing these services and to cut their responsibilities for them. Townships were geared to ensuring that workers had minimal shelter, transport to and from work each day and sufficient health care to maintain production.

The enforced segregation of black workers, their confinement to townships often far removed from their workplaces, and the political controls over their residential areas had contradictory effects. These factors militated against worker organisation and strengthened the hand of employers. But they also transformed urban townships into frontlines of resistance to apartheid, turning struggles over housing and transport and demands for democratic local government into challenges to state power.

This chapter examines how housing was used to control the urban working population and why transport to and from work featured regularly as an issue engaging workers in struggle. The final part surveys the wages and working conditions of these workers in the period reviewed, and the unemployment that was part of their experience.

Housing

In the bantustans
A freeze on the provision of accommodation for African workers in the main urban centres in favour of building houses in the bantustans was part of the battery of measures in the late 1960s to reduce the number of Africans living permanently outside the bantustans.[2] In 1970 only two bantustan towns had a population of more than 50,000; in 1979 there were nine such settlements (three of which, Umlazi and KwaMashu in KwaZulu and Mdantsane in the Ciskei, had been included in bantustans simply by shifting boundaries). There was also a proliferation of smaller towns with 2,000 to 10,000 residents and by 1979 over 1.5 million people lived in such towns.[3] In the same period there was a reduction in the African populations of 197 towns outside the bantustans.[4]

The policy of economic decentralisation involved the building of bantustan towns close to industrial centres. The ten largest bantustan towns were situated between 4 and 35 kilometres from white towns or industrial centres.[5] These townships had few amenities and were physically and socially isolated from other urban communities: 'Most ... lack an economic base and none of the homeland towns can be regarded as an urban area in the full sense of the word. They are little more than appendices to or dormitory towns for "white" urban areas.'[6]

New policies of 'orderly urbanisation' and industrial deconcentration led to a shift in the provision of housing in the 1980s. Building programmes were concentrated in large dormitory townships outside, but close to, bantustan borders. These townships were meant to act as satellites of the main cities, and to shift population and industry away from these centres.

Despite the bantustan building programmes, housing shortages in these areas were acute, due to increases in population arising from forced removals and the evictions of unemployed labour from the main centres. There was an estimated bantustan housing shortage of 170,000 dwellings in 1977. By 1983 this had risen to 258,000 units, according to some sources.[7]

Contract workers
Traditionally contract workers were housed in hostels or single-sex dormitories. The building of this accommodation in townships outside the bantustans was financed both from public funds and by employers. By 1985 288,000 African men were housed in over 200 single sex-hostels

or barracks throughout the country. Six hostels, located mainly in the PWV area, housed 3,600 women contract workers. The largest hostels each housed over 10,000 men.[8] Including the 400,000 miners housed in compounds, almost three-quarters of a million contract workers had to live in these stark, overcrowded institutions without privacy or basic comforts, separated from family and community.[9]

Contract workers outside the mines commonly lived in two types of hostels: those built by township administrations and white municipalities, generally older and with minimal facilities; and employer-built dormitories, which varied in facilities. Although the abolition of the Influx Control Act of 1986 removed the 1968 regulations enforcing the contract labour system, single male workers from the bantustan areas were still housed in these institutions in the absence of other forms of accommodation and because of the general housing shortage as the decade closed.

The state-built hostels were primitive. Many hostels had broken windows, toilets with open sewerage sluices and no partitions for privacy, and communal cold-water showers; many lacked electricity, cooking facilities, heating and water. A 1985 study of Cape Town hostels showed that an average of 22 people shared single toilets, some of which had been out of order for as long as five years. As a result many shower-blocks were turned into toilets, forcing men to wash at taps outside in the open or to make use of buckets. Most hostels lacked internal taps. The men used primus stoves for cooking, and warmed the rooms in winter by placing sheets of zinc on the stoves.[10] A 1986 study on the health of hostel inmates found that 'any communicable disease was likely to spread very easily and quickly in conditions of overcrowding. Upper respiratory tract infections, as well as skin diseases were frequent.'[11]

Tension was high in most of these hostels, induced by lack of privacy and raids by police looking for 'illegals'. Employer-built hostels were subject to the same invasions but generally had better conditions. However, they were usually more tightly controlled, as one report on hostels in Cape Town noted:

> High jackal-fences encompass employer hostels. Each company employs a caretaker, whose duties include seeing to it that unauthorised persons do not gain entry to the hostels ... Workers at these hostels complain that it is a lot more difficult for their wives or girlfriends to visit them than at council [Administration Board] hostels. Apart from the caretakers and the jackal-fences, the employers or their representatives occasionally visit the hostels during the day to check

whether there are unauthorised persons. When this happens visitors, more especially women visitors, must seek sanctuary in the nearby shrubs.[12]

A newspaper reported that in hostels built by the parastatal Iron and Steel Corporation (ISCOR) to house its contract workforce in 1978:

> The intention was to create a hierarchy of dedicated steelmen. This hierarchical structure is built into each flat, where there is a prefect with a bedroom to himself, three assistants sharing a slightly larger bedroom and another six men in the third bedroom. The pecking order extends to the positioning of the more senior man's bed, so he can control the room's light switch. And it's all worked out by computer, programmed by a sophisticated personnel information system ... Each man's progress, abilities and personal details right down to the size of his boots, are stored in the computer's memory for instant recall. He is given a new merit rating after every 75 shifts and the computer knows precisely where he is and what he is doing ... each working day. To make the system's control complete each flat is linked by intercom to the house father's cottage and to the central administration block ... One feels that it was planned by a team of clinical psychologists, economists and social anthropologists, who tried hard to consider all the angles.[13]

Domestic workers
Many domestics lived in townships as the lodgers of tenants occupying family housing. In Johannesburg a small number of women were housed in women's hostels in nearby townships. But the majority were isolated as the live-in servants of white employers occupying separate quarters – so-called servant's rooms – usually in the back yards of employers' houses.[14] While this spared them having to find accommodation in the townships, it intensified control by employers and meant that domestics could be called on to work at any hour. Although in the late 1980s conditions improved in response to organisation by domestic workers, in many cases quarters were still not provided with bathroom facilities, hot water or electricity. Conditions were generally worse in urban flats, where special rooms were set aside for domestics behind the buildings or on roofs, and all the workers in a block shared the same amenities.

Live-in servants were cut off from their communities and families for long periods. Unlike contract workers, they were also isolated from contact with fellow-workers. Recreational opportunities and social contacts were often denied them in white suburbs far from churches, community centres and friends. Municipal by-laws made it illegal for them to have husbands, lovers or their children living with them. Some local authorities introduced regulations which compelled employers to keep keys to their domestic servants' quarters, enabling the police to make spot checks for people living there illegally.

Workers living permanently outside the bantustans
Workers with rights to live permanently outside bantustans generally lived in family houses in townships. The freeze on the building of new family housing led to severe accommodation shortages throughout South Africa. According to the Riekert Commission there was a national shortage of 468,000 township houses for African families, with an immediate backlog of 141,000 units in the late 1970s.[15] Independent researchers placed the shortage at 832,000 units by 1987.[16] Between 1980 and 1985 an average of only 8,000 new homes were built each year.[17]

The shortage of housing led to widespread overcrowding. A 1987 survey of 32 townships in the PWV region found that there was an average of 11 people living in each four-roomed house. Outside the PWV, other surveys found greater occupation densities. In Uitenhage (Eastern Cape) some houses had 42 occupants and in Kimberley (Northern Cape) up to 30.[18] The average township house is a four-roomed structure, constructed of cheap materials and in most cases lacking ceilings and floors, which tenants are expected to provide themselves. Although most houses in the larger townships are supplied with water, only 13 per cent had electricity in 1986.[19] Researchers for the Carnegie Inquiry into Poverty in 1984 found that 'scant attention is being paid to the serious qualitative state of black townships ... Many urban black houses are in a serious state of disrepair and a gigantic programme of renovation is needed to make these houses decent habitations.'[20]

Because in the period covered African townships were regarded as temporary outposts of the bantustans, no facilities which could imply permanence were provided, especially recreational facilities. Their principal landmarks were the buildings concerned with administration and control. Townships could be isolated easily in times of resistance. Houses were built in parallel rows, back to back, or in concentric circles. Entire townships or parts of a township could be sealed off (as could hostels), allowing police and military units to sweep through in house-to-house searches.

The restrictive housing policy led to the establishment of squatter camps in all the major urban centres. In the 1980s at least 7 million people were believed to live in squatter settlements of one kind or another; they included both workers illegally outside the bantustans and legal workers who could not find housing.[21]

The largest squatter settlements, with a combined population of over 1.25 million, were located around Durban. The giant Winterveld squatter camp in the Bophuthatswana bantustan became a refuge for illegal and homeless workers from Pretoria and the rest of the PWV complex: it accommodated at least a million people in 1984. Some 400,000 squatters lived in Cape Town in 1988, including between 70,000 and 100,000 in makeshift shacks of tin and board at Crossroads. In the larger townships of the PWV, new forms of squatting developed with residents building illegal structures in the back yards of existing houses.[22]

In squatter camps contract workers lived side by side with those with permanent residence rights, illegal workers with legal residents, Coloured and Indian workers alongside Africans, in defiance of the fundamental divisions of apartheid. Action against them was often particularly severe, taking the form of raids, demolitions and forced removals by police and sometimes army personnel.

Administration, finance and services

In 1971 governance of African townships outside the bantustans was transferred from white municipalities to local Administration Boards (later called Development Boards), acting on behalf of central government. The Boards were also charged with enforcing controls on movement and they formed a single system of central state domination over every aspect of the lives of African workers, from labour placement to housing, welfare and services in the townships.

The townships were required to be self-financing. The state made no direct contribution to the funding of housing, services or amenities. The self-financing principle was informed by the view that the workers in the townships were there temporarily. Housing, transport and services in the urban townships were treated as costs of labour to be borne, by residents and employers, through levies. In 1985 employer levies amounted to about 16 per cent of the income of the Boards. The rest was raised from township residents through direct and indirect charges.

Between 1960 and 1980 the self-financing of black townships depended heavily on the state-sponsored sale of alcohol to Africans through a statutory monopoly. Giant beer halls and liquor outlets were built and were in most cases the only recreational facilities in these areas.

The profits were channelled into the revenues of the Boards. In the mid-1980s liquor outlets in some townships were privatised, but the boards retained controlling interests in consortia producing sorghum beer. The other main sources of revenue were rentals paid by occupants of houses and hostels. Rents were based on the size of accommodation and bore little relation to its quality.

The narrow base of township finance led to impoverished conditions and minimal services and, after the mid-1970s, to recurring and intense conflict between township administrations and residents. Beer halls and liquor outlets were among the primary targets of demonstrators during the 1976 uprising and in subsequent protests. They were burned to the ground and stocks destroyed. The increases in rents to which administrations resorted to recoup this loss of revenue also met with resistance. After 1979 there were widespread and sustained rent boycotts, plunging the administrations into still deeper financial crisis. In the 1984-5 financial year, for example, only six of the 13 Development Boards were operating with surpluses. [23] By mid-1986 rent boycotts had spread to 31 townships, creating arrears of over R250 million.[24]

Restructuring of administration
In a bid to resolve the financial crisis and to align policies for the administration of townships with other policies, the government revised its approach to housing and local government. By the early 1980s it was conceding that the acute housing shortage was interfering with its aim of fostering the growth of a settled, skilled urban labour force. Restrictions on the building of family housing were lifted and a limited percentage of state funds redirected to townships for housing programmes. The government continued a process begun in the 1970s of easing restrictions on Africans owning their own homes, extending provisions for 30-year leases to 99-year leaseholds, and introducing freehold purchase rights in 1986. Private companies were encouraged to build houses in townships for their employees and there were moves towards the legalisation of some squatter camps, allowing residents to construct their own homes around basic site-and-service schemes.

The government also set in motion a programme to reduce its dependence on rents as a source of income. In 1983 it announced moves to sell off 80 per cent of its housing stock to African tenants. The government hoped that rentals would be replaced by rates for which home owners would be liable. At the same time the state would dispose of its responsibility to maintain what had in most cases become obsolete housing stock in need of maintenance and upgrading. The sale of housing progressed slowly. By mid-1988 only a quarter of homes had been sold after several years of concerted campaigning. Aside from widespread political opposition to the scheme, residents could not afford to buy them.[25]

New rent increases were introduced in July 1984 for those who had not bought their homes. They were met by widespread and intense resistance, with boycotts sweeping the PWV townships in the second half of 1984.

Changes in housing policy were accompanied by a restructuring of local government. Unlike the Coloured and Indian populations, who were allowed to elect representatives to the tricameral segregated chambers of parliament introduced in 1984, Africans in the main industrial centres were not permitted to participate in central government. New structures were created to represent them, elected community councils in 1977 and then the town and village councils, brought into existence by the Black Local Authorities Act of 1982. By increasing their administrative powers the government hoped to satisfy the political aspirations of the African population outside the bantustans.

However, the councils were now directly responsible for implementing unpopular measures like rent increases and eviction of tenants. They remained dependent on the same narrow sources of income and their powers were limited. The Boards were retained as agents of the councils, carrying out functions such as the enforcement of pass laws, education and the construction of housing, in particular that for contract workers. Central government retained a right of veto over council decisions and could impose measures the councils failed to implement, including rent increases.

The councils manifestly failed to co-opt any significant section of the African population. Opposition was intense. Elections for councillors in November 1983 were widely boycotted and less than 20 per cent of those eligible to vote did so. The councils were surrounded by controversy, with councillors earning much higher pay than those they were supposed to represent and with less scrupulous councillors granting themselves trading licences and priority access to housing. In the uprisings which began in September 1984 councillors came under sustained attack. The homes of many were burned down, several were physically assaulted and at least four were killed. By mid-1985 many councils had ceased to function and their functions were taken over by government officials.[26]

Coloured and Indian areas

In the 1950s and 1960s Coloured and Indian workers and their families were subject to mass removals under the Group Areas Act of 1947, as the state sought to achieve total residential segregation and division of the working class. Hundreds of thousands of Coloured residents were removed forcibly from the inner-city areas and suburbs of Cape Town to inhospitable and remote mass housing estates, as were Indian residents in Durban. Provision of housing in the new estates lagged behind the rate of evictions and severe shortages arose. In the mid-1970s, for example, some 200,000 Coloureds were living in squatter camps around Cape Town.[27] In 1986 the Coloured housing shortage was officially estimated at 52,000 units and that for Indians at 40,000.[28]

Housing and services in Coloured and Indian areas were financed by white local authorities, with services subsidised from general rates. However, because Coloured and Indian residents were not represented in these authorities, projects in their areas were generally accorded low priority. These communities were instead represented by elected management committees which carried out limited functions of local government. The elections for these committees were marked by low polls.[29] Housing in Coloured and Indian areas was co-ordinated by the National Housing Commission. Funds were provided to white local authorities by the National Housing Fund and repaid from rents.

In the 1980s new patterns of housing emerged in the Coloured and Indian Group Areas, in a move away from an earlier emphasis on sub-economic housing. Rapidly inflated construction costs and declining real wages meant that most tenants in the new housing schemes simply could not afford their rents: after 1981 there were repeated struggles against rent and service increases in the Cape Town and Durban areas. Many tenants were forced to squat. In Durban, where the local authority provided mass housing schemes at relatively low costs, new housing was still too expensive for most Indian workers. A survey conducted among residents of Chatsworth in 1981, for example, found that in order to pay rent half the residents spent less on food and essentials than was minimally necessary. An increasing number of people had taken to renting garages or outbuildings, or were squatting.[30]

Local government in the late 1980s

Faced with rent boycotts, popular rejection of councils and management committees and an unresolved financial crisis, the government began implementing long-standing plans to further restructure local government through the Regional Service Councils Act of 1985. Regional Service

Councils (RSCs) were established in some parts of the country as an extension of local government intended to co-ordinate the provision of services by the segregated local authorities in each locality. They were made up of the representatives of councils in African townships, management committees in Coloured and Indian areas and white municipalities, with a chairperson appointed by the provincial administrator.

The new bodies set out to increase direct state control over local authorities and expand the financial reserves available to them. The RSCs drew their finances from the existing incomes of the individual local authorities but in the provision of housing and services were free to redistribute funds from one authority to another within their area. At the same time, reserves were increased by imposing two additional levies on local businesses, a regional services levy (calculated as a proportion of a company's total wage and salary bill) and a regional establishment levy (a percentage of the turnover of each firm). The revised system of finances was aimed at resolving the financial crisis in local government by transferring many of the costs of the welfare of black labour to the private sector.[31]

It was widely feared, however, that the increased levies on employers would act as a constraint on wage increases. More importantly, the discredited councils and management committees were retained intact as institutions of political control within the new system. The potential of the African councillors nominated to the RSCs for influencing the distribution of resources was minimised by the allocation of voting power in the RSCs. Votes were distributed per delegate in proportion to the value of the services consumed by the residents of each area. The representatives of the wealthier white areas were therefore likely to be able to retain effective control. At the same time checks were built into the allocation of votes to prevent black authorities acquiring a majority. No single authority would have more than half the votes.[32]

Getting to work

Transport patterns and conditions

By forcing black urban workers to live in segregated townships generally far removed from their work, the apartheid system transformed transport into a key feature of the system of labour relations.

The development of transport patterns reflected the ways in which population controls were enforced, and the use of transport as an instrument of those controls. According to a research report by the

Council for Scientific and Industrial Research (CSIR), over a period of 25 years commuting patterns were transformed from mainly short distances to medium and long distances by the Group Areas Act, bantustan consolidation and population removals.[33]

A 1985 survey found that over 400,000 commuters travelled distances of more than 30 kilometres a day. Eighty per cent of black commuters spent an average of two and a half hours a day travelling. The remaining fifth spent between three and a half and seven hours of each day travelling. These statistics compared unfavourably with European countries, where the average distance travelled was less than 14 kilometres and time spent on transport averaged about an hour.[34]

In many townships workers rose before dawn to be on time for buses, allowing for inevitable delays. Most left for work while it was still dark. At night townships, which were mostly not electrified, were unsafe for commuters, particularly on pay days. A 1987 survey of 16 PWV townships found, for example, that more than half the commuters had experienced violence in the course of travel.[35]

Commuters travelling from far-flung bantustan dormitory towns to industrial centres spent more time on buses than other workers. Residents of KwaNdebele who worked in the PWV area left home in the dark and returned home late at night. According to a 1982 survey, 13 per cent left their homes between 2 a.m. and 3 a.m. in the morning to be at work on time, while only 8 per cent left after 5 a.m.[36] On average they spent more than 40 hours a week on buses:

> Once on the bus, several passengers ... put towels over their heads and fall asleep almost as soon as the bus pulls off. Some passengers cover themselves in blankets, others doze off with their head on the seat in front of the passenger next to them. The bus seats are hard and cold air seeps in through the windows. Occasional sharp stops or jolts of the bus wake the passengers suddenly pressing them against one another.[37]

Many of the KwaNdebele workers slept on the floors of the crowded buses or developed the art of sleeping standing up. Most had no time for recreational or leisure activity at all.[38]

Travelling time was increased by waiting for buses which were not already full and by breakdowns because of the strain on services. In a 1981 attitude survey in Mdantsane, 70 per cent of workers identified transport as their most serious problem.[39] Delays of up to two hours were common and commuters regularly arrived late for work; buses were dirty and broken windows never repaired. Shelters were non-existent and the service did not correspond to workers' shift times.

Under local authority ordinances, black bus stations were sited on the outskirts of the central business districts of most larger cities, so that after arriving in town commuters still had to walk to work.[40]

Finance of transport

Unlike housing and other services, public transport was not viewed as self-financing and bus and train services were heavily subsidised by the state. Employers also contributed to costs in the form of a levy for each worker employed. The level of employer levies fell dramatically between the mid-1970s and 1983, when they were tripled.[41] There were sharp increases in state subsidies with the growth of bantustan dormitory townships and commuter workforces.[42]

Aside from the state-owned railways, and in Durban where local authorities provided a bus service, private commercial operators dominated the transport sector outside the bantustans and were the recipients of the state and employer subsidies. In the bantustans seven bus corporations predominated, partly owned by the parastatal Corporation for Economic Development.[43]

From the 1940s on the state encouraged the monopolisation of the transport sector. Bussing was contracted out to a small number of licensed private monopolies by the National Transport Commission. They were in a powerful position to set their own profit margins without fear of competition and to force cost increases on commuters. The monopoly also worked against African entrepreneurs and black taxi companies who might have provided a cheaper and more efficient service. Alternative forms of transport were until the late 1980s restricted by the withholding of licences.

Commuters were not represented at hearings of the local Road Transportation Boards, which set fares. The Boards invariably ruled in favour of the companies. In spite of the high level of state subsidisation and the increase in employer levies in 1983, commuters still bore a high and rising share of their transport costs. In 1985 they contributed about half the cost of their fares; state subsidies accounted for about 37 per cent and employers only about 13 per cent.[44]

In the early 1980s, the state cut subsidies to commuters. In 1985–6, for example, rail subsidies were drastically cut while those for buses were increased by less than 1 per cent.[45] The costs of transport were therefore borne increasingly by commuters and fares rose after 1983.

Fare increases took place against a background of declining real wages after 1981. A 1985 survey showed that African households were spending well above 10 per cent of their income on transport. Commuters in the bantustans were even worse off. In KwaNdebele, for example, fares consumed 17.5 per cent of the average commuter's income.[46]

Resentment against transport costs and conditions were manifested during every period of heightened resistance to apartheid. After the bus monopolies were established in the 1940s commuters frequently resisted increases through bus boycotts, and buses were among the first targets of demonstrators. In the first three months of the 1976 Soweto uprising, 573 of the 962 buses owned by the Public Utility Transport Corporation (PUTCO) in the Transvaal were damaged in stoning incidents. Twenty-eight were entirely burnt out.[47] In the protests which began in the second half of 1984 PUTCO saw 20 of its buses totally destroyed in one year alone.[48] The state and bus companies were sensitive to bus boycotts, the state because they extended worker organisation beyond the factory floor, and bus companies because they directly threatened profits and reduced their claims to annual subsidies which were calculated as a proportion of the number of tickets sold.

During the 1980s the transport system was beset by crises. The number of passengers declined, chiefly because of increased unemployment and a preference by commuters for more efficient taxis and mini-buses.[49] Several government commissions and studies by state research bodies looked into these problems, notably the Welgemoed Commission (1983), the National Transport Policy Study (1982–3) and the National Institute for Transport and Road Research of the CSIR in 1984.[50]

The Welgemoed Commission recommended that the monopoly on public transport be retained, but that subsidisation of services be gradually phased out. Although the Commission recommended that the state clamp down on unlicensed taxis and other alternative forms of transport, the National Transport Commission suggested that more privately owned taxis and mini-buses be licensed. This would reduce the state's commitment to subsidisation:

> Taxis and micro-bus (combi-taxi) services should be regarded as a necessary adjunct to the development of more adequate public transport services in the major urban centres, but the number of permits issued in each centre should continually be reviewed in order to keep these as close to the optimum as possible and to minimise any destructive competition with other transport services.[51]

Prior to 1984, the state pursued a generally repressive policy towards taxis and mini-buses owned by black entrepreneurs, licensing only a few and allowing them to operate only in restricted areas – usually inside townships. The authorities clamped down on unlicensed 'pirate' taxis. A more liberal policy was pursued after 1984; the number of licensed taxis and mini-buses doubled between 1985 and 1986.[52] However, the government's commitment to the monopoly on bus services continued.

The other major revision in transport policy was the state's aim to reduce subsidies by transferring responsibility for local and regional services to the new Regional Service Councils. Transport was no longer solely financed by the state but partly funded from taxes imposed on employers under the new system. In the past employers resisted increased levies. Inevitably, under the new system, an increasing proportion of transport costs would be borne by commuters themselves, because employers resisted greater responsibility by trying to hold down wages as the new taxes were imposed. The new system reinforced discrimination against workers from bantustan areas, favouring those living closer to their places of work who could make use of cheaper transport.

Wages, cost of living and unemployment

As well as maintaining the division and control of the workforce, the transport system reinforced the denial of basic rights to the black population, the restrictions on their movement and discriminatory reservation of jobs for whites. These all helped to force the black industrial workforce into largely manual and semi-skilled work and allowed employers to set the generally low wages paid to black workers.

Before 1973 African wages in manufacturing were static or had declined in real terms. After that real earnings increased substantially, fuelled by exposés of conditions in foreign companies investing in South Africa and by the resurgence of the trade union movement. Pay increases at the mines, following a dramatic rise in the gold price, pushed up the general level of wages, and minimum wages for unskilled workers increased by about a quarter between 1973 and 1984.[53] Nevertheless, the wage gap between white and black remained. In 1981, for example, white workers' wages increased by the same percentage as Africans. The National Manpower Commission reported in the same year that the absolute difference between the earnings of whites and those of other groups was growing, due to the continued concentration of whites in skilled, highly paid job categories.[54] The entry of some black workers into skilled occupations formerly monopolised by whites did not significantly increase the aggregate earning power of black workers. The minimum wages for artisans declined in real terms by a quarter between 1973 and 1984, partly because of lower wages paid to black workers entering skilled work (see Table 6).[55]

Real earnings
The increase in total earnings which occurred did not involve an equal increase in wage rates. The government maintained that between 1973 and 1981 real wages increased by an average of 5.2 per cent each year and by 58.2 per cent over the entire period.[56] However, the increases partly reflected earnings from longer hours of work or temporary bonus payments and employer contributions to pension funds rather than higher hourly rates. Between 1970 and 1981, for example, an average of 11.7 per cent of working hours in manufacture was in the form of overtime, accounting for about a fifth of monthly pay packets.[57] When overtime pay is excluded the wage increases amounted to less than 1 per cent between 1978 and mid-1981.[58] Moreover, the increases of the early 1970s were made from a very low base. After four years of wage increases, average monthly earnings of African workers were still only 75 per cent of the most conservative estimates of the Poverty Datum Line.[59]

After 1981 real wages continued to rise in response to shop floor pressures, although more slowly, until 1983, when recession saw a relative retreat from strike activity. Declining living standards caused a rash of strikes in the first half of 1984, again increasing real earnings. After 1985 and until the close of the decade, however, recession and political crisis rapidly reduced earnings, except in strongly unionised sectors where wage increases kept level with inflation. By March 1986 real wages of all workers, skilled and unskilled, had fallen by over 7 per cent and in 1987 they continued to fall outside unionised sectors.[60]

Unemployment and inflation severely eroded the earnings of African families and their dependants as workers lost jobs in mass retrenchments and lay-offs in the motoring, metals and other sectors of manufacturing after 1981. In the 1980s from having two or three wage earners many households were reduced, to dependence on a single wage. Inflation affected the cost of basic necessities. Prices of maize products, bread, milk and sugar increased by between 7 and 25 per cent each year during the early 1980s. Between 1980 and 1985 food prices more than doubled, rents increased by 123 per cent and the cost of public transport rose by 218 per cent.[61]

Wages

Accurate evaluation of industrial wages during the period reviewed is difficult. The government published only broad sectoral figures, of doubtful reliability. However, the legally enforceable minimum wage rates laid down by official wage regulating machinery allows a more detailed picture to emerge.

The main institutions determining minimum wages were Industrial Councils and Wage Boards. Their defects and their bias against black workers and in favour of employers, white workers and the state are explored in Chapter 5 below.

Industrial Councils brought together registered trade unions and employer organisations to negotiate minimum wages annually (or less frequently) for a particular industry. The agreements became legally binding. Some Industrial Councils were national in scope, others were regional or even restricted to individual towns. In 1985 there were 101 such agreements in operation, covering manufacture, construction, liquor and catering, personal services such as laundries and hairdressing, local government, transport, aspects of commerce and a range of other activities.[62]

Industrial Councils set wages for industries in which trade unions had organised workers, as only registered unions could be represented on councils. Minimum wages in industries or sectors which were, for the most part, not organised were determined by Wage Boards. For example, no Industrial Council existed for civil engineering (which included road and dam building, construction of airports and so on). Wage Boards were appointed by the Minister of Manpower and were composed of state functionaries. They investigated wages and other conditions of employment, heard evidence from interested parties and made recommendations to the Minister which were then published as legally enforceable wage determinations or labour orders. Domestic servants, farm workers, small employers and several categories of public service employment were excluded – workers in these sectors had no statutory wage protection at all.

In 1985 there were 229 wage determinations in force. Each covered one magisterial district, but workers in isolated and largely rural towns and villages were seldom covered and employers could pay any wages they saw fit in these areas. Neither Industrial Council agreements nor wage determinations applied in the bantustans.[63]

Industrial Council agreements and wage determinations for the period reviewed were systematically studied by the South African Labour and Development Research Unit (SALDRU) in Cape Town. Data concerning agreements and determinations current in June 1986 in selected sectors of the economy, and covering the hourly rates of most of the African workforce shows some of the factors which influenced the level of wages. In the case of Industrial Councils, figures did not reflect the actual wages earned by workers. Employers could pay above these levels and unions in manufacture often succeeded in negotiating higher wages with individual employers. Wage determinations reflected actual wages more accurately, as they covered unorganised sectors (see Graph 3.1).

Building sector

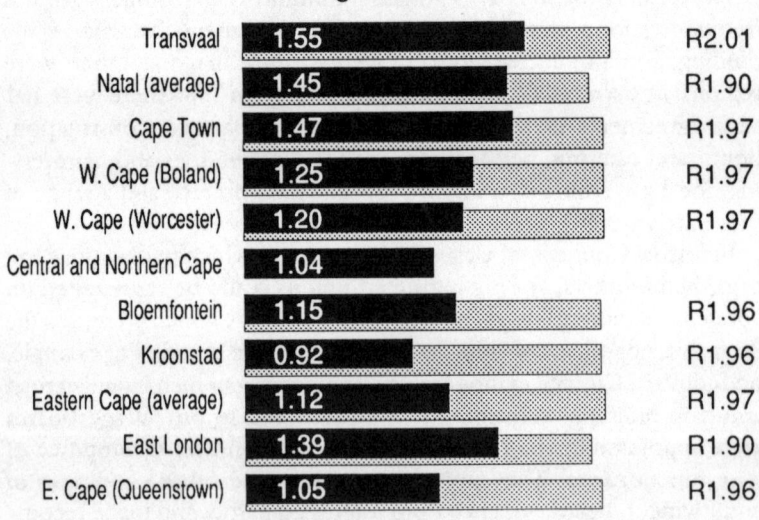

Transvaal	1.55	R2.01
Natal (average)	1.45	R1.90
Cape Town	1.47	R1.97
W. Cape (Boland)	1.25	R1.97
W. Cape (Worcester)	1.20	R1.97
Central and Northern Cape	1.04	
Bloemfontein	1.15	R1.96
Kroonstad	0.92	R1.96
Eastern Cape (average)	1.12	R1.97
East London	1.39	R1.90
E. Cape (Queenstown)	1.05	R1.96

Motor sector

Motor transport: Transvaal	1.25	R1.96
Motor transport: Transvaal	0.98	R1.90
Auto: Eastern Cape	2.70	R1.90
Auto engineering (SA)	1.24	n/a
Motor manufacture (SA)	1.50	n/a
Motor: Other (average)	1.14	n/a
Motor vehicle body (SA)	1.50	n/a

Textiles sector

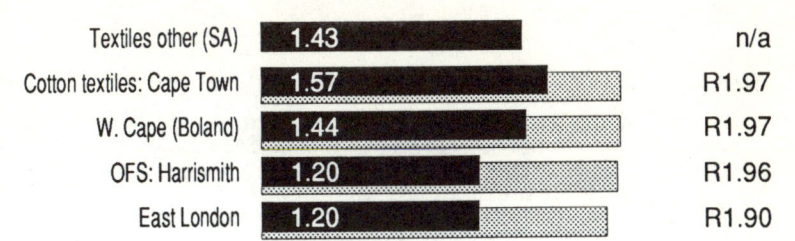

Textiles other (SA)	1.43	n/a
Cotton textiles: Cape Town	1.57	R1.97
W. Cape (Boland)	1.44	R1.97
OFS: Harrismith	1.20	R1.96
East London	1.20	R1.90

Selected foods sector

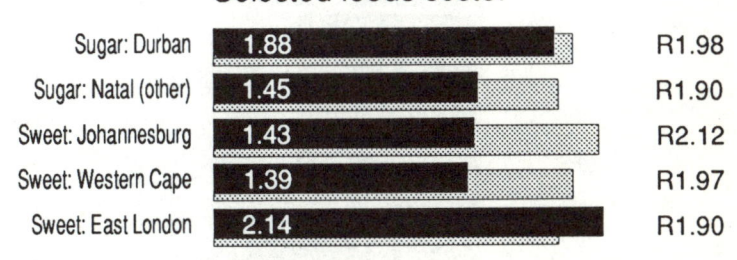

Sugar: Durban	1.88	R1.98
Sugar: Natal (other)	1.45	R1.90
Sweet: Johannesburg	1.43	R2.12
Sweet: Western Cape	1.39	R1.97
Sweet: East London	2.14	R1.90

Liquor and catering sector

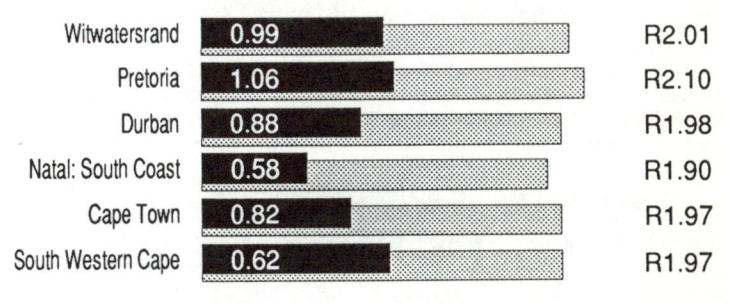

Witwatersrand	0.99	R2.01
Pretoria	1.06	R2.10
Durban	0.88	R1.98
Natal: South Coast	0.58	R1.90
Cape Town	0.82	R1.97
South Western Cape	0.62	R1.97

Steel sector

South Africa	1.90	R1.97

Chemical sector

Western Cape	1.74	R1.97
Transvaal	1.82	R2.01

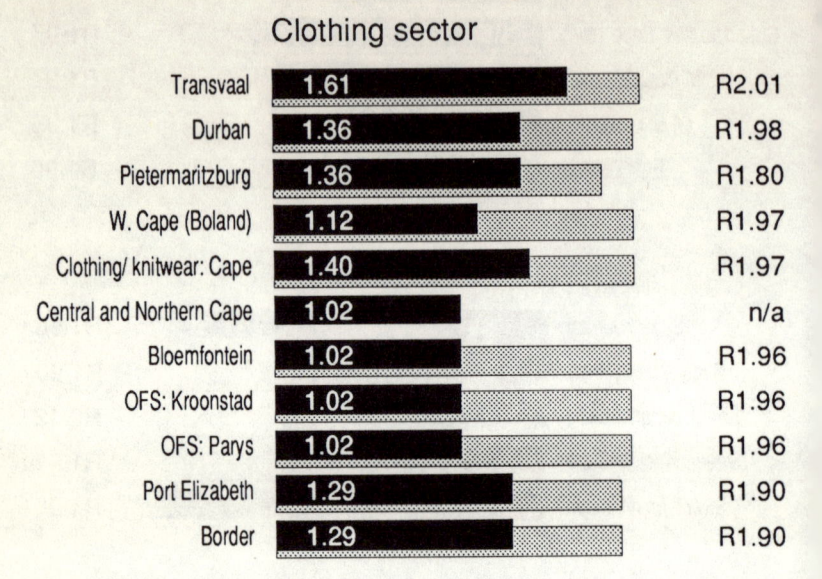

Clothing sector

Region	Wage	HSLL
Transvaal	1.61	R2.01
Durban	1.36	R1.98
Pietermaritzburg	1.36	R1.80
W. Cape (Boland)	1.12	R1.97
Clothing/ knitwear: Cape	1.40	R1.97
Central and Northern Cape	1.02	n/a
Bloemfontein	1.02	R1.96
OFS: Kroonstad	1.02	R1.96
OFS: Parys	1.02	R1.96
Port Elizabeth	1.29	R1.90
Border	1.29	R1.90

Graph 3.1: Hourly wages (rands) set by Industrial Councils for labourers in selected sectors and regions current in June 1986, compared to regional Household Supplemented Living Levels (HSLLs)

Notes: n.a. denotes that no HSLL was provided by the IPR for the region concerned.
Sources: Institute for Planning Research (IPR) 1986, p.62; Pillay, D. *et al* 1985; *SALDRU Labour Research Series, Monitor of Minimum Wage Measures*, 2nd Quarter 1986, pp.48–53.

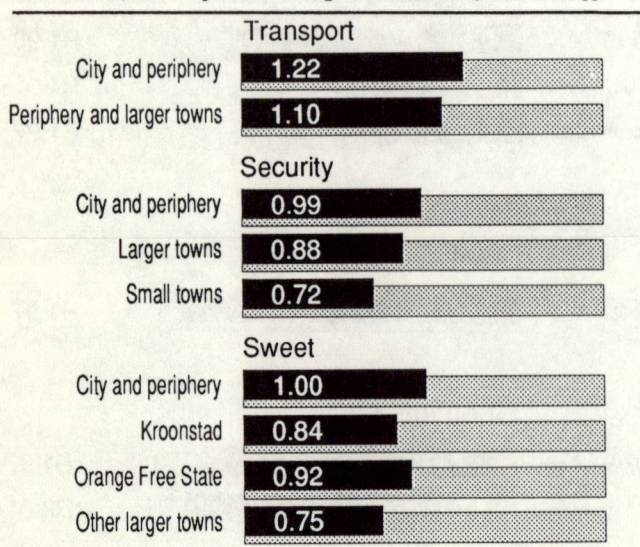

Transport

Region	Wage
City and periphery	1.22
Periphery and larger towns	1.10

Security

Region	Wage
City and periphery	0.99
Larger towns	0.88
Small towns	0.72

Sweet

Region	Wage
City and periphery	1.00
Kroonstad	0.84
Orange Free State	0.92
Other larger towns	0.75

In the Towns and Cities

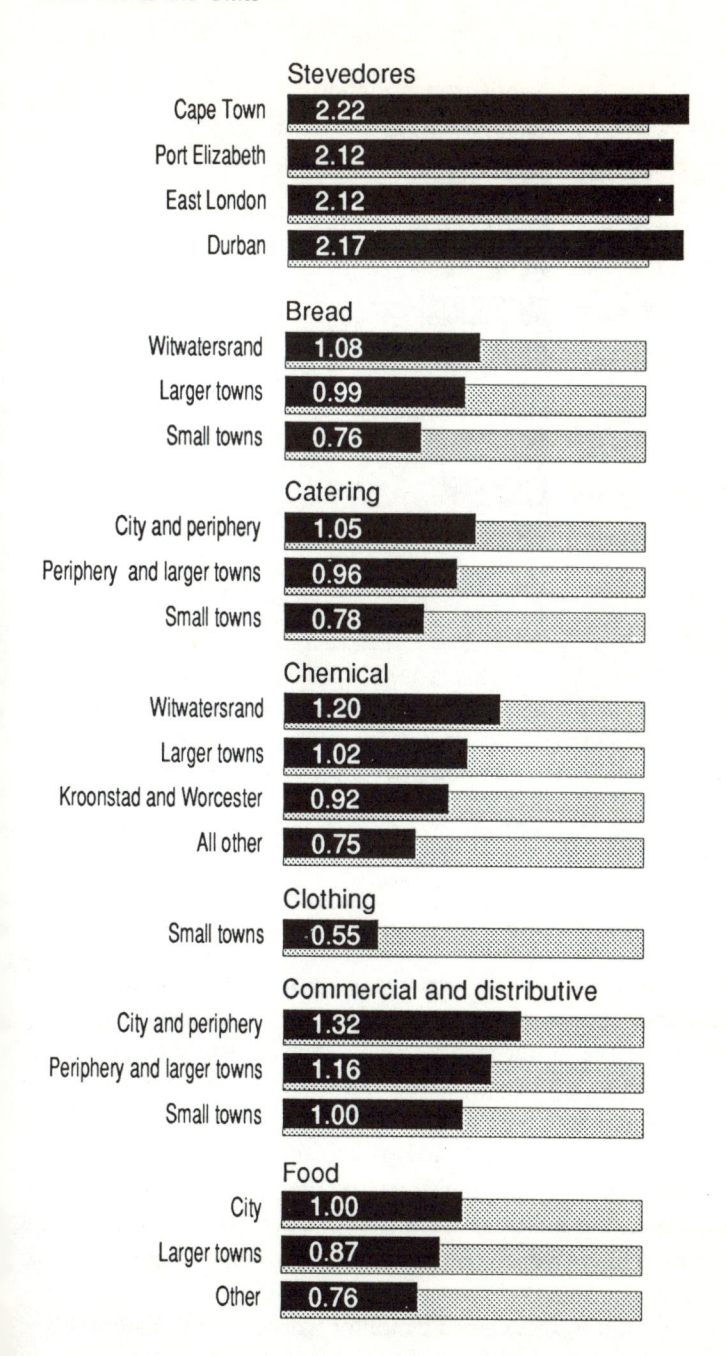

Stevedores
- Cape Town: 2.22
- Port Elizabeth: 2.12
- East London: 2.12
- Durban: 2.17

Bread
- Witwatersrand: 1.08
- Larger towns: 0.99
- Small towns: 0.76

Catering
- City and periphery: 1.05
- Periphery and larger towns: 0.96
- Small towns: 0.78

Chemical
- Witwatersrand: 1.20
- Larger towns: 1.02
- Kroonstad and Worcester: 0.92
- All other: 0.75

Clothing
- Small towns: 0.55

Commercial and distributive
- City and periphery: 1.32
- Periphery and larger towns: 1.16
- Small towns: 1.00

Food
- City: 1.00
- Larger towns: 0.87
- Other: 0.76

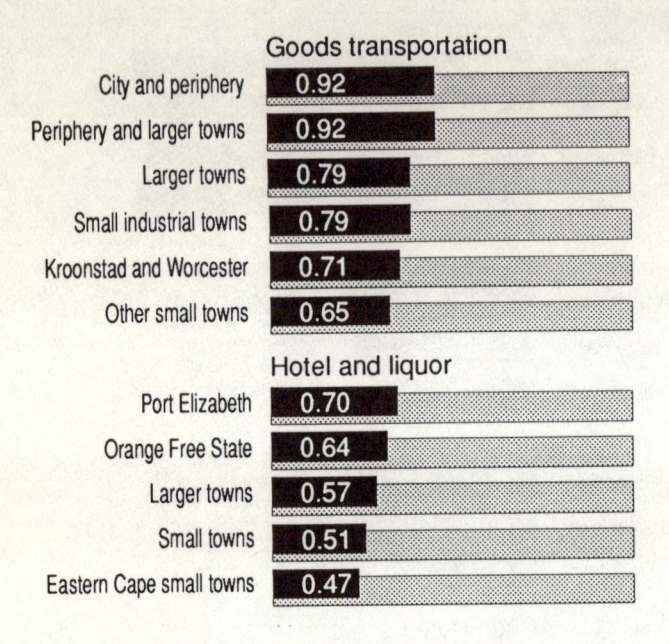

Goods transportation

Region	Wage
City and periphery	0.92
Periphery and larger towns	0.92
Larger towns	0.79
Small industrial towns	0.79
Kroonstad and Worcester	0.71
Other small towns	0.65

Hotel and liquor

Region	Wage
Port Elizabeth	0.70
Orange Free State	0.64
Larger towns	0.57
Small towns	0.51
Eastern Cape small towns	0.47

Graph 3.2: Hourly wages (rands) set by Wage Boards for labourers for selected sectors and regions current in June 1986, compared to the average Household Supplemented Living Level (HSLL) of R1.96

Notes: HSLLs provided by the IPR do not correspond to regions covered by Wage Determinations. The HSLL used here is an average of the Johannesburg and Pietermaritzburg HSLLs, the highest and lowest in the country respectively.
Sources: Budlender *et al*, 1985; Institute for Planning Research (IPR) 1986, p.62; *SALDRU Labour Research Series, Monitor of Minimum Wage Measures*, 2nd Quarter 1986, pp.63–70.

The monitoring showed great regional variations in wages for the same broad categories of work, particularly in the building and clothing industries and the liquor and catering sectors. There were also wide differentials in wages between different sectors of the economy. The effect is most marked with regard to wage determinations, where wages paid in the main cities and their peripheries were higher than those in towns and outlying areas. In the chemical industry, the commercial and distributive trades and in the food industry, workers in some small towns earned only about three-quarters of wages applicable on the Witwatersrand.

The minimum wages earned by motor workers in the Eastern Cape (aside from being the highest in the country) were uncharacteristically high for that region, reflecting the impact of successful strikes there between 1979 and 1983. Wages for motor workers in the Transvaal were between 46 and 36 per cent of those in the Eastern Cape. Much of the Transvaal motor industry was located around Brits and Rosslyn, both adjacent to the Bophuthatswana bantustan and drawing on a less organised commuter workforce. In the metals sector the impact of struggles led by the Metal and Allied Workers Union (MAWU) in the early 1980s was reflected in higher minimum wages. The impact of worker organisation can also be seen in the East London food industry, where struggles led by the South African Allied Workers Union in the early 1980s caused employers to raise wages in an attempt to pre-empt further trade union mobilisation.

The wage determination for stevedores was the highest negotiated in June 1986. Wage determinations mostly covered unorganised industries, but dock workers organised by the General Workers Union (subsequently merged with the Transport and General Workers Union) agreed with employers that the annually negotiated wage increase for the industry be published as a binding labour order, to prevent undercutting.[64] These exceptions aside, wages were generally highest in the urban areas of the Transvaal, followed by those of the Western Cape and Natal, with lower minimum wages in the Eastern Cape and outlying areas of other provinces.

The data show that in general, unorganised workers earned up to a quarter less than those covered by Industrial Councils. The position of workers falling under Wage Boards was further weakened by the infrequency of wage determinations. Between 1973 and 1981, new determinations were set on average only once every three and a quarter years.[65]

The data also show that wages were universally low. With the exception of Eastern Cape motor workers, East London sweet workers and stevedores, workers in all other sectors and regions earned minimum wages well below the Household Subsistence Level (HSL), which was calculated on the basis of the essentials required by a black family of six for a minimum existence. The lowest wages were in the liquor and catering trades (hotel and restaurant employees and bar personnel), among nightwatchmen in the security industry and in clothing factories in small towns. Unorganised workers in catering, for example, could earn less than a quarter of the HSL.

Women workers

In 1979 the South African Women's Legal Status Committee listed 240 job categories in which minimum wages for men and women differed

– women's wage rates were between a fifth and a quarter less than those of their male counterparts in the same categories at work.[66] The Labour Relations and Wages Act of 1981 abolished formal discrimination based on gender in minimum wage agreements and all new agreements at Industrial Council level. The exceptions were nursing and teaching (sectors where women predominated), which were exempted from the new legislation.

However, wage discrimination was maintained by redefining categories of work in which a majority of women were employed, and ranking them on lower wage scales than the equivalents for men. The fact that a majority of women workers were employed in agriculture and domestic service also held down the overall wages of women workers.

Some 800,000 African women, approximately 15 per cent of the African workforce, worked as domestic servants in the mid-1980s. A detailed study of domestic service in the Grahamstown area in 1980 found that the absence of legal protection made domestic workers especially vulnerable to exploitation. More than a quarter began work without knowing what they would be earning. Fear of dismissal meant that they avoided asking for increases and they received irregular increases at the whim of employers, if at all.[67] Domestic workers' wages varied widely from region to region. In 1987 the average wage earned was R98 per month, with domestics in the larger cities earning between R80 (Cape Town) and R110 (Transvaal areas), but only R59 in rural areas.[68]

Even in manufacture women worked in lower paid jobs and industries. The pattern of industrial agreements and wage determinations shows this clearly. Women constituted 82 per cent of African employees in clothing, where wages were up to 50 per cent less than in industries where a majority of men were employed (motoring, metals and chemicals). Women's wages also grew more slowly than those of men. In Soweto the real earnings of women declined between 1979 and 1981 by a quarter, compared with just under 10 per cent for men.[69]

Against the background of prevailing low wages, employers and the state opposed a statutory national minimum wage. In 1986 the Temporary Removal of Restrictions on Economic Activities Act was passed, empowering the State President to deregulate industries or regions covered by Industrial Council agreements and wage determinations – that is, to suspend prevailing minimum wage regulation. The legislation, intended to stimulate the development of small businesses, could be extended to areas where the industrial deconcentration programme was being applied, creating conditions similar to those in the bantustans, where there was no wage protection. Wage determinations were suspended under the legislation during 1986 for specific establishments in three categories – commercial and distributive trades, hotel and liquor trades, and security services, all of them sectors where the lowest wages already pertained.

In a second development in 1987 the government set up a deregulated free trading zone in Kew, near Johannesburg. In the first such move within a major industrial area, wage regulating measures and certain clauses of the Basic Conditions of Employment Act were suspended. Trade unions condemned the move, fearing it might be the first in a series of steps to fragment collective bargaining in urban areas.[70]

Unemployment

The economic recession which set in during 1981 made unemployment one of the most pressing problems facing workers. Unemployment was not, however, a new phenomenon. The recession exacerbated a permanent structural feature of the economy.[71]

Structural unemployment had several roots. One was the apartheid system: the collapse of the subsistence economy due to the contract labour system, the creation of the bantustans and forced removals produced a permanent pool of unemployed labour. Another cause was the structure of the economy. Rapid economic growth after the wave of industrialisation in the 1940s was not matched by a corresponding increase in the rate of employment. Between 1946 and 1970 the annual growth of output was 5.2 per cent, but employment increased by only 2.7 per cent a year.[72] In the late 1960s and early 1970s industry became increasingly capital intensive in an effort to maximise productivity and compete on international markets. The introduction of capital-intensive technology was particularly thoroughgoing because black labour was so unorganised: 'Unemployment was brought about precisely because domestic and foreign investors were able to introduce capital-intensive investments without the kind of opposition that one finds in the West.'[73]

Between 1946 and 1972 real fixed capital stock increased more than fourfold at an average of 5.7 per cent per year.[74] Between 1970 and 1980 the capital:labour ratio in non-agricultural sectors increased by 43 per cent. In manufacture it increased by 51 per cent and in mining by 64 per cent. The size of the workforce contracted as the machines were deployed.[75]

Job reservation and the 'colour bar' were further causes of structural unemployment. Even as shortages of white skilled labour arose, black workers were only allowed in a strictly controlled fashion to move into posts previously monopolised by whites. Until the late 1970s, when the policy was modified to some extent, the government preferred to import white skilled workers from abroad rather than permit African advancement. Between 1965 and 1972, immigrants increased the size of the white skilled labour force by 30–40 per cent.[76]

Decentralisation and deconcentration policies also contributed to structural unemployment because of restrictions on the employment of Africans in the centres of economic activity. From the mid–1960s to the end of the 1970s decentralisation created only 23,000 new jobs. But during one year in that period, 1968–9, the number of workers prevented by restrictions from accepting work in the industrial centres was 26,700.[77]

These factors combined to make unemployment a structural feature of the economy. Since 1960, even in boom periods, it has never fallen below 16 per cent. The rate remained more or less constant between 1960 and 1981 but then rose to above 20 per cent.[78] Calculations of unemployment differed according to the definitions used. The government calculated the unemployed in 1986 at 519,000, but this accounted only for the officially registered unemployed. Most unemployed workers did not register as there were few benefits attached to doing so, and the bantustans, which accommodated the majority of the unemployed, were not included in the statistics. Studies by independent academics put unemployment in 1986 at between 4.8 and 6 million workers: half of all economically active Africans. These figures were derived by adding the estimated quarter of a million new job seekers per year to an independently researched level of unemployment in 1981 of between 2 and 2.3 million, which was widely regarded as authentic and was confirmed by other surveys.

A net decrease, according to government sources, of 181,000 jobs in manufacture since 1981, the removal of a quarter of a million workers from farms since 1979 and unemployment in 'independent' bantustans were the key factors behind the drastic increase in unemployment after 1981.[79]

Unemployment was concentrated in the bantustans, to which the unemployed were confined by controls on movements, and was five and a half times higher in non-urban bantustan areas than in bantustan towns. Outside the bantustans, unemployment was particularly high in the towns and cities of the Eastern Cape. In 1986, 56 per cent of the black population in the Port Elizabeth–Uitenhage area were out of work.

Denied skills training, women tended to be laid off before men. In some areas of the country unemployment was almost twice as high among

Table 3.1 Average monthly earnings by group in main sectors of the economy, 1974–1984 in rands

Sector	White 1974	White 1984	Coloured 1974	Coloured 1984	Indian 1974	Indian 1984	African 1974	African 1984
Mining	563	1,751	137	560	170	928	45	332
Manufacturing	449	1,668	118	487	128	595	88	415
Electricity	494	1,532	132	491		843	100	429
Construction	445	1,657	160	573	213	946	84	333
Trade	290	1,121	98	386	136	611	66	285
Transport and communications	407	1,381	118	447	164	854	82	388
Finance and insurance	400	1,317	154	733	210	961	118	561
Government and public services	394	1,309	141	561	199	913	74	373

Source: Annual Report on Apartheid, 1986, p.31.

Table 3.2 Reduction in employment for selected economic sectors, 1981–1985

Sector	Year 1981	1985	Job Change	% change
Mining	637,664	636,982	–682	–.11
Manufacture	787,600	703,800	–83,800	–10.64
Food	113,000	108,200	–4,800	–4.25
Textiles	71,900	61,500	–10,400	–14.46
Clothing	33,100	30,800	–2,300	–6.95
Paper and wood	60,200	55,500	–4,700	–7.81
Chemicals	53,800	49,100	–4,700	–8.74
Metals	349,200	247,600	–101,600	–29.10
Electricity	28,100	36,200	8,100	28.83
Construction	239,200	204,000	–35,200	–14.72
Trade and accommodation	349,716	355,953	6,237	1.78
Transport & communication	210,709	173,425	–37,284	–17.69
Government & services	489,738	518,774	29,036	5.93

Source: South Africa 1986, Tables 7.7–7.9.

women as it was among men. In the Pilanesberg area of the Bophuthatswana bantustan, for example, the proportion of women who had been out of work for longer than two years rose from 4.3 per cent in 1977 to 53.8 per cent in 1984. The corresponding figures for men were 8.3 and 38.5 per cent. But the disparities were even wider when it came to the length of time people in the area had been unemployed. For the women the mean time was six and a half years; for men, three years and eight months. In the Port Elizabeth–Grahamstown area in 1986 30 per cent of unemployed women and 21 per cent of men had been unable to find jobs for more than two years.[80]

Among youth (about 60 per cent of the population in the 1980s) there were high levels of unemployment. The National Manpower Commission estimated in 1982 that two-thirds of Coloured youths, and 60 per cent of Indian youths under the age of 30, were unemployed.[81] In 1986 more than half of African school leavers were unable to find any sort of work.[82] The recession severely eroded employment in particular sectors. Table 3.2 shows the decrease in employment in key sectors between 1981 and 1985.

The resources which unemployed workers could fall back on were meagre. The unemployment insurance system in South Africa was underdeveloped and discriminated against lower paid, unskilled workers. An official Unemployment Insurance Fund (UIF) contributed to by employers (47 per cent), the state (5 per cent) and workers themselves (47 per cent) was created in terms of the Unemployment Insurance Act of 1966. However, domestic and agricultural workers were excluded from its ambit and had no protection against the consequences of unemployment. Workers who had not initially worked for a period before becoming unemployed were also not eligible for the UIF.

There was a dramatic increase in UIF claimants after 1981, paralysing the administration and even threatening it with bankruptcy. During the first four months of 1985 the Fund's expenditure exceeded its income by R6.5 million each month and it was calculated that its accumulated reserves would last less than a year.[83] To relieve these pressures, in December 1985 employers' contributions to the Fund were increased and the government was forced to boost reserves with an additional one-off contribution.

Under the UIF workers were paid at 45 per cent of their last wage and only for six months. Aside from these inherent shortcomings, the administration of the Fund was inefficient and collapsed in some parts of the country. In 1985 workers in Natal and the greater Witwatersrand area experienced delays of between six months and a year before they received their first payment. Elsewhere the average waiting period was six weeks.[84] In 1982, separate unemployment insurance funds were established in the 'independent' bantustans, and contributions of workers deemed to be 'citizens' of these territories were transferred from the Central Fund to the new schemes. The bantustan schemes were similarly characterised by incompetence and delays.

Shopfloor relations and working conditions

The industrial colour bar
The first laws barring black workers from employment in certain categories of work were enacted in the 1890s. In later decades the 'industrial colour bar' was reinforced by law and supporting practices such as closed-shop agreements. The 'job reservation' system introduced in 1956 effectively prevented black workers from moving into more skilled jobs and occupations for about 20 years.

In 1979 the government's Wiehahn Commission, appointed to investigate labour relations, recommended the abolition of statutory job reservation. The demand for skilled labour had outstripped what the white labour force could provide and employers' organisations had been calling for the relaxation of barriers to African job advancement. The government accepted almost all of Wiehahn's proposals, with the result that laws preventing Africans moving up the skills ladder were scrapped in all sectors except mining.

In the 1980s, in an attempt to reduce the skills shortage, the state and employers concentrated on the training of skilled African labour. But the impact of the measures was limited by the shortcomings of the apartheid education system, inadequate facilities for the training of African artisans and resistance by white trade unions. As the colour bar was shifted, white unions used their power to try to protect their members' privileges.

Job reservation
Before statutory job reservation was scrapped in the early 1980s most skilled occupations were reserved for whites. Practices included:

- Reservation of a class of work or specific occupations for whites only;
- fixing a maximum percentage of African workers allowed employment in a particular industry;

- fixing a ratio of African workers to white workers in a particular industry;
- prohibiting the replacement of white workers by Africans.

Statutory job reservation was effected through Section 77 of the Industrial Conciliation Act of 1956. It empowered the Minister of Labour to prohibit Africans from doing specific kinds of work in an industry if it might create 'inter-racial competition'.[85] It extended bans on the employment of African artisans in the mining and construction industries to other sectors of the economy. Between 1956 and 1975, 28 determinations reserving jobs for whites were promulgated under the Act.[86] The Apprenticeship Act of 1922 empowered apprenticeship committees – made up of employer representatives and white trade unions – to block the registration and hence training of Africans. A consequence of this, as Table 3.3 clearly shows, was that in the metal, engineering, electrical and motor trades whites still constituted over 80 per cent of artisans and apprentices in 1985.

White trade unions supplemented these legal restrictions by closed-shop agreements with employers. The agreements barred workers who were not members of the relevant unions from particular jobs. This was a simple expedient to exclude Africans, who were not allowed to join registered trade unions before 1980. White unions also concluded agreements with employers which fixed ratios of black to white employees. Agreements of this type were applied in the engineering, motor and print industries.

These practices continued into the 1970s and 1980s: of the closed-shop agreements concluded or revised in 1976 and 1977 more than a third specifically barred African job advancement.[87] These mostly involved white trade unions, but craft unions organising Coloured artisans also prevented the advancement of Africans into some industries, through closed-shop agreements, especially in the Western Cape. In the building and furniture trades, for example, in contrast to other sectors, there were high proportions of Coloured artisans, as Table 3.3 shows.

The skills shortage
By the 1960s shortages of skilled labour were becoming apparent. Attempts were made to address the problem without threatening the white monopoly of the upper echelons of industry. White labour was recruited from abroad at the rate of 30,000 people per year between 1956 and 1975.[88]

A more enduring response was to shift the colour bar upwards, allowing Africans to move into jobs previously monopolised by whites. Wholesale exemptions were made to the reservation statutes. Of the 28 determinations made between 1956 and 1975 only five were still in force in 1977.[89] Another expedient was to reclassify jobs. On the railways, for example, Africans were brought in to do shunting work in the 1950s. They were defined as 'shunters' mates', a status below that of 'shunters', who were exclusively white.[90] In construction, jobs done by whites were broken down or diluted, allowing African workers to perform tasks such as primary painting, plastering and basic carpentry, without threatening white job descriptions, wages and working conditions.

White unions used job reservation as a bargaining chip with employers, gaining higher wages and extended benefits in exchange for allowing black workers into white jobs. White building artisans, for example, were guaranteed a 20-year period of preferential employment and increased wages for conceding the dilution of their tasks.

Towards the end of the 1970s there were signs that the rise of black trade unions would threaten the privileges of white workers, eroding their bargaining strength. Mechanisation and technological innovation also made many of the skills monopolised by white workers redundant and created a demand for entirely new skills. This led to job fragmentation, and to de-skilling and re-skilling of existing occupations. Employers took advantage of the changes to replace skilled white workers with lower paid semi-skilled black workers. In manufacture the ratio of black to white workers increased from 2.75:1 in 1960 to 3.6:1 in 1976.[91]

State and employer responses
In the late 1970s a more comprehensive policy to redress the skills shortage was called for. Part I of the Wiehahn Commission report, published in 1979, warned that any sustained economic upswing would cause serious shortages of skilled labour which could threaten economic recovery and growth.[92]

The Commission recommended the repeal of Section 77 of the Industrial Conciliation Act of 1956 and the phasing out by 1983 of the five remaining job reservation determinations.[93] The Commission was divided over closed-shop agreements. A majority report called for the abolition in principle of the closed shop, while representatives of white labour wanted to retain existing agreements. However, the Commission recommended that no changes be made to established labour practices

Table 3.3 Occupational breakdown of the economically active population by race and sex, 1985

Occupational category/ Sector	Total	Whites Male	%	Female	%
Professional, semi-prof, technical	541,957	220,011	41	116,878	22
Managerial, executive and admin	174,428	145,332	83	19,799	11
Clerical	641,481	99,638	16	303,805	47
Sales and related	267,891	67,151	25	63,741	24
Manufacture, transport and related above labourers:					
Processing metal/plastics/machine parts, operators in motor industry	239,920	17,446	7	1,466	1
Building and construction	221,543	6,172	3	18	0
Processing of wood/furniture	66,799	861	1	53	0
Textiles and clothes	177,223	868	0	1,257	1
Food, drink and tobacco	90,698	3,172	3	1,712	2
Leather and shoes	29,735	396	1	184	1
Glass, cement and bricks	56,217	925	2	13	0
Chemical and rubber	61,587	5,043	8	695	1
Printing and paper manufacture	30,752	1,033	3	1,699	6
Other semi-skilled	349,625	71,385	20	8,992	3
Service capacities	610,946	82,691	14	37,168	6
Labourers	682,947	615	0	417	0
Artisans:					
Metals and engineering	104,406	88,124	84	51	0
Electrical trades	47,826	41,829	87	87	0
Motor trades	42,550	34,179	80	30	0
Building trades	58,005	18,724	32	16	0
Printing trades	12,142	7,819	64	607	5
Furniture trades	5,782	764	13		0
Food trades	4,924	3,088	63	364	7
Diamond cutters/jewellers	1,361	972	71	65	5
Miscellaneous	14,137	6,039	43	5,317	38

Source: South Africa 1985, pp.7–30.

	Coloureds			Indians				Africans			
Male	%	Female	%	Male	%	Female	%	Male	%	Female	%
19,198	4	27,800	5	13,605	3	7,814	1	52,679	10	83,972	15
2,051	1	633	0	3,360	2	191	0	2,477	1	585	0
29,411	5	38,504	6	33,601	5	15,608	2	94,212	15	26,702	4
9,649	4	23,366	9	9,861	4	6,974	3	44,807	17	42,342	16
25,599	11	11,378	5	5,487	2	1,129	0	166,114	69	11,301	5
25,564	12	171	0	1,080	0	15	0	187,718	85	796	0
10,568	16	2,935	4	2,265	3	4	0	39,848	60	10,265	15
9,401	5	48,307	27	6,237	4	19,677	11	31,553	18	59,923	34
8,698	10	6,958	8	2,175	2	826	1	52,202	58	14,955	16
5,528	19	5,563	19	4,707	16	2,327	8	6,892	23	4,138	14
4,564	8	2,093	4	575	1	6	0	43,102	77	4,939	9
7,233	12	2,050	3	2,142	3	118	0	42,551	69	1,755	3
7,935	26	3,577	12	2,687	9	38	0	13,202	43	581	2
37,292	11	11,873	3	1,147	0	2,076	1	192,722	55	13,868	4
33,782	6	38,104	6	9,284	2	3,394	1	242,819	40	163,704	27
59,201	9		0	6,127	1	1,124	0	549,332	80	51,914	8
8,510	8	21	0	2,395	2	3	0	5,290	5	12	0
2,843	6	36	0	1,246	3	8	0	1,750	4	27	0
3,995	9	19	0	1,936	5		0	2,385	6	6	0
27,409	47	6	0	4,223	7		0	7,571	13	56	0
2,166	18	92	1	717	6	13	0	603	5	53	0
3,021	52	46	1	888	15		0	1,008	17	55	1
419	9	12	0	311	6	31	1	631	13	68	1
239	18	9	1	6	0	8	1	58	4	4	0
1,724	12	414	3	186	1	101	1	236	2	120	1

without consensus within the relevant Industrial Councils (where unions representing skilled workers were entrenched). The government, in a White Paper which followed Wiehahn, adopted the minority view on the closed shop: existing agreements would be retained but no new ones established. These provisions were included in the 1980 Industrial Conciliation Amendment Act.

Part II of the Wiehahn report, published in 1980, dealt with the training of artisans. Its recommendations were made law in the Manpower Training Act of 1983 which standardised practices and introduced some changes. All aspects of training were centralised under a National Training Board, set up under the control of the National Manpower Commission. The Training Board was to identify training needs, and to encourage better use of existing institutions and create new ones. Provision was made to indenture African apprentices. The Act relaxed training regulations, allowing workers to pass trade tests on the basis of practical experience and not only through formal courses. The number of Africans registered for apprenticeships increased from none to 14 in 1980, 211 in 1981 and 582 in 1986, but they still accounted for only 6 per cent of apprenticeships in 1986.[94]

Education and training
The state and employers also raised the level of technical and vocational training in the early 1980s. Curricula were restructured to place greater emphasis on vocational training. Fourteen departmental training centres (with a further 16 planned over the next five years) were established outside the bantustans to provide for technical training at secondary school level. Further provision was also made for more advanced technical training at technical college and technikon level – a technikon is 'an educational institution which provides management, technical and artisanal skills courses at post-secondary school level'.[95]

Despite these changes, the development of skills training for black workers was slow and the provision of facilities for them continued to be discriminatory. In 1986 there were still only 43 technical colleges and industrial training centres for Africans, compared to 72 for whites; there were only three technikons for Africans, compared to eight for whites. Five times as much was spent on white technical and advanced technical education in 1986–7 than on African.[96] In 1985, 81 per cent of students at technical colleges were white (a higher proportion than in 1970) and whites made up 78.5 per cent of those at technikons.[97]

Training for Africans continued to be inferior, because of discriminatory expenditure and segregation. Technikons were only allowed to determine their own admissions policies in 1987, while technical colleges in white areas continued to be closed to Africans, except under ministerial exemption. A 1988 study concluded that segregation placed severe obstacles in the way of Africans seeking technical education, because standards were often low, employers failed to provide training facilities for African workers, black workers were forced either to travel further afield to study or to take up correspondence courses, and state resources were being wasted on the maintenance of separate institutions.[98]

The advancement of white labour received as much attention as black training, with an expansion of training facilities for whites, both men and women, and increased incentives to immigrant white labour.[99] Immigration restrictions were relaxed to allow potential immigrants to enter the country as workseekers without firm job offers if they had qualifications which were in short supply. The government also subsidised the fares of immigrant workers by 80 per cent.[100]

The abysmal state of the primary and secondary education provided for black children, the repression of struggles by pupils for improved conditions and the small number of black students in higher education were the bedrock of continuing inequalities in employment and the de facto retention of the industrial colour bar.

In 1986–7, in spite of significant increases to the education budget, six times as much was spent on the education of white pupils as on Africans, and less than 13 per cent of African pupils completed secondary education.[101] Tertiary education was similarly discriminatory. Until the 1980s black students could only study at white universities if the courses for which they registered were not available at a black university. Only 1 per cent of the population, 58 per cent of them white, received any form of tertiary education.[102]

Consequently, the increase in training facilities for blacks had only a marginal impact. Large numbers of Africans were trained as semi-skilled machine operatives and in sales, supervisory and clerical categories; artisanal, skilled and highly skilled jobs, however, were still dominated by whites (see Table 3.3), especially in metals and engineering and the electrical and motor trades.[103] Africans were almost entirely absent from managerial and administrative occupations and formed a small minority of workers in all professional and technical capacities. They still constituted 88 per cent of all workers employed as labourers in the least skilled occupations. The remaining 12 per cent were Coloured or Indian.

New divisions in the workforce
The advancement of a limited section of the African workforce reinforced divisions caused by the contract labour system. Workers with permanent residence and employment rights outside the bantustans had prior access

to newly opened skilled occupations. Contract workers remained concentrated in manual and unskilled capacities.

The gender stratification of the workforce was also reinforced. Women moved into the lower rungs of the skills ladder as men moved upwards. The percentage of black women in industry increased from 14.5 per cent in 1973 to 22.3 per cent in 1981, but nine times as many women as men were involved in service jobs (domestic service, laundry, office cleaning, etc.). Only 12 per cent of the female labour force was involved in urban industrial occupations, and then only in particular sectors of manufacture.[104] Table 3.3 shows the distribution of African women in the workforce. They were almost entirely absent from managerial and executive positions. There were twice as many African women as men in professional, semi-professional and technical posts, the majority of them in nursing. However, African women were entirely absent from artisan posts and apprenticeships and only occupied semi-skilled positions in significant numbers in the textile and clothing sectors, the food industry and the making of leather goods and shoes, which were all low-paid industries closely related to the household tasks and craftwork traditionally performed by women.

The development of the clothing and textile industries illustrates graphically how the shifting colour bar affected women. Black women entered the clothing industry in larger numbers when white women, who dominated the industry in the 1950s and 1960s, then moved out of the industry or up the skills ladder. In 1960 there were 3,745 white women in the industry. In 1980 their number had dropped to 362. They were followed out of the industry by Coloured women (6,185 in 1960, dropping to 2,437 in 1980) and to a lesser extent by African men (3,636, dropping to 2,054). African women then responded to the shifts in the market and the search for cheaper labour. In 1960 there were 4,207 black women employed in the clothing industry, but by 1980 their numbers had more than tripled to 15,368.[105]

Conditions at work

In most industrialised countries legislation guaranteeing minimum conditions of employment emerged from decades of struggle. In South Africa the virtual proscription of African trade unions until the late 1970s and the repression of other forms of organisation produced working conditions reflecting the history of oppression and the divisions imposed on workers.

With the rise of the independent trade union movement in the late 1970s, workers were able to challenge management prerogatives and improve their conditions in some sectors of manufacture. However, only a small percentage of workers were unionised. Conditions changed little in smaller industries, factories and plants, especially those located away from the main urban centres and in the bantustans.

Legislation laying down minimum conditions at work was weighted against African workers. The Basic Conditions of Employment Act passed in 1983, which amended previous legislation, continued to exclude farm workers, domestics and employees of state institutions. Discriminatory practices were still found in most workplaces. Outside the realm of multinational companies and some larger South African companies, facilities like toilets and canteens were generally segregated even where white and black employees worked together.

Working hours

The Basic Conditions of Employment Act set the working week at a maximum of 46 hours excluding overtime.[106] However, it applied only in industries not covered by Industrial Councils. In two-thirds of Industrial Council agreements in 1985 hours were longer, especially in transport and the liquor and catering sectors (see Table 3.4).

In 1981 shift workers accounted for almost a third of the hours worked in manufacture, concentrated in the rubber, paper, textile and chemical industries.[107] The health problems associated with shift work, especially fatigue, were exacerbated by apartheid conditions. Long commuting distances – imposed by enforced segregation – and the absence of transport outside working hours often meant that shift workers were further deprived of sleep. No separate legislation existed providing for minimum hours of shift work. The Department of Manpower determined conditions on the basis of individual applications by employers.

Domestic and agricultural workers not protected by the Act worked the longest hours. The long hours of farm workers are detailed in Chapter 2 above. A study in 1980 of domestic workers in Grahamstown revealed an average working week of 61 hours.[108] In 1982 The Domestic Workers' Association (DWA), based in Cape Town, recorded 16-hour working days among its members, while in the same year the Johannesburg-based Domestic Workers Education Project (DWEP) found an average of 12 hours per day among its members. The situation had not improved by 1985, when a South African Domestic Workers' Association (SADWA) survey revealed that a 10–12 hour day was still the norm in the Johannesburg area.[109]

Table 3.4 Maximum work hours in Wage Determinations and Industrial Council agreements, current in 1984

Hours	No. of Wage Determinations	No. of Industrial Council Agreements
40	3	19
42		17
43	4	10
44		18
45	33	28
46	154	52
48	16	2
50		2
54		6
55		2
56	13	
57		
58	6	
Total	229	157

Source: D. Budlender *et al* 1985, p.71.

The Basic Conditions of Employment Act restricted overtime to three hours per day and no more than ten hours per week in industries not covered by Industrial Councils. Overtime was technically voluntary but workers were vulnerable to pressures which might make them loath to refuse, especially in times of recession. This was one of the grievances of contract workers in Johannesburg's municipal services who struck in 1980. At the Orlando Power Station they worked compulsory overtime shifts; they were expected to fill in for absent workers in any job category, even after having worked two consecutive eight-hour shifts.[110]

Extremely exploitative conditions existed in occupations involving night work, especially cleaning (where predominantly women were employed) and security services (mainly contract workers). In a survey of Johannesburg cleaning workers in the mid-1980s, the Transport and General Workers Union (TGWU) found that the women worked eight-hour shifts each night, cleaning office blocks, shops and supermarkets. The long shifts and travel time allowed the women less than five hours sleep a day. Most suffered from sore eyes, headaches and high blood pressure, and had stomach ailments relating to irregular eating habits.[111]

Before the Basic Conditions of Employment Act was passed women were prohibited from doing night work. However, ministerial exemptions were so frequent that women came to dominate the cleaning sector and to work night shifts in garment and textile plants.[112] The Act also limited the hours security guards and nightwatchmen might be employed to 60 hours a week.[113] Prior to these changes they routinely worked between 72 and 84 hours a week.

Health and safety

According to government sources 15,218 workers were reported injured in South African factories in 1984, 451 of them fatally. These statistics excluded state-owned railways and harbours, for which figures were not provided. They also excluded the mines. Separate statistics showed that on average a quarter of those injured each year were permanently disabled.[114] There were no conclusive statistics for the incidence of internal injuries arising from dust, gas and chemicals, or from exposure to heat and noise.

Management attitudes to health and safety were shaped by discriminatory health and safety legislation which offered black workers little statutory protection. The Workmen's Compensation Act of 1941 (as amended) exonerated employers from any costs relating to injuries on their premises above a fixed monthly levy paid to the Workmen's Compensation Commissioner (WCC). The WCC paid out medical and other expenses, including compensation, arising out of claims by injured workers. The Act specifically excluded the possibility of an injured worker suing an employer for negligence, although where negligence was proved to be the case the injured employee was liable for extra compensation. The Act did not provide for action against negligent employers beyond an increase in levies on 'accident-prone' factories.

Compensation under the Act was inadequate and discriminatory. According to one study, 'Because of the wage gap between blacks and whites, compensation is de facto racially determined. For the same injury a black worker will almost always receive less compensation money than a white worker.'[115] Compensation was also specifically restricted to physical injuries and diseases arising from exposure to toxic substances (chrome ulceration, dermatitis and lead poisoning). However, it was often difficult for workers to prove such exposure as symptoms often occurred years after contact. Only a small number of industrial diseases were compensatable. Lung cancer – which can be caused by a number of industrial carcinogens, including asbestos – was excluded.[116]

Employers who recorded few or no accidents in their plants were entitled to rebates on levies they contributed to the fund. Intended to encourage safety precautions, the provision had in many cases the opposite effect, with managements failing to report accidents or covering them up. There was also nothing in the Act to prevent employers from dismissing injured workers.

Occupational health and safety were long neglected largely because of the repression of trade unions. The Erasmus Commission, set up by the government in 1978 to investigate the occurrence of occupational diseases, found that industrial hazards and illnesses were widespread. There was a lack of management concern and workers had little control over the conditions:

> ... it has regrettably to be stated categorically that ... industrial health not only occupies a secondary position in industry in this country, but that industrialists have put very little time, money and organisation into the prevention of occupational diseases. This applies to the prevention of industrial accidents as well.[117]

The Commission found state controls inadequate. The Factory Inspectorate, falling under the Department of Health and charged with enforcing health regulations in factories, was desperately understaffed. Only 29 of the 66 posts for inspectors were filled.[118] The Commission also found that large sections of the workforce were exposed to harmful and toxic substances in their daily work. It also paid attention to the most common industrial hazard – noise. Again its findings were alarming: 230,000 workers were threatened with deafness because they worked in conditions above the legal decibel limit. Less than 10 per cent had ear protectors or had been properly informed of the dangers to which they were exposed.[119]

Although the Commission's investigation of chemical hazards was thorough, the dangers of dust in working environments were excluded from its brief. The extent of brown lung disease (caused by inhaling cotton dust) among textile workers was only revealed after an investigation by the National Union of Textile Workers (NUTW). In the factories it surveyed, 16 out of every 100 workers were found to have signs of the disease, some in an advanced stage.[120] A similar union survey of workers involved in brick production found that over 12 per cent had signs of tuberculosis.[121] A Metal and Allied Workers Union

(MAWU) survey of metal foundries on the Witwatersrand in 1984 found that less than a third of managements monitored dust levels.

Although the Erasmus Commission's findings were an indictment of conditions in South African factories, it avoided making substantive recommendations and its report was imbued with apartheid ideology:

> It was generally felt that it was essential for the Republic to do its own research in view of the fact that its workers consisted of different races and that local conditions differed so widely from those in most other countries. The Commission also felt that the formation of standards and threshhold values for industry required the greatest accuracy and care, not only for the protection of the worker and the public, but also because they have financial implications that may have serious and sometimes disastrous consequences for an industry.[122]

The Commission recommended that 'threshold values for different substances serve only as guides' and that they should have no statutory status.

It was largely because health and safety became issues around which the trade union movement could mobilise that the government introduced legislative reforms in the early 1980s. In 1983 the Machinery and Occupational Safety Act was passed, under whose terms new minimum safety standards in factories and plants could be promulgated. It also amended previous legislation which had specifically excluded workers from any direct say over their own safety and health. For example, under previous legislation details of rules and measures concerning protection were not publicly available and access to them depended on the whims of the factory inspectorate. A secrecy provision enabled management and the Department of Labour to withhold information from workers.[123]

The Act strove to limit the role of trade unions and shop stewards in enforcing safety conditions. It provided for a dual system of safety representatives and management-appointed safety committees to monitor conditions. Safety representatives, who made monthly safety inspections on the premises, had to be selected from the ranks of employees. But managements appointed them and were able to nominate supervisors and middle-level managers rather than shopfloor workers. Elected safety committees made representations to managements on the basis of their own independent investigations. The committees were vested with advisory powers only and had no rights to make decisions, nor were they afforded the means of enforcing their recommendations. There were no procedures to report back to workers on the shopfloor, whom the Act attempted to exclude from the issue of health and safety.[124]

Domestic workers were for the first time accorded some protection by the Act, although the new provisions were difficult to enforce. Employers were compelled to report any serious accidents involving domestics to an 'inspector of manpower', the police or the relevant local authority. Employers were also barred from employing pregnant domestics for four weeks prior to the expected date of delivery and for eight weeks afterwards. A victimisation clause protected domestic workers from dismissal for revealing dangerous conditions.

Trade unions adopted differing tactics in response to the Act. Some boycotted the legislation, insisting that employers negotiate safety issues with existing elected shop steward committees. Others pressed for elected workers to be represented on safety structures, which would allow unions the right to inspect premises and to gain access to information about safety standards. After 1983 health and safety began to feature as issues in labour disputes, as workers began to seek redress for the dangers they had faced for so long on the shopfloor.

4   At the Mines

As a major exporter of gold, diamonds, coal and other minerals, South Africa lay at the centre of the world mineral market for much of the period between 1960 and 1980. The country's economy was tied to the fortunes of the mining industry, particularly that of the gold industry. In 1984 mining produced 18 per cent of South Africa's GDP and in 1985 it accounted for 80 per cent of the country's export earnings.[1]

Basic conditions

Roughly one in eight African workers was employed in mining in 1985. Of the 743,065 miners, 12 per cent were white, 86 per cent African and 2 per cent Coloured or Indian. Three-quarters of the mine labour force was employed at gold mines, about an eighth on coal mines and the rest at diamond, platinum, asbestos and other mines.[2]

Heavily reliant on exports, mining was vulnerable to price fluctuations on the international market. Mining houses therefore could not maintain profits by setting the price consumers paid. The extraction of profit rested instead on ensuring a supply of cheap labour. Gold mining was very labour intensive and expensive in South Africa, as the gold deposits had a low ore content and the mines were among the deepest in the world, with rock faces worked up to 4 kilometres below the ground.

These factors produced a highly exploitative system of labour relations with dangerous working conditions and low pay. A coercive system of labour recruitment was built up on the basis of the contract labour system. The seven major mining companies amalgamated themselves into a powerful employers' federation, the Chamber of Mines, which through a centralised labour recruiting organisation, the Employment Bureau of Africa (TEBA), recruited labour from within South Africa and its neighbouring states. Centralised recruitment eliminated competition for labour among the mining houses and allowed them to pay uniformly low wages. They submitted quotas to TEBA and each mine received the complement it required. They recruited predominantly in the bantustans, where during the 1970s many labour bureaux were closed to other categories of work. In 1985, 97 per cent of all African mine workers were still recruited on contract.[3]

Recruiting agencies also reached into South Africa's neighbouring states, mainly Lesotho, Malawi and Mozambique and to a lesser extent Botswana and Swaziland. Workers were brought to South Africa on the same basis as those recruited in the bantustans, and had to return to their countries on completion of their contracts. Contract labour remittances were an important source of revenue for Southern African states, especially Lesotho.[4] During the 1970s a system of compulsory 'deferred pay' was in operation. Part of the workers' pay was transferred directly into a state account, to be held there awaiting their return. In the case of Malawi, for example, 60 per cent of workers' pay was transferred in this way: this became a source of great resentment among miners and led to protests.

By recruiting labour from neighbouring countries the mining houses avoided having to raise wages inside the country to attract South Africans away from better prospects in manufacture. After 1975, however, the supply of labour from neighbouring countries declined. Malawi cut its supply after more than 60 Malawians were killed when an aircraft owned by a recruiting agency crashed. In 1973 Malawians constituted 29 per cent of the African labour force on the gold mines – by 1977 this had fallen to 5 per cent and by 1986 to 4 per cent. The independence of Mozambique in 1975 led to a rapid reduction in recruitment from that country. The Mozambican component of the African workforce fell from 22 to 10 per cent in 1977 and 9 per cent in 1985. Recruitment from Zimbabwe also declined after 1980 when the newly independent government refused to renew its recruiting contract with the Chamber of Mines.

As a result the South African component of the African labour force increased from 21 per cent in 1973 to 61 per cent in 1986.[5] Of the remainder, 19 per cent was drawn from Lesotho and a total of 20 per cent from Botswana, Mozambique, Malawi, Swaziland and Zimbabwe.[6]

Wages
Following the drop in recruitment from outside South Africa, pass-law controls were intensified in the bantustans to force South African workers to the mines. But some mining houses also felt compelled to increase wages. The Anglo American Corporation, encouraged by the rising international gold price, broke with the Chamber of Mines'

policy of uniform pay and increased its wages in 1972, forcing the other companies to follow suit.

Before 1972 the value of the real wages of miners had been eroded by inflation to below that paid at the end of the nineteenth century. Thereafter a continually rising gold price and competition for labour saw wages increase dramatically until 1983, when a fall in the gold price and a recession changed the stance of the mining companies. The average monthly wage of a gold miner, only R18 per month in 1972, had risen to R425 in 1986, more than quadrupling his real earnings.[7]

However, despite this change, in 1986 miners still earned only 73 per cent of the average wage of workers in manufacture and in 1987 the cash wages of the first four mining grades (85 per cent of all those employed) were still less than the Minimum Living Level.[8]

The leap in black wages between 1971 and 1980 failed to reduce the wage gap between black and white miners. While Africans were denied the vote, and barred from membership of registered trade unions until the early 1980s, white workers ran powerful unions and voted political parties into power which reserved the most skilled jobs in the industry exclusively for them. The Chamber of Mines claimed that it provided a policy of equal pay for equal work, but job reservation and other constraints denied African workers skilled jobs. In 1984 white miners earned more than five times as much as Africans.[9]

Job reservation
Until 1987 black miners were prevented from performing 13 categories of work in terms of the Mines and Works Act of 1911 and related laws. White miners occupied all higher-paid posts, from management down to locomotive drivers and blasters – black workers were prevented from rising above the level of team leader. Mining companies coped with shortages of skilled labour by allowing the colour bar to 'float' upwards. White miners were promoted into newly created supervisory categories and black workers took over their jobs. White unions were persuaded to relinquish their monopoly of some tasks in exchange for increases in pay, a shorter working week and other benefits. These changes involved amendments to legislation or the development of informal practices. For example, black workers took over many of the tasks at the rock face, drilling holes and preparing rock faces for blasting, but the actual ignition of explosives was reserved for whites who held blasting certificates. While black workers increasingly did the same work as whites, they were not paid the same rates because they were legally disqualified from holding the certificate required to do the work.

In the early 1980s, the state tried to resolve the skills shortage in manufacture, but the political and trade union power of the white miners made it more cautious about the mining industry. The Wiehahn Commission, which investigated labour relations and reported in 1979, had recommended that statutory job reservation at the mines be abolished, subject to negotiation between the Chamber of Mines and trade unions. As black trade unions in the form of the National Union of Mineworkers (NUM) were only permitted access to the mines in 1983, this allowed the virulently right-wing Mine Workers Union (MWU), the largest of the white unions, to obstruct the changes proposed by the Chamber of Mines. The MWU was particularly resistant to opening certificates of competency in blasting to blacks, as most of their members were qualified blasters.

At its 1985 Congress, against a backdrop of increased militancy at the mines, the NUM, representing black miners, resolved to put the issue of job reservation on the bargaining table along with wages and conditions, and threatened if necessary to take strike action to have it removed.[10] In mid-1986 the Mines and Works Act was redrafted, opening the 13 work categories to any 'competent' persons. But the Act did not define competent persons. Instead it empowered the Minister of Mineral and Energy Affairs to decide the conditions of competence, in consultation with mining employers and trade unions, including the MWU. In July 1988 regulations spelling out the requirements for obtaining certificates of competency were finally gazetted. Candidates would have to be able to communicate orally and in writing in one of the official languages (English or Afrikaans). The regulations empowered special advisory committees to recommend the minimum educational qualifications and 'other requirements' which would allow black workers to obtain certificates. The composition of these 'advisory committees' was weighted against black miners, each consisting of three government officials, two employer representatives, two representatives of 'people holding the relevant certificates' (i.e. white mining unions) and two others.

Groups with entrenched vested interests in job reservation in the mining industry were therefore still afforded by the 1988 draft regulations the power to block African advancement, and the regulations fell far short of the NUM's demand that 'requirements for qualification should be a matter between employers and unions, and should depend on workers' abilities to do the job'.[11]

Working conditions, health and safety

The journey of black miners into the shafts was a catalogue of humiliation and regimentation in the period reviewed. It began with the recruitment of workers in the bantustans or neighbouring countries. On arrival at the mine, they underwent compulsory medical examinations in which they were forced to strip in front of white medical staff and overseers, even though only their eyes, ears and chests were examined. On most mines a short period of training followed in which they were taught 'Fanakalo' – a hybrid of English, Afrikaans and African languages, which developed out of the need of employers and supervisors to direct and control workers whose languages they did not speak. Further training consisted of acclimatisation to conditions underground, from which white workers were exempted. Every day for a week African miners were marshalled into heated, windowless, acclimatisation chambers, for seven hours at a time. While in the sealed rooms they underwent a regimen of exercises and received no water or food. This corresponded to conditions at the rock face, where there were no lunch or tea breaks. Then followed a short period of instruction in work methods and safety. Preliminary training lasted between one and three weeks. By contrast, in Britain miners were given more than three months' basic training in the same period.[12]

Underground working hours were long. Black miners worked on average eight and a half hours per shift, six days a week. White workers worked five and a half to six hours per shift, leaving the shafts before black workers.[13] Time spent on the job by black workers was extended by unpaid time travelling from the compound to the rock face and back. Shaft networks extended for miles under the ground; rock faces were sometimes located hours away from the lift shafts. Temperatures ranged between 37 and 40° Centigrade, with high humidity.

A typical daily shift was described in a 1980 interview with a Transkei migrant worker in the following terms:

> We must wake up very early. We must be at the face to start work at 7 a.m. If you want breakfast you must get up at 3 a.m. If you get there late they say – no more, it is finished ... The compound is close to the bank. We walk there. There are so many people to be taken down. Thousands. We wait and they take us down about 5 a.m. There are two lift cages. One goes up while one comes down. They take 20 upstairs and 20 downstairs. If you go down 20 stations it takes half an hour ... On the way we must stop and get into another lift cage which goes down again.

> From the station it is far to the face where we work. It is an hour's walk from station to face. We must be there by 7 a.m. to start ... When we get to the face it is my job to spray water to settle the dust ... It is hard work. It is very hot and you sweat so much. We are all wet with sweat. We work in trousers, boots and helmets. Sometimes people just fall down where we're working. It's just too hot ... We have no tea time. No food. No rest time, we must work right through. We stop work at 4 p.m. Before we stop we must put the dynamite charges in the holes we have drilled. The whites do that. We then walk back to the station and they blast the face. Nine hours work.[14]

Segregation was widespread on mines well into the early 1980s. Lift cages raising workers to the surface were segregated: blacks had to wait until all the white miners had gone up. Cases of black miners having to spend the night underground because the white lift operator had knocked off were not uncommon. From 1982 the lift system was the cause of several strikes at the mines.

Conditions at the rock face were very uncomfortable and dangerous:

> The shovellers must ... shovel the rock to where the tram lines begin. Sometimes this is far. The passages are too narrow. They shovel the rock from one man to the next in a line, from one spade to the next. Maybe the line is long. Two, three, four hundred yards. We work in the dark. Just with a helmet light and battery on your belt. You can see the gold in the rock in the light ... The mines are dangerous. Many people die from accidents. The roof can fall. Most die from explosions in the walls when smoke comes out and kills them. There are injuries from the drills, from flying stones or they cut off fingers, toes or whole arms ...[15] We drink the water for the drills because it is an hour's walk to the station for water. The water is bad. We also have no toilets. We just do it there.[16]

South African mines are among the most dangerous in the world. Since the turn of the century at least 46,000 workers have lost their lives underground. Between 1973 and 1985 more than 9,000 fatalities occurred, an average of 750 deaths per year. The number of reported injuries was also extremely high, roughly 17,000 per year up to 1983. Between 1983 and 1987 a further 50,000 sustained permanent disabilities.[17] In the 1980s fatalities at South African coal mines were six times higher than those in Britain and more than one and a half times higher than in the US.[18] Although large numbers of workers were killed in single incidents, such as explosions or rock bursts, daily accidents caused by rockfalls accounted for most deaths.[19] The Erasmus Commission, appointed by the government in 1976 to look into industrial disease, found that very little attention was paid to the health and safety of miners. The Nieuwenhuizen Commission, appointed specifically to look at mine safety confirmed these conclusions when it reported to Parliament in March 1982 that only one government safety inspector was employed to cover 700,000 workers.[20]

The post of 'team leader' is crucial to safety, but until 1987 the Mines and Works Act reserved training in safety procedures solely for whites. Team leaders could not take decisions about safety without the consent of supervisors. They could not, for example, without permission withdraw a team from any area which they felt was dangerous.[21] White supervisors were meant to ensure that sites were safe. However, studies showed that they spent little time at the rock face, coming into the stopes sometimes only two or three times a week – and at some mines even less frequently. The 1987 changes in the Act formally abolished job reservation at the mines but, as noted above, still placed obstacles in the way of African candidates for certificates of competency – including training in safety procedures.[22]

Another factor undermining safety was the bonus system. A white miner received bonuses for the extent of rock face worked by teams under his supervision. Black workers got bonuses for the quantity of holes drilled or rocks moved. There was no limit to how much white miners could earn from bonuses, although black miners were restricted to an amount equal to a third of their salary.[23] For many white supervisors, bonuses came before safety and they might refuse to halt work or remove miners from areas which black team leaders felt were unsafe.

Inquiries into disasters on mines repeatedly revealed neglect of safety procedures by mining companies and white officials. Sixty-eight miners were killed in an underground methane explosion at the Hlobane colliery near Vryheid in 1983. Although the colliery had a four-star safety rating (five-star was the top rating), evidence was presented to an official inquiry of widespread neglect of safety procedures. There was insufficient ventilation to remove methane gas; an overseer had scored out a report of dangerous gas levels a week prior to the explosion; no special precautions were taken before mining the dyke which was the source of the explosion; safety lamps were inadequate or defective; holes in the ventilation system had not been blocked off; only half the equipment used in the affected section of the mine had been flame-proofed. According to the attorney appearing for the families of the deceased miners, a total of 21 safety regulations had been broken at the mine, some repeatedly.[24]

At the Kinross gold mine in September 1986, 177 miners died in underground passages after inhaling highly toxic fumes when flames from a burning gas cylinder ignited polyurethane lining the passage walls. This substance was removed from all mines in the US in 1980 and is banned in British mines.[25] In 1987 there was a further series of mine disasters, including one at the St Helena gold mine near Welkom in which 62 miners were killed.

Many other practices in mines undermined safety. Protective clothing was inadequate. Companies were required by law to provide workers with free helmets, but workers had to pay for protective boots, overalls and socks. Companies were not legally required to provide goggles and ear plugs. Miners, unlike manufacturing workers, were not protected by law from excessive noise levels. Few mines even took elementary steps to reduce noise. One of the main sources of accidents was that workers failed to hear rockfalls. An NUM study published in 1986 found that most drills were not even equipped with inexpensive silencers.[26]

Mine workers were not protected by the provisions of the Machinery and Occupational Safety Act of 1983, which applied solely to manufacturing workers. Instead of providing for the election of safety stewards, as occurred in some manufacturing firms, mining companies opted for the forum of the government Prevention of Accidents Committee. It was established in 1913 but black unions were only allowed access to it in 1983, when they were permitted representation by one delegate as against 30 from the management.[27]

The Chamber of Mines frequently refused unions representing black miners access to its reports and studies of safety levels. It would not allow the NUM to study inquiry records and reports compiled by the management of the West Driefontein gold mine, where 11 workers were killed in rockbursts in 1983, and in 1985 it refused the union access to 42 unpublished reports on safety on the grounds that 'they might not be used objectively'.[28]

Official inquiries into accidents discriminated heavily against workers. Whether an inquiry was held was left to the discretion of the government Mining Engineer. The scope of the inquiry was restricted to those who 'may be held responsible' for the accident, most commonly team leaders, supervisors or individual workers. Unions could not present evidence, although they could attend. Only the mining companies were made privy to any recommendation for improved safety resulting from the findings. Workers were often simply not consulted or informed.[29]

From 1984 the NUM made a point of attending all inquiries into accidents on coal and gold mines. The union formed its own Safety Department and in 1985 held its first National Safety Conference in Johannesburg. The department attempted to educate workers about their limited rights under the Mines and Works Act, including the right to refuse to work in dangerous conditions or to perform work reserved for trained white personnel. Through actions at the mines and through the courts, miners began to secure safer conditions. In 1985 the Industrial Court upheld the right of underground workers to refuse to work in dangerous conditions. The ruling came after a case where the management of the West Driefontein mine suspended 17 miners who refused on safety grounds to work.

Strike action over safety issues was frequent in the second half of the 1980s. Miners marked the 1983 Hlobane disaster with a work stoppage. In 1985, 1,800 miners struck at the Rietspruit Colliery when a colleague was crushed to death. At Vaal Reefs, 18,000 miners came out in May of the same year to back up their refusal to perform blasting work, officially reserved for whites. In its strongest single response yet, the NUM brought out a quarter of a million miners to mark the death of the 177 miners killed in the disaster at Kinross in October 1986.[30]

Asbestos

Information about the effects on health of asbestos mining and the incidence of asbestosis and mesothelioma, lung diseases contracted from inhaling asbestos fibres, were actively suppressed in South Africa until the mid-1980s. Only 6,677 workers were still employed in asbestos mining at the end of 1985. It was a declining industry, many mines having been abandoned in the 1970s, but South Africa remained the world's largest producer of blue asbestos, a highly dangerous carcinogenic substance. It was banned in Sweden and could only be used with special permission in Britain. The International Metal Workers Federation has actively campaigned for a world-wide ban.[31]

Information about asbestos-related diseases in South Africa began surfacing in 1981. In November of that year a British television programme exposed very high levels of asbestos dust pollution at mines and factories near Prieska in the Northern Cape: 'black employees working in plants and mills thickly encrusted with blue asbestos dust, without respiratory protection, and the countryside and watercourses stained blue with dust'.[32] Around the same time Dr Neil White, a Cape Town health researcher, disclosed that 33 cases of mesothelioma had been diagnosed in Prieska in the 18 months before November 1981.

Thirty people had died in the town and in the 42 years previously about 900 cases had been diagnosed. In a sample survey of about 1,000 former employees of the local asbestos mine, he also found that over a quarter had contracted asbestosis.[33]

Following a strike by miners at the Penge asbestos mine in the North Eastern Transvaal in 1984, more disconcerting information came to light when figures kept by the mining company were leaked to the press. They showed that 780 miners had received compensation for asbestosis over the previous decade. In 1983, 130 workers (almost 10 per cent of the workforce) had contracted the disease, while the fibre count in the air was 16 times higher than the South African statutory limit and 325 times higher than that for Britain. In spite of five visits to the mine in 1983 by the government Mining Engineer, who each time found fibres in excess of legal limits, no action was initiated. Steps were taken to improve the situation in 1984, but 80 per cent of the workers were still working in fibre levels higher than the British limit. Equally alarming was the disclosure that waste from Penge and other mines (some abandoned many decades before) had been dumped in the open veld, exposing some 200,000 people to disease. Newspaper reporters found children playing on the dumps: 'Fibres littered the roads in the area, the local people used the dumps to build asbestos cement houses and there was a school next to a huge dump.'[34]

Legislation providing for the compensation of workers who contracted diseases at the mines was blatantly discriminatory. Workers on mines and in ore-processing plants were compensated under the Occupational Diseases in Mines and Works Act. Compensation was paid in proportion to earnings and so for African miners was low. A white worker would in 1984 have been entitled to a lump sum of R17,889 for a first degree disease. If his condition deteriorated to a second degree he would be entitled to a further payment of R8,945. By contrast a Coloured worker would be entitled to only half these amounts, and an African miner would have received a single payment of only R1,491.[35]

Accommodation

African miners were generally housed in compounds. By law mining companies could only house 3 per cent of their workers in family quarters, although some mines were exempted from this regulation. On most mines family housing was usually reserved for the more skilled workers.[36] Over 98 per cent of mine workers were still accommodated in single-sex hostels in 1985.[37] Conditions in the hostels varied. At a few mines workers lived in shared rooms with common rooms, canteens and recreational facilities. However, mass dormitories were the norm at most mines, with anything between eight and 20 men sleeping in triple steel bunks or concrete bunks built into the walls. Washing facilities were often large halls with overhead showers and rows of toilets without partitions.[38]

Common to all compounds, whatever their facilities, was a high degree of regimentation and control — they were aptly described as 'quasi military institutions'.[39] They were normally fenced off and guarded. At several mines numbers were painted on the roofs of barracks to facilitate control from the air. In some compounds the lights were centrally switched off at 11 p.m. and switched on again at 5.30 a.m.[40]

Mining companies employed their own security forces. They were used to crush strikes, setting dogs on workers, using teargas and opening fire on demonstrators. One company, Gold Fields, had a security force of 5,900 men, with 774 guard dogs. They patrolled the company mines and were hired out to other mines.[41] Anglo American owned a helicopter equipped with spotlights, which could drop teargas. At the Stilfontein mine, teargas systems were connected to ventilation shafts in liquor outlets, hostel kitchens and administration offices. A similar system at Western Deep Levels mine was dismantled in 1985, following adverse media publicity.[42]

Tension levels at the mines were not relieved by the division of the workforce into different language groups who were then housed in separate quarters: Sotho-speaking, Xhosa-speaking, Zulu-speaking and so on. The ban on trade union organisation at the mines until 1982 meant that workers had no organised means of expressing their grievances or changing their situation. Throughout the 1970s frustrations led to violent clashes, often between workers speaking different languages or between those from different areas. As a result of the divisions enforced by management and the stress under which workers lived, minor differences could escalate into violent confrontations.[43]

On most mines authority and discipline were enforced through a hierarchy of officials within each of the groups into which workers were split. Typically, every 16 men within a barracks 'elected' an *isibonda* — a sort of room prefect or foreman — who was responsible for allocating cleaning and cooking tasks and for general discipline. *Isibondas* representing 30 to 40 rooms within a compound system were directly subordinate, in turn, to management-appointed *indunas*. Their role was to act as policemen, walking beats armed with knobkerries and enforcing discipline. They also settled minor differences and negotiated with the white compound manager. *Isibondas* and *indunas* were often 'rewarded' for their complicity. They were accommodated in smaller dormitories or individual rooms. On mines owned by Anglo American the *induna* system was replaced by a system of room prefects and 'unit supervisors', which was run on similar lines.[44] Discipline took many forms, from fines to arrest and isolation. In the 1970s a common form of discipline was the manacling of offenders to mining fixtures overnight. Workers were also forced to sleep on the floor as a punishment.[45] In 1985 the International Metal Workers Federation revealed that on at least one mine, Transvaal Alloys, workers were being physically punished for striking. They were forced to accept whippings by white supervisors, or face dismissal.[46]

Struggles at the mines

The contract labour system inhibited the awareness of collective strength, and the highly controlled living environments and brutal repression of worker organisation obstructed unionisation at the mines. Spontaneous strikes over wages, food, working conditions and housing occurred repeatedly in the first half of the century, and there was mass resistance to recruitment and desertion from contracts. In the 1940s the African National Congress (ANC) and the South African Communist Party organised a section of the mining workforce into trade unions. The African Mine Workers Union (AMWU) was formed clandestinely, mobilising around wages and inadequate food rations. In 1944, War Measure 1425 prohibited gatherings of more than 20 persons on proclaimed mining ground, but workers held meetings outside the compounds.[47] Rising militancy among miners culminated in 1946 in a general strike by 74,000 workers in response to an AMWU call. It was brutally repressed. Leaders were arrested, mine compounds sealed off and at one mine the workers were driven underground at bayonet point. Nine workers were killed and over 1,000 injured in clashes with police. The defeat of the strikers began the decline of trade unionism at the mines, although spontaneous strikes, protests and covert activities continued for the next three decades.

Strikes and protests intensified in the 1970s, chiefly around the issue of wages. Anglo American wage increases, instead of placating miners, fuelled feelings of powerlessness and frustration. Workers were not consulted about the increases; they perceived them as in no way compensating for the accumulated disadvantages of the preceding 50 years.

Wages, along with job reservation, the *induna* system, the quality of food and conditions in hostels were the source of successive strikes and disturbances in the 1970s and early 1980s. The level of violence rose, with attacks on property, especially hostels, clashes between miners and attacks on *indunas* and *isibondas*. Miners from neighbouring states often requested repatriation as a form of protest.

Sociologists argued that the destruction of mine property, attacks on *indunas* and clashes with other workers were a form of industrial sabotage committed to

> reduce tension or frustration, or on the other hand, to assert some form of direct control over one's work or life. Unplanned smashing and spontaneous destruction are signs of a powerless individual or group and ... they principally occur in industries which are in an almost 'pre-trade union' state. The current wave of unrest at the mines, with its so-called faction fights, seems to be, in some instances, a clear case of industrial sabotage.[48]

During this period there were many casualties arising both from violence among workers and repression of worker organisation by police. Twelve miners were shot dead at the Western Deep Levels mine in Carletonville in September 1973, during a wage dispute.[49] A further 64 died in 1974 when resistance was particularly intense, following Anglo American wage increases.[50] In 1975, 69 workers were killed and 251 injured; in the first half of 1976 a further 25 died with 146 injured. In 1975 deferred pay was a major source of dissent. Workers from neighbouring states struck at seven mines. The state responded by repatriating 20,000 workers and ten miners were killed in violence.[51]

This high level of resistance prompted the government to establish an inter-departmental Commission of Enquiry into Riots in the Mines in March 1975. Its findings were never published but were subsequently leaked. It concluded that the contract labour system was the source of labour unrest. It described miners as highly conscious politically and said that they would 'co-operate to an increasing degree to realise their political aspirations':

> The Black worker is aware of what is going on around him and of events elsewhere in Africa and in the World. He ... is becoming more and more aware of himself and the important part he plays in the mining industry. He is aware of the enhanced gold price and that the industry is dependent on him and very vulnerable – seen from the labour point of view ... We must constantly bear in mind that

the Black worker himself is very susceptible to communist influences and that everything possible has to be done to protect him from those influences.[52]

The inquiry also concluded that the 'unusual and unnatural circumstances in which the migrant workers find themselves' in the compounds and hostels contributed towards a feeling of insecurity and caused boredom and frustration which in turn led to violence.[53] The Commission did not, however, recommend improvements in conditions. Instead it advocated greater repression of miners, including the presence on each mine of a 'trained security unit equipped with patrol dogs, teargas, batons and where practicable an armoured car'. It also called for 'regular and effective search parties for weapons in hostels and compounds'. The divisive structuring of the compounds was to be retained to undermine unity, because otherwise, 'in the event of trouble or a riot, it is likely the entire labour force will band together and the mine concerned will therefore be most vulnerable.'[54]

Miners became even more militant after the mid-1970s. While wages remained the central grievance, other issues were taken up and forms of resistance diversified. There were many cases of workers refusing to undergo acclimatisation training. In June 1979 miners at Randfontein dropped hoppers down lift shafts to protest at delays in being hoisted to the surface. Some workers broke their contracts and returned to the bantustans as a form of protest. Instances of miners staging work stoppages in mine passages and underground sit-ins increased.[55] In May 1982, for example, 1,600 workers struck underground at the Buffelsfontein mine near Stilfontein to protest at hoisting delays. They returned to the surface after 25 hours underground. In 1982 the introduction of a new, compulsory, death benefit scheme was met with several strikes, when management began deductions without consulting workers and before the scheme was formally introduced.

In July 1982 accumulated frustrations erupted in a national strike involving some 70,000 miners. Whereas previous disputes had tended to be short (a few hours or a day), the 1982 strike lasted three or four days at some mines. In total 12 gold, platinum and coal mines were affected in the Transvaal, Orange Free State and Natal.[56] At issue was an annual Chamber of Mines wage increase which was too little to prevent a decline in real earnings. The previous year workers had received increases of between 15 and 20 per cent, and with inflation at 16 per cent miners' real earnings were once again declining. At mines owned by Anglo American, Consolidated Investments and Rand Mines, higher increases were awarded, fuelling the anger of workers at other mines.

State and employer responses were ruthless. Police and mine security guards baton-charged and opened fire on strikers. At the Venterspost gold mine police were sent into the shafts to arrest miners who had blocked underground tunnels. At West Driefontein four miners were shot dead and the body of one hung upside down from the compound gate. At the Kloof gold mine thousands of strikers were herded at gunpoint onto a nearby football field and forced into buses which took them to the bantustans.[57]

Unions come to the mines

The 1982 strike proved a landmark in the unionisation of miners. During the 1970s the trade union movement had been preoccupied with building its presence in heavy industry and manufacturing. SACTU had set up clandestine discussion and education groups at the mines, but there was only a semblance of organisation in the 1982 strike. Even though it ended in defeat it generated a climate of militancy in the face of harsh repression.

The Black Allied Mining and Tunnel Workers Union (BAMTWU) Union was founded in 1982 at some coalfields in Northern Natal. Asbestos miners at the Penge mine (North Eastern Transvaal) were organised by the Black Allied Mining and Construction Workers Union (BAMCWU) in the same period. The South African Mine Workers Union (SAMWU) was formed in 1983, run by a steering committee of several general unions; it established a presence on the West Rand gold mines and at Rustenburg platinum mine.[58] The most important development, however, was the emergence of the National Union of Mineworkers (NUM), at that time affiliated to the Council of Unions of South Africa (CUSA). Founded in 1982 with an initial membership of 40,000, it grew rapidly after the strike. By January 1986 it was claiming a signed-up membership of 250,000: about one-third of the black workforce (see Appendix 1). It established a base in the gold mines, but later expanded to copper and diamond mines, with strongholds in the Orange Free State, the Western Transvaal, Witbank and Namaqualand.[59] The union had to organise semi-clandestinely at first, recruiting among miners who visited townships outside working hours.

The 1982 strike also changed management tactics towards the miners' organisations. The frequently violent nature of protests in the previous ten years and the scale of the 1982 events demonstrated the failure of prevailing methods of repression. The Chamber of Mines decided to allow unions access to mines and compounds, as part of a more sophisticated strategy aimed at co-opting sections of the workforce into tame unions.

The Chamber sought to allow black miners to organise in ways that did not threaten the privileged position of white miners or undermine the cheap labour system. White miners' unions were encouraged to set up paternalistic 'parallel' unions for black miners and to register them with the Minister of Manpower, allowing them to negotiate on behalf of black workers. In this way, and by extending existing closed-shop agreements to cover black workers, it was hoped that black miners would be diverted away from the emerging independent union movement. But the speed with which the independent unions won members forced the Chamber of Mines to abandon this strategy, and in June 1983 it signed its first recognition agreement with the NUM, allowing it to represent certain categories of black workers.[60]

Access agreements varied from mine to mine, but they were initially highly restrictive: they prohibited mass meetings, smaller meetings in compounds, the distribution of union literature and the use of public-address systems. In the first years of its growth the NUM had difficulty reaching underground workers because of restricted access to compounds and it recruited chiefly among surface workers (mainly clerks and storemen). It extended its drive to underground workers through machine operators and team leaders. Consequently, in its first year it represented only small categories of generally better paid, more skilled workers. After 1983 underground workers came forward of their own accord, applying for membership.[61] But even by 1985 the NUM represented all sectors of the workforce at only 18 of the 44 mines where it had a presence.[62]

Even where mining companies concluded recognition agreements they continued their efforts to disorganise the NUM. According to a 1984 study their methods included the constant undermining of shaft stewards' rights to represent workers, the refusal to accept authentic medical certificates for sick union members, the dismissal of shaft stewards and members, refusal to negotiate with committees, changes in conditions of access to the mines, bargaining with unions for specific groups of workers only and the repression of strikes by mine security personnel and police.[63] Individual mining companies pursued different policies towards the NUM, with effects which could be seen in the NUM's membership: at the beginning of 1986, 80 per cent of membership was at mines owned by Anglo American. The union was much weaker at mines owned by employers taking a harder line, like GENCOR and Anglovaal.[64]

The rise of the NUM

After 1982 the NUM led miners through several key struggles, in particular the negotiations in July each year for wage increases. The union had to gain credibility as the voice of miners while avoiding provoking the Chamber into crushing it. The Chamber adopted a consistently hard line in the negotiations after 1982, each time seeking to exploit the union's weaknesses in order to cut it down before it could consolidate.

In 1983 the NUM, whose membership at the time was only 60,000, demanded a 30 per cent wage increase and eventually settled for half that – an amount that fell short of inflation. In 1984, with membership closer to 100,000, it adopted a more confident approach. It began by demanding a 25 per cent increase against an employer offer of 10.9 per cent.[65] In four months of bargaining the NUM exhausted all avenues of negotiation and after a ballot decided on a strike. At the last moment the Chamber lost its nerve and increased its offer. The NUM was however unable to convey this information to its members in time and 40,000 miners struck.[66] Mine managers refused to negotiate with shaft stewards committees, calling in security units and police. Ten miners were killed, compounds were sealed off and workers were dismissed en masse at several mines. The strike was violently put down even though the union had fulfilled all the conditions for a legal strike.

Hardline employer tactics continued in 1985. In April 17,000 workers were dismissed from Anglo American's Vaal Reef complex near Klerksdorp and Anglovaal's nearby Hartebeesfontein mine after strikes and go-slows over job reservation. The workers were forcibly bussed back to the bantustans and neighbouring states and then selectively reinstated to weed out active union members. When the negotiations for the annual wage increases began in July the NUM, with a signed-up membership of 250,000, was in a stronger position than ever before. Widespread political resistance throughout South Africa had made itself felt in the compounds. By May 60,000 miners had been involved in industrial action and resistance was taking diverse forms, including boycotts of concession stores and liquor outlets on mine property. Mining houses claimed that there had been several incidents of industrial sabotage. The NUM had also committed itself to more militant action, including a work to rule until the Mines and Works Act was abolished and physical retaliation to assaults by white miners.[67] Wage negotiations began in a charged atmosphere. After two weeks of talks the NUM declared an official dispute.

In July GENCOR unilaterally imposed increases without further reference to the union, and at five of its mines 27,000 miners went on strike. The strike was broken using tried and tested methods.[68] Meanwhile the NUM announced that it would call a strike in August at the 27 remaining gold mines and collieries. Its decision was backed by a membership ballot which showed strong support for strike action.[69] Anglo American backed off and increased its offer. The other mining houses refused to budge. The union had succeeded in splitting the Chamber's united front for the first time. About 28,000 miners struck at GENCOR, Gold Fields and Anglovaal. However, in the face of repression the strikes collapsed after one day, showing that the NUM was thinly spread outside its Anglo American strongholds.

The NUM was again the target of repression, particularly at Gold Fields where it was weak. At East Driefontein and Hartebeesfontein its membership was depleted by mass dismissals. At other mines, shaft stewards and union members were weeded out in selective rehiring. The strike showed that effective industry-wide action required considerable expansion of membership and structures and in 1986 the NUM committed itself to building its membership at GENCOR and the other mines with a hardline policy towards unions.[70]

The momentum of struggle was maintained in 1986, with more miners taking action and a further diversification of tactics. By February 26,000 miners had participated in strikes, consumer boycotts and protests about wages, working conditions, quality of food and prices in concession stores and beer halls. In that month, on gold mines on the West Rand, 42,000 miners participated in walkouts and underground sit-ins in response to the arrest of mine shop-stewards and the introduction of productivity bonuses.[71]

The 1986 annual wage negotiations took place against a background of the political resistance that had been sweeping the country since late 1984 and which had had an increasing impact at the mines. Miners participated in a generalised stay-away to commemorate May Day.[72] A national State of Emergency was imposed in June. By the end of the year about 2,700 union officials and members were known to have been detained, including the NUM vice-president Elijah Barayi. During 1985 more than 100,000 workers had been involved in a range of disputes over mine conditions, wages, accommodation and repression of striking workers by police and mine security forces. The year 1986 saw the situation exacerbated by the State of Emergency and stoppages and stay-aways by trade unionists frequently revolved around the consequences of the state's security legislation and the presence of security forces in the townships.[73]

The Chamber of Mines, mindful of the deteriorating political situation, was reluctant to provoke further conflict and adopted a more flexible approach towards the NUM's wage demands in July. They again broke ranks. Anglo American, GENCOR, Johannesburg Consolidated (JCI) and Rand Mines' gold division raised their wage offers, which were eventually accepted by the NUM. Gold Fields and Rand Mines' colliery division, however, stuck with lower offers, prompting a strike by 30,000 miners at Gold Fields mines in October.[74]

In 1987 the Chamber and the NUM finally locked horns in an all-out confrontation. The NUM was spurred by the growth of its membership beyond Anglo American mines and the inflationary erosion of wages for the fourth successive year. The Chamber was determined to curb the union's influence as the continuing State of Emergency succeeded in reducing the level of open popular resistance. Negotiations deadlocked and the NUM called a legal strike, bringing out some 340,000 miners – two-thirds of the mining workforce – in the largest strike in the country's history. It also became the longest miners' strike, lasting over three weeks. The members of the Chamber adopted uniform negotiating stances and used repression to end the strike.[75]

By the third week 320 miners had been injured in clashes with mine security guards and police. More than 300 had been arrested or detained. At Vaal Reefs security guards tried to force workers down the shafts with sjamboks and clubs. At the President Steyn gold mine at least 44 miners were injured: in one incident police randomly opened fire on miners waiting for buses and taxis. At Western Deep Levels miners were forced underground with teargas and rubber bullets. At the Braken mine, over 2,000 miners staged a six-hour underground sit-in after being forced down the shafts with teargas and dogs. Similar sit-ins occurred at the Harmony and Kloof gold mines. Violent clashes between miners and mine security forces occurred on at least six other mines.

The scale of the repression forced the NUM to call off the strike after three weeks without gaining concessions on wages. However, it made some gains on fringe benefits and leave. Although employers dismissed over 50,000 workers, the union retained much of its organised strength. The strike cost the mine employers an estimated R250 million in lost production revenue, well in excess of what it would have cost to meet the NUM's wage demand. The 1987 strike taxed the NUM's resources to the full. In 1988 the union sought to regroup and consolidate its strength. The Chamber for its part was loath to risk a repeat of the previous year's confrontation. The annual wage increase was agreed without resort to strike action.[76]

The impact of the NUM was considerable. It organised the largest group of miners in the history of the industry. It caused splits between the mining companies, widened the range of issues around which miners mobilised and successfully challenged management and white miner control, in particular in the area of safety. But the obstacles it faced at the close or the decade were still formidable, not least the compound system and the isolation of miners from other workers.

In all fundamental respects repressive labour control policies were maintained it at the mines in the 1970s and 1980s. The improvement of wages and the upgrading of living conditions at some mines did not alter the generally highly repressive and regimented conditions. The readiness of employers to use violence against striking miners was a major obstacle to worker organisation at the mines.

PART III

5 Industrial Law

Industrial legislation in South Africa has been continually adapted to economic and political change. There were particularly extensive changes in the 1980s. Through all the changes, however, industrial law retained the constant objective of channelling all disputes into the official bargaining machinery which, with its complex network of rules and regulations, sought to weight bargaining procedures in favour of employers and the skilled, predominantly white, labour force and against the interests of African workers. It also aimed to restrict trade union activity to workplace issues and obstruct their involvement in broader challenges to apartheid.

Restructuring

Until 1979 African workers were barred from membership of registered trade unions which alone had access to official bargaining machinery. By lifting the restrictions in 1979 the state hoped to incorporate African unions and circumvent the growing industrial militancy of African workers. The checks and controls built into the official machinery had brought about decades of relative industrial quiet among white, Coloured and Indian workers.

Independent trade unions – most of which had a majority of African members – took advantage of the reforms during the early 1980s to extend their organisation, but they also resisted attempts to institutionalise and defuse industrial conflict. As mentioned in previous chapters, however, many workers were not included in the reforms: domestic and agricultural workers and those in essential services were excluded, while in the bantustans there were different and separate controls.

The inclusion of African workers into the official bargaining machinery followed the report of the Wiehahn Commission. Under the Industrial Conciliation Act of 1956, then in force, separate registered unions representing white, Coloured and Indian workers were allowed to bargain at industry-wide level, through the Industrial Councils (see Chapter 3 above).

Registered trade unions were open only to workers officially defined as 'employees' and the Act excluded African workers from this definition. Representation of African workers was instead channelled through factory-based works committees and liaison committees. Works committees, established under the Bantu Labour Settlement of Disputes Act of 1953, were elected by African workers and could bring grievances to the attention of management. Employers were, however, under no legal obligation to bargain with the committees, agreements concluded with them were not legally binding and committee members had no legal protection from victimisation.

After strikes in the early 1970s liaison committees were introduced by the Bantu Labour Relations Regulation Act of 1973, which replaced the 1953 legislation. Composed of an equal number of employer and worker representatives, they could negotiate legally binding agreements. But they were not directly elected. Management appointed the chairs and nominated half the worker representatives. The committees were widely rejected by workers as favouring employers.

Workers organising outside these structures were subject to repression, with police frequently intervening in strikes. Striking workers were arrested or dismissed and contract workers on strike were forcibly removed to the bantustans. Union organisers were harassed, detained and restricted. Nevertheless a rising level of industrial action in the early 1970s brought increasing numbers into unofficial, independent unions. Whereas in 1969 there were only 16,040 workers in unregistered unions, their number had risen to 60,000 by 1978.[1]

Between 1973 and 1980 the independent unions pressurised managements to recognise and negotiate with union-affiliated factory committees rather than the liaison committees. These tactics represented a new ethos and political consciousness on the shopfloor. Disputes took place in strategic sectors like transport, and with the economy emerging from cyclical recession in 1979 the stage was set for a renewed strike wave, as workers sought to make up the cumulative decline in real earnings over the previous five years.

The Wiehahn Commission commented:

> Employers are under sustained pressure to recognise and negotiate with black trade unions and often also to encourage their formation. The pressure is particularly severe on those companies which have overseas principals, many of whom are being required to implement the various codes of employment practices in their South African operations. Evidence submitted to the Commission shows that the

number of companies which now recognise trade unions and negotiate with them – mostly subsidiaries of foreign corporations – is increasing apace.²

... Black trade unions not being registered and therefore being outside the statutory industrial relations system, could well bring extreme stress to bear on the existing statutory system – a development which could within a very short space of time pose a grave danger to industrial peace. A very real danger exists that this development is in the process of creating, by precedent, an informal system which it might in the long run not be possible to dismantle or restructure.³

The Commission was also concerned at increased political consciousness and organisation among workers and their involvement in wider struggles. In Natal, the 1970s were marked by repeated struggles around transport as commuters boycotted buses in protest at fare increases. In the Western Cape squatters bitterly resisted controls on movement and government housing policies. During the nation-wide uprising in 1976–7 there were worker stay-aways by between 75 and 80 per cent of the workforce in Johannesburg and Cape Town in support of broad political demands (see Chapter 8 below).

The Commission feared that trade unions could become a political force involved in struggles to overthrow apartheid. Unregistered trade unions were becoming a permanent feature of industrial relations, enjoying 'moral and financial support on a broad front'. The fact that they were not prohibited, although excluded from the provisions of the Industrial Conciliation Act, was an 'incentive to foreign labour and political organisations' to give them aid. Furthermore they were used as 'vehicles for change' by other non-labour organisations.⁴ Abroad, the United States and countries of the European Community, faced by campaigns by international trade union bodies and anti-apartheid groups pressing for multinationals to withdraw from South Africa, were compelled to introduce codes of conduct recommending that subsidiaries of companies registered in their countries should recognise black trade unions, negotiate minimum conditions and abolish discriminatory policies.

The most urgent need to restructure industrial relations arose, however, from changes in the economy exacerbating the skills shortage. The Commission noted:

The increasing opportunities for black workers to advance into job categories previously occupied by non-blacks will soon give rise to the anomalous situation where black workers working side by side with non-black workers in the same skilled occupations find themselves excluded from the statutory trade union system purely on grounds of colour. Increased vertical labour mobility by job advancement through education and training, particularly of the black labour force, will place the statutory trade union system under extreme stress if the exclusion of the black worker from the system is perpetuated.[5]

Recommendations of the Wiehahn Commission

The Wiehahn Commission departed from previous government strategies. It rejected further restriction of unions which 'would have the effect of driving Black trade unionism underground and uniting Black workers not only against the authorities, but, more important, against the system of free enterprise in South Africa'.[6] It recommended instead that African workers be included along with other workers in the industry-wide bargaining machinery by redefining African workers as 'employees', registering African trade unions and granting them access to Industrial Councils. It argued that allowing African unions to register under specific conditions would make it possible to control them more effectively. These conditions would include a ban on affiliation to political movements, restrictions on the right to strike and subjection of unions to the Industrial Council system.

The Commission argued that:

Black trade unions are subject neither to the protective and stabilising elements of the system nor to its essential discipline and control; they in fact enjoy much greater freedom than registered unions, to the extent that they are free if they so wish to participate in politics and to utilise their funds for whatever purposes they see fit.[7]

It would be far healthier if Black trade unions were admitted to registration at an early stage in order to encourage logical groupings – be it in the form of amalgamations, federations, confederations or less formal terms of association – on industry lines. Such a natural and organic development would have the beneficial effects of countering polarisation and ensuring a more orderly process of collective bargaining, in addition to exposing Black trade unions more directly to South Africa's trade union traditions and the existing institutions, thus inculcating a sense of responsibility and loyalty towards the free market system.[8]

An Industrial Court would also be established as a forum for adjudication in industrial disputes. It would create a body of legal precedents around employment practice, which would gradually reduce the potential areas of conflict between workers and employers.

1979 legislation

Most of the recommendations of the Wiehahn Commission were made law through the Industrial Conciliation Act No. 94 of October 1979, and some others in the Labour Relations Amendment Act of 1981. The powers of the Industrial Court were upgraded in a further amendment to the Industrial Conciliation Act in 1980. But the industrial relations system remained highly restrictive in several important respects. African workers in agriculture, domestic service, state and local authority employment, and certain categories of workers in educational institutions, were still excluded from the definition of 'employee'.

For example, workers employed by the state-owned South African Transport Services (SATS), which ran the country's rail network and harbours and was the largest single employer outside the mining sector, did not fall under the legislation. The Minister of Transport, empowered under separate legislation to determine conditions of employment in the industry, refused to recognise representative black trade unions in SATS.

The 1979 Industrial Conciliation Amendment Act also introduced new controls on registered unions. Registration of a new union would initially only be provisional. Final registration was subject to a period of observation in which the union was assessed according to complex criteria of representativeness. The Act also introduced further restrictions. The government accepted the minority view of five signatories to the report and excluded contract workers from membership of registered trade unions. It barred unions which constituted themselves on non-racial lines from registration, again accepting the minority view of one of the signatories.

The Act retained severe restrictions on the right to strike. Strikes during the currency of a wage determination or Industrial Council agreement remained illegal. Workers in essential services were prohibited from striking. Essential services were broadly defined and included all municipal workers and those in passenger transport. In other sectors workers could only legally strike when a series of protracted procedures had been exhausted. Registered unions had to pursue disputes within the relevant Industrial Council and, failing agreement, accept mediation or arbitration by a person or body agreed upon by both parties. In industries where no Council existed and in the case of unregistered unions, disputes had to be referred to a Conciliation Board, an *ad hoc* body appointed by the Minister of Manpower and consisting of an equal number of employer and worker representatives.

Failing resolution through these channels, a process which could take months, a dispute had to be declared in writing and a 30-day 'cooling off' period observed before workers could legally strike. For members of registered unions, a further stipulation applied: a ballot had to be held to gauge whether there was majority support for strike action.

Workers had little incentive to follow these procedures. Aside from their complexity, there was no statutory protection against dismissal for workers legally on strike. Throughout the 1980s many legal strikes were met with mass dismissals of strikers. Because of these impediments illegal strikes continued to proliferate after the new Act was passed.

Union responses
The majority of independent trade unions opposed the criteria for registration, especially the bar on non-racial unions and contract workers, and the discretion allowed to the Industrial Registrar to determine which unions should be registered. Particularly worrying were the clauses on the representativeness of unions which left discretion almost entirely to the Registrar: unions conciliatory to management might be registered in place of independent ones.

The unions were also concerned that once registered they would be subject to considerable control, and that at a later stage new controls might follow the initial ones. Registration entailed submitting their constitutions to the Registrar and opening their finances to inspection by the Department of Manpower. The unions feared that registration would dissipate the basis of their strength: the worker-controlled, democratically run factory committees on the shopfloor.

The new legislation also severely restricted the training facilities of registered unions. Many independent unions had built up their own programmes to school union activists in industrial relations and broader political issues. The Wiehahn Commission had noted that unregistered unions were making use of material of 'uncertain origin and questionable ideological motivation'. The legislation stipulated that all trainees and training institutions of registered unions should be registered and industrial relations training should take place at approved centres only.[9]

Some unions registered; most of these did so reluctantly and threatened to de-register if certain restrictive criteria, chiefly the bans on non-racialism and contract workers, were not dropped. Other unions refused to register. Opposition to the legislation defined shopfloor struggle between 1979 and 1981 as independent, unregistered unions tried to force employers to deal with them and to drop registration as a condition for plant-level negotiations. There were several bitter struggles. In some, unions allied with student and community groups, who collected strike funds and organised widely supported, often successful, consumer boycotts (see Chapter 6 below).

Employers resisted demands for recognition by unregistered unions. The government backed them with repressive actions ranging from the arrest and forced removal of striking workers to the detention of union officials and the banning of union meetings.

During 1981, however, the tide began to turn in favour of the unions. By the end of that year employers in various parts of the country had been under some 18 months of sustained shopfloor pressure for recognition. Some employers broke ranks and recognised unregistered unions, while major employer federations urged the state to drop the issue of registration and make legislative provision for companies to deal with unregistered unions.

The strikes and employer pressures forced the government to revise some of the controls, continuing a process of making piecemeal concessions which it had begun as early as 1980 when it had backed down on the issue of excluding contract workers from membership of registered unions.

1981 legislation

In 1981 the Wiehahn Commission published the fifth part of its report, including an assessment of developments between 1979 and the first half of 1981. The report expressed concern that the 'dualism' of the system had been retained, with many independent unions still outside the official machinery. Attempts to pressurise unions into registering had further alienated them from official bargaining structures, set off disputes and threatened to politicise industrial relations. This was particularly apparent in the rash of illegal strikes, consumer boycotts and other forms of extra-union support.

Informing the analysis of the Commission was the view that new labour legislation needed to take account of the growth of strong representative unions which had not registered. These could not be ignored by the state or employers, nor could they be prohibited or forced to register. Unions which chose not to register had to be brought into the system through incentives and the extension of some of the controls which previously applied to the registered unions to unregistered unions.[10] The Commission argued:

Under an approach which rather seeks to remove obstacles and which links demonstrable benefits to registration it would be a fair assumption that any organisation which refuses to take advantage of the benefits, but which still purports to represent worker interests, has objectives well outside the sphere of industrial relations.[11]

These sentiments informed the Labour Relations Amendment Act of 1981, which repealed the most severe restrictions on registered unions, including the ban on non-racial unions and provisional registration. Some of the remaining controls on registered unions were extended to cover unregistered unions as well, including the stipulation that they submit their constitutions, lists of membership and an annual audit to the Industrial Registrar. Unregistered unions were also prohibited from affiliating to or financially supporting a political party. The controls were also extended to trade union federations.

The Act sought to limit industrial action outside the official bargaining machinery still further, by increasing the penalties for illegal strikes to a fine of R1,000 or imprisonment for one year. It prohibited unions from 'granting financial assistance to a striker with the object of "inducing" or "enabling" him to take part in an illegal strike'. In an attempt to curb extra-factory support for strikers, the Act extended the definition of a trade union which would fall under its controls from 'an association of employees whose primary purpose was to regulate relations between employees' to 'any association that involves itself in such activities at all'.[12] The implication was clear: non-union organisations would be prevented from involving themselves in disputes. The Intimidation Act (No. 72) of 1982 further restricted strike action by defining the offence of intimidation very widely. Any person who without 'lawful reason' and with 'the intention to compel any person either to perform or act or to abstain from doing any act or to abandon a particular standpoint' by using threats of violence might be guilty of intimidation.[13]

The 1981 legislation tightened state monitoring of industrial dissent by requiring that all strikes and disputes had to be reported to the National Manpower Commission. These controls were further consolidated in 1985 by new amendments, stipulating that any agreements reached between unions and employers would only be legally enforceable if the parties concerned had supplied the Department of Manpower with details of their constitutions, membership and office addresses, and had maintained their financial affairs in good order.[14] No new industrial relations legislation was passed between 1985 and 1987.

The more restrictive aspects of the 1981 Labour Relations Amendment Act were not widely applied. A relatively small number of workers were prosecuted for striking illegally and the state failed to act against unions making use of strike funds in disputes. The Intimidation Act was used more frequently but the state seldom intervened in disputes prior to 1987, when the political climate changed (see below). However, the state made widespread use of legislation providing for detention without trial, and banning of meetings and individuals, to curb unions which in its view had 'objectives well outside the sphere of industrial relations'.

After the 1981 Labour Relations Act registration receded as a shopfloor issue. Employers concentrated instead on refusing to negotiate at plant level, insisting that minimum wages and working conditions be set in industry-wide negotiations in the Industrial Councils. Most independent trade unions, however, objected strongly to participating in Industrial Councils, although many were eventually forced into tactical participation by economic and political forces (see Chapter 6 below).

The Industrial Court

The Industrial Court was intended to function as the final forum of appeal in industrial disputes which were not resolved by the conventional channels; and it was also to be a substitute for legislation enforcing fair employment practices. Working conditions and safety of industrial workers were controlled by the Basic Conditions of Employment Act and the Machinery and Occupational Safety Act, both of 1983, which amalgamated and amended existing laws. But the contract between employer and employee, and in particular the prerogatives of management to hire and fire labour, remained firmly within the ambit of common law.

The drafters of the Wiehahn report hoped that the court, by pronouncing on the fairness of certain management procedures, would reduce the issues around which disputes were sparked off and bring a broader area of management–worker relationships within the sphere of official procedures. The benefits to unions of making use of the court would act as a strong incentive for unions to enter into Industrial Councils, as the court only had jurisdiction over unresolved disputes which had first been referred to these structures, or over disputes involving unregistered unions which had first been referred to a Conciliation Board.

The Court's judgements were to be legally binding and eventually to constitute a body of case law defining fair employment practices. However, the guidelines on how this was to be done were initially vaguely formulated. An 'unfair labour practice' was defined as 'any practice which the Court regards as unfair'. Independent unions were wary of the Court at first because of this vagueness, while its status as a lower court made its authority uncertain. Falling under the Department of Manpower, rather than the Department of Justice, it could be overruled by higher courts. Furthermore, it was staffed by Department of Manpower officials who frequently had little knowledge of labour law and relied largely on personal notions of fairness. By 1982 the Court had dealt with only 62 cases.[15]

Several developments caused the unions to make greater use of the Court after 1981. One was recession: they turned to the Court as a means of limiting management prerogatives without having to expose their membership to dismissal through shopfloor action. Amendments to the Court's status also slowly encouraged unions to use it. In the 1980 Industrial Conciliation Amendment Act, the Court's power was enhanced in order to make it more attractive to independent unions. The Act defined an 'unfair labour practice' more precisely as:

any practice involving any change in practice at the workplace which has or may have the following or similar effects:
– that any employee may be unfairly affected or that his employment opportunities, work security or physical, economic, moral or social welfare may be prejudiced or jeopardised;
– that the business of any employer may be unfairly affected or jeopardised;
– that labour unrest may be created or promoted;
– that the relationship between employer and employees may be detrimentally affected.[16]

The definitions could be used against workers as well as employers, but they gave the Court scope to restrict management practices.

Most importantly, in September 1982 the Labour Relations Amendment Act gave the Court powers to award 'interim relief' to an aggrieved party. Dismissed workers could be reinstated or compensated pending the ruling on their appeal.[17] In 1983 use of the Court increased. Unions used it on 170 occasions and were successful in subjecting to legal regulation some areas of formerly unfettered managerial discretion, including the right arbitrarily to dismiss employees. The Court also instructed companies to conduct retrenchment procedures fairly.[18]

From 1984 trade unions again became more critical and selective in approaching the Court. After the succession of rulings in favour of workers in 1983 the Department of Manpower impeded the functioning of the

Court, usually by refusing to appoint Conciliation Boards in disputes involving unregistered unions and thereby blocking their access to the Court. New, usually temporary, chairmen were appointed to oversee the Court. Their rulings contradicted each other, as did those of the court's *ad hoc* officials travelling around the country hearing cases locally. The Court's inferior judicial status was also emphasised when the Supreme Court ruled that it was 'merely a government agency from which there was no meaningful right of appeal'.[19]

Between 1984 and 1986 many of the Court's new rulings were detrimental to unions. Examples include: a ruling that contract workers could be dismissed without notice because their contracts were temporary; the Court failing to reinstate unfairly dismissed workers because too much time had elapsed between the dispute and the court hearing; its refusal to order individual employers to negotiate in good faith; and its failure to rule against closed-shop clauses, which prevented representative independent unions from negotiating on behalf of their members. Counterposed to those were only four new legal precedents in favour of unions: two ordering mining companies to reinstate dismissed strikers, one against the use of lie detectors on workers and one compelling a company to negotiate in good faith.

In spite of these weaknesses trade unions continued to use the Industrial Court mainly as a tactic to counter management during recession, and to effect reinstatement of workers, by making use of precedents set by the Court. In 1986 almost 2,000 cases were heard.[20]

Political clampdown
Between late 1981 and early 1985 the government left the regulation of shopfloor relations largely to employers, unions and the Industrial Court. But it stepped in with repressive actions when unions engaged in broader political activity. During the 1985 and 1986 States of Emergency, unionists and shop stewards who had built links with civic associations and other political organisations were detained. In late 1987 there was a dramatic rise in the level of arrests and trials of strikers on charges of intimidation, public violence and other offences.[21] The government published a draft amendment to the Labour Relations Act to restrict severely the right to strike, which became law in 1988.

The shift of strategy appeared to be part of a wider policy of repressing political organisations following the sustained national uprising of 1984-6. The mood in the townships often spilled over onto the shopfloor and strikes increased each year from 1984, rising above the 700 mark in 1986 and involving almost half a million workers. In

1987, 9 million work days were lost in shopfloor action, compared to 1.3 million in the previous year.[22] At the same time, influenced by the political ferment, strikes were increasingly militant in character, especially those in the public sector, where there were often violent confrontations with the police. In other sectors there were factory occupations, sympathy strikes and consumer boycotts, as well as physical attacks on strike-breakers.[23]

The trade union movement was drawn into a more clearly defined political role, backing and sometimes initiating stay-aways behind broad political demands. As political organisations were repressed under the consecutive renewals of the States of Emergency in 1986, 1987 and 1988, the workplace increasingly provided a channel for mobilisation which had been closed off in the townships.

In July 1988 the new Labour Relations Amendment Act set out to hem in the unions on the shopfloor and restrict their scope to mobilise. It also sought to win back terrain seized by the unions in the previous eight years. Among several restrictive clauses the Act outlawed sympathy or solidarity strikes and allowed employers to sue unions for company losses and damage to property sustained during illegal strikes. In terms of the Act workers could not strike over an issue dealt with in a wage determination or Industrial Council agreement for 15 months after the gazetting of the relevant agreements. At plant level it was illegal for workers to strike over any issue which had already been the source of strike action in the preceding 12 months.

The functioning of the Industrial Court was also affected by the Act. Unfair labour practices were much more tightly defined in ways aimed at winning back management prerogatives, which had been successfully challenged by unions through the court. Selective re-employment of workers after a strike was no longer an unfair labour practice; nor was the dismissal of workers with less than one year's service; nor the dismissal of workers without first holding a disciplinary hearing; retrenchments were fair where the retrenched workers were selected according to 'reasonable criteria' (a clause which allowed employers discretion to retrench without consulting unions). Under the Act it was an unfair labour practice for a union to call a consumer boycott in support of a dispute, and any unlawful strike in itself constituted an unfair labour practice. The Act also set up a 'special labour court' to hear appeals arising from hearings of the Industrial Court. While enhancing its legal status, this removed it from the jurisdiction of the Supreme Court.[24]

In 1988 there was a decline in the level of strikes, for the first time since 1984, as unions took stock of the new climate.[25] Employers also began making use of the Act's restrictive clauses. Between July 1988 when the Act was passed and February 1989, four companies brought actions against unions for losses sustained during illegal strikes.[26]

Bantustans

The Wiehahn dispensation did not apply in the bantustans, where either there was no bargaining machinery or separate and usually more repressive industrial relations legislation existed. As part of the central government's decentralisation programme it suspended wage determinations and Industrial Council agreements in the bantustans by issuing Proclamation R84 in 1970, effectively scrapping minimum wage regulations in an attempt to encourage investment. This situation persisted in the non-'independent' bantustans except for KwaZulu, and in the 'independent' bantustans of Ciskei, Transkei and Venda. KwaZulu and Bophuthatswana had rudimentary wage regulating structures.

Legislation was frozen at the point at which 'self-government' was imposed on each bantustan. The status of 'self-government' gave the bantustan authorities powers to pass certain laws. Unless the authorities created new regulations after self-government, the legislation which applied in the rest of South Africa at that date was still in operation.

The bantustans of Lebowa, Gazankulu, Qwaqwa, KwaNdebele and Kangwane all became 'self-governing' before the Wiehahn dispensation. No new regulations were implemented and the old works committee system still applied in each of these areas. The only 'self-governing' bantustan to introduce new regulations was KwaZulu. Its Industrial Conciliation Amendment Act No. 10 of 1981 was similar to the 1979 Wiehahn legislation, providing for almost identical bargaining structures and registration procedures. It differed from the legislation of the central government by allowing unions to affiliate to political bodies. This was done specifically to allow for the creation of the United Workers Union of South Africa (UWUSA), which was affiliated to Inkatha, the political grouping based on the KwaZulu bantustan structures.[27] UWUSA was established to counter the influence of the independent unions which had strongholds in the industrial complex of Isithebe and the townships around Durban and in parts of Northern and Southern Natal within the bantustan boundaries, thereby posing a challenge to Inkatha's political control of the region.

Bantustans which had 'independence' imposed on them – Transkei (1976), Bophuthatswana (1977), Venda (1979) and Ciskei (1981) – were empowered to repeal legislation passed by the central government and to create their own bargaining structures. Some introduced additional restrictive measures which inhibited worker organisation. These included laws providing for the banning of meetings and organisations and detention without trial.

The Transkei Labour Relations Act No. 13 of 1977 restricted bargaining to in-house liaison committees similar to those in the pre-Wiehahn era. No provision was made for industry-wide bargaining or trade unions. Strike action was made virtually illegal and disputes were mediated or arbitrated by bantustan labour inspectors and magistrates. The authorities also banned several independent trade unions by proclamation.[28]

A similar liaison committee system was provided for in the Venda Labour Act of 1981. The authorities were overtly hostile to trade unions. The official responsible for manpower, when introducing the legislation, stated that the bantustan had 'not yet reached a stage of development that could entertain trade unions'. Such a stage would come, but 'we will only allow it when we are sure such unions have no outside influence'.[29]

The Bophuthatswana Industrial Conciliation Act No. 8 of 1984 barred unions from the area unless their head offices were based there. It also stipulated that officials of such unions must be 'citizens' of Bophuthatswana. Several unions which had a presence in the bantustan were affected by the legislation and effectively prohibited from operating there.[30] Under the legislation there were strict criteria for the registration of unions, including a prohibition on affiliation to political parties or bodies.[31] Unions allowed to register had access to official bargaining machinery which was broadly similar to that created by the Wiehahn dispensation.

The Ciskei authorities regarded the supply of contract labour as the bantustan's main 'export' commodity and in 1984 banned the main union in the region, the South African Allied Workers Union (SAAWU), following a prolonged bus boycott in which it played a leading role (see Chapter 8 below). The 1953 Labour Relations Act still applied in the bantustan as the authorities took no steps to amend it. It predated even the works committee system and excluded workers from any form of collective bargaining whatsoever.[32]

The authorities in the 'independent' bantustans all passed legislation providing for detention without trial, the banning of meetings and organisations and the restriction of individuals, which severely affected the possibilities for organising workers.[33]

6 The Struggle for the Right to Organise

Low wages were the root cause of the vast majority of industrial disputes in South Africa in the 1970s and 1980s. But in acting to redress low pay and poor working conditions, workers were confronted by the problem of getting employers to deal with genuinely representative structures, be they factory committees, elected representatives or unions. Organisation around wages and conditions was transformed into a struggle for the legitimacy of trade unions.

Chronological overview

The 1970s
The government maintained a consistently hostile attitude to worker organisation after its clampdown on SACTU in the early 1960s. Although never formally banned, SACTU was forced into a clandestine role by repression as the authorities tried to make African workers negotiate through works committees or under the tutelage of conservative unions.

There were few strikes and they were harshly dealt with. Strikers were routinely dismissed or arrested and pickets violently dispersed. Between 1955 and 1960, the era of SACTU, an average of some 5,800 workers were involved in strikes each year. Following its repression this fell to an annual average of only 2,000 during the 1960s, even though the size of the workforce increased.[1]

In the early 1970s the tide began to turn. There was a gradual increase in the frequency of strikes as African workers responded to the severe decline in their standard of living over the previous decade. Foreign investors responsible for the burgeoning of manufacture had taken advantage of a disorganised, badly paid workforce. In 1971 a strike by 15,000 contract workers in Namibia paralysed essential services in the territory's capital, Windhoek. Its effects spilt over into South Africa and during 1972 stevedores struck for higher wages in the port of Durban. Cape Town dockworkers followed with a work-to-rule and a ban on overtime.[2] In the same year Johannesburg bus drivers struck for higher wages. The strike was brief but it disrupted production over a wide area as commuters failed to get to work. Although all these actions were repressed, employers were prompted into pushing up wages.

These small advances set the stage for the strike wave which gripped Durban in January and February 1973. At the time the city and its environs contained the largest concentration of manufacturing industry outside the PWV area. The close proximity of factories contributed to the rapid spread of a wage dispute at Coronation Brick and Tile. More than 100 individual plants were affected as over 160,000 workers downed tools.[3] The strikes were an emphatic rejection of the works committee system. Most of them lasted at most only two or three days. In most cases employers gave in to demands, which were largely for higher wages, and, in the wake of the strikes, Wage Boards and Industrial Councils moved to review the earnings of African workers in an attempt to stem further militancy.

Durban was a critical breakthrough for worker resistance and a stimulus to the re-emergence of independent trade unions with majority African membership, mostly formed in the areas around Durban and Johannesburg. They attracted a ready following. The government, however, remained hostile to autonomous worker organisation.

A recession between 1974 and 1979 prevented the new unions from consolidating their structures. Strikes declined from their 1974 peak of 384 to only 90 by 1977 (see Table 6.1). Unions tried to gain management recognition of democratically elected factory committees with rights to negotiate in-plant agreements, but all the strikes for this demand were decisively defeated. In 1974 strikes at the Leyland motor plant and at Nautilus Marine (employing dock workers), both in Cape Town, collapsed when employers refused to deal with union-affiliated factory committees and the workforces were summarily dismissed. In 1976 many workers were interrogated by police from the Security Branch and pressurised to implicate officials of the National Union of Textile Workers (NUTW) and Textile Workers Industrial Union (TWIU) for incitement to strike following a dispute at Natal Cotton and Woollen Mills over the activities of police spies on the shopfloor. Three union officials were subsequently charged and two detained without trial.[4]

In the Transvaal in March 1976, 29 strikers were severely injured when police wielding pick-axe handles broke up a gathering of workers outside the factory gates of Heinemann Electric during a dispute over recognition of a factory committee affiliated to MAWU.[5] At Armourplate Safety Glass, workers striking against the retrenchment of colleagues were summarily dismissed even though they had followed the intricate conditions for a legal strike.

Table 6.1 Number of strikes and stoppages, per year, 1970–1987

Year	No. of strikes	No. of strikers	Working days lost	Conciliation Board hearings	Cases heard in the Industrial Court
1970	76	4,146			
1971	69	4,451			
1972	71	9,224	14,167		
1973	370	98,379	229,281		
1974	384	59,244	98,583		
1975	274	23,306	18,709	29	
1976	245	28,013	59,861	22	
1977	90	15,304	15,471	35	
1978	106	14,160	10,558	32	
1979	101	22,803	67,099	28	5
1980	207	61,785	174,614	22	18
1981	342	92,842	226,550	19	38
1982	394	141,571	365,337	38	49
1983	336	64,469	124,594	52	190
1984	469	181,942	379,712	98	475
1985	389	239,816	678,273	141	801
1986	793	424,340	1,308,952	1,294	2,042
1987	1,148	591,421	5,825,231		

Note: The figures used in the table account only for strikes and disputes. They exclude stoppages, lockouts and similar incidents.
Sources: South Africa 1987, *Annual Survey of Race Relations*, Tables 5.3.2; 5.4.1; 5.5; ibid. 1981, p.209; ibid. 1982, pp.183; 185; ibid. 1983, pp.200; 205; ibid. 1984, p.330; ibid. 1985, p.195; ibid. 1987/8, p.667; *Hansard Debates* February 1984; *Citizen* 20 February 1985; *Star* 2 March 1987; *Weekly Mail* 3 April and 22 May 1987.

Repression in 1976 continued when the government detained and banned key union organisers. In March, members of the TWIU and NUTW were charged by the state for incitement to strike; others were detained. In November the same year six organisers in the Trade Union Advisory and Coordinating Council (TUACC) unions were banned. Small victories were achieved, however, when some subsidiaries of multinational companies, responding to pressures abroad, recognised committees affiliated to independent unions.[6]

The 1980s

Work-to-rules, go-slows, stoppages and strikes increased dramatically in the 1980s. The face of industrial relations was transformed by factory

Table 6.2 Reasons for strikes, 1980–1986

Reasons	1980	1981	1982	1983	1984	1985	1986
Wages	79	149	186	112	164	148	246
Wages and other reason	9	15	23	17	17	14	
Union matters	20	26	21	21	47	28	27
Disciplinary measures	29	52	60	71	97	57	113
Working conditions	46	35	20	42	44	42	125
Other or unknown	24	65*	84	73	100	100	269
Total	207	342	394	336	469	389	780

Notes: * Of these 50 were concerned with the issue of pensions.
Sources: Annual Survey of Race Relations 1981, p.209; South Africa 1982, p.224; South Africa 1984, p.373; South Africa 1986, Table 5.4.4; *SA Barometer,* Vol.1, No.5, 8 May 1987.

struggles for higher wages and union recognition, and challenges to the centralised and bureaucratic nature of bargaining, shopfloor controls, day-to-day discrimination and poor working conditions.

Many of these strikes helped build unity between different categories of workers. The divisions which apartheid set out to impose were undermined. Contract workers and commuters were organised alongside those with rights to permanent residence outside the bantustans, and non-racial unity was forged between African, Coloured and Indian workers. Unions also sought alliances with other groupings opposed to apartheid and seminal strikes were sustained by community support. The increase in strike activity occurred at the same time as a resurgence of resistance to apartheid, which in turn stimulated more shopfloor activity.

Strikes and disputes during the 1980s are examined chronologically below, before struggles for the right to organise are dealt with in more detail.

1980–81 A politically more confident workforce, the implementation of the Wiehahn commission's recommendations and a renewed upswing in the economy at the end of 1979 were factors fuelling a wave of strikes for increased wages. During the recession living standards had again fallen. The real earnings of textile workers, for example, had declined by 15 per cent between 1977 and 1980. When municipal workers went on strike in 1980 they were responding to a 13 per cent decline in living standards in the same period.[7]

The shift in the government's industrial relations strategy allowed unions space to establish themselves; there was a rapid growth of membership and a proliferation of new unions. Shopfloor struggles were increasingly cast in the mould of resisting attempts to force unions to register. There were several strikes over demands for union recognition, or a combination of demands for better wages and union recognition. In the early 1980s the number of strikes per year doubled and then tripled over the levels of the 1970s while the number of workers involved increased more than sixfold between 1978 and 1981 (see Table 6.1).

Wages were pushed up. In a critical shift of strategy some employers broke ranks and began recognising unions which refused to register. Whereas in 1979 only two companies had signed recognition agreements with unions, 17 did so in 1980.[8] Those unions which had been established before 1980 were now able to use recognition agreements to consolidate and extend their shopfloor presence (see Table 4.1).

The revival of shopfloor struggle was stimulated by a resurgence of broad anti-apartheid campaigns. There was an extended school boycott which affected most of the country, and protests and boycotts over the cost of housing and transport. These struggles over particular aspects of life under apartheid began to link up with each other and with workplace action. Local trade union struggles helped shape strategies of resistance. In the Western Cape consumer boycotts were launched to support striking workers and there was also a general stay-away by workers in support of the school boycott and a boycott of buses. During 1981 some trade unions participated in the alliance of organisations which campaigned to boycott the twentieth anniversary celebrations of the founding of the South African Republic. They also boycotted elections for the government-created South African Indian Council later that year.

1982–3 At the end of 1981 the state clamped down on trade unionists who had participated in campaigns beyond the shopfloor. During 1982 and the first half of 1983 the level of open political resistance fell, partly because of repression and partly because organisations sought to consolidate. Political mobilisation on a national scale only began to revive in the second half of 1983, although intense local struggles around rent and fare increases continued (see Chapter 8 below).

The economy entered a renewed, deeper recession which eroded workers' living standards and in many cases reversed gains made in the 1980–1 strike waves. After the 1981 Labour Relations Amendment Act extended restrictions on registered unions to those which had refused to register, employers stopped trying to force unions to register and sought instead to make them negotiate in industry-wide Industrial Councils. Employers hoped in this way to undermine the shopfloor strength of the unions.

For unions already established in their industries the focus shifted after 1981 from battles for recognition to struggles over the content of agreements and attempts by management to introduce clauses – particularly no-strike provisions – restricting union activity. Unions also contested employer pressure to negotiate in Industrial Councils. However, employers now proved more resilient, strengthened by the slump conditions.

In the second half of 1982 and in 1983 the shadow of retrenchment hung over industrial action. Weaker, newer unions abandoned aggressive strategies for improved wages and conditions for a defence of jobs and retention of membership. The effects of the recession and its delayed impact in specific sectors of the economy brought about a more complex pattern of strikes. In 1982 the number of strikes increased, with a higher number of workers involved than in previous years (see Table 6.1). Unions were still able to use the organisational gains made in the previous two years to bring out large numbers of workers. The refusal of metal workers to negotiate in the Industrial Council accounted for a significant proportion of these strikes. However, in contrast to the preceding years, the majority of strikes ended in defeat for the unions. The nature of strikes also changed. Forty-eight per cent of strikes during 1982 centred around wages and related issues in 1981 the majority concerned recognition, dismissals and conditions.[9]

The full impact of the recession began to be felt in 1983. A 15 per cent decline in strikes (see Table 6.1), and a halving of the number of workers involved, signalled a retreat by unions from shopfloor confrontation: at least one-third of the 1983 strikes were spontaneous and occurred without overt union involvement or in industries without previous organisation. The larger, more established industrial unions adopted cautious strategies, seeking to consolidate and conserve membership. Whereas in 1982 the Federation of South African Trade Unions (FOSATU), which represented the majority of established industrial unions, was involved in 60 per cent of strikes, in 1983 it was involved in less than one-third of actions.[10]

Established unions concentrated on negotiating fair retrenchment procedures and building on existing agreements to include new areas of concern such as health and safety. There was greater recourse to the Industrial Court and applications for Conciliation Board hearings increased as unions sought gains without exposing their membership to dismissal through strike action (see Table 6.1).

Many of these trends were reversed at the end of 1983. Almost half the year's strikes took place in December. The cumulative drop in living standards over the previous 18 months caused an explosion of strikes for higher wages in the mining, chemical and distributive sectors.[11] Declining wages were exacerbated by a 10 per cent increase in the General Sales Tax on consumer goods. Drought was impoverishing the unemployed dependants of workers living in the rural bantustans, whose numbers had been swelled by an additional 158,000 workers retrenched during the previous year.[12]

1984–5 The year 1984 saw the highest number of strikes yet in a single year and the largest body of strikers (181,942). In the first half of the year half of all strikes centred around wage demands. Most of the remaining actions were over unfair dismissals, many resulting from worker claims for improved wages. But the recession strengthened the hand of employers; over half the workers involved in strikes in the first half of January 1984 were dismissed.[13] There were even indications that employers provoked strikes as a pretext to dismiss workers and weaken union structures.

The recession also sharpened tensions outside the factory gates. Township rents and transport costs increased, adding to the effects of declining earning power. There had been a steady growth of township civic associations and between 1982 and 1984 there were several local struggles against fare hikes, rent increases and poor services, some of them prolonged and bitter. In addition, from 1983 school boycotts occurred with increasing frequency (see Chapter 8 below).

Trade unions were deeply affected by the developments sparked off by the rent and education boycotts in the townships of the Vaal Triangle in September 1984. As the protests developed into an uprising against the township administrations and spread across the country, the regime responded by sending troops and police to restore control by armed force. The violent occupation of the townships became a partial State of Emergency in 1985 and a country-wide State of Emergency in 1986. As trade union members were drawn into local township struggles, the unions came under increasing pressure to involve themselves in broader resistance, in particular through consumer boycotts and stay-aways.

In 1985 shopfloor strikes declined by 17 per cent. However, the number of workers involved increased by 31 per cent in other words, more workers were involved although there were fewer strikes. Much of the increase was accounted for by disputes involving miners. The impact of the National Union of Mineworkers (NUM) pushed the number of workers involved in strikes above the 200,000 mark as miners sought to make up for their accumulated disadvantages. The NUM became the largest constituent of the Congress of South African Trade Unions (COSATU), which was formed at the end of 1985.[14]

The drop in the number of strikes, however, demonstrated how the recession continued to affect shopfloor struggles. For the most part only the industrially based unions which had established and consolidated their membership before the recession were able to make further strides. Unions in the metals, motoring, chemicals and food sectors accounted for most disputes, which tended to be concentrated around the annual mid-year wage negotiations in Industrial Councils. Strikes against wage levels proposed by employers in the councils often turned into trials of strength lasting several days or weeks. Many of the older unions had by the mid-1980s established a presence in particular sectors and backed up their demands in particular factories by calling company or sector-wide sympathy strikes among their members.

1986–8 Although in 1986 there was a dramatic rise in both the frequency of strikes and the number of workers involved in them, prompted again by the recessionary erosion of earnings, fewer workers were involved in each strike than had been the case in 1985. There was again conflict at the mines. The major industrial unions refined their tactics in the annual rounds of Industrial Council wage negotiations, workers making use of factory occupations and sit-ins to prolong strikes and increase pressure on employers.

In 1987 the level of shopfloor action rose to more than 1,000 strikes in one year, with more than half a million workers involved in them.[15] There were several key disputes, including a bitter confrontation between miners and the Chamber of Mines. Unions made a concerted effort to break into the public sector, where labour organisation had been repressed for most of the early 1980s, and there were prolonged and bitter recognition disputes on the state-owned railways and in the postal sector. These were trials of strength and the average duration of strikes increased from 3.1 days in 1986 to 9.9 days in 1987. With inflation at 20 per cent, wages remained the major cause of disputes in other sectors.

The pattern of disputes reflected the impact of a 'living wage' campaign initiated by COSATU. Its affiliates put uniform wage demands in a series of strikes, concentrated in the well-organised food, chemical and metal industries.[16]

Shopfloor activity was increasingly militant. The State of Emergency severely restricted community and political organisations, and according to a survey by a firm of industrial relations consultants 'led to their expectations and style being projected onto the union movement ... The emergency ironically had the effect of encouraging trade union activity, and channelling it into a political perspective.'[17] The government and employers expressed concern at this 'politicisation' of shopfloor relations. The Minister of Manpower spoke of 'the total onslaught' having been extended to the labour terrain.[18]

Early in 1988 there came the first signs of a downturn in strike activity, which declined to a quarter of the level of the previous year the lowest level of shopfloor activity since 1983.[19]

The drop in activity was partly a response to a concerted state and employer backlash against the union movement. The Labour Relations Amendment Act was the most public sign of this, but a rapid increase in anti-union action by employers and the authorities in the form of lockouts, dismissals, court interdicts and police intervention in disputes had been discernible since at least mid-1987. The Institute of Industrial Relations gave a figure of approximately 1,424 union officials and members detained or arrested during 1987 under security legislation, labour legislation and emergency regulations.[20]

In the first half of 1988 the government imposed a wage freeze on the public sector and called on employers in the private sector to resist wage demands. In the face of these pressures unions were inclined to be cautious.[21] Where unions did engage in strike action, employers proved resilient and, as in the previous three years, union wage targets were not met.

Events in the townships continued to overshadow those on the shopfloor. Alliances constructed between unions and political organisations in 1984 and 1985 were the basis of union participation in regional and national stay-aways. There were 47 such stay-aways in 1985 and 1986. One study found that strike action around shopfloor issues had accounted for only 22 per cent of work days lost in 1986 the rest were lost in stay-aways. In June 1988 hundreds of thousands of workers stayed away from work to protest at the impending Labour Relations Amendment Act, to be promulgated on 1 September.[22]

The scale of these protests led one study to conclude that:

> The declining number of strikes ... [in 1988] does not necessarily mean a similar decline in worker militancy, which has taken a different form and direction with more overt political overtones. The stay-away ... was to some extent a manifestation of this.[23]

Thus while state repression and the actions of employer led to some caution on the shopfloor, most unions continued to play a political role and significantly influenced opposition politics. As the year closed

COSATU initiated discussions on the formation of an anti-apartheid front to unite the broadest possible range of organisations and sought out new co-operation with the smaller National Council of Trade Unions (NACTU) (see Chapter 8 below).

Struggles over registration and recognition

In this section the way in which strikes have affected the growth of the trade union movement and the rights of organised workers are looked at in more detail.

Union positions on registration
There was initially no united union response to the issue of registration which arose when government strategies focused after 1979 on incorporating unions into the official industrial relations machinery. Most of the unions which later formed CUSA (see Chapter 7 below) decided that it was pragmatic to register even though they opposed the controls. One issue which did not greatly concern them was the ban on non-racial trade unionism contained in the 1979 legislation. Rooted in the black consciousness movement, they excluded whites from posts as officials or organisers and had few non-African members. The remaining unions, the Western Province General Workers Union, known after 1982 as the General Workers Union (GWU), the Food and Canning Workers Union (FCWU), the African Food and Canning Workers Union (AFCWU) and the unions in FOSATU, had a strong commitment to non-racialism. Among them they had substantial Coloured and Indian membership and employed white officials and organisers. They were united in their opposition to the restrictions on non-racial membership and to the exclusion of contract workers from membership of registered unions.

After the government removed the restrictions on contract workers in 1980, FOSATU unions decided to apply for registration although they implied they would de-register if other restrictive aspects of registration, including the ban on non-racialism, were not also removed. FOSATU believed that the advantages of registration would compensate for the remaining controls. Registration would contribute to its shopfloor strength, by making it easier to obtain recognition agreements. Employers would be forced to bargain with its affiliates and they would be able to expand their presence in the sectors in which they were based. FOSATU also feared that if its unions resisted registration more conservative unions, hostile to the interests of African workers, would be registered in their place. The presence in its ranks of two registered unions influenced the federation's decision. The long-established National Union of Motor Assembly and Rubber Workers of South Africa (NUMARWOSA) and the Western Province Motor Assembly Workers Union (WPMAWU) (both representing Coloured workers) had not encountered any substantive interference in their internal workings because of their registered status.

The FCWU, AFCWU and GWU, however, continued to reject registration. For these unions, acceptance of government controls would compromise their hard-won autonomy and shopfloor strength, which lay in democratic factory committees, and their accountability to their members. If employers were to be made to recognise unions, then this had to be through the building of shopfloor strength rather than legislative fiat.

In the Eastern Cape SAAWU, formed in 1980, and other general unions took a strongly non-collaborationist approach. They refused to register 'as long as racially exclusive laws existed' – 'If we were to register into the institutionalised labour system we would be acknowledging support for the present labour laws.' Many of the general unions were at the same time actively committed to resisting apartheid beyond the shopfloor and their refusal to register accorded with their rejection of the legitimacy of the government.[24]

Differences over registration were the source of sometimes acrimonious debates between the unions in FOSATU on the one hand and the food and canning unions, the GWU and SAAWU on the other. Only after the 1981 amendments to the Labour Relations Act did some of these unions again move closer together.

Recognition strikes by unregistered unions
Between 1980 and 1981 unions which refused to register were involved in a series of bitter strikes aimed at winning recognition. Wages, dismissals and working conditions were often the immediate causes of strikes, but once a route for negotiation was sought, workers insisted that employers negotiate with their unregistered unions. Employers initially resisted the pressures. The government backed up their stance with repressive action and put pressure on wavering employers.

The first major recognition strike coincided with the publication of the Wiehahn report. In April 1979 workers in the Fattis and Monis pasta and milling factory at Bellville near Cape Town walked out when five fellow-workers (all members of AFCWU) were dismissed for circulating a petition requesting a wage increase, regular lunch and tea breaks and three weeks' annual leave.[25]

The militant way in which the dispute developed anticipated future strikes. It involved and united Coloured and African workers, contract workers and permanent residents. When it became clear that management would neither recognise nor negotiate with AFCWU, nor reinstate the striking workers, community organisations, student bodies and other political groupings in the region launched a strike fund and began a consumer boycott of the company's products. The boycott later spread to other parts of the country and was a key element in forcing the company to recognise AFCWU and negotiate the reinstatement of all the sacked workers after a struggle lasting almost seven months. It was the first time in more than a decade that an unregistered union had been recognised.[26]

A second seminal battle for recognition was fought in Cape Town, this time by the GWU. Workers struck at two local meat factories in May 1980, demanding that management recognise factory committees affiliated to the union. At one of the plants management refused to negotiate with unregistered unions. At the other, where the factory committee was composed of African and Coloured workers, they were prepared to recognise the committee if it were composed of Africans only. Workers at 20 other abattoirs and meat firms left their plants in a one-day solidarity protest, but were locked out when they tried to return to work.

Using the tactics of the Fattis and Monis dispute, community and other organisations launched a consumer boycott of red meat, a strike fund was set up and efforts were made to discourage scab labour. The meat workers met with firmer employer resolve than in the Fattis and Monis strike and the government intervened more overtly. Late in May the employers met the Deputy Minister of Co-operation and Development and issued a joint statement saying that they had decided on a common line of action to settle the dispute. Shortly after this meeting two officials of the GWU were detained. Other unionists and voluntary workers were detained later. Pamphlets issued by the union were banned and several strikers were arrested in police raids on hostels and removed to the Transkei bantustan. The government also raised the floor price of red meat by a quarter to help meat conglomerates resist the strike.[27]

In mid-June, all meetings (outdoor and indoor) were banned. Although aimed chiefly at breaking the school boycott which was going on at the same time, it severely undermined organisation of support for the strike. It was no longer possible to hold meetings to co-ordinate the boycott and this, together with the detention of GWU organisers, left the boycott committees leaderless.[28] The meat workers conceded defeat in August.

A breakthrough finally came in the Eastern Cape in the same year. The formation of SAAWU had led to a rush of recognition strikes in factories in the East London area between March and September 1980. SAAWU confronted not only a co-ordinated management–state offensive, but also repression by the Ciskei bantustan authorities who banned most of the strike report-back meetings. Over 100 workers were convicted on charges of incitement to strike. Meetings were baton-charged by riot police, and SAAWU officials were detained.[29]

In October the Minister of Manpower flew into East London, urging employers to hold out until new legislation was promulgated to deal with unregistered unions, and the East London Chamber of Commerce later issued a statement saying employers would not deal with unregistered unions. But at the height of the strikes SA Chloride broke ranks with other employers and signed a recognition agreement with SAAWU after a ballot had shown that it had 95 per cent support among workers.[30] Chloride's response was part of a wider trend emerging among employers who were being subjected to sustained shopfloor pressure. In late 1980 prominent employer associations, the Federated Chamber of Industries and the Afrikaanse Handelsinstituut, began advising their members to recognise representative unions. By mid-1981 many employers were doing so.[31]

Recognition strikes after 1981

The unions which had most vigorously resisted registration experienced spectacular membership gains during this period. Membership of the food and canning unions rose from 1,500 in 1978 to 10,000 by early 1982, GWU's by 5,000 and SAAWU's by almost 60,000 (see Table 4.1).

In 1981, with the passing of the Labour Relations Amendment Act of that year, the government conceded its failure to force independent unions to register and the distinctions between registered and unregistered unions became blurred. After 1981, struggles were dominated by the industrial affiliates of FOSATU, in the metals, motoring and other sectors. Having chosen to register, they concentrated their energies on resisting employer strategies to weaken them by trying to force them to bargain through the Industrial Councils.

But basic recognition battles, including those by industrial unions, continued well into the 1980s. Employers continued to attempt to use in-house liaison or works committees. Many employers, especially in small firms, particularly those based in rural areas or smaller towns and therefore less vulnerable to the waves of urban worker militancy, refused outright to deal with worker bodies.

In April 1981 a strike for higher wages and the recognition of NUMARWOSA flared up at the Pretoria plant of the Sigma motor company. It signalled the beginning of a long period of militancy in the motor industry in the Pretoria area. Prior to the strike, management at Sigma had tried to channel all negotiations through a liaison committee. In mid-April 4,000 workers walked out of the plant. One of the largest strikes at the time, it lasted for nine days. In spite of dramatic falls in production, workers won only a partial victory. Employers recognised the union but 18 of the 20-member workers' committee which co-ordinated the strike were dismissed and when ensuing talks on wages deadlocked Sigma unilaterally implemented its own increases.[32]

Also in 1981, the South African Chemical Workers Union (SACWU) sought recognition from fertiliser manufacturers Triomf. The company delayed resolving the issue and then in November 1982 retrenched union members and replaced them with contract workers freshly recruited from the Ciskei bantustan. However, Triomf was forced to recognise SACWU after the union threatened to take the case to the Industrial Court which was then generally favouring unions.[33]

Workers failed to secure a victory in a long-running recognition dispute at the British-owned British Tyre and Rubber (BTR)–Sarmcol plant at Howick a small town near Pietermaritzburg in Natal. Described in a British newspaper as 'one of the worst examples of white management victimisation in modern South African labour history', it led to the most bitter single dispute of the mid-1980s.[34] MAWU sought recognition from management in 1983, but after two years of inconclusive negotiating the 1,000-strong workforce struck in May 1985. Management dismissed the strikers and brought in new workers from outlying areas, most of them sympathisers of the Inkatha organisation. In 1987 BRT–Sarmcol management recognised UWUSA, Inkatha's surrogate union set up to counter the influence of COSATU, of which MAWU was a key affiliate.

MAWU used a range of tactics to try and win the reinstatement of its BRT–Sarmcol members. These included threatened sympathy strikes at other subsidiaries of the company and a failed legal challenge in the Industrial Court. Through its international contacts MAWU also sought to put pressure on the BRT–Sarmcol head office in London. The strike was notable for the support it generated both in South Africa and in Europe. The union and community groups organised a worker stay-away in Howick and Pietermaritzburg in July 1985 in support of the strikers' demands, which an estimated 70 per cent of the workers in the area observed. In Howick local businesses were at the end of 1986 still 'battling to re-establish themselves' after a year-long black consumer boycott in support of the strikers.[35]

Struggles against the TUCSA closed shop
After 1982 FOSATU unions seeking to expand their presence in the clothing, textiles, printing, packaging and motor-components sectors came up against the conservative Trade Unions Council of South Africa (TUCSA) which competed for African members. TUCSA was a federation of unions representing for the most part skilled and semi-skilled white, Coloured and Indian workers. Its origins were in the artisan and craft unions of the early twentieth century which had signed closed-shop agreements with many employers. In the Western Cape a large proportion of the Coloured workforce had been incorporated into TUCSA in this way, presenting a formidable obstacle to independent unions. Closed-shop agreements also included African workers employed in some industries. They were organised into 'parallel' unions, with their registered parent unions ostensibly negotiating conditions on their behalf. Often, however, TUCSA used the junior status of the parallel unions to control the rate of African unionisation, hold down their wages and block their access to more skilled categories of work (see Chapter 7 below).

FOSATU unions were involved in intense recognition battles with employers who refused to suspend closed-shop agreements even where the FOSATU unions were clearly more representative. TUCSA unions blocked FOSATU's NUTW in the clothing, textiles and leather sector, while MAWU and the Paper, Wood and Allied Workers Union (PWAWU) experienced difficulty in gaining access to the motor and paper-producing industries, respectively, in some parts of the country.[36]

In one of the longest-running recognition battles, the giant textile manufacturer, Frame, was forced to recognise the NUTW at its Pinetown Frametex plant in early 1985 after a 12-year struggle involving repeated stoppages and a major legal injunction in support of recognition. The company would deal only with TUCSA's TWIU, even though it was eventually shown to represent only one third of the workforce, and it victimised officials and members of the NUTW.[37]

In the Western Cape emergent unions in the textile industry faced similar problems. Attempts to democratise the TUCSA-affiliated Garment Workers Union, which dominated the clothing industry with its closed shop, failed in the early 1970s. In 1984 an attempt was made to set up a rival, democratic Clothing Workers Union (CLOWU). Its unsuccessful struggles for recognition led to the first industrial action in the Cape Town clothing industry in 67 years.

In spite of these setbacks and difficulties, by the mid-1980s most employers in manufacturing had recognised independent unions. At the mines, however, employers resisted pressures to deal with the NUM well into the 1980s (see Chapter 3 above). Unions also experienced difficulties in the public sector where there were bitter struggles with high levels of state repression. Employers in bantustans, strongly encouraged by the bantustan authorities who feared unions as a threat to their power, similarly refused to deal with unions.

Organisation in the public sector

Employers in the public sector exploited several factors which disadvantaged workers. Workers in local government, the health service and some state-owned enterprises were included in the 1979 revisions to the Industrial Conciliation Act, but as essential service employees it was illegal for them to strike. In terms of the Act all disputes in such services which could not be resolved through negotiation had to be referred for compulsory arbitration (see Chapter 5 above).

The majority of workers employed in the public sector were traditionally on contract and vulnerable to dismissal and removal to the bantustans if they engaged in stoppages. Even though the 1968 Bantu Labour Regulations, which institutionalised the contract labour system, were abolished in 1986, the public sector continued to employ a majority of single male workers from the bantustans, who in the absence of other accommodation continued to be housed in the structures originally built for contract workers. The housing in municipal compounds of workers employed by local government also made it difficult for trade union organisers to gain access to the workforce. Unions trying to recruit Johannesburg municipal workers in 1986, for example, were hampered because organisers who clandestinely gained access to compounds were arrested on charges of trespass.[38] Local government in both black and white areas and the state-owned railways were the frontlines of recognition battles in the public sector. These were highly strategic areas of the economy and the government actively resisted advances by representative unions. Instead it set up closed-shop agreements with its own pliable in-house unions. It also used harsh repression to break strikes. By mid-1988, with two or three exceptions, most disputes in the public sector had led to decisive union defeats.

The handling of two key disputes in the two years after the implementation of the Wiehahn dispensation – one in the Johannesburg municipality, the other in Port Elizabeth harbour – set the tone for following years. Workers employed by the Johannesburg municipality at a power station struck in July 1980 in support of demands for higher wages and recognition of their fledgling union, the Black Municipal Workers' Union (BMWU). Of the 14,810 employees of the municipality 13,492 were Africans, almost all of whom were workers on contract, and within four days most had come out in sympathy with the power station workers.[39] The state responded ruthlessly to the strike. Representatives of the municipality travelled to Pretoria to meet with the Minister of Manpower. Within hours the industrial registrar registered a management-sponsored in-house union, the Union of Johannesburg Municipal Workers, which represented the municipality's salaried employees and had no following among contract workers. Management began dismissing workers who refused to return to work. Thirteen thousand were forcibly bussed back to the bantustans. Riot police sealed off the municipal compounds and in some instances workers were forced back to work at gunpoint. Key BMWU organisers, including its president, Joe Mavi, were detained and brought to trial on charges of sabotage. (They were subsequently acquitted.)[40]

The municipal workers' strike came at the height of the early recognition battles and the harshness of the state's tactics arose partly from its determination to force through its registration policy. The treatment of striking railway workers employed in the Port Elizabeth docks by SATS in 1982 showed, however, that there was no change of heart. The workers struck in support of demands for the recognition of the GWU. SATS refused to deal with the union and instead promoted the growth of its in-house Black Staff Association. Responding to accusations that it was fostering a 'sweetheart' union which could not claim to represent railway workers, SATS stated:

> Why can't a union be a sweetheart union? There is nothing wrong with unions of this type. The railways is [sic] a conservative family type organisation ... There is no room ... for maverick unions ... GWU should leave the railway workers alone. The existing unions are quite capable of looking after the interests of all railway workers.[41]

In August 1982, with clear majority support, the GWU issued management with an ultimatum to start negotiating. When this lapsed some 1,000 rail workers began a go-slow. State reaction was swift. Nine hundred workers were sacked on the spot and forced into buses which took them back to the townships. They were issued with termination pay and rail warrants back to the bantustans. Most refused to accept these and led a fugitive existence in Port Elizabeth, avoiding arrest under the pass laws. SATS had already decided to retrench employees over the age of 60 and the strike provided an opportunity to lay off workers. Four hundred of the dismissed workers were not replaced and five years were to pass before an independent union was again able to establish a significant presence among rail workers.[42]

There were also rumblings in the health service. In the mid-1980s there were several strikes in hospitals around the country, usually in support of wage demands. Particularly where nurses and other medical staff were involved, workers were able to put the health authorities under some pressure. For example, because of their skills health workers were often reinstated after dismissal during strikes, but repression meant that their more substantive grievances were not addressed and representative unions had difficulty organising.

In the second half of the 1980s repression remained the stock response to stoppages and strikes in local government. In 1985, 200 Potchefstroom municipal workers were arrested for illegally striking and in 1986 entire workforces were dismissed in disputes in Empangeni, Richards Bay, Kagiso and Thokoza. The George municipality paid off 215 African contract workers after a dispute and announced that in future it would employ only Coloured labour.[43]

Some modest successes were achieved. It was shown that independent unions had built a presence in the public sector, though by early 1988 they had still to penetrate state-owned companies and the municipalities of the major industrial cities. In March 1986 the Welkom Town Council agreed to recognise the Orange Vaal General Workers Union (OVGWU) and to reinstate 13 workers dismissed in a strike. The TGWU also concluded a small number of recognition agreements with the Johannesburg City Council (after five years of negotiations) and with authorities in some Natal and Transvaal towns. The South African Black Municipal and Allied Workers Union (SABMAWU) engaged in bargaining in Transvaal towns, but was not recognised. This union was behind a rare victory for local authority workers in 1986. Staff employed by the Tembisa Town Council were dismissed in May for heeding two political stay-aways called by local political and community groups. The council was forced, however, to reinstate them; community support for the strikers and popular antipathy to the council was so strong that no scab labour was forthcoming.[44]

In 1987 unions organising postal workers also made breakthroughs for the first time. Between April and September, upwards of 20,000 black workers struck at depots and post offices in the Witwatersrand area and in the Eastern Cape demanding wage parity with white workers, an end to racially discriminatory employment practices and recognition of their union, the Post and Telecommunications Workers Association (POTWA). In September the strikes were called off when the Minister of Communications agreed to establish formal mechanisms to negotiate with POTWA and wages were increased for certain categories of black workers. The Minister also undertook to 'achieve' wage parity.[45]

During 1987 railway workers won their first and long-awaited victory against SATS. A dispute was sparked off in March among railway workers at the SATS City Deep depot in Johannesburg, around what was perceived to be the unfair dismissal of a worker. The dispute spread to other parts of the Witwatersrand, Transvaal and the Orange Free State. Demands for the reinstatement of the dismissed worker were extended: employers should issue a statement of intent to abolish racism in employment practices and they should recognise the South African Railway and Harbour Workers Union (SARHWU). By the fourth week more than 22,000 workers were out on strike at over 80 depots and sympathy action was spreading as far afield as East London, Bloemfontein and Komatipoort. It was the largest ever strike in the public sector.[46]

SATS refused to deal directly with SARHWU. Leading union officials were detained and more than 300 strikers were charged with 'gathering illegally'. On 22 April the deadline by which workers had been ordered to return to work expired, the strikers were dismissed and SATS began taking on unemployed white workers to replace them.[47]

Police shot dead three strikers after breaking up a SARHWU meeting in Germiston and five more were shot in the streets of Johannesburg when riot police intercepted a march of workers on their way to the site of the Germiston shootings.[48] Police then laid siege to COSATU headquarters, where SARHWU was based, and carried out a six-hour search of the premises. Railway workers were assaulted, union records seized, doors to offices broken down and equipment destroyed. More than 400 people in the building were detained.[49]

A more bloody response had rarely been seen outside the mining industry and prospects of the railway workers winning reinstatement seemed remote. But, in June, SATS agreed in negotiations with union lawyers to reinstate the strikers. The company's about-turn was prompted by the prospect that a SARHWU application to the Supreme Court for the reinstatement of the workers would succeed on the grounds that the Minister of Transport had exceeded his legal powers by issuing a special gazette empowering him to dismiss striking SATS workers.[50] There were also signs that private sector employers, worried about wider effects of the dispute, had placed pressure on SATS to concede. Although the main demand of the strikers recognition of SARHWU was not met on that occasion, the outcome was a victory, leaving the support base of the union intact with the prospect that it could consolidate and extend its presence.

The role of the bantustans
In early recognition struggles, emerging unions came up against hostile bantustan authorities who feared that the unions would become a focus of opposition, filling the vacuum left by the repression and banning of most political organisations in the bantustans.

SAAWU members were repeatedly harassed and intimidated by the Ciskei authorities when they returned from the factories of East London to their homes in Mdantsane. The impending 'independence' of the bantustan at the end of 1981 had far-reaching implications for SAAWU members, who stood to lose their South African citizenship and hard-won rights of work and movement associated with it. Broader political organisation was only to emerge in the area later, and SAAWU was propelled into the role of opposing 'independence' alongside its quest for a shopfloor base. The Ciskei authorities were consequently centrally involved, along with employers and central government in attempts to repress the union in its early recognition struggles.[51]

The union negotiated eight recognition agreements during 1981. But during a strike for union recognition at South African Television (SATV) strikers were shown a list of unemployed workers drawn up by the bantustan authorities and told that there were replacements waiting to take their jobs. Similarly, after a strike at Dunlop Flooring in November the Ciskei authorities assisted management in replacing strikers who had been dismissed. The new applicants were all screened by the Ciskei Central Intelligence Service.[52]

The government, employers and bantustan authorities selected a strike at the East London plant of Wilson Rowntree in February 1981 to try and break SAAWU. The dispute concerned the arbitrary dismissal of a worker which led to further sackings when others took protest action.

Strikers also demanded recognition of SAAWU: employers dealt officially only with a TUCSA affiliate, the registered Sweet and Food Workers Union. SAAWU called a consumer boycott of sweets produced by the company, but despite wide support the workers were defeated after a year on strike. During that year scores of workers and union officials were detained under emergency proclamations in force in the bantustan and under the Internal Security Act.[53] A document drawn up by a local official of the Security Branch was circulated to employers in East London, suggesting ways of undermining SAAWU. It advocated that managements force unions to register, encourage the growth of TUCSA unions and keep records of unemployed workers with whom they could replace strikers.[54]

After the imposition of 'independence' on the Ciskei in December 1981 the bantustan authorities stepped up their harassment of SAAWU and other trade unions, and refurbished their labour-recruiting agencies. A Department of Manpower was created with a computer into which details of individual workers were fed, including any history of involvement in strikes. Employers were offered a workforce which would not resort to 'desertions', 'walkouts' and 'insubordination'.[55]

The Bophuthatswana bantustan authorities also opposed emerging unions. In 1984 miners struck at the Union Carbide vanadium mine in the bantustan, demanding recognition of the NUM. Shortly afterwards the bantustan administration introduced legislation barring unions based outside the bantustan boundaries in an attempt to prevent the NUM and other unions gaining a foothold. When the NUM tried to organise the GENCOR Impala Platinum mine the company refused to deal with it because it did not comply with the legislation.[56] In January 1986, 23,000 miners (two-thirds of the workforce) struck for higher wages, and were dismissed en masse the largest dismissal in South African labour history up to that date.

In Natal, in areas in and around the KwaZulu bantustan many of the unions affiliated to COSATU were well entrenched by 1985, and were seen as a threat by Inkatha which sought to counter COSATU's influence by setting up UWUSA in May 1986. This provided some employers with an opportunity to undermine the representative unions with which they had been forced to deal. In mid-1986 the FAWU, which represented most workers at the Pietermaritzburg and other plants of Clover Dairies in Natal, challenged management over its opposition to formal recognition. Management responded by promoting UWUSA, allowing it access to the plant to recruit (a facility denied to

FAWU). These actions sparked off disputes: 240 were dismissed during a strike in June 1986 in a management attempt to break the union.[57]

However, UWUSA generally had great difficulty penetrating plants organised by COSATU unions. This failure prompted vigilante activity, emanating from Inkatha and UWUSA, against COSATU affiliates. Union organisers and members became targets of assaults, murders and arson attacks in the course of 1986, and this continued and intensified in the following years.[58]

Struggles against official bargaining machinery

Industrial councils
Although many employers in the manufacturing industry had recognised unregistered unions, they agreed to negotiate with unions at plant level only over selected issues. They insisted that all substantive issues, notably wages, be discussed in the Industrial Councils where agreements for whole sectors or industries were hammered out. Their object was to move bargaining away from the shopfloor, where employers were most vulnerable to worker pressure, to the councils, which were constituted of an equal number of employer and employee representatives. Employers and skilled workers could easily combine against lower paid, less skilled workers. Furthermore, existing members of the councils could veto the entry of new parties (i.e. independent unions) and retain closed shops. Independent unions entering councils for the first time confronted interest groups with years, sometimes decades, of experience.

Most independent unions had built an industrial presence factory by factory, with strong representative shopfloor structures immediately accountable to members. For these unions negotiating in councils would mean, in the words of one unionist:

> busying oneself talking miles from the point of mobilisation, overextending limited resources greatly, and in no time losing track of the points where employers can be legitimately pressurised ... Emerging trade unions ... are determined to retain direct worker control over the union side of the bargaining table and to keep the unit in respect of which bargaining is taking place, down to a size where there can be effective report backs on negotiations, democratic channels for the workers affected to state their attitude to proposals made in the course of such negotiations and generally to ensure by the time one concludes any bargain, that the majority of workers affected thereby

are in favour of an agreement being concluded on the terms finally proposed.[59]

The question of whether or not to participate in councils was an invidious one for unions. A council set wages and conditions for all workers in a sector, even if workers were not represented in its deliberations. By staying out of councils unions abandoned the possibility of influencing negotiations, but by participating they could be party to terms which disadvantaged their members. Most emerging unions decided against participation, at least until they had built up sufficient strength to counter employers and unions representing skilled workers. However, by 1983 the recession had increased the capacity of employers to hold out against plant-level actions and some of the emergent industrial unions, notably in the metal and paper industries, reconsidered tactics and joined the councils. These were unions which had experienced rapid membership growth, sometimes across several regions. To confront employers more effectively they felt the need to channel militancy and organisation into simultaneous industry-wide actions: councils were a logical focus for this. These unions were also influenced by the experience of the motor unions which had participated in Industrial Councils before the Wiehahn dispensation.

Motor industry

While negotiating in the councils, the motor unions took strike and other actions against offers put by employers in the councils. They backed up their challenges by continuing to press for a widening of issues negotiable at plant level. One of the first major struggles against the Industrial Councils, after the Wiehahn dispensation, occurred in 1980 in Uitenhage in the Eastern Cape. Motor workers downed tools in rejection of an employer wage offer in the council, and some 3,500 members of NUMARWOSA and the Union of Automobile Workers (UAW) struck on 16 July.[60] In the following days another 5,000 workers in component industries, including the Goodyear Tyre factory in Uitenhage, downed tools. Police teargassed workers returning home and later people in the townships erected barricades.

The strikes in the Uitenhage components plants immediately affected production in motor companies in nearby Port Elizabeth. A shortage of parts forced Ford's Cortina plant and General Motors to shut down. By 20 July 10,000 workers were on strike.[61] At a special meeting of the Industrial Council for the motor industry on 24 July, employers raised their wage offer and agreed to further increases over the next few months. It was an unqualified worker victory.[62]

In 1982 the National Automobile and Allied Workers Union (NAAWU) (an amalgamation of NUMARWOSA and other motor unions) co-ordinated the first sector-wide shopfloor action against an employer wage offer in the council. There were five months of continuous action in support of a R3.50 per hour 'living wage' against an employer offer of R2.15. Between April and September there were 26 separate strikes, sit-downs and go-slows involving 52,589 workers.[63] At Ford, cars emerged from the assembly lines painted in the wrong colours. Workers made frequent use of go-slow tactics, assembling one car an hour against the usual target of 12 to 15. After employers rejected a union compromise offer NAAWU withdrew from the Industrial Council. Volkswagen, General Motors and Ford were all closed for various lengths of time. Most factories were only able to commence normal production in August. However, strengthened by the recession, employers remained intransigent.[64] Ford used the strike to retrench 507 workers and the council rate was unilaterally imposed. In September NAAWU again brought out workers, this time in the first company-wide strike in support of demands for wages above those agreed in the council.[65]

The accumulating impact of the recession prevented NAAWU from consolidating its challenge to the Industrial Council, and motor companies warned workers that strikes were an incentive to hasten automation programmes. Many companies introduced short-time working. Volkswagen shelved its expansion programme in Uitenhage and attempted to weaken NAAWU's Eastern Cape power base by relocating part of its operation to the Transvaal.[66] In 1985 one of the largest companies in the Eastern Cape, Ford, announced it was ending its operations in Port Elizabeth following a merger – 2,000 workers were retrenched.[67]

Despite setbacks in the Eastern Cape, NAAWU and other smaller motor unions continued to win concessions in the Pretoria area where the Transvaal motor industry was concentrated. In 1984 workers at Alfa Romeo at Brits successfully won recognition for NAAWU following a strike – a crucial victory, because it gave the union majority representation for the entire motoring industry.[68] BMW agreed to negotiate wage increases at plant level with NAAWU in June 1984 after a ten-day strike. These were significantly higher than the prevailing minimum rates set at council level and later in the year similar concessions were won in plant-level negotiations at Toyota in Durban.[69] In June 1986,

BMW and NAAWU agreed on a 40-hour working week, the first such agreement in a motor assembly plant.[70]

In the Eastern Cape there were also small gains. A rash of strikes in 1985 ended with employers awarding interim monthly pay increases until talks in the council could resolve wage disputes. In the three years after 1985, unions in the motor sector continued to extract concessions in Industrial Council negotiations, although employer offers seldom met union demands.[71]

Chemical sector
A key struggle against the Industrial Council in the chemical sector was fought out in 1980 at the Boksburg plant of Colgate Palmolive. In an earlier dispute, management had agreed to recognise the Chemical Workers Industrial Union (CWIU) but refused to negotiate on pay or conditions unless the union joined the council. When employers refused to discuss wage demands the union set in motion procedures for a legal strike (the first time in the post-Wiehahn era an independent union had done so). All other options were duly exhausted, and the prescribed ballot showed workers overwhelmingly in favour of striking. But when the union declared that it would call a boycott of Colgate products (toiletries whose sales are heavily reliant on black consumers) the company backed down and agreed to negotiate. The success at Colgate, in the heartland of the heavily industrialised East Rand, spurred further industrial action in the metal industry in the area in 1981 and 1982. It was here that the most sustained challenges to the council system took place.[72]

The metal industry
South Africa's iron, steel and engineering concerns are largely owned by a small number of companies (among them Anglo American, Barlow Rand and GENCOR) organised into a powerful employers federation, the Steel and Engineering Industries Federation of South Africa (SEIFSA). SEIFSA adopted uniform strategies towards labour. In guidelines drawn up in 1981 it advised its members to grant only those unions party to the National Industrial Council for the Iron, Steel, Engineering and Metallurgical Industry (NICISEMI) access to plants and to restrict 'points of negotiation' with unions which remained outside the council.[73]

MAWU refused to join the council and between July and November 1981 was at the centre of a strike wave involving some 25,000 workers which swept the East Rand metal factories. One-third of the strikes were about wages, the rest concerned union recognition, dismissals, the action of foremen, and workloads.

MAWU introduced a strategy of demonstration stoppages, encouraging workers to return to work as soon as management agreed to negotiate. It met with qualified success. Few employers conceded to demands, but in more than half of the disputes strikers were reinstated, so that the union preserved its strength. It used victories to extend its presence and the pressures had some effect. SEIFSA revised its guidelines in 1982 and advised employers to conclude in-house agreements on selected issues with unions in their plants whether they participated in the council or not. But employers still refused to negotiate over substantive issues, especially wages, outside the councils.

Between February and May of 1982 there were further strikes on the East Rand, fuelled by price, fare and rent increases and drought in the rural areas. In 15 stoppages where MAWU was involved, more than half were in support of wage demands higher than those set in the councils.[74]

The recession, however, favoured employers. SEIFSA advised its members not to negotiate with strikers and to dismiss those who failed to return to work. The strike wave peaked at the end of April at Scaw Metals when 2,800 workers were dismissed after an 11-day strike, without gaining concessions on the issue of wage demands.[75] MAWU's strategy of challenging wages imposed by NICISEMI was undermined and the union was forced to reappraise its strategy.

In 1983 MAWU decided in favour of tactical participation in the council, becoming the first independent union to do so since Wiehahn. MAWU was having difficulty consolidating its rapidly growing membership, and struggles in several plants at the same time had overextended its resources:

> All the strikes were over the same issues wages, pensions, job security and retrenchment. Although the strike wave assumed industry-wide proportions the strikes themselves were fragmented. Workers in different factories did not unite in their demands ... MAWU needs a focus around which workers could unite in their demands. Industry-wide bargaining is needed for this level of mobilisation ...[76]
>
> Employers are solidly united behind SEIFSA. We need to be solidly united to face SEIFSA ... The Industrial Council is the only place we can face employers nationally and our much greater size makes this easier now than two years ago.[77]

The decision to participate was tactical: MAWU would not be party to any agreement or actions with which its members did not agree; it would insist on facilities to report back during negotiations and it would withdraw from the council if necessary.[78]

MAWU's tactics were soon put to the test in the annual wage negotiations in NICISEMI. When employers refused to allow it to suspend the proceedings and report back to its membership, MAWU withdrew from the council and subsequently rejected wage increases imposed in its absence. It attempted to increase the council's minimum rates by separate negotiations and action at shopfloor level, but encountered firm resistance.[79]

In 1984 MAWU and three other metal unions formed an alliance to frame common demands. All four were affiliated to the International Metal Federation (IMF) and had been brought together in a South African Co-ordinating Council of the international body. Aside from MAWU, two of the unions represented black workers. The other, the South African Boilermakers' Society (SABS), organised chiefly among white skilled workers but in the wake of the Wiehahn dispensation and the collapse of the colour bar it had begun recruiting black workers. It argued for the rate for the job, hoping in this way to prevent its skilled white membership from being undercut by cheaper black labour. For the same reasons it actively sought co-operation from the black metal unions. Its decision to co-operate with the black unions was at the same time a sign that white workers' wages were also being eroded by inflation.

At Anglo American's Highveld Steel foundry, SABS and MAWU agreed in 1984 to strike together to win across-the-board increases above those proposed in the council. The strike followed worker ballots: 92 per cent of MAWU members and 70 per cent of SABS members voted in favour of striking. Joint shop stewards meetings were held and report-backs on negotiations with management were also held jointly.[80] Anglo refused to increase its wage offer, but in the course of the negotiations it did allow the unions access to the company's accounts, thus widening the area of plant-based negotiations.[81] At another metal plant, Hart Limited in Durban, workers scored a similar victory in 1984 when the company agreed to widen the plant-level issues over which it was prepared to bargain.

During 1985 employers were at their most intransigent and proposed a year-long freeze on wages because of 'prevailing severe recessionary conditions and rapidly escalating costs'.[82] Although this position was later revised and small increases conceded, they fell far short of MAWU's demands. The union declared disputes and pressed for plant-level increases at 70 key factories. These were larger plants, mostly in

MAWU's Transvaal strongholds; some were subsidiaries of multinationals. The union felt that at these plants international pressure would ensure that workers were less likely to be dismissed.[83]

There were strikes at several key metal concerns, some spilling over into 1986. New worker tactics emerged. There were factory occupations for the first time; one at Haggie Rand lasted two weeks. Most ended only when employers secured eviction orders. The occupations intensified pressure on employers and made it difficult to dismiss workers, lock them out or bring in scab labour.

Again MAWU could claim some modest successes: areas of plant-level negotiation were widened and some additional wage increases granted. Most strikers were reinstated, but most larger companies still refused to bargain over substantive issues at shopfloor level.

In the 1986 annual Industrial Council wage negotiations MAWU members rejected the employer offer. In contrast to the previous year when it had selected certain companies for industrial action, MAWU decided to pressure employers at almost all the plants where it had support. This initially took the form of a co-ordinated one-hour stoppage, then a ban on overtime work and finally a national one-day stoppage.

Some employers broke with tradition and proposed negotiations over wages at plant level even while negotiations were still proceeding in the council. This was, however, not a concession in principle to the long-sought demand for plant-level bargaining. Rather it represented a sophistication of employer tactics, designed to fragment MAWU's national campaign. It succeeded. In factories where MAWU was weak or its structures relatively new, its members broke ranks and agreed to wage offers lower than those demanded by MAWU in the council. This undermined the national focus of the union's challenge to NICISEMI.[84] In the union's own estimation, not all its members had 'understood the NICISEMI negotiations and the significance of demands sent to the Industrial Council' and it undertook to conduct an education campaign among its members.[85]

During the 1987 Industrial Council wage negotiations the National Union of Metalworkers (NUMSA), formed after the merger of MAWU and several motor unions earlier in the year, was isolated. Fifteen of the 16 unions participating in the talks, including NUMSA's partners in the IMF South African Co-ordinating Council, accepted SEIFSA's wage offer. The union balloted for a strike and received majority support from its members. Some 60,000 workers were set to strike at 500 plants. However, on the day before the strike was scheduled to begin, the Minister of Manpower approved the national agreement for the metal industry and extended its provision to parties which had not agreed to it, making any strike action illegal. NUMSA called off the strike rather than expose its members to employer and state retribution.[86]

In 1988 the union reassessed its tactics, agitating for a joint stand by the IMF-affiliated unions. Three of the IMF partners, all representing black workers and affiliates of the National Council of Trade Unions (NACTU), fell in behind NUMSA. The unions agreed to hold joint general meetings to formulate demands and to report back on negotiations. The four unions were backed by a combined membership of 120,000, as against the 80,000 of the remaining unions in NICISEMI. The Minister of Manpower would not, as in 1987, be able to impose an agreement which did not have majority support.[87]

The unions' revised tactics paid off. Negotiations deadlocked, the IMF unions balloted their membership for a strike, and in August more than 30,000 workers from the four unions struck at 111 factories.[88] During the second week of the strike, more than 50 factories broke ranks with SEIFSA directives and entered into plant-level negotiations.[89] Although similar concessions had in 1986 fragmented MAWU's national campaign, the 1988 strike was sufficiently broad to maintain momentum.

Although SEIFSA made no substantive concessions on wages, it offered to backdate its increase by two months and conceded other demands, including the swapping of 1 May and 16 June for other public holidays. Crucially, it agreed to look into changing the collective bargaining system to give recognition to NUMSA as the major union. For the first time NUMSA signed the national agreement.[90]

On balance MAWU (later NUMSA) gained significantly by joining the council; it rapidly increased its membership, strengthened its organisational structures, mobilised metal workers on a national level, laid the ground for greater unity with other metal unions and altered the balance of forces in a strategic industry.

Other sectors
In only two instances apart from the motor industry were FOSATU and later COSATU affiliates able to shape the councils to their advantage or significantly undermine their power. In 1983 NUTW joined the Transvaal Knitting Council. It was in a strong position because it had a majority presence in the plants covered by the council. Employers who had negotiated industry-wide increases with the union before it joined the council agreed to suspend the closed shop of TUCSA unions which had kept NUTW out in the first place.[91]

In pulp and paper manufacturing, PWAWU was able to weaken the council in its sector. PWAWU represented most African workers and joined the council in 1984 when it failed to get employers to negotiate substantive issues at plant level. Its experience highlighted dramatically just how the councils were weighted against the interests of African workers. Even though it represented 60 per cent of the 10,000 workers employed in the industry, it was alloted only one council seat and found itself consistently outvoted by employers and the three smaller unions representing white workers. The union argued unsuccessfully for representation on the council to be allocated proportionately according to size of membership.[92]

PWAWU withdrew in August 1985 and the council subsequently collapsed. The union was then confronted by new dilemmas. Council membership had given a national focus to its wage demands. Outside the body it faced the danger that employers would offer widely differing wages. In the paper industry there were also, as in others industries, disparities between rural and urban wages. To overcome these obstacles, the union adopted a strategy of company-wide pressure. Its breakthrough came in early 1987 when a strike took place simultaneously at five plants of Mondi Board, forcing the company to agree to uniform increases at all its plants.[93]

Industrial Council struggles: assessment
Union campaigns against the Industrial Councils yielded contradictory experiences, depending on the circumstances particular to each industry. The experiences of MAWU and PWAWU highlighted some of the dilemmas of unions with large memberships. Both were forced by a combination of growing and dispersed memberships on the one hand, and strong employers on the other, to join councils, as a way of giving an industry-wide focus to bargaining and consolidating their challenge to employers. But employers manipulated the structures of the councils to try to weaken union challenges at crucial junctures. The motor unions succeeded in getting employers to bargain outside the council, but recession and the decline of the Eastern Cape motor industry meant that they were unable to achieve the increases they sought.

But the struggles against the councils provided a focus for mobilisation and recruitment of new membership. Through their choice of tactics unions seldom exposed their members to dismissal; they preserved and extended their bases, an achievement all the more remarkable in the hostile climate of recession.

Industries not covered by Industrial Councils
In those sectors not covered by Industrial Councils minimum wages were arbitrarily set through wage determinations; levels were usually

lower than the levels set by councils (see Chapter 3 above). Organisation in these sectors was difficult and strikes were illegal during the currency of wage determinations unless stringent criteria had been met. As explained in Chapter 5 above, in the case of a dispute workers had first to apply for a Conciliation Board hearing. If that failed to resolve the issue, strike action could be resorted to once a secret ballot had shown majority support for this.

Despite these difficulties, unions were able to put employers under intense pressure to raise wages in one sector not covered by a council, the retail sector. The sector employed mostly young, urbanised workers with, in the words of one union official, 'a relatively high degree of education that goes with a well developed politics. They mirror the socio-political situation in the townships.' This made for a militant workforce. Supermarkets and other retail outlets were also acutely vulnerable to pressure. According to an employer, 'factories can close for a day during a strike and make up for lost production later. But retailers must stay open every day and the unions have recognised this factor.'[94]

Workers in the retail sector also benefited from the presence of a single union, the Commercial Catering and Allied Workers Union (CCAWUSA), which became a focus for unified organisation. It rose to prominence in 1982 during a wave of successful wage strikes in 12 branches of the OK Bazaars supermarket chain around Johannesburg which triggered similar disputes at branches of Woolworths. CCAWUSA, which was involved in 42 of the 48 strikes, expanded its membership from 7,000 in 1980 to over 21,000 by the end of 1982, which made it one of the largest industrial unions of the time (see Table 4.1).[95]

In 1986 there was an intense ten-month period of strikes, sit-ins and wild-cat stoppages affecting all major chain stores. In April more than 6,000 workers were involved in a five-day legal wage strike at Pick 'n Pay, covering at least 45 stores in all areas except the Western Cape.[96] Negotiations had been especially bitter and the Conciliation Board failed to resolve the deadlock. After initially demanding a monthly average increase of R216 against the R43 offered by employers, the union eventually dropped to R90 and later accepted R85. Workers were able to bring particular pressure to bear by sitting-in at stores, hindering attempts to keep shops open with skeleton staffs of white workers.[97]

A longer strike began a few months later at stores of OK Bazaars over wages and the 'backdoor retrenchment' of 2,000 workers, which broke an agreement with the union to observe fair procedures. The strike lasted ten days and took in 137 of the company's 202 stores. Over 1,000 workers were arrested, 161 of them detained under State of Emergency regulations.[98] Workers tried to use the tactics developed in the Pick 'n Pay dispute by sitting-in and occupying premises, but the emergency regulations hampered them. Police were called to some stores to evict strikers; in others management spread large amounts of pepper on the floors to prevent workers from congregating.[99] In the final settlement OK agreed to a R100 across-the-board increase; although this was R60 short of the union's original demand, OK also agreed to implement a minimum wage and increase staff discounts.[100]

These strikes were drawn-out trials of strength. Workers were not sustained by strike funds and often the increases which they won did not cover what they had lost in earnings. But they showed that employers were vulnerable to pressure and the unions conserved their membership for future battles.

Rolling back employer and government controls

Strikes transformed shopfloor relations and gave workers new confidence. Employers found that workers challenged their prerogative to hire and fire, to set conditions of work, or to retrench. Workers demanded a say over pensions and benefits. White supervisors found they could no longer abuse their black colleagues. Women workers won new rights, especially in the retail sector.

The government's ability to manage industrial relations on its own terms was also challenged. The collapse of its policy of forcing unions to register and the unions' qualified use of the councils were the most visible proof of this. But workers also challenged the operation of the state pensions scheme and taxes. In short, workers won terrain on many fronts.

Most of the gains were made in the period 1979–82, before the onset of the recession, which employers used to introduce restrictive clauses into recognition agreements limiting the freedom to organise on premises and introducing 'no-strike' contracts. The threat of retrenchments allowed them to step up production levels without resistance. Some unions, particularly longer-established ones, sustained their shopfloor challenges, shifting strategies from militant confrontations and trials of strength over wages and related issues to the improvement of workplace conditions, particularly those of health and safety. Although retrenchments placed unions on the defensive, many succeeded in negotiating fair retrenchment procedures with the more 'enlightened' employers.

The first major strike to challenge management controls in the workplace in the post-Wiehahn period took place at Ford in Port Elizabeth in October 1979. Although it centred on specific grievances, including wages, the strike involved a fundamental challenge to racially discriminatory practices. A survey by two academics before the strike, which Ford itself commissioned, highlighted issues which anticipated the dispute. A cut-back in working hours meant that between 80 and 90 per cent of the workforce lived below the Poverty Datum Line. The survey also found that even though the company had formally committed itself to training and promoting blacks this was not being implemented quickly enough. Discrimination was still practised at the plants.[101]

Union organisation was new and the FOSATU-affiliated UAW had made little impact at Ford. Most of the workers identified instead with the Port Elizabeth Black Civic Organisation (PEBCO), a civic association based in the townships.[102] Its chairperson, Thozamile Botha, was a Ford Cortina employee. When he was dismissed, allegedly for frequent absences from work in pursuit of PEBCO activities, some 700 workers downed tools in protest at what they regarded as victimisation. Ford backed down fairly quickly and Botha was reinstated.

But the dismissal awakened a deeper sense of grievance which rapidly triggered new incidents. During November Ford, General Tyres and some smaller industries were hit by a wave of strikes. Over 1,000 workers protested at overtime rates and racist remarks by white workers and managers; they demanded higher wages, recognition of the PEBCO-aligned Ford Workers' Committee and integration of factory facilities. After a contest lasting well over a month, Ford management finally conceded on the substantive demands.[103] The government tried to influence events by detaining several strikers, including Botha. Banned on his release, Botha later fled the country.

Undoubtedly, the fact that most of the Ford workers were skilled and hence not easily replaced by scab labour contributed to their victory; but the strike was also an early demonstration of the efficacy of shopfloor organisation and solidarity challenging controls and discrimination.

Racism in the workplace

A number of disputes were sparked off by racist abuse from white managers, foremen and workers, and by humiliating racist controls. In 1984 unions threatened to take action if Pick 'n Pay, the supermarket chain, continued to subject workers to lie-detector tests in what management called 'an effort to curtail stock shrinkage'. The following year 400 workers employed by the chemical concern, Triomf, were dismissed after a stoppage in support of a worker who refused to undergo management breathalyser tests. Only 30 were reinstated.[104]

A dispute in the food sector in 1985 further highlighted the racism of many white managers and supervisors. A black security guard (a member of the FCWU) was dismissed at the Olifantsfontein plant of Dairy Belle, a manufacturer of milk, juices and yoghurts. It was a clear case of victimisation: he had trapped two members of management passing through the factory gates with stolen products. Most of the workforce struck in support of demands that he be reinstated; they were themselves dismissed. There was a sympathy strike at one of the company's other depots and the union threatened a national boycott of Dairy Belle products. Other unions in the distributive sector said they would refuse to handle the company's products. The company was forced to concede because of falling production and distribution levels.[105]

Actions by white workers also sparked several disputes which had varied outcomes, depending on local circumstances. In September 1985 black workers employed at a Johannesburg branch of the Edgars clothing chain staged a sit-in strike demanding the transfer of a white controller who used abusive and racist language. When they were dismissed, sympathy strikes spread to more than 20 other outlets of the chain in the Reef area. Further dismissals took place, placard demonstrations outside branches of Edgars were broken up and 62 strikers were arrested. The union representing the workers, the Federal Council of Retail and Allied Workers (FEDCRAW), responded: 'This cold and heartless group has condemned over 400 workers and their families to poverty for the sake of protecting a single white racist.' However management ultimately capitulated and reinstated the strikers. The decisive factors were a threatened boycott of its products and an effective publicity campaign which embarrassed the company. The racist controller was put on probation.[106]

White worker assaults on their black colleagues also triggered some prominent disputes. In late 1984, the Food and Beverage Workers Union (FBWU) launched a boycott of the products of the Dairy Maid Ice Cream Corporation. This followed the company's dismissal of about 300 workers who stopped work in support of demands for the dismissal of a white employee who had assaulted workers. The company refused to reinstate 90 workers, almost all of them union members and activists. In a more successful action after simultaneous strikes by 800 workers employed by ASEA Cables at three of its plants in October 1986, management was forced to dismiss a white artisan who had assaulted a black shop steward.[107]

The position of women
The resurgence of trade union organisation also resulted in changes in the status of black women on the shopfloor in some sectors. Although constituting the majority of workers in garments and textiles, the food industries and the distributive and retail trades, women had little influence in the union movement. Their presence was not reflected in union leadership, for example. In 1983 FOSATU women shop stewards formed a group within the federation to press for attention to issues affecting women workers. These included sexual harassment in the workplace, maternity leave and equal pay for equal work.[108]

The issue of maternity leave figured most prominently in disputes. Before the revival of the new union movement in the 1980s, many employers simply dismissed pregnant employees. The more enlightened were willing to re-employ mothers once the birth had taken place, but often at lower wages and in different posts to the ones they had left. The first breakthrough against these practices came in the retail sector.

In July 1983, 70 workers struck at the Killarney branch of Checkers supermarket chain, demanding the dismissal of a manager who, among other things, had manhandled a cashier, insulted black workers and dismissed a number of pregnant women. Workers at 20 other branches struck in sympathy. After negotiations with CCAWUSA, the chain agreed to remove the offending manager.[109]

These early stirrings against sexism in the workplace were built upon when CCAWUSA negotiated a maternity agreement with OK Bazaars in 1984. Pregnant employees would be allowed to take 12 months' unpaid maternity leave, and later return to their jobs. The union improved upon this in 1985, when Metro Cash and Carry gave pregnant workers the option of 12 months' partly paid maternity leave. They would receive a third of their salary for seven of these months. They would also be allowed time off to feed their children and attend ante- and post-natal clinics.[110]

Subsequently other unions agreed various forms of maternity leave. The CWIU alone concluded 20 agreements in the Transvaal during 1986, one of which guaranteed six and a half months on full pay; in 1987 the first industry-wide agreement was concluded in the metal industry.[111] In 1988 an agreement was reached in the motor industry, guaranteeing women six months' partly paid maternity leave and re-employment. In the same year CCAWUSA signed the first 'parental rights' agreement with the Pick 'n Pay supermarket chain, allowing both mothers and fathers leave to care for children.[112]

In the six years after the 1984 agreement between CCAWUSA and OK Bazaars, most COSATU unions won job guarantees for pregnant women. Union organisers came to regard discussion of maternity benefits as an integral part of general negotiations. Members of the TGWU had difficulty in gaining recognition for paid maternity leave, but had made progress through the 1980s on the right of pregnant members to keep their jobs. Among hindrances to an equal position in the workforce and in the unions, women identified the failure of men to share domestic tasks. This seriously curtailed women's ability to participate in union meetings. At COSATU's 1989 conference women from a wide range of affiliates voiced these and other obstacles to their progress within union structures. In the face of resistance from male delegates the conference adopted a resolution on 'women's leadership' committing the federation to encourage the election of women shop stewards on the factory floor. The conference failed, however, to adopt a resolution condemning sexism in the federation. Noting the need for women's organisations, the Conference resolved to work for the revival of the Federation of South African Women (FEDSAW), which in the 1950s and early 1960s had articulated the demands of women in the workforce.[113]

Retrenchment
Attempts by unions to protect their membership against the threat of lay-offs were a major cause of industrial action after 1981. The impact of the recession on the trade union movement was uneven. It did not necessarily retard new organisation, as one union offical argued:

> In an advanced industrialised country ... workers might consider far more carefully and conservatively the potential risks of joining a union struggle in the midst of a recession ... Black workers in South Africa are generally not risking a well paid satisfying job, as certain of their counterparts in the advanced industrial societies might conceivably be doing ... while there can be no doubt about the fact that unemployment has increased substantially in the past month[s] it is equally true ... that unemployment levels were so high during the preceding boom that the threat of unemployment is not perceived as being substantially greater now than in the immediate past.[114]

However, after 1981 retrenchments began to feature as a prominent issue in disputes.[115] In October 1982 MAWU shop stewards, concerned at the laying off of 1,700 workers in the metals sector, met to pool ideas on how to combat retrenchments. A strategy was formulated whereby unions would demand that impending lay-offs be negotiated with unions a month in advance, overtime work be suspended, and dismissed workers be given redundancy pay. Similarly, at its national conference in 1982 CUSA recommended the suspension of overtime, a halt to the recruitment of new labour, the introduction of short time and the early retirement of pensionable workers. Where retrenchment was unavoidable, joint management–worker committees were to meet to select who would be retrenched. The emphasis would be on protecting contract workers' jobs.[116] Agreements usually adopted the principle of 'last in, first out': unions sought guarantees that the longest employed workers would be the last dismissed.

Industrial action over retrenchments led to some novel agreements. Following a stoppage at Kelloggs cereal manufacturers in April 1982, when six workers were retrenched, employers agreed to allow the shop-steward committee to investigate manning levels in the plant. Six empty places were found and workers were taken back at the same rates of pay and without changes in conditions of service.[117] The GWU gave priority to protecting contract workers and at a marine engineering firm members with permanent residence rights offered to accept retrenchment in place of 13 contract workers. Similarly at Dorman, Long, Swan and Hunter in Cape Town, workers organised by GWU agreed to go on three months' unpaid leave on a rotating basis to avoid retrenchments. [118]

In 1983 unions won a seminal victory when the Industrial Court ruled that retrenchment without adequate notice constituted an unfair labour practice: workers had to receive proper warning of dismissal, recognised trade union representatives should be consulted on pending dismissals, workers should have adequate opportunity to seek alternative employment, and the 'last in, first out' principle was endorsed.[119]

By the mid-1980s the battle against arbitrary retrenchments had been won at many plants where unions and employers had longer-standing relationships. Most subsequent disputes concerned how retrenchments would take place or were protests against employers who side-stepped agreed procedures.

Many unions negotiating retrenchment agreements tried to get employers to introduce short time as an alternative to lay-offs. At PG Glass in October 1985, CWIU members unilaterally introduced their own short-time schedule when employers refused to do so. They clocked in half an hour later in the mornings and left earlier each day.[120]

Employer refusal to consider short time was also the source of a five-week contest at 46 outlets of Foschini, a clothing chain, in May 1986. CCAWUSA called a legal strike over the retrenchment of 274 workers and many stores were the targets of sleep-ins. The strike was eventually resolved by mediation after unions threatened to launch a consumer boycott. Foschini agreed to severance pay and an additional pay award based on length of service for the retrenched staff.[121]

Pensions

As we have seen, the issue of deferred pay was one of the major sources of strikes at mines in the early 1970s. Workers in other sectors showed that they, too, opposed government and employer dictates on how their money should be used particularly with regard to pension payments.

In 1981 the government introduced the Preservation of Pensions Bill aimed at company pension schemes. A number of employers had made it a condition of contract that workers contribute to company schemes. The bill proposed that workers would not be able to withdraw accumulated pension rights before retirement age (at 65), even if they were dismissed from their jobs. When leaving one job for another, they would have to transfer their benefits to the pensions scheme of their new employer, or retain them in the fund of their previous employer. One of the motivations of the state was to stabilise a crucial source of investment income as part of its drive to sustain economic growth.

Workers opposed the bill. Many used pension funds as a source of short-term savings. They wanted access to these when they lost their jobs, so that they could fall back on them while unemployed. Workers also mistrusted the efficiency of the pay-out system. For example, would pensions schemes be able to trace pensioners removed to the furthest outreaches of the bantustans?[122] Employers were, for the most part, in favour of the bill; it would allow for longer-term investment of pension funds and it would encourage a more stable labour force as workers would be less inclined to change jobs.

News of the bill triggered a wave of strikes between April and November 1981; it was the largest single cause of strikes that year. They were concentrated in Natal but also affected the Eastern Cape and the Transvaal. The strike wave extended into 1982, when there were a further 27 strikes around the issue, particularly in the sugar-milling industry.[123] Workers demanded that employers pay out their pension contributions immediately before the bill became law. Employers responded in various ways. Some paid out without workers having to resort to strike action, while others paid out after stoppages. Some employers refused to pay out, arguing that maintaining contributions was a condition of contract. In certain plants workers were forced to resign before being paid out and management used the opportunity to retrench or to root out activists.[124]

In the Eastern Cape one of the pensions strikes, at the Firestone tyre plant in Port Elizabeth in January 1982, gave rise to new shopfloor tactics. When employers succeeded in breaking the strike and 160 of the 1,500 dismissed workers were not rehired, the union representing those dismissed, the Motor Assembly and Components Workers Union of South Africa (MACWUSA), decided to broaden the campaign into a sympathy strike, the first in the post-Wiehahn era. Workers at Ford Cortina refused to handle tyres from Firestone. Within two hours, no more cars were coming off the production line. Workers also came out on strike at other motor plants. After 17 days of strike action, the deadlock was broken, with Firestone agreeing to the immediate reinstatement of some of the dismissed workers; the rest would be phased in at monthly intervals.[125]

In November the Minister of Manpower announced that the bill had been scrapped. It was an historic victory, one of the few occasions when workers had directly forced the hand of the state.[126]

Workers were unsuccessful in challenging further legislation affecting access to their pay. There was a similar wave of strikes involving over 20,000 workers at the end of 1984 and beginning of 1985, over changes in taxation. Workers opposed a new system of automatic tax deductions from their monthly pay packets. Although the Taxation of Blacks Act actually reduced the tax for which Africans were liable, by bringing it into line with that paid by whites, the Act became the focus of intense anger. It brought home the reality that while tax on blacks and whites was levied at the same rate, blacks were politically excluded from a say in how it would be spent.[127]

Disinvestment

During 1985 motor workers were confronted by a new phenomenon. A combination of recession and international campaigns for disinvestment caused some multinationals to withdraw from the country. When Italian-based Alfa Romeo's Brits plant in the Transvaal was closed, for example, 580 workers went on strike until the company agreed to negotiate with NAAWU over severance pay, the future of pension payments and other matters.[128]

The responsibilities towards their employees of companies withdrawing from South Africa lay at the heart of a strike at the American-owned General Motors (GM) plant in Port Elizabeth in November 1986. GM's decision to sell its local subsidiary to South African interests was made without consulting workers. There were no guarantees that the new owners would pursue the same industrial relations policy, that retrenchments or redundancies would not follow the sale or that worker benefits would not be prejudiced.[129] GM would make no concession on the strikers' main demand, that they be awarded severance pay based on length of service.[130] The strike was broken when the company obtained a court order to evict 500 strikers who were occupying the plant.[131]

New tactics, new trends

Company-wide strikes
The emergence of company-wide strikes, and the co-operation on common demands of different unions in the same sector, resulted from the growth of unions beyond their initial bases and their use of more sophisticated tactics.

The first company-wide strike of the 1980s took place in September 1983. Over 3,000 workers struck simultaneously at three plants of Autoplastics, in Pretoria, Cape Town and Port Elizabeth. NAAWU, the union behind the strikes, had an agreement with employers to negotiate pay for all the plants simultaneously; failure to agree on an increase prompted the dispute.[132]

Many company-wide actions were pioneered in the chemicals sector, with the growth of SACWU. There was no national Industrial Council in the sector and hence no minimum wage rate: companies paid different wages from plant to plant. The union sought uniform wages throughout the industry. In January 1985, for example, some 2,000 SACWU members struck over wages and the victimisation of unionists at four plants of Plascon Paints. Although they failed to move employers, a similar strike the following year brought a resumption of negotiations over wages and the reinstatement of dismissed workers.[133]

In June 1985 sympathy strikes were legitimised by a ruling of the Supreme Court. It rejected an application by AECI requesting that a threatened wage strike at its Newcastle plants and sympathy strikes planned at four other centres be declared illegal. The court found that the strike was legal because the union had followed statutory procedures. In the event SACWU did not press ahead with the strike and AECI took pre-emptive action at Newcastle, retrenching workers and threatening to dismiss anyone who went on strike.[134] In 1986, however, the union did bring out its members at seven separate AECI plants, again over wage demands.[135]

In some sectors different unions united around common demands. A celebrated example occurred at Dunlop in 1984. When 1,200 workers at its Durban plant were dismissed after legally striking to win the reinstatement of workers dismissed in an earlier dispute, sympathy strikes were organised by the two FOSATU-affiliated unions, MAWU and CWIU, at the Ladysmith and Benoni plants of Dunlop. The company was forced to reinstate the Durban workers.[136] In the second half of the 1980s cross-union co-operation became more common, as greater unity was achieved within the union movement. Co-operation between NACTU and COSATU affiliates in the metal sectors was a key factor, as we have seen, in winning concessions from employers during the 1988 Industrial Council wage negotiations.

Factory occupations
In 1985 workers began to occupy premises during disputes. The occupations took two forms: sit-ins (short-term demonstrations on the shopfloor) and sleep-ins (longer-term occupations, some of which lasted weeks). Occupations initially proved effective. They prevented employers from locking strikers out or easily replacing them with scabs. As workers stayed near their machines, employers also feared that any precipitate action could result in damage to equipment. Workers were sustained by support committees, often relatives and friends, who brought them food and information.

The first such occupation took place at the end of 1985 during strikes at Kelloggs in Springs, at a Nampak plant in the paper sector, and at the cosmetics manufacturers Cheseborough Pond at Wadeville on the East Rand. The Nampak occupation lasted two and a half weeks, forcing employers to concede to PWAWU demands over unfair dismissals and shifts. At Kelloggs, Sweet, Food and Allied Workers Union (SFAWU) members were also successful in winning the reinstatement of a dismissed worker. Cheseborough Pond workers sustained their occupation for three days and two nights. They also won concessions on wages and demands for May Day to be a paid public holiday.[137]

Sit-ins and sleep-ins were employed as part of MAWU's campaign for higher wages during its 1986 Industrial Council negotiations. Two thousand workers 'slept-in' for almost three weeks at Haggie Rand, and there were occupations at ASEA Cables and eight other metal plants.[138]

As these tactics proliferated in the food, chemicals and paper sectors, and in the struggles in the retail sector in 1986, there was a backlash. Employers sought and often obtained eviction orders. In some disputes workers defied the orders and there were confrontations with police brought in to evict them.[139]

Strike tactics

In spite of their achievements after 1980, most unions had yet to win the right to strike without fear of dismissal. Employers more often than not either dismissed strikers or used the threat of dismissals to break strikes, especially in sectors where less skilled or contract workers predominated. Unions repeatedly declared their disillusionment with the revised Industrial Conciliation Act, which allowed employers to dismiss workers even where the procedures for legal strike action had been scrupulously followed. They also challenged the absence of any obligation on employers to negotiate in good faith in such situations. In 1985, Corobrik – makers of bricks – refused to negotiate further with the GWU over wages, even though the union had mobilised the Western Cape's largest ever legal strike, taking in five plants of the company. The union concluded from this that:

> Unless the Industrial Conciliation Act is revised to give management and workers equal bargaining power, there seems to be absolutely no incentive for workers to go through the long and arduous procedures laid down in the law ... The legislation ... grants workers the right to strike but leaves room for managements to wield power that will always outweigh that of workers.[140]

Some unions did win the right to strike in agreements with management, or gained tactical concessions in agreements. A wage strike at Natal Thread by NUTW members in June 1983 ended with employers undertaking that in the event of another strike the workforce would either be dismissed in its entirety or reinstated in its entirety. The union's objective was to prevent employers selectively rehiring dismissed workers after disputes, to weed out union activists. FOSATU's PWAWU signed an identical agreement with the Carlton Paper Corporation in October 1983, and in 1985 NAAWU concluded an agreement with Rowan, which undertook not to dismiss strikers for at least a month after a legal strike.[141]

Aside from those which occurred as part of the bargaining within Industrial Councils, the majority of strikes after 1980 were illegal, as workers, no longer feeling the need to observe the law or the official bargaining processes, asserted their will through organised strength.

Building unity
One of the most significant achievements of the trade union movement in the 1980s was to organise workers along non-racial lines and unite different categories of workers through shopfloor action. The process was uneven and developed more in industries where unskilled or semi-skilled workers of different apartheid-defined groups worked closely together.

Unions countered divisive tactics on the part of employers and government by creating an ethos of non-racialism, and by building a relative degree of solidarity among contract and other workers. They also consolidated their bases in industries with a majority of contract workers. Advances in the organisation of Coloured workers in the Eastern Cape and among Indian workers in Natal helped break the grip of the conservative closed-shop unions and gave organised substance to non-racialism.

The 1979 Fattis and Monis strike was marked by strong unity between Coloured and African workers: of the 88 on strike, 68 were African (40 of whom were contract workers) and 20 Coloured, most of them women. The contract workers in particular came under pressure. The hostels in which they lived were raided by police and some were convicted on charges of being in Cape Town illegally; a Ciskei bantustan official was brought in to try to 'persuade' them to return to work. Even though 23 contract workers eventually did so, the remaining 17 held out for the duration of the strike.[142]

Unity between African and Coloured workers in the Western Cape developed further in 1980 when there was a strong response in both communities to a stay-away call in simultaneous support of a school boycott and of striking meat workers. However, although the food and canning unions brought African and Coloured workers together in the Western Cape rural areas, it took longer for other independent unions to build a following among Coloured workers, many of whom were under the influence of TUCSA unions.

In May 1981 a major wage dispute involving the largely Coloured workforce, organised by the FOSATU-affiliated WPMAWU at Leyland motor manufacturers, represented a break with past trends. It was the culmination of a long struggle to democratise the WPMAWU.

Democratic unionists succeeded in pulling it out of TUCSA in the 1970s and it later affiliated to FOSATU, a crucial first step in breaking the TUCSA monopoly in the area.[143] The strike was supported by an alliance of groups, including some in African areas.[144] By the mid-1980s independent unions were making modest gains among Coloured workers in the Western Cape, putting TUCSA unions on the defensive. In the Eastern Cape the motor unions became a powerful force among Coloured workers.

The independent unions found it difficult to organise contract workers. The overriding factor in the government's determination to crush the 1980 strikes by Cape meat workers and Johannesburg municipal workers, and the 1982 SATS strike, was the objective of stopping union advances in the organisation of contract labour. Contract workers remained vulnerable in situations of industrial conflict even where they followed the letter of the law. For example, a legal wage strike by chemical workers at AECI in January 1984 was defeated when management threatened to dismiss the predominantly contract workforce.[145]

A similar tactic was used against workers at the South African Coal, Oil and Gas Corporation (SASOL) oil refinery during late 1984 when the 6,000 strong workforce, drawn from ten different bantustans and all employed on contract, participated in a stay-away in the PWV area, called in November to support local school and rent boycotts and to demand the removal of troops and police from the townships. On the first day of the stay-away armoured vehicles and police surrounded the hostels, and the workers were all dismissed and removed to the bantustans.[146] FOSATU and CUSA threatened to bring all their affiliates out in a national strike if the workers were not reinstated. In the complex negotiations that followed, the CWIU obtained the reinstatement of 70 per cent of those dismissed and half of the shop stewards involved.[147] It was an historic victory: the unions had been able for the first time to force a state employer to reinstate a predominantly contract workforce.

Some unions managed to build strong organisational unity in industries employing both contract workers and permanent residents. This was most marked in the metal industries on the East Rand, where MAWU had a strong following among contract workers in hostels in local townships. By the time of the 1981 metal industry strikes, the distinctions between migrant and urban workers were dissolving as both participated in shop-steward structures.[148]

Unity was also forged in parts of the chemical, pulp and paper and food industries. Through this process, according to one writer:

One of the fundamentals on which South African capitalism has been developed is being challenged – the notion that migrant labour is, by its very form, necessarily cheaper than urban labour. This is particularly true when a union is organising in an industry which employs a combination of the two labour forms, as the union then can argue for the equalisation of wages. In effect, the union movement has challenged one of the basic ways in which the working class is fragmented, and has been adopting a path that tends towards the homogenisation of the working class.[149]

Building alliances
A hallmark of the revival of worker organisation after 1980 was the growth of alliances, albeit often temporary, between trade unions and other organisations. Community support usually took the form of strike funds, discouragement of scabbing, and consumer boycotts. Some of these alliances provided a basis for greater co-operation between unions and political organisations in wider campaigns against apartheid.

Again, the successful 1979 Fattis and Monis strike showed the way forward. A consumer boycott was taken up initially by students at the University of the Western Cape, with a largely Coloured student body, followed by students at the predominantly white University of Cape Town, African pupils, the South African Council of Sport (SACOS), the Black Sash and the Western Cape African Chamber of Commerce (WCACC). The Western Cape Traders Association (WCTA) also played a crucial role – its 2,300 members, shop owners in the Coloured areas of Cape Town, took Fattis and Monis products off their shelves.[150]

The 1981 Leyland strike in Cape Town also drew on this local tradition of community support. The union organised support committees in the areas where workers lived. A strike fund was set up and food parcels collected. After an initial period of optimism the workers' position quickly worsened. Organisations in the Cape Town area were overextended as many were already involved in other campaigns. Because of these and other logistical problems, it took over three weeks for support work to take effect in some areas. With 600 workers on strike the union needed R200,000 weekly to sustain the strike, but the strike fund was only able to raise R35,000. By the third week some workers were beginning to trickle back to work.[151]

Overall, consumer boycotts rarely contributed decisively to worker victories in the early 1980s. The success of the Fattis and Monis boycott can be attributed to the newness of the tactic, the absence of other political activity diverting the attention of the supporting organisations, and the strong support of local traders.

The boycott tactic was revived in 1984 during a dispute at a Johannesburg plant of Simba Quix, crisp manufacturers, where three workers had been arbitrarily dismissed. When management refused to negotiate, the entire workforce came out on strike in August and were themselves dismissed.[152] SFAWU called a boycott of crisps produced by the company. Most of the affected workers lived in Tembisa and other East Rand townships where residents had been struggling against high rents and the town councils. Workers and shop-steward councils had been drawn into these struggles and close working relationships had developed between unions and political organisations, particularly those of school students (see Chapter 8 below).

Thirty organisations backed the Simba Quix boycott including most of the independent trade union movement, the United Democratic Front (UDF), the Azanian Students' Organisation (AZASO) and the Congress of South African Students (COSAS), while traders in the East Rand townships refused to stock Simba Quix products. The threat of the boycott was enough to make the company back down and most of the dismissed workers were reinstated in negotiations which followed.[153]

Simba Quix's response showed that conditions had changed: employers could be made vulnerable to consumer pressure. Closer relationships between individual unions, and between unions and community organisations, meant that thousands of consumers could be mobilised to boycott products. After this success, boycotts were used repeatedly in the retail sector, in the dairy industry and at the mines, where miners refused to shop at company concession stores. These boycotts met with varying degrees of success, depending on local conditions, but the alliances which they threw up sometimes cemented relations between unions and broader political organisations. Boycotts were the initial stepping stones to the mass stay-aways and other jointly organised campaigns against apartheid in the second half of the 1980s (see Chapter 8 below).

Less visible, often informal support also proved crucial to sustaining strikes. During the 1980 strike by Johannesburg municipal workers, for example, residents of nearby townships sheltered striking contract workers who would otherwise have been sealed off in their hostels.[154]

Support for strikers, particularly in townships where many of the residents worked for a single employer, discouraged strike-breaking. This helped bring victories in the 1980 strikes by Eastern Cape motor workers, in the dispute at Sigma in 1981, and in several other actions.

Similarly, in one of the longest strikes on record, 249 workers dismissed by B & S Metals at Brits in September 1982 for staging a go-slow won a celebrated victory with community support. For a year they sustained their strike, meeting every day to keep up morale and even selling their possessions to survive. MAWU successfully campaigned among workers in the surrounding areas not to break the strike, even though unemployment was high in the rural environs of Brits. In September 1983 management agreed to reinstate the workers after the Industrial Court had ruled that their dismissal constituted an unfair labour practice.[155]

7 Trade Unions

As the trade union movement developed, it reflected and in some cases reinforced the divisions of South African society but it also, especially in the decades under review, expressed the political necessity of overcoming those divisions.

The established trade union movement

The independent, predominantly African, trade unions which emerged in the 1970s and early 1980s did so alongside an established trade union movement which represented largely skilled white, Coloured and Indian workers and which was often hostile to the new unions. With few exceptions, unions had by the 1970s become broadly identified with the interests of the more skilled sections of the labour force. They were committed to maintaining the privileges won for their members in the preceding decades.

There were three broad, and partly overlapping, strands:

- 'craft' or 'craft-diluted' unions preserving access to skilled occupations through closed-shop agreements;
- white 'racist' unions monopolising skilled occupations through the exclusion of black workers from trade union membership;
- a more complex category of racially mixed unions which had become identified with the interests of skilled workers.[1]

'Craft' unions and 'racist' unions
The predecessors of the craft unions of the 1970s were formed between the 1880s and the 1920s by carpenters, printers and skilled miners. Later they took in some skilled grades in manufacturing. These unions tried to prevent employers from undercutting and replacing their members with cheaper black labour, or diluting and fragmenting their work and employing African workers to take over aspects of their jobs. Their aim was to protect their access to skilled work and higher rates of pay. The high point of these struggles was the 1922 rebellion, when a strike by white miners resisting the employment of cheaper black labour sparked

wider resistance and commandos of white workers fought running battles with government troops.[2]

The employment of African labour was also opposed by racist unions which drew many of their members from rural Afrikaners moving from the least productive farms into the newly industrialised cities in the early twentieth century. They encountered competition for jobs from cheaper African labour moving off the land in a parallel process of migration. This situation was exploited by racially exclusive unions set up by the emerging Afrikaner nationalist movement, which drew many into campaigns for the statutory reservation of skilled and semi-skilled jobs for whites and the exclusion of blacks from apprenticeship training.

Many of the members of these unions also participated in the 1922 rebellion. The state responded to the rebellion by seeking to accommodate the trade union movement. In 1924 the Industrial Conciliation Act established the Industrial Council system which institutionalised collective bargaining. The craft unions responded with a conciliatory attitude to employers. In exchange for restrictions on the right to strike and an agreement to maintain discipline over rank and file workers, they established a monopoly of skilled occupations by means of closed-shop agreements or agreed ratios of skilled workers to unskilled workers.

However, changes in the production process in the 1960s threatened the craft unions. Some skills were replaced by mechanisation, fragmentation or the dilution of skilled jobs into semi-skilled occupations, which were filled initially by semi-skilled whites, then by Coloured and Indian workers and later by Africans. To preserve the status of skilled whites the craft unions recruited semi-skilled workers, hoping through the closed shop to control the pace of the dilution of their occupations. They also sought guarantees from employers that the rate for the job would be paid regardless of colour. With these guarantees vested in Industrial Council agreements, employers had little incentive to employ African labour in occupations controlled by the craft unions and the movement of Africans into skilled jobs was slowed.

The white racist unions, for their part, threw their support behind political parties advocating racial segregation and helped bring a government to power in 1924 which legislated a colour bar in mining and heavy industry. In 1948 white workers were similarly instrumental in bringing to power the National Party, which was committed to extending the colour bar into manufacture. The expansion of manufacturing during and after the Second World War had brought many black workers into industry as operatives, creating conflicts between employers and less skilled white workers over the allocation of jobs. The National Party government also introduced legislation repressing trade unions representing Africans. Whereas the craft unions relied in the main on closed shops to protect their privileged access to jobs, the racist unions relied on statutory job reservation.[3]

The successors to the early racist unions could in the 1970s and 1980s be found in the mining, metal and related industries and in government services and the public sector, while craft unions organised largely within the skilled occupational strata of the mining, motor, building, metal and engineering industries. Craft unions represented 275,000 workers in 1984.[4] Many white racist unions were affiliated to the South African Confederation of Labour (SACLA), with the South African Iron and Steel Workers Association (SAISWA) constituting the bulk of its membership. In 1985 SACLA represented 120,800 white workers.[5] Some craft unions with exclusively white membership were also affiliated to SACLA. Most mixed-membership unions either remained independent or were affiliated to the Trade Unions Council of South Africa (TUCSA), which combined several craft unions with industrial unions and staff associations.

Mixed unions and TUCSA

Although most mixed unions did not explicitly restrict membership by categories of colour or skill, many nevertheless became identified with the interests of skilled workers and were hostile to the organisation of African workers except under restrictive conditions. Many were established to organise within specific occupations such as engineering, furniture-making or electrical work. The effect of the statutory colour bar in slowing the advancement of African workers into these occupations meant that these unions came to represent the interests of skilled white, Coloured and Indian workers.

There were also several unions with large semi-skilled Coloured and Indian memberships in textiles, catering, food and other sectors; these unions had no African members and were registered. Through access to the Industrial Councils they developed conciliatory attitudes to management, institutionalised negotiation procedures and negotiated closed-shop agreements, automatically securing control of their industries. They became bureaucratised and unresponsive to their memberships and they generally lacked shopfloor structures.

Most of the unions in this category were affiliates of TUCSA. Now defunct, it will be remembered for its antipathy to the emerging independent unions. TUCSA reflected the contradictions of its composition:

white-collar unions and professional associations in the public sector and local government; craft unions mostly in the metal and motoring industries; skill-dominated racially mixed unions and bureaucratised, closed-shop unions representing large semi-skilled memberships in the textile and related industries. Its attitudes to the organisation of African workers, sharpened by the resurgence of independent African trade unions after 1973, was always equivocal.[6]

TUCSA was founded in 1956 following a split in the South African Trades and Labour Council (SAT & LC), a federation of racially-mixed unions, some of which also had African branches. The split occurred over the question of how to respond to the introduction of the 1956 Industrial Conciliation Act, in particular to its exclusion of Africans from membership of registered unions and the way it forced non-racial unions to split into segregated branches. A small number of the federation's affiliates continued to organise African workers, but most, including those which went on to form TUCSA, decided to comply with the legislation, shed their African branches and divide along segregated lines.

In 1956 the unions which went on to form TUCSA and shape its subsequent policies were responding to what they perceived as a threat to the vested interests of their skilled members. Employers constantly sought to dilute and fragment the jobs of TUCSA's skilled membership, replacing skilled workers with unorganised semi-skilled or unskilled African labour. For these reasons TUCSA policy vacillated on the organisation of African workers, and at times it excluded African workers from its ranks. At other times it sought to control the rate of black advancement by organising African workers into subordinate 'daughter' unions controlled by the 'parent' affiliates.

In 1959, three years after the exclusion of African workers from its ranks, TUCSA set up a commission to look into the organisation of African workers, but no concrete proposals emerged. Under pressure from the International Labour Organisation, it decided in 1962 to allow African unions to affiliate. By 1966, 13 unions with 7,000 members had done so.[7] But in 1967 a TUCSA conference resolved again to disqualify African unions in response to pressure from the state and the predominantly white unions in its ranks:

> It is the considered opinion of the conference that the Bantu Labour (Settlement of Disputes) Act has failed to stem the tide of Bantu performing semi-skilled and skilled work at greatly reduced rates of pay, whether it be the result of mechanisation, automation or

otherwise. This has greatly reduced the bargaining power of the registered trade unions.[8]

Then in 1968 the TUCSA annual conference overturned its previous decision and allowed African trade unions to re-affiliate, only to expel them once again the following year.

In 1973, in response to the Durban strikes, TUCSA embarked on a strategy of organising 'parallel' unions. These were set up to organise African workers in industries where TUCSA affiliates operated – under the tutelage of and subordinate to the interests of the existing registered unions. Most parallel unions were paper organisations only, without shopfloor structures or union organisers. The secretaries of the registered unions tended to act for both the registered parents and the parallels.[9] Anecdotes from the period indicate how little autonomy they were afforded. In 1976, for example, the secretary general of the African Tobacco Workers Union was an office worker employed by the registered union to fetch the post and make tea.[10] Union dues were deducted from members' wages, sometimes without their consent.

The changes implemented after the Wiehahn report in 1979 fundamentally altered the climate in which the TUCSA unions operated, although the unions in TUCSA welcomed the Wiehahn dispensation. The abolition of job reservation and the rapid expansion of the emerging unions, particularly in the motoring, metal and other strategic industrial sectors, severely undermined the strength of the established unions. The independent unions grew and employers became more responsive to their militant shopfloor tactics. The struggles against Industrial Councils in favour of plant-level negotiations further shifted the ground away from the established unions.

Many craft unions were forced to open their membership to African workers with similar skills, and to demand equal pay for all workers. They hoped thereby to control the rate of African advancement into their occupations. The response of the SABS, a major TUCSA affiliate in the metals sector until 1983, is a case in point. It amended its constitution in 1980 to include African workers, although separate branches were set up to represent different groups.[11]

TUCSA also intensified its parallel union strategy, sought to register its parallels and, actively assisted by employers, established closed shops affecting thousands of African workers. Its membership peaked in 1983 when it claimed to represent over 500,000 workers in 57 unions. TUCSA was hostile towards the emerging independent unions in sectors where they competed with its parallels. In 1982, TUCSA's president called for the prosecution of illegal strikers and urged employers not to be intimidated by the emergent unions.[12]

Responding to calls by the FCWU for a national protest stoppage after the death in detention of the trade unionist Neil Aggett in February 1982, TUCSA 'unhesitatingly' distanced itself from:

> any calls for industrial action in connection with this specific tragic event because it cannot subscribe to strikes, work stoppages and other forms of industrial activity not connected to the employer/employee relationship and also because it does not believe in any hasty and emotional reaction to events which have not been completely clarified.[13]

TUCSA's continued hostility to the organisation of African workers caused several of its affiliates, notably those with semi-skilled membership, to disaffiliate. These unions faced the inevitability of having to organise African workers to maintain their bargaining strength. They included the SABS, the Motor Industry Combined Workers' Union, the Engineering Industrial Workers' Union, the National Union of Distributive and Allied Workers and the National Union of Furniture and Allied Workers. TUCSA's claimed membership declined to 340,000 by 1984.

Concerned at the loss of affiliates, TUCSA began adopting stances more critical of the government at its 1984 and 1985 conferences. Resolutions were passed condemning bannings and detention without trial; calls were made for the abolition of the pass laws and an end to forced removals. The more critical stance on the Congress floor was not, however, reflected in the elections for office bearers. The federation's policy-making structures continued to be dominated by unions hostile to the organisation of African workers.[14]

In 1985 the disaffiliations snowballed. TUCSA lost much of its industrial base, reducing its claimed membership by more than half.[15] Not only was it under challenge from the independent unions, but its members were caught up in the struggles of the period. TUCSA affiliates with large semi-skilled memberships, notably the garment and textile unions, were radicalised by these events and changed their organising styles and political positions. However, the federation failed to reflect the changing mood or develop a coherent response to the detention of trade unionists and the deaths of union members in township conflicts. While emergent union groupings called for the dismantling of apartheid and refused to negotiate directly with the government, demanding economic sanctions instead, TUCSA was working within the government framework. It supported gradual reform, took part in official commissions of inquiry and opposed sanctions, prompting further defections.[16]

By early 1987 the federation was made up largely of associations representing white-collar, professional and supervisory workers such as building society officials, municipal employees, mine surface officials and technicians. At the end of that year, robbed of a base in any significant industrial sector, TUCSA resolved to disband. Some of its former affiliates were drawn into COSATU. Others remained autonomous, leading to an increase in the number of unaffiliated unions – by early 1987 they represented more than half the organised workforce.[17]

The racist unions were even more threatened by the rise of the independent unions. Traditionally reliant on statutory job reservation to guarantee their monopoly of jobs, they resisted opening membership to workers of other groups. Some tried to set up 'parallels' but they were weakened by the growth of independent unions, except in the mining sector. They bitterly opposed the Wiehahn dispensation and the abolition of job reservation. SACLA experienced several splits and disaffiliations over how to respond to the reform of labour relations. Many racist unions turned their attention to mobilising support for extreme right-wing political parties which aimed to remove the government and reinstate the old status quo.[18]

Rise of the independent unions

In the mid-1980s two trade union federations emerged which between them united most of the country's independent unions. In November 1985 the Congress of South Africa Trade Unions (COSATU) was launched after four years of discussions. It spanned 20 sectors of the economy, and accounted for half a million members. COSATU was committed to non-racialism, a bedrock principle to which each of its 33 affiliates subscribed.[19]

In October 1986 a second smaller federation was formed, the National Council of Trade Unions (NACTU), with 23 affiliates and some 144,000 members. It drew together unions which subscribed to the political traditions of black consciousness. They had withdrawn from the talks leading to COSATU's formation, rejecting non-racialism as a precondition for unity.

The two federations accounted for almost all the independent unions which had emerged in the 1970s and the early 1980s – the greatest upsurge of worker organisation in South African history.

Historical forebears

There have been several periods in which economic and political conditions accelerated African trade union organisation in South Africa. A labour movement sprang up with the onset of industrialisation in the 1920s in the form of the Industrial and Commercial Workers Union (ICU). It was a general union drawing workers from several sectors and reached a membership of around 100,000. By 1927, however, a combination of repression, internal splits and undemocratic leadership had caused it to decline. A second wave of unionisation commenced towards the end of the 1920s. Members of the Communist Party helped build new industrially based unions alongside the existing registered unions which organised white and Coloured workers. Out of these new unions came the Council of Non-European Trade Unions (CNETU), which by 1945 claimed a national, predominantly African, membership of tens of thousands of signed-up members in 119 unions.[20]

When the SAT & LC split in the face of the 1956 Industrial Conciliation Act, some of its former affiliates, committed to non-racial organisation, joined with the CNETU unions and newer African unions set up since the war to form SACTU. SACTU initially had 19 affiliates and 20,000 members; but by 1962 its membership had grown to 55,000. It dominated the organisation of African workers between 1955 and 1964.[21]

SACTU's organisational strategies and policies were shaped by the need to respond to the implementation of apartheid policies by the National Party: the extension of racial segregation into all spheres of life; further restrictions on the freedom of movement of the black population; and the repression of trade unions and political organisations. In the eight years of its above-ground activity SACTU more than doubled its membership and the number of affiliates reached 51 unions in spite of increasingly severe restrictions on its right to organise. Its activities extended beyond the shopfloor – it stressed the link between factory organisation and the broader struggle for national liberation.[22] On the basis of these convictions it entered into a formal alliance with the major political movements opposed to apartheid under the leadership of the ANC. SACTU committed its membership to the resistance campaigns of this Congress Alliance in opposition to the implementation of new apartheid legislation between 1955 and 1960. These included mass defiance of laws segregating social amenities, the burning of passes and several mass worker stay-aways to underscore political demands.

After the declaration of a State of Emergency in 1960 and the banning of the ANC, SACTU itself became a target of sustained repression. Over the next two years, 48 of its leaders were banned and another 31 detained.[23] By 1963 many of its unions had retreated into their strongest bases. In that year SACTU abandoned legal forms of organisation and its leadership went underground or into exile. It then established an external mission and operated clandestinely, underpinning and seeking to shape the political direction of successive waves of worker organisation inside South Africa. Its tradition of 'political' trade unionism was a strong influence on the general unions which were formed in the early 1980s, and thus a factor influencing the political direction of COSATU which drew on SACTU's tradition of political struggle.

Revival of the independent union movement
The first grouping of independent unions, composed largely of industrially based unions, arose in the wake of the 1973 strikes. Most were founded in the industrial concentrations around Johannesburg and Durban, and were eventually absorbed into the Federation of South African Trade Unions (FOSATU) and the Council of Unions of South Africa (CUSA). They established themselves between 1973 and 1979 in the face of overt state hostility to worker organisation and a largely recessionary climate. The new unions adopted cautious strategies, seeking to build and consolidate in individual factories and plants. These concerns and the absence of broader legal political organisation caused them to be wary of involvement in wider resistance campaigns until as late as 1983. They concentrated instead on shopfloor issues. Their experience of organisation and the structures which they had painstakingly built in the factories placed them in a strong position to take advantage of the Wiehahn reforms and the improved economic climate between 1979 and 1981. They rapidly expanded and by 1984 had organised a majority of workers in some sectors. By the early 1980s they had also established cross-factory, and later cross-union, local and regional structures. These new structures were increasingly drawn into campaigns of resistance to apartheid and moved some of the unions gradually to take on a political role.

Later in the 1970s the second new grouping of trade unions emerged, mainly regionally based and structured as general unions drawing membership from several sectors. While some established footholds in manufacturing industries, most were located in service sectors such as cleaning, catering and local government, where wages and working conditions were bad and organisation weak. They were politically more militant than those in the earlier group, having been formed in the climate of heightened political activity which followed the 1976 uprising. After 1980 political resistance began to take on a more coherent form. New community organisations, tenants' associations, youth, student and women's groups emerged in all the major urban centres and participated in renewed national political campaigns. In contrast to the pragmatism of FOSATU and CUSA, the newer unions favoured direct involvement in broader political struggles and, like SACTU before them, stressed the inseparability of shopfloor struggles from campaigns against apartheid. After the formation of the United Democratic Front (UDF) in 1983 several of the new unions affiliated to it.

The militant political profile of the general unions exposed them to intense state repression. Their initially large memberships were eroded after 1982 by the recession, which hampered their ability to organise across industries and had its most severe impact on some of the sectors in which they organised. By the end of 1985 a combination of repression and recession had weakened their organised strength and influence compared to the industrial unions of FOSATU and CUSA, which weathered the storm more successfully.

These two groupings accounted for most of the unions which formed COSATU in 1985. However, at least three other unions also influenced the shape of the trade union movement in the late 1970s and the 1980s. These were the Food and Canning Workers Union (FCWU), based in the Western Cape, an old SACTU affiliate and survivor of the repression of the 1960s; the General Workers Union (GWU), also based in the Western Cape, formed in the same period as the industrial unions of FOSATU and CUSA, but structured as a general union; and the Commercial Catering and Allied Workers Union (CCAWUSA), which was formed in the early 1970s, remained independent and was an important force in the retail and distributive trades.

In the following section, each of these major groupings is analysed, focusing on the sectors they organised, the major struggles in which they participated, the nature of their organisational structures and their wider impact on worker organisation.

Unions formed between 1973 and 1976

Industrially based unions in Natal and the Witwatersrand emerged from earlier forms of activity among workers: workers' advice bureaux; benefit funds; worker newspapers distributed by student support groups;

projects to train shop-stewards; and, in the Pietermaritzburg area, attempts by former SACTU activists released from imprisonment to revive trade union activity in the region. The new unions grouped themselves into associations which pooled resources and co-ordinated activities. But hostile state policies and recession reduced their membership and in the mid-1970s the need for a larger national federation had become clear. FOSATU was launched in April 1979 after two years of negotiation and discussion, but it failed to draw GWU and FCWU, based in the Western Cape, or CCAWUSA and several industrial unions in the Transvaal aligned with the black consciousness movement. Some of these unions formed CUSA the following year.

Federation of South African Trade Unions (FOSATU)
FOSATU drew in most of the unions formed after the Durban strikes, namely CWIU, MAWU, NUTW, TGWU, PWAWU, SFAWU and the Glass and Allied Workers Union (GAWU).

Two older registered unions, NUMARWOSA and WPMAWU, with predominantly Coloured membership, also joined. Formally affiliated to TUCSA, they had been democratised in the early 1970s. Another two registered unions also joined FOSATU, namely the Chemical and General Workers Union (CGWU) and the Eastern Province Sweet, Food and Allied Workers Union (EPSF&AWU). The founder unions were reduced to ten when the motor union NUMARWOSA and its African parallel, the UAW, merged in 1981 with the WPMAWU to form the National Automobile and Allied Workers Union (NAAWU). The EPSP&AWU merged into SFAWU and the CGWU into CWIU respectively.

The unions in FOSATU were therefore drawn from several traditions ranging from the large registered motoring unions, experienced in industry-wide forms of negotiation, to unregistered unions struggling for recognition of their plant committees. During its early years FOSATU avoided direct involvement in political activity as it wanted to build strong and entrenched shopfloor structures. Its cautious political profile also owed much to the diversity of its membership. Although a tight federation, FOSATU contained a range of political views, and included many Labour Party adherents among its Coloured membership and Inkatha members in Natal, organisations hostile to more radical political movements.[24]

As the federation grew and consolidated it began taking up issues beyond the shopfloor; the shift was in part a response to pressure from rank and file members exposed to political and community struggles in the areas where they lived. However, by the time the federation was dissolved in 1985 and its constituent unions absorbed into COSATU, it had not formally affiliated or aligned itself to any of the broader existing political organisations – instead it conducted independent political campaigns.

FOSATU's membership expanded from 94,614 in 1981 to 139,917 in 1985.[25] Five years of shopfloor struggles and the expansion of the unions from their Transvaal and Natal bases into other regions meant that by 1985 FOSATU affiliates had become the majority unions in the motor, tyre and rubber industries as well as in chemicals, metal and engineering, paper and printing, furniture, transport sectors and (outside the Western Cape) textiles.[26]

The most prominent of FOSATU's affiliates was the MAWU. It expanded from its early bases in Durban and pioneered many of the organising styles and structures later adopted by the federation as a whole. It consolidated its base in the metal foundries on the East Rand in struggles during 1981 and 1982.[27] Like other FOSATU unions it continued to expand its membership nationally in spite of recessionary conditions and lay-offs, increasing to 36,789 by 1986 (see Table 4.1). The highly strategic metals sector was a crucial testing ground for employer tactics against unions, placing MAWU at the forefront of struggles over wages and conditions (see Chapter 6 above).

PWAWU was formed in 1973 in the Transvaal and experienced major growth only after 1981, when it moved into the paper mills in Southern and Northern Natal, organising 60 per cent of the sector's workforce. In the second half of the 1980s it moved into the furniture and printing industries.[28]

CWIU was formed in 1974, initially in Southern Natal. Between 1980 and 1982 it opened new branches in the Northern Transvaal and the rest of Natal, later in the Eastern Cape and then in Cape Town. It organised in the hard-chemical, petroleum, rubber, plastic, pharmaceutical and glass manufacturing sectors of the chemical industry. It confronted the powerful multinational companies AECI and Sentrachem and the parastatal SASOL, the latter a major player in a key strategic industry because of its involvement in the conversion of coal to petroleum. CWIU built up a majority membership at SASOL plants (all in the Transvaal) in spite of attempts to break the union in 1984, when the workforce was dismissed en masse for its participation in a stay-at-home (see Chapter 6 above).[29]

Another FOSATU union, NAAWU, had organised more than half the employees in the Eastern Cape and Pretoria motor assembly plants, but it was initially weak in the widely dispersed components sector with only 1,000 members in a workforce of 80,000 employees. However, the union had built up a 50 per cent presence in rubber and tyre plants by late 1984.[30]

TGWU was initially based in the Durban docks but redefined its constitution in 1979 to cover other sectors, notably the goods-transport industry, municipal workers and bus drivers. It opened a branch in the Transvaal where it built a presence among bus drivers, in goods-transport companies and among cleaning staff in city office blocks. Organisation along general rather than industrial lines took place in municipalities and local authorities and among security guards, and after 1984 among cleaners, although the core of the union remained its base in transport.[31]

SFAWU was formed in 1974 in Springs and initially was based in four factories. It split in 1979 over affiliation to FOSATU, with part of the membership forming a new union, the FBWU, which affiliated to CUSA. In 1980 the union expanded to Southern Natal, becoming a force in local sugar mills. Later it moved into other sectors of the food industry, including milling, baking, dairy, sweet manufacture and brewing, and in 1981 a third branch was opened in Natal. By 1985 it had a national presence, based in 65 factories across the country.[32]

With FOSATU's remaining affiliate, NUTW, expanding in 1984 to the Western Cape from its base in Natal and its smaller presence in the Transvaal, the hegemony of TUCSA in the clothing and textiles sector in the region was for the first time seriously challenged.

Structures

The hallmark of the new unions was their emphasis on worker control through the development of strong shopfloor structures directly accountable to workers. Within FOSATU constitutional provision was made for worker control of affiliates at all levels, through emphasising decision-making power at local and regional levels.

FOSATU decided in 1981 to establish shop-stewards' councils, later known as 'locals'. The councils began as informal forums for the local discussion of strategy, and drew together shop-stewards from plants in a particular area. During the metal strikes of 1981-2 on the East Rand, MAWU experienced phenomenal growth and its organisational resources were severely stretched by the speed with which strikes spread from plant to plant. A shop-stewards' council was set up to consolidate new membership and to spread the burden of co-ordinating industrial action.

Members were drawn from the shop-steward committees and factories already organised by MAWU.

The East Rand council initially met monthly, but eventually weekly meetings had to be held. The success of this strategy on the East Rand was demonstrated by the subsequent growth of organisation. In 1980 only two factories were organised by MAWU. By the end of 1981, 23 factories had been included and were sending representatives to the shop-stewards' council.[33]

MAWU's experiment on the East Rand was used as a model and councils were set up in other parts of the country. They often cut across different unions, strengthening organisation as stewards exchanged experiences and looked at ways in which workers in different factories and unions could support each other's struggles.[34]

In 1982 FOSATU's Congress amended its constitution to provide for 'locals' in all regions. They became powerful forces for worker organisation and brought about a gradual change in the political complexion of the federation. They helped to concentrate attention on broader problems facing workers, drawing the unions into housing, transport and education struggles.[35] The locals backed rank-and-file pressure on the federation to take up national political issues and after 1982 FOSATU began to conduct its own political campaigns (see Chapter 8 below).

FOSATU was a disciplined federation with a policy of close co-operation among its affiliates at all levels. Key resolutions taken at the National Congress were binding on its affiliates. These committed its members to non-racialism, worker control through the weighting of decision-making structures in favour of delegates rather than officials, the objective of establishing a single union in each industry, the right to factory-level bargaining through democratically elected shop-steward committees, and a decision not to affiliate to or support any single political organisation.[36]

Council of Unions of South Africa (CUSA)
Most of the unions not affiliated to FOSATU joined CUSA when it was formed in 1980. While committed to a non-racial labour movement in the long term, the new federation disagreed with FOSATU on how this would be achieved. CUSA objected to the presence of whites in the FOSATU leadership, alleging that they dominated the federation. It committed itself instead to building 'black leadership'. At its 1982 national conference it enlarged on this position:

CUSA operates in a country which is racialist, undemocratic and which exploits the larger Black ... community. Racially disadvantaged people need re-education and training so that they can take their rightful place in their community. CUSA believes therefore that we need to develop a leadership which serves the community. We believe in developing the awareness and consciousness of the Black community which has been denied its rightful leadership role in South Africa.[37]

In 1985 the federation had 11 affiliates, with its strongest unions based in the mining, transport, chemicals, food and beverages sectors. Its most prominent affiliate (after NUM left CUSA in 1985) was SACWU, which until the mid-1980s was larger than FOSATU's CWIU. It pioneered early struggles in the chemicals sector, especially in its stronghold, the conglomerate AECI, where it had 8,000 members by 1986.[38]

Other important CUSA affiliates were FBWU and the Transport and Allied Workers Union (TAWU), which became a significant force in bus corporations in the PWV area and the Lebowa, Bophuthatswana and Qwaqua bantustans. By 1986 it had a membership of roughly 10,000.[39]

In the second half of the 1980s CUSA's Building, Construction and Allied Workers Union (BCAWU) made breakthroughs in the building and construction sectors of the East Rand, consolidating itself as the predominant union among building workers in the PWV area, with a membership of around 10,000.[40]

By the end of 1985 CUSA had nine affiliates (see Table 4.1 for a list and membership). CUSA unions, with the exception of NUM, refused to affiliate to COSATU when it was formed because of the new Congress's commitment to non-racial organisation and the continued presence of white organisers in some of the larger affiliates. In 1986, CUSA's nine affiliates were joined by three unaligned unions: the Electrical and Allied Workers Trade Union (EAWTU), the National Union of Furniture Workers (NUFW) and the Media Workers Association of South Africa (MWASA).

CUSA's structures were grounded, like FOSATU, in plant-based shop-steward committees, although the federation had no formal local and regional structures.

Non-aligned unions
The Western Province General Workers Union, or WPGWU (later the General Workers Union – GWU) and the Food and Canning

Workers Union (FCWU), both based in the Western Cape, were participants in talks which resulted in the formation of FOSATU, but declined to join because they felt that their structures were still too weak to sustain participation.

Of the two Western Cape unions, the FCWU was the oldest. Founded in 1941, it survived the repression of SACTU by retreating into its Western Cape rural base for most of the 1960s and 1970s. The union had been forced to split by the 1956 Industrial Conciliation Act and until 1985 was formally composed of two branches, the registered FCWU with a Coloured membership and its unregistered parallel African Food and Canning Workers Union (AFCWU), with an African membership. In stark contrast to the registered TUCSA unions, the FCWU retained a strong commitment to worker unity and non-racialism. It functioned to all intents and purposes as a single entity, and refused to register its African counterpart in terms of the Wiehahn dispensation because of the controls inherent in the registration package. It only did so in 1985 when it once more became, in letter as well as spirit, the single non-racial union it had been in the early 1950s.

FCWU's base was in large food packing and processing plants, and it also organised some farm workers on agricultural co-operatives. It was a predominantly Coloured union. A large proportion of its members were women, although it also represented a minority of mainly migrant African workers. It later organised Africans in the Transvaal and Natal food industries. By 1983 it had a membership of 16,000 in 84 factories.[41] It placed great emphasis on functioning as a democratic worker-controlled union, with factory committees negotiating directly with management. These in turn formed regional or local branches which took responsibility for new organisation.

The WPGWU was formed in 1976. It was initially organised along general rather than industrial lines and aimed to build itself into a regional union among African workers, who formed only 15 per cent of the labour force in the Western Cape. Most were on contract with only temporary status in the region, and the fluctuating nature of the union's base made it difficult to organise on industrial lines. In spite of difficult conditions the union quickly built a presence across industries in Cape Town's construction sector, the meat industry and in public services. Its stronghold, however, was in the docks. The defeat of the meat workers in 1980 put paid to its hopes of significantly expanding beyond the docks and it concentrated on organising the stevedoring industry in other parts of the country. By 1982 it was recognised by employers in the East London, Port Elizabeth and Durban docks, giving it control of the entire stevedoring industry. The decisive defeat of the 1982 SATS strike frustrated the union's plans to move into the railways and in 1982 it redefined itself as an industrial union, confining itself to transport workers outside the railways, with a general section in the manufacture of building materials.[42]

The union bitterly opposed registration. But, like the AFCWU, it found itself hampered by its unregistered status – it could not, for example, have its members' contributions deducted automatically from their wages. Wages and conditions in stevedoring were set by labour orders, which were irregular and applied only to larger employers. The union increasingly felt the need to channel its energies into industry-wide bargaining, but its unregistered status disqualified it from applying for the establishment of an Industrial Council for the sector. In 1985 it finally applied for registration.[43]

The Commercial and Catering Workers Union (CCAWUSA), founded in 1975, initially worked closely with the TUCSA-affiliated National Union of Distributive and Allied Workers (NUDAW) to organise Africans in catering, but later became more autonomous. It came to prominence in 1981-2 during a series of struggles in chain stores in the PWV area (see Chapter 6 above). By 1986 it had 50,000 members (see Table 4.1). Transvaal chain stores remained its strongest base, but it had branches in all the other major centres of the country.

CCAWUSA registered at an early stage, and because its membership was confined to African workers it was not constrained by the restrictions on non-racial organisation. Only in 1984 did it open its ranks to Coloured and Indian workers, and it became fully non-racial in 1985 when it aligned itself with COSATU.

Unions formed after 1976

Most of the new unions formed in the second wave of 1970s unionisation were regionally based. They established close relationships with local political organisations and in the heightened political climate of the 1980s many participated in campaigns of resistance. They grew rapidly during recognition struggles between 1980 and 1982: by 1985 there were 24 general unions based in the Transvaal. Three of them – SAAWU, the General and Allied Workers Union (GAWU) and the Municipal and General Workers Union of South Africa (MGWUSA) – had a loose working alliance.

After 1983 several unions formed alliances with community organisations and affiliated to the UDF. They drew their membership from industries where the lowest wages and harshest working conditions prevailed: the security industry, cleaning firms, local government and the public service, liquor and catering trades and building industries.[44] State hostility to independent organisation in these sectors and the unions' often militant political stance made them the targets of state repression. Members of SAAWU and the UDF were particularly harassed by the state during 1983, with many trade unionists and hundreds of others detained during the East London bus boycott. UDF members were also detained during the white referendum on the new government constitution and the boycott of local council elections in African townships. SAAWU members maintained the bus boycott for over two years; and many more were charged and convicted for a variety of offences relating to the boycott (see Chapter 8 below).[45]

The South African Allied Workers Union (SAAWU)
SAAWU was the most prominent of the general unions. Its origins lay in the black consciousness movement. The Durban branch of the movement's labour wing, the Black Allied Workers Union (BAWU), broke away in 1979 and regrouped as SAAWU, arguing that black consciousness had served its political role but failed to meet the needs of the new period. It advocated a non-racial approach to organisation: 'As long as you contribute towards the country's wealth, you are a worker. Even if white workers are privileged they are workers. They must sacrifice their privileges and join us'.[46] SAAWU's original base in Durban was weakened by continuing divisions and ceased to be its main area of operation. The union's strongest growth took place between 1980 and 1982 in East London, where it became a significant political force.

SAAWU operated as a general workers' union. It was influenced in this by the absence of any other labour organisation, the presence of numerous different industries in East London and the fact that it had a regional base. It was active in several industries: chemicals, sweets, beverages and transport in the Eastern Cape, and chemicals and milling in the PWV area. At its 1984 Congress it claimed a membership of 100,000 organised into 18 local branches; in 1980 it had had only two branches and 5,000 members.[47]

This rapid expansion followed a decision by South African Chloride in 1980 to recognise the union, thereby becoming the first company to recognise an unregistered union. It was involved in six strikes for demands for recognition in that year and in a further 17 disputes involving 14,000 workers in 1981.[48]

East London's proximity to the Ciskei and the location of Mdantsane within the bantustan boundaries propelled SAAWU into opposing the Ciskei authorities, particularly when 'independence' was imposed at the end of 1981. The bantustan authorities banned the union in 1983, during the protracted and bitter bus boycott in which SAAWU played a leading organisational role. These restrictions were compounded by the actions of the central government, denying the union access to halls and other meeting places in East London. The union was nevertheless able during 1983 to expand from its existing bases to East London's textile industries where over a third of the local workforce was employed.[49]

By 1987 SAAWU had spread outside East London. There were local branches in Natal, the Eastern Cape and the Transvaal and in Bloemfontein in the Orange Free State.[50] SAAWU organised through factory committees which were represented at local and regional branches. It also called mass meetings to discuss issues raised at branch level, although this became increasingly difficult after 1983.

For SAAWU there was an inextricable link between shopfloor organisation and broader political resistance. It was one of the first unions to affiliate to the UDF and at its 1984 conference it resolved that its individual branches would also affiliate to local UDF structures.[51]

Other general unions

SAAWU worked closely with the General and Allied Workers Union (GAWU), a Transvaal-based general union with footholds in the West Witwatersrand area and Kuruman, near Vryburg in the Northern Cape. Founded in 1980, it organised in the brush and copper-processing industries, in mining, among office cleaners, hospital workers, scooter drivers, petrol attendants and some transport workers. It also established a presence in the steel industry in the Transvaal. Broadly sharing the political perspectives of SAAWU, it participated in wider political campaigns.[52]

Other general unions emerged between 1980 and 1984, from local strikes. The National Federation of Workers was formed in 1980 as a non-racial grouping of several small general unions. It organised initially in the iron and steel industries, especially in the Richards Bay area, and among post office workers and domestic workers. It later adopted a strategy of organising workers in small towns in Natal, radiating out from Richards Bay, with some success. At its height it had some 11,551 members.[53]

MACWUSA was launched in the Port Elizabeth motor industry during the 1979 Ford strike as a rival to the FOSATU-affiliated UAW. It was set up by workers unhappy with UAW's handling of the strike, but it remained confined to the Ford Cortina plant in Port Elizabeth and the Firestone Plant in Uitenhage, although it had some footholds in Durban and the Sigma plant in Pretoria. It developed a close relationship with community organisations in Port Elizabeth,[54] where it formed a sister-union, the General Workers Union of South Africa (GWUSA), to organise workers in sectors outside the motor industry. GWUSA drew members from metals, textiles, bakeries, hospitals, dairies, the beverage industry and from among clerical workers.[55]

The Municipal and General Workers Union of South Africa (MGWUSA) emerged from the remnants of the Black Municipal Workers Union (BMWU) which led the Johannesburg municipal workers strike in 1980. Many of the workers dismissed in the 1980 strike returned to Johannesburg in 1981, seeking jobs in other sectors and in 1982. MGWUSA constituted itself as a general union to cater for their interests.[56] It restricted itself to organising workers only where other unions had no presence and eventually it fell back on its base in the Johannesburg municipality.

The independent black consciousness tradition
A smaller group of general and small industrial unions based largely in the Transvaal and adhering, like CUSA, to the black consciousness philosophy, eventually formed the Azanian Congress of Trade Unions (AZACTU). Most were formed with the assistance of the Azanian People's Organisation (AZAPO) between 1982 and 1984. They rejected the existing federations and groups, because of 'the need to promote, develop and maintain authentic, black working class leadership' and 'the need to encourage the spirit of solidarity and unity within the black working class and black community'. Later, in opposition to COSATU's non-racialism, they merged to form the NACTU.[57]

AZACTU's most prominent affiliate was BAMCWU, with a claimed membership of 20,000 in the cement, quarrying, construction and mining industries. Initially set up in Pietersburg, and later Phalaborwa, it moved to other mining towns in the Northern Transvaal. It built a strong base among asbestos miners at Penge, where several bitter disputes over wages, union recognition and safety occurred. Later another AZACTU affiliate, the Black Allied and General Workers Union (BLAGWU) was formed in the same region.[58]

Another affiliate of AZACTU, the South African Black Municipal and Allied Workers Union (SABMAWU), was an offshoot of the BMWU. It organised among employees in local government, particularly those employed by councils in the townships, and was at the centre of some successful strikes. AZACTU's 1,500-member Insurance and Allied Workers Union of South Africa (IAWUSA) was the first of the independent unions to organise black white-collar workers in banks and other finance institutions.[59]

The quest for unity

Thus, by the mid-1980s the trade union movement consisted of several complex and diverse strands, many of which were united through the formation of COSATU in 1985. Achieving this unity was a prolonged process.

The emergence of COSATU

By the second half of 1981 there were several factors acting as a spur to wider unity. The recession had increased retrenchments, eroded the strength of unions and forced them to adopt defensive strategies, and many officials of the most militant unions were detained at the end of that year.

But real obstacles to wider unity remained. They included the different organising styles and political profiles of the general and industrial unions and differences between FOSATU and CUSA over the involvement of whites in unions. There were also differing strategies towards registration and negotiations in Industrial Councils. Serious rifts had developed over 'poaching' of members and demarcation of territory. In Port Elizabeth there was still mistrust between the FOSATU-affiliated NAAWU and its breakaway rival, MACWUSA, dating back to the 1979 Ford strike.

Progress towards unity required the resolution of structural, tactical and political differences during a series of 13 meetings over four years.[60] After intensive spade work by key unions a summit was convened in August 1981, at Langa in Cape Town, to discuss a common approach to the challenges facing the unions. All the major unions and federations were involved and they found several areas of broad agreement. The meeting rejected the Industrial Council system in its existing form and affirmed the need to set up regional solidarity committees to promote regional co-operation among the unions.[61] The unions also endorsed a statement objecting to registration. Moreover, the conference also resolved to resist the banning and detention of trade unionists in the Ciskei bantustan.[62]

A follow-up meeting was held in April the next year at Wilgespruit near Johannesburg. New developments had a bearing on the talks. Although the 1981 Labour Relations Amendment Act had extended uniform controls to all unions, registered and unregistered, thus diminishing the basis of differences, the general unions retained their objection to registration on grounds of political principle. MACWUSA and GWUSA attacked FOSATU for failing to explore the possibility of de-registering in order to bring its position into line with most other unions. The two unions withdrew from the meeting over these differences.[63]

The detentions of trade unionists at the end of 1981 hampered the setting up of regional solidarity committees. By the time of the Wilgespruit meeting they were functioning only in Cape Town. On a national level no real advances towards practical co-operation had been made. Nevertheless the mood remained optimistic, sustained by the national stoppage to mark the death in detention of the trade unionist, Neil Aggett, in which there had been co-operation between many of the unions.[64]

There were two new developments at Wilgespruit. Acting on decisions at its Congress two weeks earlier FOSATU presented a proposal to form a national trade union federation and indicated its willingness to disband if this occurred. Most of the other unions rejected the proposal as premature, except for GWU which gave it qualified support.[65]

Differences over registration presaged more substantial conflicts between industrial unions and general unions. These were reinforced by the differing political perspectives which began emerging as resistance revived during 1983, in particular over the question of whether unions should affiliate to national political bodies like the UDF, and make alliances with community, student and other groupings. The meeting deadlocked; unions resolved to seek mandates from their members on how to act on the proposal to form a federation and the issue of registration.

The idea of a formal federation was increasingly attractive to FOSATU because of its national presence in key economic sectors. In 1982 it resolved to focus on consolidating its presence in these sectors. Similarly, after its Congress in July 1982 GWU concentrated mainly on organisation in the docks, although it retained a presence in building materials and some other sectors. It had no practical objections to a federation.[66]

The general unions had less to gain from a federation. They were regionally based, with membership spread across industries. They were ill-prepared for the type of federation which FOSATU was proposing in which there would be a single union for each sector; they would be swallowed by the larger industrial unions and their political positions diluted. The general unions favoured the achievement of unity through an initial period of building cross-union structures at regional and local levels. In their view this was not only a matter of expediency, but of principle – unity should be built from local levels upwards, rather than imposed from above. They wanted to see a return to the Langa resolution on regional solidarity committees.

The next meeting took place on 4 July 1982 in Port Elizabeth. Immediately before the meeting seven general unions with broadly similar perspectives (SAAWU, GAWU, OVGWU, MACWUSA, GWUSA and the South African Textile and Allied Workers Union, or SATAWU), had met and drawn up a list of principles which they felt should bind the affiliates of any prospective federation.

The differences discernible at Wilgespruit crystallised into more clearly opposed positions at the Port Elizabeth meeting. The general unions put forward their set of principles, which included: rejection of registration; an endorsement of bargaining at shopfloor level instead of through the Industrial Councils; non-racialism; involvement in community issues; worker control of trade unions; rejection of reactionary organisations, and the principle that the federation's policy be binding on affiliates. The other unions felt that there could be no return to the Langa resolutions, including the statement on registration, as these had been superseded by the proposal to form a federation. The rejection of Industrial Councils was similarly opposed by FOSATU and other unions.[67] The meeting ended without any progress being made, and nine months were to pass before further advances were possible.[68]

In this climate SACTU issued one of several statements which appealed to unions not to allow the issues of registration and Industrial Councils to be elevated to matters of principle, and called for a distinction to be made between principles and tactics.[69]

Intensive lobbying and background discussion led in April 1983 to further attempts at reaching agreement about a federation. The unions, including CUSA for the first time, met at Athlone, Cape Town, to discuss a single item: the formation of a new union centre. There were much larger delegations than at previous 'summits', with a higher proportion of worker delegates than officials. The discussions were less polarised. The general unions withdrew from the position that registration and Industrial Councils were non-negotiables, although they still sought the establishment of local and regional structures to foster unity at rank-and-file level before a wider federation was formed. The remaining unions were critical of this approach, in particular FOSATU which pointed to its shop-stewards' councils as an attempt to achieve exactly these objectives. The industrial unions, including CCAWUSA and those in CUSA, felt that unity could only be built through the process of forming the federation itself.

In spite of these differences, a feasibility committee with representatives from the key industrial and general unions was set up to formulate structures for a new federation. All the different strands of the union movement were represented.[70] The feasibility committee met twice in 1983. But a major stumbling block now emerged over demarcation, the process of deciding which unions would organise in what sectors. It was agreed that at a meeting scheduled for October 1983 all the unions should provide membership figures and lists of the industries in which they were organised. Where unions found they were organising in the same industry it was agreed that they would try mutually to minimise overlapping and competition for membership.

The general unions were slow to provide details on demarcation. In particular, SAAWU was severely hampered by the brutal repression during this period of its members in the East London region. This failure to provide figures exacerbated tension between the general and industrial unions. At a meeting in March 1984 to review progress on demarcation the industrial unions decided that those not demarcated along industrial lines should be excluded from the feasibility committee because they were 'not ready or able to join the federation' which was proceeding on the basis of one industry, one union. Between March 1984 and June 1985 discussions about the proposed federation continued, but without the general unions. Swift progress was made – a sub-committee was formed to draft a constitution and a date for a launch, fixed for October 1985.[71]

Events outside the factory gates helped sustain the momentum towards unity. The impact of repressive action against education and rent boycotts in the Vaal Triangle in September 1984, and the national uprising which ensued, deeply affected rank-and-file union members, drawing them into local struggles. Greater unity was fostered among members of different unions at grassroots level and between local branches of unions and community organisations. A broad range of organisations participated in stay-aways, consumer boycotts and other activities, and pressures built up for the general unions to be drawn back into the unity talks. The ANC and SACTU backed these pressures with several background initiatives and statements stressing the need for all unions to join a federation organised along industrial lines.

In June 1985 an invitation was extended to the unions outside the unity talks to attend a meeting in Soweto to redraft the constitution of the proposed federation. The meeting was held in August. The general unions returned and the black consciousness unions aligned around AZACTU attended for the first time. Broad agreement was reached on the need to establish an industrially based federation in which individual unions would later merge to form a single affiliate for each economic sector. But the retention of non-racialism as a guiding principle of the new federation proved a major stumbling block for CUSA and the AZACTU unions. They withdrew, although in the process CUSA lost NUM, which elected to remain in the talks.[72]

After four years of discussion COSATU was launched in Durban in November 1985 at a conference followed by a mass rally. The new federation acquired 500,000 signed-up and 450,000 paid-up members, making it the largest federation in South Africa in terms of membership. It included the former affiliates of FOSATU, the GWU, FCWU, CCAWUSA and a small number of other general unions and unaligned industrial unions. The largest affiliate was the National Union of Mineworkers (NUM), which claimed a membership of 100,000 and which disaffiliated from CUSA to join COSATU. The new federation's five fundamental principles were non-racialism; one union, one industry; worker control; representation on the basis of paid-up membership; and co-operation between affiliates at national level. Elijah Barayi, vice-president of NUM, was elected President of COSATU; Chris Dlamini, president of FOSATU, first vice-president; and Jay Naidoo, general secretary of SFAWU, general secretary.

COSATU was structured as a tightly disciplined federation with policy-making functions located in a bi-annual National Congress and a Central Executive Committee (CEC). Local shop-stewards' committees, which had been the bedrock of FOSATU's organisational successes, were incorporated as integral components of the wider federation. They were charged with ensuring and monitoring the implementation of COSATU national policies, resolutions and campaigns. They were also to address themselves to problems in their area of operation by linking up with local organisations. By 1987, 41 such locals had been formed country-wide.[73] Representation in the Central Executive Committee was weighted in favour of large industrial affiliates as an incentive to the smaller general unions to merge. Each union with under 15,000 members was entitled to two representatives and larger unions to four.

From the founding resolutions it was clear that COSATU envisaged playing a political role. There were calls for an end to the State of

Emergency, the withdrawal of troops from the townships and the lifting of the bans on organisations and individuals. Other resolutions rejected the bantustans and the apartheid education system, committed the federation to fight to scrap the pass laws and expressed support for international pressure on South Africa, including disinvestment. The conference also supported policies with a more immediate bearing on shopfloor organisation, including equal pay for women workers, full maternity rights and child-care facilities, opposition to sexual harassment in the workplace, and the right to strike with full freedom of association, including the right to picket. It resolved to campaign for a national minimum wage.[74]

While not formally affiliated to any political organisation, COSATU's political perspectives were a synthesis of different positions in which the industrial unions had stressed the consolidation of a shopfloor presence prior to participating in broader political campaigns and the general unions had stressed the need for alliances between unions and community organisations. In the keynote address the Convener of the Congress, Cyril Ramaphosa, stated:

> We all agree that the struggle of workers on the shop floor cannot be separated from the wider struggle for liberation...
>
> If workers are to lead the struggle for liberation we have to win the confidence of other sectors of society. But if we are to get into alliances with other progressive organisations, it must be on terms that are favourable to us as workers. When we do plunge into political activity, we must make sure that the unions under COSATU have a strong shopfloor base not only to take on the employers but the state as well.[75]

These broad principles were incorporated in a binding resolution adopted by the COSATU Executive Committee in February 1986.

Mergers
COSATU had been established around the principle that its constituent unions would merge to establish a single affiliate in each of the following industrial sectors: food and drink; textiles, clothing and leather; mining; paper, wood and printing; metals, motor assembly and components; chemical and petroleum; commercial and catering; transport, cleaning and security; local government; and domestic workers. It would also create new unions to organise workers in agriculture and construction.

Progress was slow. By mid-1986 only two mergers had met the original six-month deadline. Building on negotiations which took place before COSATU's formation, the former FOSATU affiliate TGWU merged with GWU to form a new transport workers' union (30,000 members) which retained the name Transport and General Workers Union. In the two years after its formation it gave priority to the establishment of Industrial Councils in the cleaning and security sectors, and to the extension of the Industrial Council for goods transport in the Transvaal to the entire country, giving bargaining and organisation a sector-wide focus.[76]

The former FOSATU affiliate, SFAWU, merged with FCWU and members from GWU and the Retail and Allied Workers Union to form the Food and Allied Workers Union (FAWU), which had 50,000 members in June 1986.[77] The newly merged TGWU retained its 6,000-odd membership in municipalities pending the formation of a single union in local government. Similarly, GWU retained its 4,000 odd membership in the Western Cape building supplies industry, pending the creation of a COSATU affiliate of building workers.[78]

The most strategic of the mergers took place in the motoring and metals sectors in May 1987. Seven unions merged to form the National Union of Metalworkers (NUMSA), including MAWU and NAAWU and their formerly bitter rivals the United Metal, Mining and Allied Workers Union of South Africa (UMMAWUSA), and MACWUSA. The Motor Industries Combined Workers Union (MICWU), a former TUCSA affiliate, was also drawn in, as were some members of GAWU and TGWU. With 136,000 members, NUMSA was second only to the NUM in size and strength.[79]

In May 1986 a number of smaller unions and associations representing domestic workers agreed to merge after two years of discussions. The 50,000 strong South African Domestic Workers Union (SADWU) was formed from the old SADWA, the Natal-based National Domestic Workers Association and two Eastern Cape unions, the Port Elizabeth Domestic Workers Union and the East London Domestic Workers Union. Soon after the merger, SADWU decided to affiliate to COSATU.[80]

A fourth and important merger occurred in January 1987 when membership drawn from seven largely general unions merged to form a new affiliate, the Construction and Allied Workers Union (CAWU). The largest number of members came from GAWU and others were drawn from MAWU, GWUSA, the Brick and Allied Workers Union (BRICKAWU) and TGWU. It gave COSATU a base of 30,000 members in the construction industry, which until then had largely been the preserve of CUSA's BCAWU.[81]

At a Congress to launch a merged union in the retail and distribution sectors in June 1987, the Hotel and Restaurant Workers Unions (HARWU), the Retail and Allied Workers Union (RAWU) and the relevant members of the general unions SAAWU and GAWU were brought into an enlarged CCAWUSA, but an internal dispute excluded the Johannesburg, Cape Town and Klerkdorp union branches.[82]

Several other mergers took place, bringing COSATU closer to its target of 13 industrial affiliates. In October 1987 PWAWU was reconstituted as the Paper, Printing and Allied Workers Union (PPAWU) after recruiting workers from the printing industry. It now had some 30,000 members.[83] In November the NUTW (formerly affiliated to FOSATU) merged with the smaller independent National Union of Garment Workers and its former bitter rival TWIU to form a new Amalgamated Clothing and Textile Workers Union of South Africa (ACTWUSA) with 68,000 members.[84]

The inclusion of TWIU was testimony to the impact of the political protest and the rise of the independent union movement on the larger former affiliates of TUCSA with majority unskilled and semi-skilled membership. They were radicalised as younger, more militant organisers and activists moved into positions of influence.

Two other former TUCSA affiliates in clothing and textiles, the Western Province Garment Workers Union, which had determined labour organisation in the Western Cape, and the Natal-based Garment Workers Industrial Union (GWIU) were similarly democratised and in December 1987 merged into the Garment and Allied Workers Union (GAWU) with 102,000 members. The merger heralded a period of militancy in the once passive Western Cape and Natal clothing and textile sectors. There were several wage strikes and the unions' membership supported the June 1988 stay-away to protest at the Labour Relations Amendment Bill (see Chapter 5 above).

In the course of 1988 GAWU and ACTWUSA discussed the possibility of a further merger. This finally took place in 1990, after a protracted period of negotiations. The new union which emerged, the South African Clothing and Allied Workers' Union (SACTWU) is one of the largest COSATU affiliates, with 190,000 paid-up members.[85]

In June 1986 members of SAAWU, the old GAWU (General and Allied Workers Union) and two independent health workers' unions merged to form the National Education, Health and Allied Workers Union (NEHAWU) with a membership of 9,000, pledged to represent workers in the health and educational sectors. In October a second merger of public sector unions took place. The Cape Town Municipal Workers

Association, the Municipal Workers Union (MWUSA, formerly MGWUSA) and members of SAAWU, GWUSA and TGWU merged to form a new union, the South African Municipal Workers Union (SAMWU), with some 17,000 members.[86]

By the end of 1988 only the completion of two mergers was outstanding. TGWU had yet to merge with SARHWU to bring about a single transport union straddling the docks, road transport and the railways. Serious political divisions within CCAWUSA had held up the completion of mergers in the retail and distributive trades.

In the intervening period CUSA and AZACTU were drawn together by their common commitment to black leadership of unions, a process given impetus by the launch of COSATU and its strong emphasis on non-racialism. In October 1986 CUSA and AZACTU amalgamated themselves into a new federation, NACTU, with a claimed membership of 170,000. It linked 23 unions, 12 from CUSA and 11 from AZACTU. The new federation intended to structure itself along industrial lines. To this end it began merging its separate unions in construction, metals and engineering and disbanded its three general unions.

Table 7.1 Profile of the independent trade union movement, post mergers, 1988

COSATU (paid-up members):	
Amalgamated Clothing and Textile Workers Union of SA (ACTWUSA)	68,507
Construction and Allied Workers Union (CAWU)	18,176
Commercial Catering and Allied Workers Union of SA (CCAWUSA)	42,221
Chemical Workers Industrial Union (CWIU)	32,739
Food and Allied Workers Union (FAWU)	65,803
National Education Health and Allied Workers Union (NEHAWU)	5,876
National Union of Mineworkers (NUM)	207,941
National Union of Metal Workers of SA (NUMSA)	156,519
Paper Print Wood and Allied Workers Union (PPWAWU)	25,046
SA Municipal Workers Union (SAMWU)	14,892
SA Domestic Workers Union (SADWU)	8,700
SA Railways and Harbour Workers Union (SARHWU)	23,685
Transport and General Workers Union (TGWU)	21,046
Total	691,151

continued

Table 7.1 continued

NACTU (claimed members):	
Black Allied Mining and Construction Workers Union (BAMCWU)	4,119
Black Domestic Workers Union (BDWU)	300
Black Electronic and Electrical Workers Union (BEEWU)	520
Brushes and Cleaners Workers Union (BCWU)	3,000
Building Construction and Allied Workers Union (BCAWU)	22,000
Banking, Insurance, Finance and Assurance Workers Union (BIFAWU)	1,050
Domestic Workers Association of SA (DWASA)	3,000
Engineering and Allied Workers Union of SA (EAWUSA)	3,000
Electrical and Allied Workers Trade Union of SA (EAWTUSA)	15,000
Food and Beverage Workers Union	17,000
Hotel, Liquor, Catering and Allied Workers Union (HLCAWU)	4,500
Media Workers Association of SA (MWASA)	5,000
Natal Liquor and Catering Workers Union	6,737
National Union of Farmworkers (NUF)	418
National Union of Furniture Workers (NUFW)	20,000
National Union of Public Service Workers (NUPSW)	2,560
National Union of Wine, Spirits and Allied Workers Union (NUWSAW)	4,881
South African Chemical Workers' Union (SACWU)	32,000
SA Laundry, Dry Cleaning and Dyeing Workers Union (SALDCDWU)	500
Steel Engineering and Allied Workers Union (SEAWU)	5,500
Textile Workers Union (TWU)	400
Transport and Allied Workers Union (TAWU)	8,000
United African Motor and Allied Workers Union (UAMAWU)	8,000
Vukani Black Guards and Allied Workers Union (VBGAWU)	2,000
Total	169,485

Sources: Work in Progress No.54, June/July 1988; *SA Barometer* Vol.2, No.10, 3 June 1988.

Towards wider unity

NACTU, unlike COSATU, followed the pattern of its predecessors CUSA and AZACTU in not insisting on uniform political discipline. Nor did it develop the strong local and regional branch structures and shop-stewards' locals of COSATU. It was therefore a much looser federation. Individual affiliates had far greater freedom to determine how they would structure themselves, while the ideological views of the federation's leadership did not always percolate down into the rank-and-file membership, which was politically more diverse. After 1984 members of unions which were to become NACTU affiliates were drawn into anti-apartheid struggles alongside those of unions which became COSATU affiliates. In some areas shop-stewards' councils had been set up which bridged both federations. CUSA unions supported most of the stay-aways initiated by FOSATU to protest at repression and mark commemorative days.

Individual affiliates of CUSA and FOSATU had also worked closely when negotiating shopfloor issues. FOSATU's TGWU and CUSA's TAWU had, for example, a long history of co-operation in the transport industry. Metal unions in the two federations had also on occasion put forward joint proposals in wage negotiations. Following an agreement not to poach each other's members, the food unions in the two federations had also begun working together more closely.

From an industrial relations point of view there were strong imperatives for NACTU eventually to join forces with COSATU. Its membership was by mid-1988 less than a quarter of COSATU's. It was only in chemicals, transport, construction and food that it had a presence of any significance, and in the longer term there were forces propelling it to join COSATU, given the tendency towards industry-wide bargaining and the need to defend members against the post-1987 employer backlash.

Like COSATU, NACTU affiliates had also become targets for repression in some parts of the country, and as in COSATU a debate surfaced in NACTU around the need to seek wider unity to withstand the state onslaught.

Something of a breakthrough was achieved in the first half of 1988 when the COSATU and NACTU leadership held joint discussions on their response to the Labour Relations Amendment Bill (see Chapter 5 above).

In May, a special COSATU conference, called to formulate responses to the Bill and to restrictions placed on 17 political organisations and on COSATU on 24 February, called for a three-day protest stay-away and resolved to build a broad alliance of organisations opposed to apartheid, including NACTU.

Ideological differences, however, still stood in the way of closer, more structured COSATU-NACTU co-operation. In December 1987 NACTU's president, James Mndaweni, had stated that COSATU's formal adoption of the ANC's Freedom Charter was a 'divisive move' planned by people who were 'against working class unity'.[87] However, in May 1988 at an ANC-NACTU meeting in Harare (Zimbabwe), the ANC stressed that adherence to the Freedom Charter should not be the defining criterion in forming a broader alliance against apartheid. The ANC and NACTU also agreed it was imperative for the labour movement to strive towards the establishment of a single united labour federation.[88]

A proposed conference of a wide range of organisations opposed to apartheid, including NACTU, was convened by COSATU in September 1988 but was banned by the authorities (see Chapter 8 below). When the Labour Relations Amendment Act finally came into operation, also in September 1988, COSATU and NACTU decided to hold a joint worker summit to discuss action against the bill and forge closer ties.[89]

But while the two federations appeared to be moving towards closer co-operation, there were still debate and uncertainty in NACTU. Shopfloor rivalry between competing industrial unions, notably CWIU and SACWU, and TGWU and TAWU, impeded progress. In September 1988 the NACTU president again restated his position that the major obstacle preventing the two federations from joining forces was COSATU's adoption of the Freedom Charter.[90]

In February 1989 NACTU's national executive decided to shelve a worker summit it had called jointly with COSATU, because of the need for its affiliates to spend more time discussing 'the exact form of unity' between the two union bodies.[91]

When COSATU decided to go ahead with the summit on 4 and 5 March, which included several prominent non-aligned unions, 11 NACTU affiliates (including BAMCWU and FBWU) broke ranks with the leadership and decided to attend. Branches and other local structures of some of the remaining affiliates also attended.[92] Thus by 1989 NACTU's future as a federation appeared to be hinging on its responses to the question of unity with COSATU.

PART IV

8 Resistance to Apartheid

Shopfloor struggles represented only one aspect of workers' challenges to the conditions controlling and shaping their lives during the 1970s and 1980s. The nature of apartheid, as this book will have demonstrated, made for a particularly direct connection between labour issues and the political and social relations determining the conditions under which black workers lived. People organised as workers were frequently involved in struggles outside the workplace, and in turn workplace organisation and activity were strongly influenced by the level of mass struggle.

The revival of the trade union movement was stimulated by wider struggles, especially after 1980. The crucial battles of the embryonic union movement against registration and the Industrial Councils were fought out against the backdrop of a rising level of political resistance. After 1984, as the political and civic spheres of organised resistance were subjected to sustained and systematic repression, the trade union movement became more clearly drawn into political struggle, and came to play a leading role in promoting a broad alliance of forces seeking the end of apartheid. In doing so it had to come to terms with fundamental questions about the relation between struggles to improve and defend working conditions and the national liberation struggle.

In this chapter these questions are examined more closely, looking at the struggles after 1976 which grew out of the living conditions imposed on black workers, and taking stock of the response of the emerging trade union movement. The period from September 1984 to 1989 is the subject of the last two sections. They focus first on the new tactics of struggle, adapted under conditions of extreme repression and based on alliances of trade unions and political organisations, and then on the relation between the trade union movement and the struggle to end apartheid.

Workplace and community

As black workers were forced to live in segregated, tightly controlled and often remote townships or hostels, social and political issues were of direct and immediate consequence to them as workers with the capacity to organise against their conditions, in particular transport to and from work, controls on movement and the provision and cost of housing.

In the 1970s and early 1980s these concerns were principally reflected in three forms of resistance: bus boycotts, resistance to controls on movement in the form of squatter struggles, and, after the 1976 uprising, struggles around rent increases and the quality of services to township residents. In some areas these merged with education boycotts by black students.

During the 1980s the different struggles became linked as the organisations in the course of local struggles formed local, and sometimes regional, alliances. The process accelerated under the impact and direction of national political campaigns calling for a unitary, non-racial and democratic system – in particular the 1981 boycott of the twentieth anniversary celebrations of the white minority Republic and a boycott of elections to the government-created South African Indian Council. The formation of the UDF in 1983, with an initial affiliation of some 200 organisations growing later to around 600, provided a legal national political structure for resistance: people involved in particular struggles over conditions arising out of apartheid could thus be mobilised openly into the national campaign to dismantle apartheid.

When mass protests over rent increases in the Vaal Triangle in September 1984, and the violent police reaction to them, sparked a national uprising, the scale of resistance was so great that the regime could retain control only by deploying the police and army in the townships and by giving them emergency powers. A partial State of Emergency declared in July 1985 was followed in June 1986 by a national Emergency, still in force three years later.

Transport
Bus boycotts have often provided epic occasions in the history of worker resistance. Whole communities refused to use buses when fares were increased. The uncomfortable, crowded and dirty conditions on buses were also the cause of boycotts, as was the perception that monopolised bus services were government companies. In these circumstances, commuters have either walked to work or made use of alternative transport: taxis, trains or private vehicles.

The use of bus boycotts to resist fare increases goes back to historic struggles in Alexandra, Johannesburg, in 1947 and 1957. In the repressive climate of the 1960s there were few similar campaigns, and the tactic was only revived in the early 1970s in Natal. Between 1972 and 1980 most of the urban concentrations and small industrial towns in Natal were affected by transport struggles. A boycott of buses by the 10,000 commuters of Madadeni and Osizweni, near the coal-mining centre of Newcastle, was an early instance of conflict between workers and bantustan authorities which became endemic in the 1980s. As part-owner of the Trans-Tugela Transport company (TTT), the KwaZulu authorities played an active role in repressing the boycott. Vigilante groups were formed to protect bus shelters and TTT ticket offices from demonstrators.[1] But the commuters won a partial victory when the Bantu Investment Corporation was forced to sell half its shares to another company which replaced the bitterly resented system of uniform fares imposed on all users with fares related to the distance travelled.

In the second half of 1980 the focus shifted to the Western Cape, where the local transport monopoly, City Tramways, put up fares on its routes for African and Coloured commuters.[2] For the first time a transport boycott occurred as part of wider regional resistance and took strength from newly formed community organisations in the region. Widespread support had been mobilised for pupils at Coloured schools boycotting classes and for striking meat workers (see Chapter 7 above). Commuters now drew on this network of support. Local bus boycott committees were set up, co-ordinated by an umbrella Bus Action Committee. The government and City Tramways collaborated to crush the protest. Tramways personnel reported the registration numbers of illegal taxis to the police. Riot police carrying submachine guns forced people onto buses and on at least one occasion baton-charged groups of people boarding taxis.

The boycott was broken when, reacting to mounting resistance on several fronts throughout the country, the government banned all meetings. Co-ordination of the boycott was hampered and although African commuters continued to walk to work for another two months, the boycott collapsed in the more dispersed Coloured areas.

As the scope of popular resistance widened in the mid-1980s, bus boycotts became less central in focusing working-class resistance, although action continued against the rising cost of transport for workers. Following the start of nation-wide protests in September 1984, fare increases were suspended in many areas for fear that they would spur further resistance in the already volatile political climate. During 1986, however, bus boycotts were revived to underscore wider political demands. In May, for example, there was a boycott in Duduza on the East Rand which lasted three months and was linked to a consumer boycott of local white businesses. Both campaigns aimed to secure the release of detained community leaders and included demands for the lifting of the State of Emergency, withdrawal of troops from the township and improvements to local services. In October a similar, seven-month boycott by commuters forced a bus company on the West Rand to suspend its operations. Organisations in Kagiso and surrounding townships near Krugersdorp had launched a boycott of the local Greyhound Bus Company because it refused to transport mourners to a funeral of demonstrators killed by police. The boycotters later also demanded that the company stop opposing licence applications by black taxi drivers, allow pensioners to make free use of the buses on pension-due dates and stop allowing troops and vigilantes to use buses.[3]

Transport struggles were also a feature of resistance in the bantustans. They were often rooted in frustration at the long distances 'commuters' were made to travel by the government's policy of forcing people to live in distant bantustan dormitory towns. Venda, Lebowa, the settlements around Durban, KwaNdebele, and especially the bantustans surrounding Pretoria were all the focus of struggles during the 1980s, many sustained for long periods. Commuters confronted the authorities in these regions head-on. Because they often had commercial interests in the local bus companies and because they were expected to maintain a supply of contract and commuter labour, the bantustan authorities often tried to crush boycotts.

One instance of this was when a boycott in Mdantsane in July 1983 met with severe repression by the Ciskei bantustan authorities. Conditions on buses owned by the Ciskei Transport Corporation (CTC) had been a source of grievance since 1981. A Committee of Ten, consisting largely of SAAWU members and shop stewards, was formed to co-ordinate the boycott. The train service running along the outskirts of Mdantsane proved crucial to the boycott's success.[4] It was used as an alternative form of transport and later, as repression intensified, as a meeting place to discuss tactics:

> Every commuter who travels the one hour journey from Mdantsane to East London is drawn into the dramatic atmosphere of the train culture ... They sing about Sebe and his fraudulent regime and they praise the power of the working class. They sing about freedom and their long history of resistance. They listen intently to speeches from workers and community organisers who explain each new development and inform them about political events happening in other parts of the country ... It is here, in these moving cocoons at the heart of

the apartheid structures ... that the future of the bus boycott will be decided.[5]

Two weeks after the bus boycott began, vigilantes of the ruling Ciskei National Independence Party (CNIP) were brought into Mdantsane from the rural areas, unleashing a reign of terror. Taxi drivers, motorists and people walking to work were beaten up and their cars confiscated. Thousands of SAAWU members were detained and held in the changing rooms of a local sports stadium, where many were severely beaten and tortured. Some women detainees were raped.[6] At railway stations the Ciskeian army barred entrances to trains and in some cases forced commuters onto buses at gunpoint. In three incidents some 20 people were killed when soldiers fired on commuters trying to board trains. By August over 1,000 people, most of them members of SAAWU, had been taken into detention and 70 people had been killed in vigilante attacks on commuters.[7]

Commuters pledged to intensify the boycott until all those detained were released and the families of the dead and wounded compensated. In August the bantustan authorities assumed emergency powers. Meetings were banned, a curfew was imposed and shortly afterwards SAAWU was banned inside the bantustan. But the boycott continued, causing the collapse of the bus company the following year.

Controls on movement

Resistance to controls on movement also helped shape the political climate in which the union movement emerged in the 1970s and 1980s. African workers defied and resisted the regulations from the moment of their inception. When regulations were tightened in the 1950s and extended to women as well as men, there were widely supported campaigns against them in rural and urban areas. Pass-burning campaigns in 1960 were only ended by violent repression, including the massacre of 69 peaceful demonstrators at Sharpeville and the imposition of a State of Emergency.

Apart from organised political campaigns there has always been widespread defiance of the controls. Hundreds of thousands of workers have travelled from the bantustans to seek work or live illegally in the cities as a matter of survival. Many have been women – wives of contract workers – with their children, who have moved to the cities to be with their husbands and closer to sources of employment. In spite of the constant monitoring and repeated expulsion of 'illegals' to the bantustans, this flow of people rendered the controls unworkable in many areas of the country, and was one of the factors forcing the government to overhaul and modify the system (see Chapter 1 above).

Denied access to officially approved accommodation, people settled illegally in squatter communities around the main urban centres. Although similar struggles occurred all around the country in the late 1970s, there was a particularly fierce struggle in the Western Cape for the preservation of squatter communities faced with demolition and expulsion. The struggle was a response to the Coloured Labour Preference Policy and the concerted attempts to reduce the local African population.

Between 1974 and 1978 squatter camps around Cape Town were razed, dispersing 60,000 illegal Africans, homeless Coloured residents and Africans with rights of permanent residence, all living side by side in defiance of apartheid policies.[8] Those legally entitled to be in Cape Town were resettled in Crossroads between the city and its airport. It quickly also became a new refuge for illegal workers. Committees were set up to organise the shack-dwellers against pass raids and the demolition of new shacks. It was a highly cohesive community, establishing its own school and creches and some essential services, and it became one of the cornerstones of resistance in Cape Town. An early victory was won when Crossroads was declared a temporary emergency camp in June 1976.

It nevertheless remained long-term government policy to demolish the camp. Surprise demolitions and raids to arrest 'illegals' were intensified. Between 1979 and 1982 there was a respite when new tactics in line with the recommendations of the Riekert report were applied. The government adopted an apparently conciliatory approach and negotiated a deal with the committee representing Crossroads residents. The camp would be demolished but legal residents of Cape Town, as well as contract workers and their families who, though illegally in the area, earned their living in a 'legitimate' way, would be housed in a new township to be built for that purpose (New Crossroads). The 'deal' was to prove the basis for serious divisions which continued to plague the community in later years.

Over the same period the authorities set out to destroy two other settlements which had arisen between 1980 and 1982. One consisted of women evicted from the disused Langa Barracks (destined for conversion into housing for permanent residents), and the other the overspill of Crossroads' illegal population who lived in makeshift plastic shelters at Nyanga Bush. By day police would tear down the structures.

By night the women would return and rebuild them. The pass laws were also used. By September, 3,666 people deemed to be Transkei bantustan citizens had been expelled from the Western Cape in police raids.[9] Most of those expelled tried to return to Cape Town; the authorities set up roadblocks on the main roads into Cape Town to obstruct them, but by the end of 1981 many had found their way back.

In March 1983 the government announced plans to remove the entire legally resident African population of Cape Town to a new site. The residents of existing townships of Nyanga, Langa and Guguletu would be resettled at Khayelitsha, 40 kilometres from Cape Town, together with residents of the squatter camps (including Crossroads) legally qualified to live in the area.

The Surplus People's Project commented:

> The process of moving Africans to Khayelitsha will be used as a filter to separate legals and illegals once and for all ... All existing squatter camps, including the Crossroads complex will be cleared ... A clear sweep will be made to clear 'illegals' out ... Only those with rights to be in the Western Cape will be entitled to live there. Khayelitsha will be the only legal place for Africans to live. So no unqualified person will be in Khayelitsha and anyone outside Khayelitsha will be moved.[10]

When in 1986 controls on movement were revised in line with the Abolition of Influx Control Act, the African townships in Cape Town were reprieved, but the fate of the squatter camps still hung in the balance. In February of that year violent clashes between police and squatters had broken out in Crossroads after rumours of the camp's imminent demolition. Resistance was so intense that police were unable to enter the camp and could do little more than seal it off.

The newer settlements became strongholds of local youth organisations affiliated to the UDF. Attacks were carried out on police and military vehicles from the midst of the densely packed shanties. In June 1986 vigilante groups, drawn mainly from the longer-term residents of Crossroads, actively abetted by police and troops, drove out most of the residents of the newer sites, torching their shacks as they fled. Supporters of the UDF were attacked, and many were killed. As many as 30,000 lost their homes and most were forced ultimately to go to Khayelitsha. It was the tragic and bitter close to one of the most sustained episodes of resistance by squatters to government restrictions on their freedom of movement.[11]

Housing costs

After the 1976 uprising new associations of tenants, youth or women and other loosely termed 'community organisations' were formed in black residential areas. The impetus came from school and campus activists who sought to build on the experiences of 1976 by mobilising residents at a grassroots level around issues which immediately affected them. Community organisations were formed in the Coloured areas of Cape Town and Indian townships of Durban around the issues of the accommodation shortage, poor housing, increased rents and related fees like electricity bills. In some cases they won concessions from the authorities, giving residents a new sense of power and laying the basis for wider forms of organisation. The Soweto Civic Association (SCA) and the Port Elizabeth Black Civic Organisation (PEBCO) were both formed in 1979. Similar organisations were subsequently formed in other African townships, particularly after 1980, when the continuing crisis around the finance of essential services and the imposition of the community council system sharpened resistance (see Chapter 3 above).

In 1981 the Cape Housing Action Committee (CAHAC), an umbrella body uniting 14 separate community organisations in the Cape Town area, was launched. During 1981 and 1982 it broadened grassroots organisation and, in co-operation with local trade unions, launched campaigns for improved maintenance of council housing and the suspension of rent increases.[12] There were similar developments in the Indian areas of Durban where the umbrella Durban Housing Action Committee (DHAC) called boycotts around rent and electricity rate increases in 1980 and 1981. In response to these campaigns the Durban City Council was forced to bypass state-appointed bodies and negotiate directly with the DHAC.[13]

Although there had been demonstrations against rents as early as 1977 in Soweto, campaigns around rents reached a new level in African areas after 1980, following the installation of the community councils. The councils, set up by the government to administer the townships in accordance with the policies of apartheid, sought to redress the deficits they had inherited from the Administration Boards by repeatedly increasing rents.[14]

In the following two years struggles against rent increases acquired an intensity which was often transformed into wider resistance to local authorities and at times met with police violence. In 1984 rent boycotts and protests at poor services acquired national dimensions. Initiated in Tumahole near Parys, they spread to Tembisa, Duduza and Katlehong on the East Rand, and by September had also taken in communities in the Vaal Triangle. Violent repressive action by police in the Vaal Triangle sparked the country-wide protests which were met by an occupation of townships by the police and army and the declaration of a State of Emergency in July the following year. The rent boycotts spread and in some areas were to last for over three years, as part of a sustained attack on the councils.

Popular resistance
After the mid-1970s there were three periods in which resistance to apartheid was transformed from struggles over specific issues into open mass action which directly challenged the capacity of the apartheid regime to maintain control. On each occasion workers participated in ways which reflected their increasing organisation and growing involvement in political struggle.

During 1976–7 a boycott of schools in Soweto was transformed into widespread unrest which quickly spread to many parts of the country. The unrest was initially fuelled by anger at the violence which police unleashed on a demonstration on 16 June 1976 in protest at the introduction of Afrikaans as a compulsory medium of instruction in schools. During the uprising three worker and student stay-aways were organised, marking attempts by the school students to strengthen their support and reflecting the scale of resistance. On 4 August 1976, 60 per cent of the Johannesburg labour force stayed away from work in response to a call by the Soweto Students' Representative Council. There was little mobilisation among workers apart from the picketing of commuters on their way to work, blockading of stations and sabotage of railway lines into the city. There were reports of tension between students and contract workers who, living isolated in barracks, were cut off from the undercurrents of resistance in the townships at large. They were the most vulnerable section of the workforce and faced eviction to the bantustans if they became involved in strike action.

The initiative for the second stay-away came from the underground ANC. It was called in support of broad demands, including the release of those detained in a state clampdown on activists. Pamphlets were distributed calling for a three-day stay-away in the Johannesburg region from 23–5 August. The first day of the stay-away met with a 75–80 per cent response.[15] On the second day police succeeded in exploiting the tensions between contract workers and permanent residents in Soweto. Twenty-one people were killed as contract workers attacked township residents.

A third stay-away, national in scope and spanning three days, was called in September after pupils in the Western Cape had begun boycotting schools in solidarity with those in Soweto. Students revised their strategy: a process of dialogue and agitation among workers started before the second stay-away was intensified. Over half a million workers took part, with an increased participation by contract workers. There was a strong response among the Coloured workforce in the Western Cape, providing for greater cohesion across apartheid divisions in the region which trade unions were later to consolidate.

During 1980 there was a second phase of open mass resistance. This time the focus was in the Western Cape, but the protests spread later to the Eastern Cape, to parts of Natal, the Orange Free State and Johannesburg. A boycott of Coloured schools in Cape Town in protest at apartheid education was supported by all major community organisations in the area. Resistance was heightened by the meat workers' strike and the bus boycott. A stay-at-home was called for 16–18 June to coincide with the fourth anniversary of the Soweto uprising and to underscore a range of demands, principally to do with the school boycott. Over the three-day period, between 50 and 70 per cent of the workforce stayed at home.[16] Support was again strong among Coloured workers in the Western Cape. There were violent confrontations between police and residents in the Coloured suburbs in the wake of the stay-away, after police shot and killed children stoning commuter buses.

The third period of mass popular protest came after a number of struggles during 1983 and 1984. After the UDF was formed there had been sustained national political mobilisation, focused on uniting all sectors of society and co-ordinating different sectors of struggle in opposition to the government's constitutional plans and in resistance to apartheid in general.

From 1983 school boycotts occurred over issues left unresolved during the boycotts of 1980. As noted above, rent increases led to rent boycotts in the Vaal Triangle, as rising prices put pressure on the already low wages of black workers. Tension was heightened by elections for the newly installed segregated tri-cameral parliament in September 1984. Under this dispensation, alongside the existing parliament for whites, two new chambers were created in which the Coloured and Indian communities were afforded a limited form of parliamentary representation. The African majority continued to be totally excluded from the central decision-making structures. Political organisations mounted a highly successful boycott of the elections – just over 17 per cent voting in the Coloured election and 16 per cent in the Indian.[17]

In the week of the elections an estimated half a million scholars stayed away from classes in support of demands for a non-racial and unitary political system.[18]

From August 1984 school students' organisations began shaping demands concerned not only with education but encompassing general economic and political issues, such as rising living costs, rejection of the new constitutional dispensation and calls for the resignation of community councils. This emphasis on broader demands reflected these organisations' desire to extend their support to those active in other struggles and their conviction that issues in the educational sphere could not be resolved in isolation from the broader context of oppression.[19]

On 3 September 1984, the day on which the new parliament was inaugurated, police violently attacked residents of Sebokeng in the Vaal Triangle who were protesting at rent increases – several residents were killed. The attack and the angry response to it initiated a period of mounting conflict as protests spread and police killings of township residents became a regular occurrence. Between 1985 and April 1990 at least 5,964 people died at the hands of the police, according to independent monitoring groups.[20]

The intensification of resistance followed similar patterns in different areas. Pupils and unemployed youths were in the forefront of resistance. The community council system, together with police and others seen as collaborators, came under sustained and often violent attack, leading in some areas to the collapse of formal administration. The occupation of townships by troops, initially in the Vaal Triangle but later more widely, and then the July 1985 State of Emergency, provided a further focus for resistance, with continuing clashes between residents and soldiers and police. By mid-1985 the authorities had only nominal control over many areas, particularly in the Eastern Cape. Once police and military patrols were withdrawn, control reverted to township residents. In some areas 'street committees' emerged and 'people's courts' were set up to rid areas of crime and enforce political discipline. There was also a rise in the level of armed activity by ANC combatants.

Union responses

It was against this background of intensifying and more complex forms of resistance that the new trade union movement emerged. As it developed it was faced with the issue of how to respond to local struggles, to national campaigns and to the periods of mass protest.

The 1950s had been an era of active alliance between trade unions and political organisations in common campaigns against apartheid. SACTU had effectively played the role of the workers' wing of the national liberation movement. But the interaction of the independent trade union movement with both local organisations and national political movements in the 1980s was more complex. Until the UDF was formed in 1983 there was no single, legal national political organisation comparable to the Congress Alliance of the 1950s to which unions could relate. Nor, until the formation of COSATU in November 1985, was there a national trade union body comparable to SACTU, which might focus the perspectives of the union movement on how it should engage with the political movement.

FOSATU
After 1982 unions in FOSATU began evolving strategies of support for struggles beyond the workplace. In its first three years the federation had concentrated on consolidating its industrial presence. Its member unions had been drawn from disparate backgrounds. The motor unions in the Eastern Cape, for example, drew largely on a Coloured membership with little tradition of community organisation or political struggle. In Natal many of the members of its affiliates came under the influence of Inkatha, which actively opposed and sought to frustrate the school boycotts and other political campaigns. These and other factors made the federation cautious about assuming a political role.

The perspectives of FOSATU unions were gradually changed in the recognition battles and struggles against the Industrial Council system. Regional and cross-union co-operation brought a greater uniformity of perspective among its affiliates, and in February 1982 FOSATU led the stoppage to protest at the death in police detention of AFCWU organiser Neil Aggett. Until then the stay-away had been the primary way in which workers had asserted political demands by withholding their labour power. The Aggett stoppage was a political gesture at the workplace and it widened the methods of struggle used by workers.

COSATU's response to community struggles was also influenced by the emergence of shop-stewards' councils. For example, Germiston MAWU shop stewards pressurised employers to intercede with local authorities to stop the demolition of squatters shacks in Katlehong. Likewise, in the Uitenhage area of the Eastern Cape, NAAWU shop stewards formed the Uitenhage Black Civic Organisation (UBCO) to take up issues affecting their members.[21]

Similar developments elsewhere gradually extended FOSATU's activity beyond the shopfloor, but until well into 1983 this mainly took the form of pressurising employers to intercede with government. Its affiliates did not enter into formal alliances with local community organisations or broader political movements, nor did they engage in any of the national campaigns of the period.

However, the growing level of resistance forced FOSATU to adopt a formal political policy at its third Congress in 1982. In a keynote speech the federation's secretary general, Joe Foster, emphasised an autonomous political role for the working class, independent of broader political groups, through the creation of a working-class movement built around and accountable to factory-based shopfloor structures. He said:

> We are ... concerned with worker leadership in a wider arena than only the union struggle. Giving leadership to the working class requires an organisational base. Without this base, then the poverty and the lack of education, information and time that workers are struggling against will be the very factors which will force workers to surrender leadership of the community to other strata in society. Our aim is to use the strength of factory-based organisation to allow workers to play an effective role in the community ... That FOSATU should be involved in community activities is correct since our members form the major part of those communities. However, as we have argued, we must do so from an organisational base, if we are truly to be an effective worker resource. Without this base, it is more likely that we will destroy a clear worker identity since workers will be entirely swamped by the powerful tradition of popular politics ... All communities are composed of different interest groups ... Under the surface of unity community politics is partisan and divided. Fosatu cannot possibly ally itself to all political groups that are contesting this arena. Neither can it ally itself with particular groups. Both paths will destroy the unity of its own worker organisation.[22]

In line with this policy FOSATU participated in broader campaigns independently. During the 1983 campaign to boycott the elections for the segregated parliament it organised its own campaign separately from the UDF. FOSATU shop-steward committees distributed pamphlets in factories demanding a universal franchise and rejecting the new constitutional dispensation. In some factories they requested meetings to allow management to hear workers' views on the new constitution and demanded that they make these known to the government.

Shop stewards also made door-to-door visits in the Coloured suburbs of Uitenhage and Port Elizabeth, where FOSATU's powerful motor affiliate NAAWU was based, urging residents not to vote. The campaign contributed to a low poll among Coloured voters in the Eastern Cape area.[23]

Local FOSATU trade unions played a central role in a boycott of buses by 46,000 commuters travelling daily to Richards Bay from the three townships of the Empangeni region of Natal in 1984. Until then most other bus boycotts had been organised by ad hoc committees linked to community organisations. The Empangeni boycott was co-ordinated by local shop-steward committees. It lasted nine weeks and resulted in a victory when the KwaZulu bantustan authorities allowed competing bus companies with lower fares to operate on certain routes.[24]

FCWU and GWU

The FCWU and the GWU sought the co-operation of local community and student organisations in 1979 and 1980 in support of striking workers, but with contradictory results (see Chapter 7 above).

During the Fattis and Monis boycott, when community organisations spearheaded the boycott of the company's products, a rift developed between the union and SACOS when the boycott was suspended. SACOS at first refused to comply with FCWU's decision to suspend the action, because it did not endorse the details of the union's agreement with management. In the meat boycott the following year WPGWU attempted to prevent a similar confrontation by insisting that the union take sole responsibility for the organisation of the boycott. However, when police detained the union officials responsible, the boycott collapsed – community organisations had not been sufficiently involved to sustain it.[25]

Both the GWU and FCWU retreated from further alliances and concentrated after 1980 on extending their industrial presence beyond the Western Cape. From 1981, as the differences about registration which had divided GWU and FCWU from FOSATU receded and talks about the formation of a wider federation began, the three bodies developed a closer relationship, gradually advancing a common political perspective.

Both GWU and FCWU argued, like FOSATU, that in formally allying to broader political movements, they would compromise their objective of representing their working-class members, because these movements encompassed other social strata and classes for whom the struggle against economic exploitation was not the primary goal. The position of the FCWU was that:

> Community organisations ... are open to workers and non-workers. In most cases the leadership in these organisations are intellectuals or people with more education.
>
> At this point, community organisations do not have a strong base of worker members ... There are people who do not want to recognise that there are class divisions among the oppressed. For us there can be no lasting alliance between workers organisations and community organisations unless this division is understood.[26]

Both FCWU and GWU declined for these reasons to join the UDF when it was formed; further reasons were because of what they viewed as the incompatibility of union structures and practices with those of political organisations. Trade-union structures were based on paid-up or signed-up membership in which all decisions were discussed and mandated by membership from the shopfloor upwards. This contrasted with the more loosely organised affiliates of the UDF with activists less directly responsible to a mass base.[27]

However, neither FCWU nor GWU adopted binding political positions as FOSATU had done in 1982 – they postponed the question of co-operation and affiliation to political organisations until after the formation of a national federation, which they thought would afford unions a stronger base from which to engage with political movements. In the 1984 elections for the segregated parliament, however, FCWU played a prominent role in dissuading Coloured voters in Cape Town and rural areas of the Western Cape from going to the polls.

The general unions
By contrast, several general unions participated in wider political campaigns and also formally affiliated to the UDF. In many cases regional factors strongly influenced the nature of their political role – for example, SAAWU's participation in the Mdantsane bus boycott in 1983. The overtly hostile attitude of the Ciskei bantustan authorities to trade union organisation also propelled SAAWU into an opposition political role. SAAWU's political policy contrasted strongly with that of FOSATU, FCWU and GWU:

> It is questionable whether trade unions with their accepted ambiguities, will represent the interests of the working class any better ... than community organisations ... To conflate the working class with union membership, is to confine the membership of the working class to union membership only, to the exclusion of dependants (husbands, wives, elderly parents and children) of those union members. Non-

unionised workers and the unemployed constitute a vast portion of the working class. The community, women's, student, youth and other organisations based within working class communities are also in a position to express the views of the working class and are also legitimate organisations of the working-class.

The responsibility of the union leadership in this situation if it has the interests of the working class at heart, demands of them that they lead the union's membership into the broad democratic front and into active participation within all its structures (regardless of their imperfections): to struggle for and ensure maximum working class participation and finally class (not just union) leadership of the broad democratic front.[28]

According to GAWU, the Transvaal-based general union:

Even those people who are not behind machines on the factory floor can be said to be waging a working class struggle if the issues which they take up in their sites of struggle, and the way in which they take those issues up, serve to undermine the class relations upon which the present society is built ... People can wage a working class political struggle around those issues which affect them and trade unions can play a role in instilling working class consciousness ... Our sphere of operation is the factory floor, but we need to address ourselves to those who are, for instance, in the rural areas. We don't have the necessary infrastructure as trade unions. Even if we come up with one union federation, we still will not have the infrastructure to reach people in those areas. We think, and this has been proven in practice, that the UDF does offer that kind of infrastructure.[29]

SAAWU, GAWU, MGWUSA and smaller general unions participated in several national campaigns between 1980 and 1982, notably the boycott of celebrations of the twentieth anniversary of the South African Republic and a boycott of elections to the government-created South African Indian Council.

The unions' participation mostly took the form of popularising the demands of these campaigns among union members, through the distribution of literature and the organisation of mass meetings. By involving workers in struggles beyond the shopfloor they helped lay the ground for the re-emergence of a national legal political movement. However, because of the dispersal of their members across several industries the general unions were seldom able to take industrial action in support of broader demands as FOSATU unions did after 1982.

The 'black consciousness' union

CUSA for its part decided to affiliate to the UDF and the black consciousness National Forum so as not to compel its members to identify with a single political position. In practice, however, its affiliation to the UDF remained a formality. It played no substantial role in the campaigns of the Front, working instead more closely with the principal black consciousness organisation, AZAPO, in some parts of the country.

The impact of COSATU

The intensification of resistance throughout the country in late 1984 and during 1985, and in particular the occupation of townships by troops, caused further shifts in relationships. Although the effects were felt nationwide, they were most visible on the East Rand among the industrial affiliates of FOSATU.

The East Rand area with its strategic industries had been a barometer for many of the key trends in the development of the union movement. The workforce and union membership were concentrated in three or four townships, which, together with the presence of shop-stewards' locals, made trade unions a particular focus for community issues.

During 1984 differences in FOSATU's most prominent affiliate in the region, MAWU, caused the union to split. One area of difference was the failure of FOSATU's political policy to address the wider struggles in the community where shop stewards lived. Many stewards had become active in community organisations affiliated to the UDF, in particular the East Rand People's Organisation (ERAPO), and a number of them, disenchanted with FOSATU's policy, broke away to form a new union, United Metal, Mining and Allied Workers Union of South Africa (UMMAWUSA).

Attitudes were also changing in another FOSATU affiliate, SFAWU. It mobilised other unions, student and community organisations to support a consumer boycott during the Simba Quix strike in August 1984 (see Chapter 6 above). Many Simba Quix workers lived in Tembisa; the choice of the boycott weapon reflected their desire to tap the high level of organisation around rent and school boycotts then in progress in the township. Local student and community groups, other trade unions and UDF affiliates were urged to form local committees and spread the boycott.[30]

According to East Rand trade unionists active in promoting support for the student struggles, there was also 'a groundswell of shopfloor support for student demands'. Restrictions on the age of students who could enter school were forcing many onto the labour market and workers had to finance their children's education from their own pockets.[31] In their view the dividing lines between the struggles of students and workers were becoming increasingly blurred.

The contacts and meetings in these areas contributed to the success of a two-day stay-away in the PWV area on 5–6 November 1984. The call was backed by 37 organisations, among them much of the trade union movement, including CUSA. The call arose both out of protest and anger at the violence of the police and their killing of protesters and other residents, and out of support for the struggles taking place in the area. The demands behind which the stay-away was organised reflected the merging of different struggles. As well as demands at the centre of the schools boycott, calls were made for an end to increased transport, rent and service charges, the withdrawal of troops from townships and the release of detainees.[32]

The stay-away was highly successful. There was an average absentee rate of 60 per cent of the workforce in the PWV area, with between 300,000 and 800,000 workers participating. Students boycotted schools en masse throughout the region and some 400,000 pupils stayed away from classes.[33]

Responses were strongest in the unionised factories of the Vaal and East Rand areas, with over 80 per cent participation, reflecting the crucial role of shop-stewards' locals and active union members in the mobilisation of support. Intensive canvassing among the high proportion of contract workers in these areas had preceded the stay-away, and support was high in factories where they were employed. Of all the industrial sectors, only the mines, isolated from the townships and newly unionised, produced a weak response.[34] This November 1984 stay-away was widely regarded as a milestone in the history of resistance; it was the largest action of its kind until then. For the first time since the 1950s a regional stay-away had been organised by a formal alliance of industrial unions and political organisations.

During 1985 stay-aways were frequently used by workers on a local or regional basis, and by the end of the year the industrial workforce in all the major urban concentrations except Durban had been involved in stay-aways. In contrast to the previous periods, trade unions played a significant, active organisational role.

The formation of COSATU in November 1985 gave further coherence to the political role of the trade union movement by drawing together its diverse and sometimes conflicting ideological trends. As different unions in particular sectors merged into single affiliates for each industry, the political perspectives of the general unions and the industrial unions had to be reconciled.

More importantly, COSATU gave the unions a single platform from which to engage with political organisations. The focus shifted away from the dissipated and strongly regional context in which they had previously related. The keynote speeches at COSATU's founding conference stressed the need to participate in campaigns and enter into alliances with other organisations from a position of strength and without sacrificing the unions' independent role.

The impact of these policies was evident in the closer relationships which developed between COSATU and national organisations like the UDF and the National Education Crisis Committee (NECC), supplementing the local co-operation between shop-stewards' councils and community organisations. In 1986 COSATU held a formal meeting in Lusaka with a high level ANC-SACTU delegation in which it was recognised that

> as a representative of our working class, COSATU is seized with the task of engaging the workers in the general democratic struggle, both as an independent organisation and as an essential component of our democratic forces of our country.[35]

A further indication of the closer identification of unions and political organisations, was the adoption in 1987 of the Freedom Charter by some of COSATU's larger affiliates: NUM, FAWU, NUMSA and CCAWUSA.[36]

New tactics under the State of Emergency

The State of Emergency declared in 1985 further enhanced the political role of the unions. It was directed in the main against the community organisations which had been prominent in organising the rent and school boycotts and the campaigns against the councils. Thousands of activists were detained and others forced underground. In the vacuum which arose shop-stewards' locals became even more of a focus for local organisation, taking up a range of issues and involving themselves in resistance actions which arose in response to the repression under the State of Emergency – stay-aways, consumer boycotts and a new wave of rent boycotts during 1986 and 1987.

Stay-aways

Although there were frequent stay-aways during 1985, all were local or regional in spite of the intensity and widespread nature of resistance.

The shifting and regional nature of the struggles, and the effects of the State of Emergency, made national co-ordination difficult.

In March 1985 community organisations in the Eastern Cape mobilised for a three-day stay-away as a response to the severe economic crisis and the repression in the region. The Eastern Cape had the highest level of unemployment of all the country's industrial centres and the motor industry had seen massive retrenchments. The stay-away also focused on increases in the price of petrol and on concerns that this would further increase prices of consumer goods and services. It was preceded by intensive door-to-door campaigning. With 90 to 99 per cent of the employed African workforce participating, it reflected high levels of support for the community organisations in the African townships.[37]

In Coloured areas the level of participation was much lower. The predominant industrial union in the area, NAAWU, organised among Coloured and African workers and while a degree of non-racial unity had been achieved in the workplace, the Group Areas Act had been a major impediment to united action in the communities where the workers lived. Community organisation was weak in Port Elizabeth's Coloured areas, unlike Cape Town's. The call for the stay-away was made by PEBCO, a predominantly African organisation.

NAAWU opposed the stay-away, arguing that national action was needed to address the demands. It also felt that if workers in smaller and less organised plants participated, they would be exposed to victimisation or dismissal. Because of the recession, local industrial unions had been forced into a defence of existing jobs, while in the townships the most prominent community organisation, the Port Elizabeth Youth Congress (PEYCO), drew its membership from thousands of unemployed youths with different concerns.[38] FOSATU unions felt they could not endorse the call because it would not be supported by their Coloured membership, a factor weighing heavily among a series of other objections, which included inadequate consultation with unions by the community organisations involved.[39]

Similar concerns arose later in the year in Natal. During a major stay-away to back the demands of the Sarmcol strikers in July (see Chapter 7 above), contrasting views about organisational structures and politics were put forward by MAWU and the UDF. MAWU did not involve UDF organisations in the planning of the stay-away because the union viewed it as an extension of shopfloor action. It mobilised community support independently of the UDF through its shop stewards. The UDF felt, for its part, that because of its own relationship with the community through its local affiliates, it should have been consulted. There were also disagreements about the efficacy of the stay-away as a weapon. Local UDF organisations felt stay-aways should be used as an exercise in mobilising people and raising their political awareness and that the demands of the Sarmcol workers should only form one of several political demands.[40]

In the PWV area the unity achieved in November 1984 was maintained. In May 1985 Andries Raditsela, an executive member of CWIU, died from brain injuries after being detained and assaulted by police patrolling Tsakane on the East Rand, where he lived. As in the case of Neil Aggett two years previously, his death was perceived as an attack on the trade union movement and both FOSATU, to which CWIU was affiliated, and CUSA called for a united response by organised workers on the day of his funeral. A call for a regional stay-away by FOSATU was superseded by a call for a national two-hour on-site stoppage to align with the more limited form of action proposed by CUSA and to allow for the widest possible response. A call was issued for workers in the Transvaal to attend Raditsela's funeral and for workers elsewhere to take some form of on-site action.

On 14 May 30,000 people attended the funeral, just over half of them residents of Tsakane. Fourteen thousand workers came from other areas. Well over 100,000 workers took some form of action ranging from lunchtime prayer and commemorative meetings to extended stoppages. In Natal the shopfloor response was the most extensive since the 1973 strikes. The Raditsela stoppages testified again to the crucial organisational role of the shop stewards and locals which mobilised the protest in less than a week.[41]

In the second half of 1985 stay-aways proliferated, particularly in smaller towns and even in rural areas. The homogeneous nature of the population in such areas, usually living in a single township and with most workers employed in one major industry, allowed community organisations, supported in some areas by local branches of trade unions, to mobilise the entire workforce. The stay-aways were often called to protest at the detention of local activists, police or troop activity, or to allow residents to attend the funerals of those killed by police taking repressive action. There were press reports of at least 16 such initiatives during the year.[42]

In September 1985, resistance intensified in the Western Cape, following the violent dispersal of an attempted march on Pollsmoor Prison to demand the release of Nelson Mandela, who was held there. Calls again emerged for a stay-away from a range of community organisations and local trade unions, to protest at the detention of activists and the activity of police and troops. The stay-away took place on 11–12

September with an average 50–60 per cent response concentrated in industries with an organised union presence.[43]

In the same month essential services in East London were paralysed when there was a strong response (as high as 98 per cent, according to some sources) to calls for a two-day stay-away.[44] In Umlazi and Lamontville in Natal large numbers of workers stayed away from work in response to calls, this time by churches, to mark 10 October as a National Day of Prayer, in a National Initiative for Reconciliation. In most other areas the day was marked by lunchtime prayer services. In Pretoria there were major stay-aways in November and December. The first was to protest at a ban on weekend funerals, rent increases and the continued presence of the police. The second stay-away (involving 80 per cent of the workforce) came in the wake of a police massacre of 12 Mamelodi residents during a protest against rent increases. Residents also stayed away en masse to attend funerals.[45]

Nation-wide stay-aways spanning several centres occurred in 1986, drawing on the new national cohesion which COSATU gave to the trade union movement. Its involvement in their organisation was critical to their scale and impact. Two major stay-aways were organised. The first was to commemorate May Day and to underscore demands that it be declared a national workers' holiday. The second demand was that 16 June, the anniversary of the Soweto uprising, also be declared a national holiday.

The demand for May Day as a workers' holiday, although supported by political organisations, was essentially a concern of the unions which had commemorated the day in 1984 and 1985 by calling public rallies and lunch-hour meetings in workplaces, educating workers about its significance and negotiating with individual employers for it to be granted as a holiday.[46] In the largest stay-away until then over 1.5 million workers responded to the May Day stay-away called by COSATU and CUSA. The extent of support is shown in Table 8.1. Workers were joined by thousands of school and university students.

In the PWV area the response – 79 per cent of the workforce on average – was weak only in the public sector (38 per cent). Its centre was in COSATU-organised factories. Between 80 and 85 per cent of gold miners stayed away from the shafts as did half of all coal miners, a reflection of the NUM's growth since 1984, when miners had not taken part in the November stay-away.[47] The pattern of high stay-away rates in unionised factories was repeated elsewhere. In the Durban–Pinetown area, a COSATU stronghold, the stay-away was 60 per cent effective and was supported by both African and Indian workers. Absentee rates in factories on the North and South coasts of Natal were approximately 50 per cent. This was the largest such action in the province, exceeding even the numbers involved in the Raditsela stoppage the previous year.[48] The influence of the unions on stay-away patterns was especially marked in the Eastern Cape. In the African townships of Port Elizabeth and Uitenhage the stay-away was almost total (99 per cent), as it had been in March 1985, reflecting the continued strong influence of community organisations, which had endorsed the May Day demands. Forty-five per cent of Port Elizabeth's Coloured workforce and 79 per cent of Uitenhage's responded – clear evidence of the support of the COSATU-affiliated motor unions.[49]

The exception to the national pattern was the Western Cape, where only 15 per cent of the workforce observed the call. African workers carried the brunt (51 per cent), but only 2 per cent of the Coloured workforce were involved. This response contrasted sharply with the mass worker support for the student-initiated stay-at-homes in 1976 and 1980 and the September 1985 stay-away, when there were strong responses in Coloured areas.[50] In May 1986, however, the region was suffering the effects of severe repression after a period of heightened protests. At the time of the stay-away, community organisations had also been set back by the destruction of the squatter community in Crossroads by vigilantes encouraged by police and troops.

Such support as there was for the stay-away in the Western Cape came mainly from COSATU-organised factories, but although the federation had built a strong presence in key local industrial sectors it accounted for only 10 per cent of the region's workforce.[51] Conservative TUCSA unions which still dominated the Coloured workforce refused to endorse the stay-away call. Community organisations in Coloured areas, hampered by repression, were unable to fill the gap and failed to mobilise support beyond the shopfloor.

Six weeks later trade unions and political organisations again called for a national stay-at-home. The stay-away, on the tenth anniversary of the Soweto uprising, centred around demands that 16 June be declared a national holiday and several wider demands, and was given impetus by the declaration of a new State of Emergency four days previously. The response closely reflected that of the May Day stay-away, and in some areas exceeded it (see Table 8.1). Again support was strongest in organised factories, but there was a poor response at the mines as NUM sought to conserve its energies for its impending wage negotiations. In Cape Town the response, although still low, almost doubled the May figure.[52]

Table 8.1 Responses to calls for stay-aways and on-site stoppages, 1982–1987

Area	1982 Aggett stoppages	1984 November stay-away	1985 Raditsela stoppages	1985 March stay-away
PWV region, Transvaal:				
Overall response	30,000	60%	55,000	
Eastern Cape:	35,000		17,500	
Port Elizabeth				
Coloured workers				0
African workers				90–99.5%
Uitenhage:				
Coloured workers				16%
African workers				97%
Natal:				
All areas	17,560		20,500	
Durban/Pinetown			17,270	
Western Cape:				
Overall response	12,400			
Coloured workers				
African workers				
Total	101,460	3–800,000	100,000	120,000

Notes: Figures given for stay-aways are calculated as percentages of the workforce in each region. The figures given for stoppages are estimates of the number of workers involved.
Sources: Brooks and Brickhill 1980, pp.208, 214, 229, 230–2; Joffe 1986, pp.1, 5, 8, 17; Lambert and Lambert, 1983, p.228; *South African Labour Bulletin*, Vol.10, No.7, June 1985, p.8; LMG (Natal), Jul/Aug 1985, p.95; LMG Sept 1985c, pp.108–9; LMG May 1985a, p.74; LMG June/Jul 1986a, pp.78–9, 80–1; LMG Aug 1986b, pp.96, 103; LMG Jul 1987, pp.53, 55; LMG Sept 1988, pp.67–8.

1986 May Day	1986 16 June	1987 May, white elections	1987 16 June	1988 6–8 June
79%	85%	70%	75%	77%
45%		35%	22%	39%
99.9%	99.5%	96–99%	99%	78%
79%		70%	77%	82%
99.8%	99.5%	96–99%	99%	93%
60.4%	na	70%	46%	77%
15%	39%	42%	40%	na
8%	26%	42%	30%	na
51%	78%	76%	75%	na
1,500,000	1,500,000	1,050,000	na	2–3,000,000

Emergency restrictions had made it virtually impossible for any organisations, including the unions, to publicly mobilise for the stay-away. Monitoring groups had put at thousands the number of those who avoided detention or arrest by going underground. Emergency regulations prevented these activists and officers of hundreds of organisations from holding meetings or even issuing statements. The massive public response in spite of these conditions showed that commemoration of the day had become deeply ingrained in popular culture.[53]

In addition to these national actions there continued to be regional stay-aways. In one of the most sustained, the workforce of the Transvaal mining centre, Witbank, stayed away from work for a week to protest at house-to-house raids by troops and police and the detentions of local activists.

The strong responses to two major stay-at-homes the following year, 1987, testified to their revival as a tactic of resistance. There were no actions around May Day. The government sought to pre-empt organisation around the issue by declaring the first Friday in May (falling in 1987 on 1 May) as a new annual public holiday to be known as 'Workers Day'. Unions and political organisations scorned the move: 'This simply means that the workers' struggle for the 1st of May – and not any other day – to be declared a Workers' Day will continue with even more vigour.'[54]

The union movement instead conserved its energies for a national stay-at-home on 5 and 6 May to protest at the holding of a whites-only parliamentary election, and to restate the broad demands of political organisations and trade unions. Upwards of half a million workers stayed away across the country. The protest gained impetus, especially in the PWV region, from the mass dismissals of striking rail workers, the police siege of COSATU House and evictions of rent boycotters in Soweto (see Chapter 7 above). The stay-away was a strategic advance over the national stay-aways which had gone before – it was sustained over two days with more workers responding on the second day than on the first. Many schools and universities were also closed. Once again the centre was in organised factories, following very closely the patterns of 1986 (see Table 12).

The 16 June anniversary was again commemorated in 1987 by trade unions and political organisations, with unions continuing to press for the day to be a holiday. In fact many COSATU affiliates had succeeded the previous year in negotiating with individual employers for 16 June to be a paid holiday, in some cases in lieu of another holiday in the calendar.[55]

Rent boycotts

In the second quarter of 1986 rent boycotts were revived on a national scale as the main form of popular opposition to apartheid. In some areas, notably the East Rand and the Vaal Triangle, they had continued unabated since September 1984. In 1986 they spread to other areas, both as a form of protest at continuing rent increases by financially bankrupt councils, and increasingly to back up broad political demands: the lifting of the State of Emergency, the withdrawal of troops from the townships, the release of detainees and political prisoners and improvements in conditions and services.

The boycotts were widely and often spontaneously supported, largely because after four years of rising inflation most residents were simply unable to afford higher rents. They proved a highly effective form of resistance in the repressive climate which followed the second State of Emergency, in which public forms of organisation were even more circumscribed than before.

Forty-eight townships were involved in the boycotts, centred on the PWV area, and towards the end of the year a further six townships were drawn in.[56] The boycotts were organised by a range of organisations including civic and youth organisations, but increasingly by street and area committees. In the Vaal Triangle, on the East Rand and some areas of Pretoria and Soweto, local shop-stewards councils also played leading roles.

In most areas boycotts were supported by more than 60 per cent of residents. By August 1986 the government had accumulated a deficit of an estimated R250 million since September 1984. R30 million was being added to the debt every month. By November, 41 community and town councils had collapsed financially, further compounding the crisis facing local authorities in the African townships.[57]

The state responded by detaining activists identified with the boycotts. In some areas electricity and water was cut off and evictions of selected residents took place. In Huhudi, Tumahole and Soweto, political activists were initially singled out for eviction. In August 1986 in White City, Soweto, at least 24 people were killed and over 100 injured as residents resisted attempts by municipal police to evict tenants. A similar clash took place in Orlando in November, when a further six people were shot dead, as police moved in to cut off electricity supplies.[58]

Rent boycotts continued in many parts of the country. In 1988, 50 townships were still affected by boycotts involving half a million dwellings, concentrated in the PWV region where early in the year arrears had mounted to over R300 million.[59] A second attempt in late 1987 by the government to introduce a bill which would force employers to deduct arrears from the wages of their employees was shelved during 1988 in the face of renewed opposition by COSATU and employers who feared shopfloor protests.

A more systematic strategy was adopted by the government to end the boycotts in the run-up to local authority elections in October 1988. Evictions and the cutting off of electricity continued in the PWV area. There was a renewed drive to sell off council housing; in some instances members of the South Africa Defence Force (SADF) were deployed to promote sales. Revisions to the State of Emergency regulations in February effectively banned several community organisations involved in the boycotts in the Vaal Triangle and Soweto, and restrictions on COSATU prohibited the federation from calling for or involving itself in rent boycotts.[60]

Towards the end of the year, the government claimed that the boycotts were declining nationally and were taking place only in Soweto and on the West Rand. It also claimed that more than a third of council housing had been sold off to tenants since the policy had been initiated in 1985.[61]

At the same time, tenants won some victories. In December 1988 the Soweto Council undertook to halt evictions and raids and, prompted by the continuing strength of the boycott and an unfavourable court ruling which brought into question its right to collect rent from certain houses in Soweto, decided to write off local rent arrears, amounting by then to R167 million. Residents of four townships in the Eastern Transvaal also won victories from local authorities, calling off rent boycotts in exchange for a reduction in rents. In some other areas, however, boycotts were still taking place as the decade closed.[62]

Consumer boycotts

Consumer boycotts emerged as a major tactic of resistance in the 1984–6 uprising, but they had been used before. A boycott of potatoes was initiated in the late 1950s to protest at the conditions in which prisoners were deployed as farm labour in the Bethal area of the Transvaal. Boycotts of businesses owned by sympathisers of the ruling National Party were also organised in response to the introduction of new apartheid laws in the 1950s. 'Black Christmases' were a feature of more recent periods of resistance, where to mourn those killed in police repression, township residents refrained from Christmas festivities and shopping.

Selective consumer boycotts were, as we have seen, also used during the revival of the trade union movement, to back up the demands of workers in labour disputes. In the 1984–6 uprising, however, boycotts were aimed at white-owned shops in support of local and often national demands such as the lifting of the State of Emergency. Although their impact varied, they proved a powerful form of resistance in centres where there was strong community organisation. With repression of all public forms of protest after July 1985, they were one of the few means of expressing resistance: 'It didn't require ordinary people to make themselves physically conspicuous or even to go into the streets more than they otherwise would.'[63]

In some areas the boycotts were also used in the campaign against community councils. Shops owned by community councillors were specially targeted. However, those aimed at white businesses were the most effective and proved a successful way of exploiting the tensions which arose within the white ruling group as resistance increased. Local chambers of commerce were forced to take up the demands of the communities involved with the central government.

The boycotts centred around many demands. In Tumahole (Parys) and Potchefstroom they were linked to calls for the reinstatement of local workers who had been dismissed for attending a funeral and others who had gone on strike. In most other areas they centred around conditions of housing, roads and services in townships, calls for the release of local detainees, and national demands including those arising from the schools boycotts, the lifting of the State of Emergency, the withdrawal of police and troops from the townships and the lifting of the bans on proscribed organisations.[64] In most areas local chambers of commerce could negotiate about local grievances, but were forced to take national demands to central government. In August 1985, 80 representatives of local chambers of commerce from around the country met and urged the government to concede to demands.

There were several phases to the boycotts. They were initiated in small towns in the Eastern Cape in the first half of 1985, where they were publicised at mass funerals. In July they spread to Port Elizabeth and later to East London. In the face of strong community support and a swift impact on business, local business leaders sought out community leaders in an attempt to start negotiations.

When the boycotts began, chain stores dependent on a largely black clientele were reporting falls in sales of up to 90 per cent. By August the boycott in Port Elizabeth was causing reductions of turnover in the main business district of between 30 and 100 per cent and smaller shops were being forced to close. The pattern was repeated in other parts of the Eastern Cape and the Border region.[65]

During 1985 consumer boycotts spread to the Western Cape, the East Rand area and later to Pretoria and Natal. In Pretoria supermarket sales were down by 40 per cent, and on the Reef trade unions reported reductions in business of between 40 and 60 per cent. A decision by FOSATU unions in August 1985 to throw their weight behind the boycotts strengthened them, particularly in the Reef area, where repression and detention of organisers had weakened their impact. In most regions community organisations played a leading role in organising the boycotts, but FOSATU unions took the lead in Natal.

Towards the end of September 1985, boycotts were called off in several smaller towns in the Eastern Cape and Natal either because they could no longer be sustained or because negotiations had ensued with local businesses and some concessions had been won. They continued in the major urban centres. In Port Elizabeth in particular local businesses continued to be severely affected. In response to pressure from the local chamber of commerce, 17 detainees from UDF-affiliated organisations were released in November and the boycott was suspended to allow for negotiations.[66]

The state tried to crush the boycotts by detaining activists and forcibly closing alternative retail outlets such as black-owned shops in townships. In Fort Beaufort and Tembisa, police detained local black business people, forcing their township outlets to close. In Colesberg the local authority cut off the township's water supply in retaliation for the boycott. In some smaller townships the lack of black-owned shopping outlets forced organisers to target only the larger retail outlets and supermarkets in the central business districts, leaving shoppers free to buy in outlying suburbs.[67]

The tactics used in the boycotts were regionally determined and there was no evidence of national co-ordination and harmonisation of demands as campaigns proceeded from area to area. Many boycotts continued well into 1986 when, as repression was stepped up after the imposition of the second State of Emergency in July, support began to dissipate.

In the national local authority elections in October 1988, white voters in several Transvaal and Orange Free State towns elected the far-right Conservative Party to run municipalities. The party reversed a relaxation in segregation of local amenities, notably public parks and recreational facilities. In Carletonville, Boksburg and Witbank this prompted a new rash of consumer boycotts by the residents of the adjacent African and Coloured townships. NUM shop stewards played a leading role in the organisation of the Witbank boycott. The consumer boycotts led to a repeat of the crisis conditions which had gripped Port Elizabeth and other Eastern Cape towns two years previously, with drastic reductions in retail sales and the collapse of some small businesses.

New forms of organisation
In the course of 1985, community organisations sought ways of extending and consolidating their support which did not rely on open forms of organisation such as public meetings. In some parts of the country, notably the Eastern Cape, street committees began to emerge. Residents of houses in a block of streets would elect representatives to a street committee. As these developed, area committees covering whole townships were formed, composed of delegates from several street committees. The area committees were in turn linked to local civic, student, youth and women's organisations.

In some areas street committees were set up by civic associations or youth groups and in other places they arose spontaneously to defend residents from attacks by police and vigilantes. By the end of 1985 structures along these lines had been created in Mamelodi in Pretoria, Alexandra in Johannesburg, parts of Soweto, and in at least seven Eastern Cape townships. In some areas they were only fragmentary; in others, especially in the Eastern Cape, they were deeply rooted in their communities.

As the leaders of most community organisations were detained or forced underground, street and area committees became the main focus of organisation. They assisted in the organisation of funerals, rent and consumer boycotts and stay-aways. The new structures even took over aspects of the running of township services when community councils collapsed, and in some cases alternative schools and creches were set up.

In Mamelodi in mid-1985, local youth groups had undertaken an 'operation clean up' to rid the area of crime and lawlessness which had arisen as police and other law enforcement agents were driven out of the townships. Campaigns such as these led to the creation of 'people's courts', again on a neighbourhood or area basis, to adjudicate disputes between residents, judge criminal activity and enforce political discipline.[68] In some areas, again particularly in the Eastern Cape, defence units were formed, carrying out attacks on police patrols and protecting activists from vigilantes and police.

The growth of street and area committees helped foster a closer relationship between shopfloor and community organisation. Their structures, methods of work and practices of seeking mandates from residents were close to those of trade unions and such developments displaced some of the doubts industrial unions had expressed about the accountability of the political leadership. The new structures also strengthened the working-class base of community organisations by rooting them in the areas where workers lived. They reflected too the leading roles played by shop stewards in setting up street committees in some areas, notably parts of Pretoria, Alexandra, parts of Soweto, the East Rand and the Vaal Triangle.

Unions and community organisations tried to forge formal links in some areas. The Springs shop-stewards' local, for example, provided for local youth bodies to send delegates to their meetings. In Phomolong, Harrismith, youth executive members of the local civic association stepped down in favour of union members in an effort to tie the organisation to the unions.[69]

One of the major objectives of the second State of Emergency, in June 1986, was to crush these new structures, especially in the Eastern Cape, where UDF affiliates and alternative structures ran townships; they reverted to government control only for the brief periods when police or army patrols entered the area. During the second emergency detentions were far more wide-ranging and aimed at pulling in those involved in the committees. Whereas in the first State of Emergency some 8,000 people were held, in the year following the declaration of the second, repression was far more extensive. Although precise figures are difficult to obtain, it was estimated that up to 26,000 people, including many leading activists and members of street committees, were detained. Shop-stewards' locals in some areas, and in some cases entire regional structures of COSATU, were swept up, notably in Brits, Empangeni, Howick, Harrismith and Kimberley. In the first month of the 1986 emergency, 224 trade unionists were held; by December the same year, 2,700 trade unionists had been reported held under the State of Emergency regulations.[70]

The impact of the repression was immediately discernible. A COSATU call for a stay-away to protest at the detentions met with a very weak response. Structures of communication such as street committees, essential to mobilising shopfloor support, had largely broken down, although they persisted or were rebuilt in some areas.

Political struggle

Repression against political organisations intensified from 1984 on, with the further expansion of armed forces deployed in response to the heightened political mobilisation. Over 80 people were killed by the end of 1984, mostly as a result of police and army actions, and detentions were markedly higher than in previous years. The general ban on outdoor gatherings imposed in 1976 was renewed for a further year and extensive use was also made of powers to ban gatherings in specific areas. In the ensuing years there was further deployment of armed forces, detentions rose even higher, and emergency powers were used to supplement the powers to ban meetings.[71]

Thus repression had a major impact on the political role of the trade union movement, but its organised strength and its role in production allowed it to escape some of the force of the emergency powers. Furthermore the Public Safety Act used to declare a State of Emergency prevented emergency restrictions being used to override certain rights under industrial relations legislation. In practice this meant that collective bargaining procedures during negotiated settlements between unions and management were not restricted under clauses relating to 'illegal' meetings and subversive statements under the Security Acts. The Public Safety Act of 1953 forbade the making of any regulations whereby 'any action relating to a matter dealt with under the Industrial Conciliation Act 1937 ... is rendered unlawful'. The Labour Relations Acts which followed the Wiehahn recommendations in 1979 maintained this fundamental clause.

Such factors left the trade union movement with relatively more space in which to operate than the political and community organisations. At the local level, when other organisations were prevented from holding meetings, shop-stewards locals were able to do so. And in 1988, when anti-apartheid organisations were prohibited from carrying on 'any activities whatsoever', COSATU was prohibited only from engaging in 'political' activities. COSATU was able to use this space to act as a national forum for the co-ordination and mobilisation of protests and the building of a broad coalition of anti-apartheid forces.[72]

Towards a coalition of anti-apartheid forces
However, a new phase in the state's counter-offensive against the increasingly militant union movement opened with the bombing and complete destruction of COSATU House in the early hours of 7 May 1987, in the wake of the May stay-away protesting at the whites-only election. In the next three months COSATU regional offices were the targets of arson or vandalism in Cape Town, Germiston, East London and Nelspruit.[73]

Up and down the country there was a wave of action against unions. There were further detentions of union members and officials, vigilante and police attacks on union activists, further bombings, arson attacks, burglaries, raids on and evictions from union offices and bans on union meetings. There was also an orchestrated smear campaign against COSATU, intended, union officials feared, to create a climate for further restrictions on the federation.[74]

In February 1988 the government effectively banned the most prominent legal anti-apartheid organisations, including the UDF and the principal youth, student and civic associations. The organisations were prohibited from 'carrying out or performing any activities whatsoever'. In a separate schedule of restrictions COSATU's political role was circumscribed. It was prevented from calling rent boycotts, opposing forced removals, advocating sanctions or other forms of pressure against the government, opposing local authorities, calling for boycotts of municipal elections or involving itself with the formation of 'alternative structures'. The federation was virtually confined to a shopfloor role.[75] These measures took place against the backdrop of the Labour Relations Amendment Bill, which aimed to dampen down shopfloor militancy and claw back terrain won in the worker struggles of the previous decade (see Chapter 6 above).

The accumulation of these pressures had a crippling impact on the union movement. In an assessment in early 1988 the COSATU Central Executive Committee highlighted the demoralisation of the federation. It noted that 'the truth is that only the Highveld and Western Cape function as active regions – the majority of regions are paralysed'.[76] The leadership called a special conference for 14 May, aimed at reviving the federation and hammering out a response to the Labour Relations Amendment Bill and the February restrictions. In a wider sense the conference would also be an occasion to weigh the strategic and tactical options facing anti-apartheid opposition.

The 1,500 delegates endorsed a call for a national three-day stay-away to protest at the bill and the February restrictions, to be followed by stoppages and other activity at shopfloor level. The conference also adopted a resolution committing COSATU to building a broad anti-apartheid alliance which would go beyond its traditional allies, the UDF and its youth, women's and civic affiliates. The alliance would aim to draw in organisations subscribing to the black consciousness philosophy as well as white liberal groups, organisations in the business sector and those in the bantustans. The decision was, in the words of one commentary, 'the first major strategic advance in the opposition since P. W. Botha's government launched its political counter-offensive to the rising tide of opposition on June 12 1986', when the national State of Emergency was imposed.[77]

Background to the May special conference
COSATU had in fact sought to build alliances with political organisations since its formation in November 1985, both at local level and nationally. Shortly after its founding Congress COSATU held formal consultations with the UDF and other national political organisations such as the National Education Crisis Committee (NECC). The propulsion of COSATU into the frontline of resistance over the next two years had further shaped its approach to alliances. Its second conference in July 1987 resolved that, while it would still not affiliate to any political organisation, it would establish disciplined alliances with community organisations which were 'mass-based, democratic and non-racial [with] a proven record of struggle, and principles compatible with COSATU'.[78]

COSATU developed close relationships with the larger national youth affiliates of the UDF, drawing on links formed during the school boycotts of 1985 and 1986. In organisational terms some local structures forged closer links with community organisations by, for example, allowing representatives of civic associations observer status within union bodies in some areas. Efforts were also made to develop COSATU's links with rural areas through the Northern Transvaal People's Congress.[79] At the May 1988 special conference itself 120 representatives of UDF affiliates, church and sports organisations attended with full speaking rights.[80] On the ground, distinctions between unions and community organisations had become increasingly blurred as COSATU was compelled to take on the mantle of restricted political organisations.

Although the formation of COSATU had brought about a degree of ideological homogeneity and sectoral unity – 33 unions merged into 14 over a two-and-a-half year period – within a formerly disparate union movement there were still often debilitating differences in the federation. The old divisions between the industrial and general unions had given way to a far more complex range of positions between and within unions. The debate was no longer about whether or not alliances were in the interests of the working class, but what form such alliances should take and the place of worker interests within the broader struggle against apartheid.

That these debates could be acrimonious was evidenced by a split in NUTW in 1986 when its Hammarsdale and Eastern Province branches broke away to form a rival union, the Textile and Allied Workers Union (TAWU). Differences over the extent and nature of NUTW's political role featured prominently in the split.[81] Similarly the 1987 split between the Johannesburg branches of CCAWUSA and those in other parts of the country was occasioned in part by differences in political perspectives. In a statement in February 1988, which preceded the special conference, COSATU's leadership was at pains to point out that 'the differences between our leadership and between some of our affiliates are paralysing our organisation'.[82]

The May special conference was charged, therefore, with the task not only of devising strategies to counter state repression and advance resistance, but of drawing together the diverse strands in the federation in a single response. Discussion at the conference centred on assessments of the strength of the state and its degree of success in repressing resistance; on whether the union movement should retreat into what legal space remained and rebuild from the shopfloor; on whether and how to consolidate and extend wider resistance.

After lengthy debate the conference adopted a position which recognised the damage done to anti-apartheid forces, but concluded that 'while the state was strong and ... has reserves of power ... it has its own weaknesses. Congress was unified on the need to engage those weaknesses so as to undermine its strength and drain its reserves.'[83]

On the question of alliances, debate hinged around whether COSATU should seek allies beyond those stipulated in the resolution of its second Congress in 1987. A resolution which merged elements of previous positions was brokered by key affiliates. The conference decided to convene a committee consisting of the COSATU executive and its existing allies as defined in COSATU's political policy, to develop a programme of action against repression and to convene a conference of a broad range of organisations to discuss repression and ways of responding to it.[84]

As an observer commented, the resolution implicitly recognised 'the centrality of COSATU's united front with its "proven allies" and placed the united front "at the core of a broad anti-apartheid alliance"'.[85] More importantly, the Congress achieved unity

> between affiliates with political differences. The common threats and problems faced by all workers and all affiliates no doubt contributed to the drive for unity ... There is a new political maturity in the federation, a recognition that the costs of division are too high.[86]

The stay-away on 6–8 June to protest at the February restrictions and the Labour Relations Amendment Bill was the largest ever, involving between 2.5–3 million workers and spanning three days – the first national stay-away to last so long (see also Table 8.1). Stay-away rates reflected previous patterns, with upwards of 72 per cent observing the call in the PWV area and high levels consistent with previous protests in the Eastern Cape. In Natal between 72 and 80 per cent of workers observed the call, the best response, yet recorded. Only in the Western Cape, as previously, was there a low-key response except in the food and construction sectors where COSATU affiliates had a strong presence. At the mines, where NUM was recovering from the 1987 strike and conserving its strength for the annual wage negotiations, there were also low turn-outs.[87]

The stay-away was a stepping stone in building the broader unity called for at the special conference. The protest was endorsed by a NACTU national shop-stewards' council, and NACTU–COSATU co-operation at federation level was the closest since CUSA's withdrawal from the unity talks three years previously. The stay-away was also supported by churches and black business organisations such as the National African Federated Chamber of Commerce (NAFCOC), the Black Management Forum and taxi owners.[88]

In September 1988 the government banned the conference of anti-apartheid organisations which COSATU had spent months organising.

The Conference for a Democratic Future

But the groundwork for this conference constituted the basis for the holding in December 1989 of the Conference for a Democratic Future organised by the principal opposition organisations, the UDF, NECC and COSATU. The conference took place against the backdrop of a revival of anti-apartheid resistance across the country.

In the first half of the year detainees in jails across the country engaged in a co-ordinated series of successful hunger strikes which forced the government to release most of those it was holding. The hunger strikes stimulated the launch in the second half of the year of the Defiance Campaign, which involved thousands in defiance of segregated facilities and the emergency restrictions; organisations restricted in February 1988 'unbanned' themselves and began functioning openly. These developments acted to consolidate the alliance between COSATU and the major anti-apartheid organisations which acted increasingly in concert with each other under the banner of the 'Mass Democratic Movement'.

A key component of the Defiance Campaign was a stay-away on 6 and 7 September to protest at the holding of elections for the segregated parliament. With 2–3 million workers observing the call it was again one of the largest such actions to date, and in Coloured and Indian areas there was once again a substantial boycott of the polls.

A further thread running through the Defiance Campaign was trade union resistance to the Labour Relations Amendment Act (LRAA). Although the Act had become law in 1988, the March 1989 summit and a later summit in August to plan action against the Act broadened union unity. National and regional anti-LRAA committees were set up. Plans adopted at the August summit jointly held by COSATU and NACTU included an overtime ban – which began in September and was still in force at the end of the year – and a consumer boycott. Although the campaign was initially planned independently of the Defiance Campaign, it contributed to the momentum of the latter in the form of a series of marches which took place in 17 centres in October, involving upwards of 150,000 people. The culmination of the campaign, these marches were organised behind a series of demands, including calls for the scrapping of the LRAA.

Responding to a range of pressures the government indicated that it might be prepared to negotiate a future constitution with representative opposition groupings. These pressures included the stagnation of the economy in the face of international sanctions, the withdrawal of investment and the protracted political instability since the late 1970s, the defeat of the SADF in Angola and the independence of Namibia, and finally the government's inability to enforce the State of Emergency regulations in the face of mass defiance.

The resignation of the incumbent State President, P.W. Botha, and his replacement by former Minister of Education and Training F.W. De Klerk, brought a change of style and tactics aimed at securing the long-term interests of the white minority and defusing resistance, including the relaxation of restrictions on some meetings and marches, and the release of key political prisoners. Organisations made use of the newly won space to revive resistance, notably in the form of mass marches and demonstrations in support of the ANC and to consolidate structures unbanned during the Defiance Campaign.

The ANC's position on the question of negotiations was adopted in the Organisation of African Unity's Harare Declaration. It stipulated a number of steps which the government would have to take in order to create a climate conducive to genuine negotiations. These included the unbanning of the ANC, the lifting of the State of Emergency and the release of political prisoners.

The Conference for a Democratic Future was held against this background drawing, together the widest ever grouping of forces opposed to apartheid. These included black consciousness organisations, members of churches, groups of white liberals, representatives from the bantustans and black business – as well as COSATU's traditional allies, the UDF, the NECC, and associated youth structures. The conference endorsed the Harare Declaration, so uniting a broad range of anti-apartheid organisations behind common demands.

The conference occasioned a split within NACTU, with several affiliates defying federation policy and identifying with the alliance which emerged from the event.

Conclusion

The formation of COSATU, then, had a far-reaching impact on the shape of resistance politics. It brought greater political and ideological cohesion to a formerly disparate trade union movement. Even where potentially divisive differences developed it proved itself – in the context of increased repression – able to forge positions which united its affiliates, and it initiated new phases of resistance. A consensus had been reached with the ANC about the independence of unions from political organisations. The sharp divisions which polarised the union movement prior to 1985 gave way to more uniform political perspectives in which there was broader agreement on the need for alliances with the community and for unions to take up political issues.

It was on this basis that there were advances in the political role of the union movement – in the shopfloor stoppages in support of political issues, in the role of shop stewards in shaping community responses to repression, in the massive worker stay-aways between 1984 and 1989, and finally in the initiatives taken by the unions themselves in the building of a wider coalition of anti-apartheid forces.

But the uprising of 1984–6, while stimulating the unions' political role, also demonstrated the limitations of unions in involving the working class in broader struggle. The lack of support for the BRT Sarmcol strikers by Indian workers, many still members of conservative unions, and similar restraints among Coloured workers in the Western Cape in the stay-aways between 1986 and 1989, showed that, in spite of past achievements, much work still needed to be done in building solidarity across apartheid divisions. The lack of support for the November 1984 stay-away and subsequently in the PWV among commuters from the Bophuthatswana bantustan, and a similar lack of response inside the bantustans, demonstrated the difficulty unions experienced in organising in these areas in the early 1980s.[89] At the same time rising levels of unemployment placed larger groups of workers out of reach of the union movement or led to rapid turnovers in union membership.

Community organisations filled some of the gaps in worker organisation to an extent. Unlike trade unions, however, community organisations had difficulty in building durable structures which could sustain the involvement of their constituencies beyond specific campaigns, and survive repression. Pupils and youth were the main forces behind protests after 1984, and it proved more difficult to involve older working residents on a permanent basis. However, the development of street committees expanded the working-class base of community organisations and their alliance with shop-stewards' locals proved a potentially powerful catalyst in deepening organisation and expanding resistance. The second State of Emergency largely halted this process.

Nevertheless the roots of community organisation were not destroyed. Even after years of emergency rule, resistance was 'characterised by a high level of (often informal) organisation and political consciousness at the local level, in some ways independent of formal national structures, and also able to survive a high level of repression'.[90] Thus in March 1988, after three years of continuing and intense repression, there was a stay-away involving up to 70 per cent of the PWV workforce to mark the anniversary of the Sharpeville massacre, despite the fact that neither trade unions nor community organisations formally issued a call for such a response. And participation in the 6–8 June stay-away of that year exceeded the combined membership of COSATU and NACTU, suggesting much wider community mobilisation than that mustered by the unions alone.

Postscript

The reforms of February 1990, with their unbanning of the ANC and other proscribed organisations, the release of political prisoners, the return of exiles and the start of negotiations to end white minority rule altered the political landscape in South Africa. For the first time in three centuries a more equitable dispensation was in prospect. In the course of the next two years key apartheid legislation was repealed, security laws were overhauled and the government began allocating greater resources to the long-neglected areas of education, housing and health.

The bleak prognosis of the late 1980s, with the trade union movement on the defensive and political organisations embattled, gave way to a more optimistic scenario. The trade union movement, for example, was, in the more open political climate, able to negotiate the repeal of the more restrictive clauses of the Labour Relations Amendment Act and win back terrain on the shopfloor. It mobilised its members in shows of force to back up the demands of the ANC at the negotiating table. Political organisations were able to regroup. In many areas of the country community organisations began negotiating more equitable distribution of resources for housing and services and a role in local government. The bantustan hierarchies began to crumble.

But cautious optimism was tempered by more sinister developments. The country was gripped by escalating political violence with a death toll in the thousands, most of the violence between supporters of the ANC and the Inkatha movement. Its roots lay in a complexity of causes, but could in part be traced back to the contest for trade union membership between UWUSA and COSATU in the mid-1980s, absorbed in the 1990s into a wider conflict between political groupings seeking to strengthen their hand in negotiations. The nature of the conflict was informed by the divisions inherited from the apartheid era. Inkatha-supporting contract workers operating from single-sex hostels clashed with township dwellers, many supportive of the ANC. Residents of squatter camps in several parts of the country were swept up in the violence, with competition over the scarce resources of housing, employment and water underpinning political allegiances.

A convincing body of evidence, collected by human rights groups and the independent media, indicated that a third force, with possible links to the security forces, was fomenting the violence, by supplying arms to contending groups and instigating attacks. They were also allegedly involved in random attacks on train commuters. The apparent aim of the third force was to destabilise negotiations and to weaken the organisation of progressive groupings. There were also recurring allegations of security force partiality to the Inkatha movement at the expense of the ANC.

At the same time the repeal of racially discriminatory legislation failed to provide compensation for the victims of apartheid and left intact the economic relations moulded by decades of apartheid social engineering. The repeal of the Land Acts and the Group Areas Act, for example, while abolishing racially exclusive ownership of land and housing, provided no recompense or aid to people dispossessed by forced removals. It preserved freehold tenure as the primary form of land ownership. There was little further reform of labour relations legislation or laws on wages and employment practice. In particular there were no early moves to provide legal protection to farm workers.

Without active measures to compensate those disadvantaged by apartheid the social relations inherited from apartheid appeared likely to remain for some time, possibly generations, to come. Even where the government moved to allocate greater resources to housing, education and health, the new resources were minuscule compared to the enormity of the accumulated backlog. In reallocating resources, a post-apartheid government was in addition likely to be constrained by continued recession, a severe shortage of essential skills in the labour force, flight of investment capital, high unemployment and little prospect of renewed economic growth. Improvement of conditions would rely largely on the independent initiatives of individual communities co-ordinated by community organisations. International development aid and attracting foreign investment capital were set to be priorities.

Thus while the reforms of the 1990s signalled the end of formal apartheid, substantive change was inhibited by the skewed social relations inherited from apartheid. The conditions described in the first part of this book persist in large measure even where the legislation enforcing them has been repealed. They constitute apartheid's formidable legacy and the ground from which a post-apartheid dispensation has yet to move.

APPENDIX

Appendix

Trade unions affiliated to COSATU and NACTU

Name of union	Acronym	Founded
CONGRESS OF SA TRADE UNIONS	COSATU	1985
Former FOSATU affiliates:		
Chemical Workers Industrial Union	CWIU	1974
Metal and Allied Workers Union	MAWU	1973
National Automobile and Allied Workers Union – an amalgamation, in 1980, of:	NAAWU	1980
Western Province Motor Assembly Workers Union, and	WPMAWU	1963
National Union of Motor Assembly and Rubber Workers of SA, and	NUMARWOSA	1967
United Union of Automobile, Rubber and Allied Workers of SA	UAW	1973
National Union of Textile Workers	NUTW	1973
Paper, Wood and Allied Workers Union	PWAWU	1974
Sweet, Food and Allied Workers Union	SFAWU	1974
Transport and General Workers Union	TGWU	1973
Independent industrial unions:		
Cape Town Municipal Workers Association	CTMWA	1950
Commercial, Catering and Allied Workers Union of SA	CCAWUSA	1975
Food and Canning Workers Union	FCWU	1941
General Workers Union	GWU	1973
Motor Assembly and Component Workers Union	MACWUSA	1980
Municipal and General Workers Union of SA	MGWUSA	1982
Retail and Allied Workers Union	RAWU	1983
SA Domestic Workers Association	SADWA	1981
SA Mineworkers Union	SAMWU	1983
SA Railway and Harbour Workers Union	SARHWU	1984
SA Scooter, Transport and Allied Workers Union		1981
SA Textile and Allied Workers Union	SATWU	1984
SA Tin Workers Union		1937
United Metal, Mining and Allied Workers Union	UMMAWUSA	1984
Former CUSA affiliates:		
National Union of Mineworkers	NUM	1982
General unions:		
General Workers Union of SA	GWUSA	1981
General and Allied Workers Union	GAWU	1981
National Federation of Workers	NFW	1980
National General Workers Union and the Retail and Allied Workers Union (Pta)	NGWU	1984
SA Allied Workers Union	SAAWU	1978

Appendix 253

Sectors	Branches
Chems/plastic/rubber/glass/petrol/coal prods	T1/SN1/NN1/EP1
Engineering/electronic equip/metals/cables/motor	T1/SN1/NN1/EP1
Motor assem/tyre/rubber/batteries/bulbs/carpets	T1/EC1/N1/WC1
Textiles/knitting/clothing/leather goods	N4/T1/EP1/WC1
Paper & pulp/printing/packaging/sawmills/furniture	T1/NN1/SN1/WC1
Sugar mills/bakeries/dairies/brewing/sweets	T1/NN1/SN1/EP1
Bus & truck drivers/SATS/stevedores/local govt/ cleaning/security guard	T1/SN1/NN1/EC1
Local govt	WC
Catering and retail trades	N3/T4/OV2/EC2/WC1
Agricultural co-ops/food manufac and canning	WC15/T4/EC3/N1
Stevedores/transport/construc and allied/engin	WC1/N1/EC2
Motor assembly	
Local govt and general	
Dairy employees, (Cape Peninsula)	
Domestic workers and cleaners	T1/WC1/N1/OFS1
Mines	
SATS	
Despatch riders	
Textiles	
Sheet and non-ferrous metals/collapsible tubes	
Mines/metals/motors	
Mines	T1/OFS1/N11/WC1
Chems/leather/retail/building/textiles	
Transport/building/local govt/services/engin	
Food distr/bakeries/dairies/services/skin & hides	
Gen incl food/building/textiles	

continued

Trade unions affiliated to COSATU and NACTU continued

Name of union	Acronym	Founded
NATIONAL COUNCIL OF TRADE UNIONS 1986		
Former CUSA affiliates:		
Brush and Cleaners Workers Union	BCWU	
Building, Construction and Allied Workers Union	BCAWU	1975
Food and Beverage Workers Union	FBWU	1980
National Union of Wine, Spirit and Allied Workers Union	NUWSAWU	1978
SA Chemical Workers Union	SACWU	1972
SA Laundry, Dry Cleaning and Dyeing Workers Union	SALDCDWU	1972
Steel, Engineering and Allied Workers Union of SA	SEAWUSA	1979
Textile Workers Union	TWU	1973
Transport and Allied Workers Union	TAWU	1973
United African Motor and Allied Workers Union		1980
Vukani Guards and Allied Workers Union		1985
Former AZACTU affiliates (industrial):		
Black Allied Mining and Construction Workers Union	BAMCWU	
Black Domestic Workers Union		
Black Electrical and Electronics Workers Union		
Engineering and Allied Workers Union of SA	EAWUSA	
Hotel, Liquor, Catering and Allied Workers Union	HOTELICA	1981
Insurance and Assurance Workers Union of South Africa	IAWUSA	
Former AZACTU affiliates (general):		
African Allied Workers Union	AAWU	1982
Black General Workers Union	BLAGWU	1983
National Union of Workers of SA Workers	NUSAW	

Sources: Star February 1986 (NUM figures); Miller 1982; Lundall *et al.* 1984; *South African Labour Bulletin*, Vol.11, No.3, January 1986, pp.69–89; *South African Labour Bulletin*, Vol.12, No.1, Nov/Dec 1986, p.52.

Appendix

Sectors	Branches
Building & construc/building materials/cement/roads	
Food/dairies/bakeries/cold storage/canning	T5/N1/EC1
Wine and spirit manufacture	
Chems/glass/explosives/rubber/pharmaceut prods	T1/OFS1/N1/WC1
Laundry/dry-cleaning/dyeing	
Steel/engineering/metal containers/plastics	N1/T6
Textiles	
Passenger & goods transport/vehicle ferrying	T1/N1/EC1
	T3/N2/EC1
Security guards	

Key:
EC: Eastern Cape/Border region EP: Eastern Province
N: Natal NN: Northern Natal
OFS: Orange Free State OV: Orange/Vaal area
SN: Southern Natal T: Transvaal
WC: Western Cape

The growth in membership of trade unions affiliated to COSATU and NACTU, 1980–86

Name of union	Initial mem.
CONGRESS OF SA TRADE UNIONS	*449,679
Former FOSATU affiliates:	
Chemical Workers Industrial Union	600
Metal and Allied Workers Union	3,900
National Automobile and Allied Workers	
Union - an amalgamation, in 1980, of:	4,171
Western Province Motor Assembly Workers Union, and	1,130(1970)
National Union of Motor Assembly and	
Rubber Workers of SA, and	
United Union of Automobile, Rubber and	
Allied Workers of SA	590
National Union of Textile Workers	*5,000
Paper, Wood and Allied Workers Union	100
Sweet, Food and Allied Workers Union	400
Transport and General Workers Union	70
Independent industrial unions:	
Cape Town Municipal Workers Association	
Commercial, Catering and Allied Workers Union of SA	261
Food and Canning Workers Union	1,500(1978)
General Workers Union	8,100(1978)
Motor Assembly and Component Workers Union	700
Municipal and General Workers Union of SA	*3,345
Retail and Allied Workers Union	
SA Domestic Workers Association	
SA Mineworkers Union	
SA Railway and Harbour Workers Union	
SA Scooter, Transport and Allied	
Workers Union	
SA Textile and Allied Workers Union	
SA Tin Workers Union	386(1973)
United Metal, Mining and Allied Workers Union	
Former CUSA affiliates:	
National Union of Mineworkers	
General unions:	
General Workers Union of SA	
General and Allied Workers Union	20,620(1983)
National Federation of Workers	
National General Workers Union and the	
Retail and Allied Workers Union (Pta)	
SA Allied Workers Union	16,000

1980	1982	1984	1986(Jan)
*3,000	5,325	13,752	20,700
*8,400	16,900	35,870	36,789
*4,500	18,390	20,257	20,338
*1,250			
*4,000			
*8,300	11,880	21,408	23,241
*3,000	5,800	11,430	11,856
*2,000	6,000	12,255	19,596
*4,500	6,050	7,330	11,000
	*10,724	10,445(1983)	11,097
7,000	*21,600	33,000	50,345
*10,000		*10,000	26,455
*13,300		8,400(1983)	10,000
*70			3,100
*3,345		6,217(1983)	9,249
			3,830
		*4,000(1983)	4,500
		*6,000	3,029
			8,220
		*2,500	4,700
			1,900
450		*800	581
			8,335
	*40,000	60,000(1983)	100,000
			2,205
			19,076
			11,551
	*4,000		6,057
*75,034	*95,000		25,032

continued

The growth in membership of trade unions affiliated to COSATU and NACTU, 1980–86 continued

Name of union	Initial mem.
NATIONAL COUNCIL OF TRADE UNIONS 1986	
Former CUSA affiliates:	
Brush and Cleaners Workers Union	
Building, Construction and Allied Workers Union	250
Food and Beverage Workers Union	
National Union of Wine, Spirit and Allied Workers Union	
SA Chemical Workers Union	600
SA Laundry, Dry Cleaning and Dyeing Workers Union	200
Steel, Engineering and Allied Workers Union of SA	
Textile Workers Union	
Transport and Allied Workers Union	300
United African Motor and Allied Workers Union	
Vukani Guards and Allied Workers Union	
Former AZACTU affiliates (industrial):	
Black Allied Mining and Construction Workers Union	
Black Domestic Workers Union	
Black Electrical and Electronics Workers Union	
Engineering and Allied Workers Union of SA	
Hotel, Liquor, Catering and Allied Workers Union	*2,300
Insurance and Assurance Workers Union of South Africa	
Former AZACTU affiliates (general):	
African Allied Workers Union	4,864(1983)
Black General Workers Union	
National Union of Workers of SA Workers	

Sources: Star February 1986 (NUM figures); Miller 1982; Lundall *et al.* 1984; *South African Labour Bulletin*, Vol.11, No.3, January 1986, pp.69–89; *South African Labour Bulletin*, Vol.12, No.1, Nov/Dec 1986, p.52.

Notes: Obtaining accurate statistics of trade union membership is notoriously difficult. A distinction needs to be made between signed up membership, which is often temporary, and paid-up membership which reflects those members who have paid dues. The latter figure is more accurate. All figures shown in the table above are for paid-up membership. Where this is not the case a * symbol precedes the figure.

1980	1982	1984	1986(Jan)
			*1,600
*5,400	*12,606	*15,900(1983)	*40,774
*6,000(1981)	*9,000	*15,000(1983)	*17,000
	*4,262	*4,326(1983)	*6,000
*9,479	*11,926	*15,000	*45,000
*1,785	3,251	*3,652(1983)	*5,700
*4,507	*17,210	*20,866	*32,382
	*4,000	*2,850(1983)	*2,850
6,248	*7,000	*9,000(1983)	*20,000
200	*4,850	*12,494(1983)	7,963
		135	*1,161
		15,000(1983)	*32,000
			14,000(Dec)
			2,001
	*10,000		3,000(Dec)
	2,696	*10,000	*30,000
		483(1983)	
			3,500(Dec)
		*5,030	7,500(Dec)
			1,500(Dec)

Key:
EC: Eastern Cape/Border region EP: Eastern Province
N: Natal NN: Northern Natal
OFS: Orange Free State OV: Orange/Vaal area
SN: Southern Natal T: Transvaal
WC: Western Cape

Notes and references

Preface

1. IDAF 1983, p.35.
2. *Survey of Race Relations* 1988/9, p.335.
3. *SA Barometer*, Vol.1, No.11, 3 July 1987.
4. *Weekly Mail*, 8 May 1987.
5. South Africa (Republic of) 1984, p.350; Pillay, P. 1985, p.27.
6. *Survey of Race Relations* 1988/9, pp.395–7.

Chapter 1: The labour market

1. Duncan 'The Legal Background' in *Sash*, May 1974, p.4, as quoted by Marchand 1977, p.18.
2. Claasens 1979, pp.54–5.
3. Pretorius *et al* 1986, p.248.
4. *New York Times*, 10 October 1983.
5. Mare 1979, p.44; Bureau for Economic Research, Co-operation and Development 1983, Table 24.
6. Lacey 1984, p.13.
7. *Survey of Race Relations* 1981, p.138.
8. Kraak 1981, p.10.
9. Hartford 1985, p.173.
10. *Financial Mail*, 15 August 1985.
11. *Survey of Race Relations* 1983, p.263.
12. *Star*, 18 April 1984.
13. *Survey of Race Relations* 1981, p.235; Monamo 1983, p.43.
14. Savage 1986, p.198.
15. West 1982, p.469.
16. IDAF 1983, p.45.
17. Cook 1982, p.22.
18. *Sunday Express*, 14 October 1984.
19. *Financial Mail*, 12 October 1979.
20. Unterhalter 1987, p.28.

21. Zille 1983, p.162–3; Bell 1986, p.282.
22. *Survey of Race Relations* 1981, pp.237–8.
23. *Survey of Race Relations* 1983, p.265.
24. *Sowetan*, 9 February 1984.
25. *Sunday Express*, 14 October 1984.
26. Lacey 1984, p.8.
27. Lacey 1984, p.9.
28. Labour Research Committee 1981, p.64.
29. South Africa (Republic of) 1978, para 4.204(d) and para 4.152(f).
30. Black Sash Johannesburg Advice Office 1980, p.3.
31. Unterhalter 1987, p.28.
32. *Survey of Race Relations* 1983, p.140.
33. *New York Times*, 10 October 1983.
34. *Survey of Race Relations* 1982, p.89.
35. Duncan 1982, p.10.
36. Monamo 1983, p.15.
37. Government official as quoted by Zille 1983, p.164.
38. Lombard 1983, p.131.
39. Hindson 1986, p.32.
40. Lacey 1984, p.12.
41. Budlender 1985, p.6.
42. Cobbett, W. 1987, p.26.
43. *Financial Mail*, 28 June 1985.
44. *Financial Mail*, 16 May 1986; *Summary of World Broadcasts*, 13 May 1986.
45. *Weekly Mail*, 22 January 1988.
46. *Sunday Star*, 5 March 1987; *Weekly Mail*, 10 July 1987; *Survey of Race Relations* 1986, pp.354–5, 1987/8, pp.468–9.
47. *City Press*, 8 October 1989; *Survey of Race Relations*, 1988/9, p.167.
48. *Cape Times*, 7 December 1989.
49. *Quarterly Countdown* No.12, First/Second Quarter 1989, p.33.
50. *Weekly Mail*, 7 June 1986.
51. Budlender 1985, pp.3–4.
52. *New Nation*, 18 August 1989.

Chapter 2: In the countryside

1. Tables 0.1(a) and (b) above; Graaf as cited by Cobbett, M. 1986, pp.11–13.
2. Cobbett, M. 1986, pp.6, 13.

3. Levy 1984, p.17; *Weekly Mail*, 31 January 1986.
4. *Rand Daily Mail*, 6 November 1984; Levy 1984, p.17.
5. Keegan 1983, pp.20–1.
6. Horner 1974, p.26.
7. Farm Labour Project 1982, p.6.
8. Horner 1974 p.26.
9. Lacey 1984, p.9.
10. Lacey 1984, p.9.
11. Lacey 1984, p.9.
12. De Klerk 1984a, p.10; *Star*, 12 March 1984.
13. Federation of South African Trade Unions 1984a, p.6.
14. *Die Burger*, 2 February 1983.
15. Cook 1982, p.20.
16. Cook 1982, p.22.
17. Cook 1982, p.23.
18. Cook 1982, p.26; Levy 1984, p.55; *Star*, 16 June 1986.
19. *Star*, 16 June 1986.
20. *Cape Times*, 2 February 1988.
21. As cited by Levy 1984, p.40.
22. As cited in *Lutheran World Information*, January 1981, p.17.
23. *Cape Times*, 7 January 1983; *South*, 8 June 1989; *Sowetan*, 19 June 1989; *Star* 24 June 1989.
24. *Debates of Parliament*, 22 September 1981.
25. Haysom and Thompson 1984, p.10.
26. Levy 1984, p.5.
27. *Sash*, February 1986, p.7.
28. *Sash*, February 1986, p.9.
29. *Sash*, February 1986, p.9; Catholic Institute for International Relations 1989, pp.1–9.
30. *Drum* as quoted by Levy 1984, p.5.
31. Levy 1984, p.48.
32. Levy 1984, p.42.
33. *Cape Times*, 12 March 1986; *Daily Dispatch*, 20 June 1986.
34. *Bulletin of Statistics*, Vol.2, quarter ended June 1987, Table 2.12; *SA Barometer*, Vol.1, No.2, 27 March 1987.
35. Seleoane 1984, p.4.
36. Farm Labour Project 1982, p.14.
37. *Voice*, 1 April 1981; *Cape Times*, 4 March 1981; *Rand Daily Mail*, 8 March 1981.
38. *AFRA Report Sheet*, No.26.
39. *Weekly Mail* 31 January 1986.

40. Farm Labour Project 1982, p.32; Levy 1984, p.14.
41. *Argus*, 5 May 1976.
42. *Rand Daily Mail*, 21 February 1985.
43. *Rand Daily Mail*, 20 February 1985.
44. *Rand Daily Mail*, 20 May 1985.
45. Farm Labour Project 1982, p.30.
46. Seleoane 1984, p.4.
47. De Klerk 1984b, p.5; *Star*, 1.9.88.
48. *Survey of Race Relations* 1986, p.414; 1987/8, p.162.
49. De Graaff 1988, pp.20–22; *Survey of Race Relations* 1987/8, pp.162–3.
50. *Daily Dispatch*, 7 September 1984.
51. De Klerk 1984a, pp.3–8.
52. *Survey of Race Relations* 1983, pp.159–60.
53. *Financial Mail*, 5 May 1989.
54. *Rand Daily Mail*, 12 September 1980.
55. Yawitch 1981, pp.28–31.
56. Haysom 1983, p.12.
57. *Rand Daily Mail*, 16 April 1982.
58. Roodt 1984, pp.327–8.
59. Streek and Wickstead 1981, p.166.
60. Keenan 1984, pp.323–4.
61. Keenan 1984, p.324.
62. Beinart 1984, p.285.
63. Surplus People Project 1983, p.161.
64. Beinart 1984, p.288; *Financial Mail*, 2 September 1988.
65. Cobbett, M. 1986, p.11.
66. *Business Day*, 6 June 1984.
67. Muller 1984, p.8.
68. Bekker 1984, p.3; Gandar and Bromberger 1984, p.11.
69. Gandar and Bromberger 1984, pp.9–10.
70. Bekker 1984, p.3.
71. Bekker 1984, p.9.
72. Human Awareness Project 1986, p.A4.
73. Wilson 1984, pp.4–5.
74. Gandar and Bromberger 1984, p.10.
75. Simkins 1984, p.7; Nattrass 1984, p.13.
76. *Guardian*, 26 November 1986.
77. *African Labour News*, November 1983; *Sash*, February 1986, p.16.
78. Bekker 1984, p.10; *Weekly Mail*, 15 April 1988.
79. *Cape Times*, 24 June 1980.

80. *Work in Progress*, No.13, July 1980, pp.23–5.
81. *Work in Progress*, No.14, September 1980, p.47.
82. *Work in Progress*, No.26, April 1983, p.50; *Work in Progress*, No.27, June 1983, p.47.
83. *New Nation*, 13 February 1986.
84. *Rand Daily Mail*, 3 March 1982; *Star*, 22 December 1985.
85. Lodge 1983, pp.279–80.
86. Lodge 1983, pp.280–1.
87. Keenan 1988, p.151.
88. Keenan 1984, p.324.
89. Makanjee 1988, p.68.
90. Keenan 1988, p.137.
91. *SASPU National*, April/May 1986.
92. *Star*, 5 May 1986.
93. Makanjee 1988, p.66.
94. Obery 1986, pp.3–11.
95. *Focus*, No.64, May/June 1986, p.1; No.76, May/June 1988, p.3.
96. *Focus*, No.79, November/December 1988, p.5.
97. Makanjee 1988, p.67; *Focus*, No.79, November/December 1988, p.5.

Chapter 3: In the towns and cities

1. Bekker and Humphries 1985, p.59.
2. Smit and Booysen 1981, p.91.
3. Smit and Booysen 1981, pp. 85–7, 111.
4. Smit and Booysen 1981, p.95; Smit *et al* 1982, p.101.
5. Smit and Booysen 1981, p.85.
6. Smit *et al* 1982, p.102.
7. *SASPU National*, Vol.4, No.2, May 1983; Smit and Booysen 1981, p.91.
8. *Financial Mail*, 12 July 1985.
9. *Financial Mail*, 12 July 1985.
10. Seleoane 1985, pp.24–30.
11. *Critical Health*, Nos 16, 17, September 1986, p.63.
12. Seleoane 1985, p.18.
13. *Rand Daily Mail*, 6 January 1978, as cited in *Workers Unity*, No.10, July 1978.
14. Bernstein 1985, p.63.
15. Bekker and Humphries 1985, p.83.
16. *Financial Mail*, 14 March 1986, 26 December 1986; *Star*, 10 April 1987.

17. *Financial Mail*, 14 March 1986; *Business Day*, 6 October 1986.
18. *Star*, 12 August 1986; *Weekly Mail*, 22 May 1987; *Star*, 11 December 1987.
19. *Citizen*, 3 May 1986.
20. *Business Day*, 25 November 1986.
21. *Sunday Tribune*, 7 August 1988.
22. *Daily News*, 10 September 1985; *Star*, 10 September 1985; *Financial Mail*, 14 March 1986; *Sunday Tribune*, 7 August 1988; Smit and Booysen 1981, pp.91–3; Cole 1986, p.33.
23. *Financial Mail*, 27 June 1986.
24. *Financial Mail*, 15 August 1986.
25. *Financial Mail*, 31 May 1985.
26. *Cape Times*, 15 June 1985; *Focus*, No.59, July/August 1985, p.1; *Financial Mail*, 17 April 1985, 14 February 1986.
27. Searll 1984, p.11.
28. *Financial Mail*, 26 December 1986.
29. IDAF 1983, p.55.
30. Corbett 1982, p.191.
31. South African Institute of Race Relations 1986, pp.5–6.
32. South African Institute of Race Relations 1986, pp.4, 9.
33. *Daily News*, 16 April 1986.
34. Witulski 1986, p.13; *Daily News*, 16 April 1986.
35. *Star*, 30 October 1987.
36. *Star*, 3 August 1985.
37. *Weekly Mail*, 7 February 1986.
38. *Star*, 3 August 1985.
39. Swilling 1984, p.48.
40. *Financial Times*, 66 May 1986.
41. *Financial Mail*, 10 May 1985.
42. Lemon 1982, p.86; Smit *et al* 1982, p.103; Mann and Segal 1985, p.2.
43. McCarthy and Swilling 1985, p.29.
44. Mann and Segal 1985, pp.20, 22.
45. *Weekly Mail*, 28 November 1986.
46. Witulski 1986, p.16.
47. Brooks and Brickhill 1980, p.186.
48. *Financial Times*, 6 May 1986.
49. Mann and Segal 1985, p.21.
50. *Survey of Race Relations* 1985, p.227.
51. As cited in Witulski 1986, p.20.
52. *Rand Daily Mail*, 12 April 1985; *Financial Times*, 1 August 1986.

53. Pillay, D. *et al* 1985, Analysis p.8a.
54. *Survey of Race Relations* 1982, p.64.
55. Pillay, D. *et al* 1985, Analysis p.8b.
56. Keenan 1983, p.184.
57. Keenan 1983, p.185; *Survey of Race Relations* 1982, p.66.
58. Keenan 1983, p.185.
59. Keenan 1983, p.185.
60. *Survey of Race Relations* 1987/8, p.290; *South African Reserve Bank, Annual Economic Report* 1986, p.14.
61. *Survey of Race Relations* 1982, pp.60–1; 1983, p.122; *Star*, 30 January 1986.
62. Budlender 1985 p.3.
63. Pillay, D. *et al* 1985, Analysis p.71.
64. Pillay, D. *et al* 1985, SALDRU Wage Rate Index p.28.
65. Pillay, D. *et al* 1985, Analysis p.78.
66. United Nations Organisation 1980, p.6.
67. Cock 1980, pp.7, 30; *Survey of Race Relations* 1980, p.88.
68. *Star*, 15 April 1987.
69. *Financial Mail*, 12 July 1985.
70. *Weekly Mail*, 20 November 1987.
71. *Star*, 3 July 1986.
72. Claasens 1979, p.61.
73. South African Congress of Trade Unions 1980a, p.4.
74. Maree 1978, p.29.
75. Maree 1978, p.28; Keenan 1983, p.189.
76. Maree 1978, p.35.
77. Maree 1978, p.42.
78. *Star*, 3 July 1986.
79. Sarakinsky and Keenan 1986, pp.18–24.
80. Sarakinsky and Keenan 1986, p.23.
81. *Survey of Race Relations* 1982, p.72.
82. *Star*, 12 September 1986.
83. *Star*, 3 October 1985; *Sunday Tribune*, 29 September 1985.
84. *Sunday Tribune*, 19 January 1986; *Star*, 4 October 1986.
85. Hepple 1971, p.39.
86. Maree 1978, p.37.
87. Maree 1978, p.38.
88. Maree 1978, p.37.
89. Maree 1978, p.37.
90. Hepple 1971, p.45.
91. Maree 1978, p.34.

92. Kooy et al 1979, p.17.
93. *Survey of Race Relations* 1983, p.132.
94. *Survey of Race Relations* 1980, p.101; 1987/88, pp.307–8; *Debates of Parliament*, 7 April 1986.
95. Chisholm 1984, p.396.
96. Bot 1988, p.65.
97. Swainson 1989, p.26–7.
98. Bot 1988, pp.II–III.
99. *Survey of Race Relations* 1980, p.107–109; Manzini 1982, p.6.
100. *Survey of Race Relations* 1980, p.93.
101. *Survey of Race Relations* 1987/8, pp.151,165.
102. Chisholm 1984, p.396; *Survey of Race Relations* 1987/8, p.181.
103. Swainson 1989, p.34.
104. Federation of South African Trade Unions 1984b, pp.6–7.
105. Federation of South African Trade Unions 1984b, p.8.
106. Myers and Steinberg 1984, p.146.
107. Adler, T. 1987, pp.94, 96.
108. Cock 1980, p.41.
109. *Survey of Race Relations* 1982, p.125; 1985, p.149.
110. Labour Research Committee 1981, p.69.
111. Barrett et al 1985, pp.54–5.
112. Barrett et al 1985, p.54.
113. *Star*, 3 July 1986.
114. *Critical Health*, No.18, December 1986, p.6.
115. *Critical Health*, No.18, December 1986, p.10.
116. *South African Labour Bulletin*, Vol.9, No.7, June 1984, p.6.
117. Seedat 1984, p.39.
118. Adler, T. 1979, p.62.
119. Seedat 1984, p.40.
120. *South African Labour Bulletin*, Vol.10, No.4, February 1986, p.86.
121. *South African Labour Bulletin*, Vol.11, No.3, January 1986, p.13.
122. As quoted by Green and Miller 1979, pp.36, 38.
123. Adler, T. 1979, p.60.
124. Myers and Steinberg 1983.

Chapter 4: At the mines

1. *Star*, 27 June 1985; *Financial Times*, 6 June 1986.
2. *Bulletin of Statistics*, Vol.20, No.2, Quarter ended June 1986, pp.2.5–2.11.
3. *Summary of World Broadcasts*, 28 November 1986.

4. *Star*, 11 December 1985.
5. *Financial Times*, 23 June 1986; *Survey of Race Relations* 1978, p.211.
6. *Survey of Race Relations* 1984, p.290; *Financial Times*, 23 June 1986; *Debates of Parliament*, 10 June 1987 cols 127–36.
7. *The Times*, 31 May 1986; Leger and Van Niekerk 1986, p.69; *Sunday Times*, 1 July 1984; *Weekly Mail*, 14 August 1987.
8. *Weekly Mail*, 14 August 1987.
9. *Financial Times*, 31 May 1985.
10. *Financial Times*, 25 January 1985.
11. *Survey of Race Relations* 1986, pp.753–4, 1987/8, pp.339–40.
12. National Union of Mineworkers 1986, p.31.
13. *South African Labour Bulletin*, Vol.11, No.1, September 1985, p.6.
14. *Work in Progress*, No.15, October 1980, pp.47–8.
15. *Work in Progress*, No.15, October 1980, pp.48–9.
16. *Work in Progress*, No.15, October 1980, p.47.
17. National Union of Mineworkers 1986, p.2; *Star*, 4 July 1985, 8 March 1986; *Weekly Mail* 28 June 1985, 23 September 1988; *Mining News*, April 1985.
18. *Rand Daily Mail*, 6 February 1984.
19. *Daily News*, 9 July 1985.
20. Diseko 1983, p.7.
21. National Union of Mineworkers 1986, pp.13–16.
22. National Union of Mineworkers 1986, p.14.
23. National Union of Mineworkers 1986, p.20.
24. Leger 1984, pp.19–20; *Rand Daily Mail*, 9 February 1984.
25. *Cape Times*, 18 September 1986; *Sunday Tribune*, 21 September 1986.
26. National Union of Mineworkers 1986, pp.26, 27, 30.
27. National Union of Mineworkers 1986, p.40.
28. Leger *et al* 1986, p.87; *Financial Mail*, 5 July 1985.
29. Leger *et al* 1986, p.87.
30. *Financial Mail*, 3 February 1984; *Sunday Times* 5 May 1985; *Cape Times* 21 September 1986: National Union of Mineworkers 1985, pp.5–6; National Union of Mineworkers 1986, pp.7, 34.
31. *Bulletin of Statistics*, Vol.20, No.2, quarter ended June 1986, pp.2.5–2.11; *Survey of Race Relations* 1982, pp.141–2.
32. As cited in Seedat 1984, p.41.
33. Seedat 1984, p.41.
34. *Star*, 27 August 1984; *New Statesman*, 19 October 1984; *Rand Daily Mail*, 24 August 1984, 21 March 1985.

35. *Rand Daily Mail*, 9 August 1984.
36. *Sowetan*, 13 March 1984; *Financial Times*, 23 June 1986.
37. *ILO Info*, Vol.22, No.4, October 1986.
38. *South African Catholic Bishops' Conference Dossier*, No.4, June 1985, p.4.
39. Webster 1978, p.12.
40. *SASPU National*, Vol.1, No.3, October 1980.
41. *Financial Times*, 6 June 1986.
42. *Sunday Tribune*, 10 November 1985; *Star*, 4 November 1985.
43. *Waarheid*, 4 December 1982.
44. Pallister *et al* 1987, p.151.
45. Plaut 1978, pp.43, 45; Pallister *et al* 1987, p.151.
46. *Morning Star*, 29 November 1984.
47. Webster 1978, p.17.
48. Webster 1978, p.18.
49. Luckhardt and Wall 1981, p.23.
50. *Work in Progress*, No.8, May 1979, pp.14–16.
51. *Work in Progress*, No.8, May 1979, p.10.
52. As cited by *Workers Unity*, No.9, May 1978, pp.1, 3.
53. *Workers Unity*, No.9, May 1978, p.1.
54. South African Congress of Trade Unions 1980b, pp.11–12.
55. *Work in Progress*, No.8, May 1979, pp.14–16.
56. *SASPU National*, Vol.3, No.2, August 1982.
57. *Zimbabwe Chronicle*, 7 July 1982; *SASPU National*, Vol.3, No.2, August 1982.
58. Thompson 1984, p.157.
59. *South African Labour Bulletin*, Vol.10, No.4, January/February 1985, p.63; *Star*, 8 February 1986.
60. Diseko 1983, pp.9–12.
61. *Financial Mail*, 21 June 1985.
62. *South African Labour Bulletin*, Vol.10, No.4, January/February 1985, pp.64–5.
63. Golding 1984, pp.108, 114.
64. *Financial Times*, 6 June 1986.
65. Van Niekerk 1984, p.16; *Star*, 8 February 1986.
66. Van Niekerk 1984, pp.16–18.
67. *Financial Mail*, 17 May 1985.
68. *Cape Times*, 2 July 1985.
69. *Star*, 18 July 1985.
70. *Star*, 3 September 1985.
71. *Star*, 14 March 1986.

72. *Star*, 14 March 1986.
73. *Survey of Race Relations* 1986, pp.235, 565.
74. *Star*, 14 March 1986; *Financial Times*, 2 July 1986; *Summary of World Broadcasts*, 9 July 1986; *Financial Mail*, 12 September 1986; *Financial Times*, 28 October 1986.
75. *Focus*, No.73, November/December 1987, p.10.
76. *Survey of Race Relations* 1987/8, p.684; 19 August 1987; *Star*, 16 September 1987; *Focus*, No.73, November/December 1987, p.10.

Chapter 5: Industrial law

1. Lundall *et al* 1984, p.2.
2. South Africa (Republic of) 1979, para 3.35.10.
3. South Africa (Republic of) 1979, para 3.35.14.
4. South Africa (Republic of) 1979, para 1.10.
5. South Africa (Republic of) 1979, para 3.35.3.
6. South Africa (Republic of) 1979, para 3.36.6.
7. South Africa (Republic of) 1979, para 3.35.5.
8. South Africa (Republic of) 1979, para 3.35.15.
9. South Africa (Republic of) 1979, para 5.58.
10. Cornell and Kooy 1981, p.52.
11. South Africa (Republic of) Department of Labour and Mines 1981, para 4.34.15.
12. Benjamin *et al* 1981, p.19.
13. *Survey of Race Relations* 1982, p.229.
14. *Financial Mail*, 21 September 1984.
15. Haysom 1984, p.115.
16. *Survey of Race Relations* 1980, p.179.
17. *Financial Mail*, 12 April 1985.
18. Haysom 1984, p.115.
19. *Financial Mail*, 12 April 1985.
20. *Financial Mail*, 15 October 1984, 30 November 1984, 15 February 1985, 8 March 1985, 15 March 1985, 8 April 1985, 12 April 1985, 24 May 1985, 20 September 1985, 25 October 1985, 8 November 1985, 29 November 1985; *Cape Times*, 18 February 1986; *Finance Week*, 12–18 June 1986; *Star*, 23 January 1987.
21. *Focus*, No.75, March/April 1988, p.8.
22. *Work in Progress*, No.52, March 1988, p.16.
23. *Work in Progress*, No.52, p.17.

24. *Survey of Race Relations* 1987/8, pp.648–51; *Work in Progress*, No.52, March 1988, p.19; *SA Barometer*, Vol.2, No.17, 19 September 1988.
25. IDAF 1989, p.16.
26. *Star*, 10 February 1989.
27. Whiteside and Haysom 1984, p.29.
28. Whiteside and Haysom 1984, p.257.
29. Whiteside and Haysom 1984, pp.252, 261–2.
30. Whiteside and Haysom 1984, p.259.
31. Whiteside and Haysom 1984, p.260.
32. Whiteside and Haysom 1984, p.263.
33. *Focus*, No.65, July/August 1986, p.5.

Chapter 6: The struggle for the right to organise

1. *Work in Progress*, No.6, November 1978, p.106.
2. *Work in Progress*, No.6, November 1978, pp.112–13.
3. Harlov 1983, p.12; *Work in Progress*, No.7, March 1979, p.32.
4. Luckhardt and Wall 1981, p.32.
5. Luckhardt and Wall 1981, p.32.
6. Luckhardt and Wall 1981, pp.32–3; *Focus*, No.8, January 1977, p.13.
7. *FOSATU Worker News*, June 1980; *Work in Progress*, No.14, September 1980, p.46.
8. National Union of South African Students 1981, p.3.
9. *Rand Daily Mail*, 15 January 1983.
10. *Financial Mail*, 7 September 1984.
11. *Solidarity News Service*, 27 January 1984.
12. *Solidarity News Service*, 27 January 1984.
13. *Rand Daily Mail*, 16 January 1984.
14. *Business Day*, 9 July 1985; *Financial Mail*, 18 October 1985.
15. *Survey of Race Relations*, 1987/8, p.667, 669.
16. *SA Barometer*, Vol.2, No.2, 12 February 1988.
17. Andrew Levy Associates as cited by *SA Barometer*, Vol.2, No.2, 12 February 1988.
18. *Survey of Race Relations* 1987/8, p.689.
19. *Work in Progress*, No.54, June/July 1988, p.5.
20. *Survey of Race Relations* 1987/8, p.632.
21. IDAF 1989, pp.21–2; *Work in Progress*, No.54, June/July 1988, p.5.
22. *Star*, 19 January 1987; *Weekly Mail*, 22 May 1987.

23. *Work in Progress*, No.55, August/September 1988, p.45.
24. Maree 1982, p.40.
25. *Work in Progress*, No.12, April 1980, p.4.
26. *Work in Progress*, No.12, April 1980, p.15.
27. *Work in Progress*, No.13, July 1980, pp.7–11.
28. *Focus*, No.31, November/December 1980, p.4.
29. Maree 1982, pp.34–7.
30. Maree 1982, p.36.
31. *Survey of Race Relations* 1980, pp.170–1; 1981, p.191.
32. *Work in Progress*, No.18, June 1981, pp.50–1.
33. *Star*, 6 January 1983; *South African Labour Bulletin*, Vol.10, No.7, June 1985, pp.9–30.
34. Tony Allen-Mills in *the Independent*, 31 March 1987.
35. *Financial Mail*, 21 November 1986.
36. Federation of South African Trade Unions 1985, pp.16–17.
37. *FOSATU Worker News*, August 1985; *Weekly Mail*, 28 August 1985.
38. *Star*, 22 February 1986.
39. Keenan 1981, p.4.
40. Keenan 1981, pp.27–46; *Focus*, No.34, May/June 1981, p.5.
41. As quoted in Lambert and Lambert 1983, pp.244–5.
42. Lambert and Lambert 1983, pp.244–6; *Work in Progress*, No.24, October 1982, pp.46–8.
43. Markham 1987a, p.90; *Rand Daily Mail*, 21 February 1985; *Summary of World Broadcasts*, 9 June 1986.
44. Markham 1987a, pp.99–102, 104–6.
45. *Survey of Race Relations* pp.675–8.
46. *Star*, 2 April 1987; *Weekly Mail*, 10 April 1987; *Sunday Tribune*, 19 April 1987; *Cape Times*, 22 May 1987; *Observer*, 19 April 1987.
47. *Focus*, No.71, July/August 1987, p.3.
48. *New Nation*, 23 April 1987; *Financial Times*, 23 April 1987.
49. *Focus*, No.71, July/August 1987, p.1.
50. *Southscan*, 10 June 1987.
51. Maree 1982, pp.36–7.
52. Maree 1982, pp.38–9.
53. *Focus*, No.37, November/December 1981 pp.1, 2, 5, 12.
54. Maree 1982, pp.46–7.
55. *Work in Progress*, No.17, April 1981, p.9.
56. *Weekly Mail*, 10 January 1986.
57. *New Nation*, 31 July 1986.

58. *Focus*, No.69, March/April 1987, p.3, No.71; July/August 1987, pp.1–3.
59. Copelyn 1982, pp.78–9.
60. *Work in Progress*, No.13, July 1980, p.27.
61. *Work in Progress*, No.13, July 1980, p.29.
62. *Work in Progress*, No.13, July 1980, p.31.
63. Lambert and Lambert 1983, pp.236–7.
64. Lambert and Lambert 1983, pp.236–9.
65. *Rand Daily Mail*, 15 September 1983.
66. Lambert and Lambert 1983, pp.236–9; *Rand Daily Mail*, 14 September 1983, 15 September 1983.
67. *Sowetan*, 4 February 1985.
68. Federation of South African Trade Unions 1984a, p.26.
69. *Survey of Race Relations* 1984, p.335.
70. *Survey of Race Relations* 1986, p.262.
71. *Star*, 26 April 1985, 27 April 1985; *Cape Times*, 27 April 1985.
72. Friedman 1987, pp.266–7.
73. *Survey of Race Relations* 1981, p.195.
74. *Work in Progress*, No.22, April 1982, p.26; *South African Labour Bulletin*, Vol.7, No.8, July 1982, p.1.
75. *South African Labour Bulletin*, Vol.7, No.8, July 1982, p.19; Lambert and Lambert 1983, p.234.
76. Metal and Allied Workers Union Press Statement, 25 March 1983.
77. Metal and Allied Workers Union 1983, pp.2–3.
78. Metal and Allied Workers Union Press Statement, 25 March 1983.
79. *Special Report of the Director-General*, International Labour Organisation 1983, p.33.
80. *Survey of Race Relations* 1984, p.332.
81. *Work in Progress*, No.34, October 1984, p.9.
82. *Rand Daily Mail*, 10 April 1985.
83. *State of the Nation*, May 1985; Community Resource and Information Centre 1985, p.4.
84. Matiko 1987, pp.33–8.
85. Matiko 1987, p.37.
86. *Survey of Race Relations* 1987/8, pp.333–4.
87. *Work in Progress*, No.55, August/September 1988, p.45.
88. Matiko 1988, p.110.
89. Matiko 1988, p.111.
90. Matiko 1988, p.112.
91. Friedman 1987, p.346.
92. *Financial Mail*, 13 September 1985.

93. Markham 1987b, pp.30–1.
94. *Weekly Mail*, 27 February 1987.
95. Lambert and Lambert 1983, p.246.
96. *Financial Mail*, 16 May 1986.
97. *Star*, 29 April 1986.
98. *South African Labour Bulletin*, Vol.12, No.2, January/February 1987, p.5; Vol.12, No.3, March/April 1987, p.17.
99. Obery 1987a, p.4.
100. *Financial Mail*, 6 March 1987.
101. *Work in Progress*, No.11, February 1980, p.20.
102. Maree 1980, pp.26–9.
103. Roux 1980, pp.3–12.
104. *Financial Mail*, 6 July 1985; *Star*, 7 May 1985; *Rand Daily Mail*, 1 December 1984.
105. *South African Labour Bulletin*, Vol.11, No.3, January 1986, pp.6, 7–8.
106. *South African Labour Bulletin*, Vol.11, No.2, October/December 1985, pp.3–4; *State of the Nation*, October/November 1985.
107. *Rand Daily Mail*, 18 October 1984, 19 December 1984; *FOSATU Worker News*, October 1985.
108. Federation of South African Trade Unions 1984a.
109. *Work in Progress*, No.28, August 1983, pp.48–9.
110. Bird 1987, p.22.
111. Bird 1987, pp.19, 22.
112. Obery 1988, p.30.
113. *South African Labour Bulletin*, Vol.14, No.4, October 1989, pp.13–35; *South*, 20 July 1989.
114. Lewis 1983a, p.21.
115. Lambert and Lambert 1983, pp.235–6.
116. *South African Labour Bulletin*, Vol.8, No.2, November 1982, pp.3–6.
117. *Sowetan*, 5 April 1982.
118. *SASPU National*, Vol.3, No.3, October 1982.
119. *Star Airmail Weekly*, 22 August 1983.
120. *FOSATU Worker News*, October 1985.
121. *Financial Mail*, 23 May 1986; *Star*, 4 June 1986.
122. *Survey of Race Relations* 1981, p.415.
123. Plaut and Ward 1982, pp.21–2.
124. *Work in Progress*, No.21, February 1982, pp.49–52.
125. *Work in Progress*, No.18, June 1981, pp.48–50; No.19, August 1981, pp.51–2.

126. *Work in Progress*, No.21, February 1981, p.49.
127. *Solidarity News Service*, 27 January 1984.
128. *Financial Mail*, 27 September 1985.
129. *Business Day*, 3 November 1986.
130. *Weekly Mail*, 7 November 1986.
131. Adler, G. 1986, pp.106, 109–110.
132. *Work in Progress*, No.29, August 1983, p.46.
133. *Sowetan*, 1 February 1985; *New Nation*, 13 March 1986.
134. *Star*, 7 June 1985; *Daily News* 16 July 1985.
135. *Financial Mail*, 13 June 1986.
136. *Financial Mail*, 21 September 1984.
137. *SASPU National*, Vol.6, No.5, December 1985; Vol.7, No.1, February 1986; *Star*, 25 January 1985.
138. *Weekly Mail*, 21 March 1986.
139. 139*SASPU National*, Vol.7, No.2, April/May 1986.
140. *Cape Times* 6 June 1985.
141. *Star*, 12 July 1985.
142. McGregor 1980, pp.125–6.
143. Evans 1982, p.20.
144. Evans 1982, pp.13, 30.
145. *Survey of Race Relations* 1984, p.330.
146. *South African Labour Bulletin*, Vol.10, No.3, December 1984, pp.31–45.
147. *Work in Progress*, No.36, April 1985, p.18.
148. Sitas 1985, p.42.
149. Cobbett, W. 1987, p.4.
150. McGregor 1980, p.127.
151. Evans 1982, pp.31–3.
152. *SASPU National*, Vol.5, No.6, October 1984.
153. *Star*, 3 October 1984.
154. Keenan 1981, p.29.
155. *Survey of Race Relations* 1983, p.203.

Chapter 7: Trade unions

1. Cooper, C. 1983 is the source of the definitions.
2. Davies *et al* 1984, p.243.
3. De Clerq 1980, pp.22–3.
4. *South African Labour Bulletin*, Vol.11, No.2, October/December 1985, p.9.
5. *Star*, 14 November 1986.

6. *South African Labour Bulletin*, Vol.12, No.11, November/December 1986, p.62.
7. Hepple 1971 p.68.
8. Hepple 1971, p.69.
9. Federation of South African Trade Unions 1980, p.87.
10. *Financial Mail*, 19 November 1976.
11. Cooper, C. 1983, pp.212–13.
12. Bennett 1987b, p.82.
13. *Survey of Race Relations* 1982, p.151.
14. *Financial Mail*, 20 September 1985.
15. *New Nation*, 10 April 1986; *Cape Times*, 30 May 1986, 1 September 1986; *Star*, 26 August 1986; Bennett 1987b, p.82.
16. Bennett 1987b, p.81; *Star*, 21 October 1987.
17. Fine 1987, p.220.
18. Cooper, C. 1983, pp.205–7.
19. *Weekly Mail*, 29 November 1985.
20. Davies *et al* 1984, p.322.
21. Luckhardt and Wall 1980, pp.37, 99.
22. Luckhardt and Wall 1980, p.99.
23. Luckhardt and Wall 1980, pp.430–2.
24. Bonner 1983, p.34.
25. Lundall *et al* 1984, Federations p.14; International Confederation of Trade Unions 1985, p.7.
26. International Confederation of Trade Unions 1985, p.8.
27. Lambert and Lambert 1983, p.219; Lundall *et al* 1984, Directory p.108.
28. *South African Labour Bulletin*, Vol.10, No.2, October/November 1984, pp.37, 43.
29. *Work in Progress*, No.36, April 1985, p.18.
30. *Work in Progress*, No.35, February 1985, p.31.
31. Transport and General Workers Union 1984, pp.14–16.
32. Sweet, Food and Allied Workers Union 1985, p.1.
33. Bonner 1983, p.31.
34. Baskin, 1982, pp.48–9.
35. Federation of South African Trade Unions 1985, p.8 table of locals.
36. Federation of South African Trade Unions June 1984b, pp.6–7.
37. Council of Unions of South African 1982, p.69.
38. *Indicator, South Africa*, Vol.4, No.1, Winter 1986, p.118.
39. *Indicator, South Africa*, Vol.4, No.1, Winter 1986.

40. *South African Labour Bulletin* Vol.11, No.5, April/May 1985 p.19; Vol.11, No.3, January 1986, p.17; *Indicator, South Africa*, Vol.4, No.2, Spring 1986, p.103.
41. Food and Canning Workers Union 1983, p.8.
42. Morris 1986, pp.101–110.
43. *Phambili Basebenzi*, May 1985.
44. International Confederation of Trade Unions 1985, Appendix 1, p.1.
45. *Focus*, No.49, November/December 1983, pp.6–7, No.50, January/February 1984, p.6, No.56, January/February 1985, p.6.
46. Van Heerden 1982, p.111.
47. *South African Labour Bulletin*, Vol.9, No.6, May 1984, p.23.
48. Van Heerden 1982, p.111; Bonner 1983, p.27.
49. *South African Labour Bulletin*, Vol.10, No.2, October/November 1984, p.26.
50. *Star Airmail Weekly*, 7 September 1984.
51. *South African Labour Bulletin*, Vol.9, No.6, May 1984, p.27.
52. General and Allied Workers Union 1984, pp.1, 4.
53. *South African Labour Bulletin*, Vol.11, No.3, January 1986 pp.75–6.
54. National Union of South African Students 1982, p.22.
55. National Union of South African Students 1982, p.23.
56. Lundall *et al* 1984, Directory p.117.
57. *South African Labour Bulletin*, Vol.10, No.2, October/November 1984, p.29; Vol.11 No.2, 1985; Vol.12, No.1, 1986.
58. *South African Labour Bulletin*, Vol.10, No.2, October/November 1984, pp.31, 32.
59. *South African Labour Bulletin*, Vol.10, No.2, October/November 1984, p.33.
60. *SASPU Focus*, Vol.5, May 1986.
61. *South African Labour Bulletin*, Vol.7, Nos 1, 2, September 1981, pp.3–4.
62. *Focus*, No.32, January/February 1981, pp.6, 12.
63. Community Resource and Information Centre 1984.
64. *Focus*, No.39, March/April 1982, p.8.
65. Community Resource and Information Centre 1984.
66. Morris 1986, p.109.
67. Community Resource and Information Centre 1984.
68. Hindson 1984, pp.93–4.
69. *Workers Unity*, No.36, June 1983.
70. Community Resource and Information Centre 1984.
71. *South African Labour Bulletin*, Vol.11, No.1, September 1985, p.31.

72. *South African Labour Bulletin*, Vol.11, No.1 September 1985, pp.32–3.
73. *Work in Progress*, No.49, September 1987, p.23.
74. *South African Labour Bulletin*, Vol.11, No.3, January 1986, pp. 50–60.
75. *South African Labour Bulletin*, Vol.11, No.3, January 1986, pp.45–6.
76. Von Holdt 1989, pp.2–3.
77. *Cape Times*, 3 June 1986.
78. *South African Labour Bulletin*, Vol.11, No.6, June/July 1986, pp.46–7.
79. Obery 1987b, pp.8–10; *Weekly Mail*, 29 May 1987.
80. *South African Labour Bulletin*, Vol.12, No.2, January/February 1987, p.19.
81. *Weekly Mail*, 30 January 1987.
82. *South African Labour Bulletin*, Vol.12, No.5, July 1987, pp.22–3.
83. *South African Labour Bulletin*, Vol.13, No.7, November 1988.
84. *Indicator, South Africa*, Vol.5, No.1, Spring 1987.
85. *South African Labour Bulletin*, Vol.13, No.2, February 1988, p.74; Vol.13, No.7, November 1988, p.84; *New Nation*, 2 March 1988.
86. *Indicator, South Africa*, Vol.5, No.1, Spring 1987.
87. *Sowetan*, 21 December 1987.
88. *Daily Dispatch*, 6 May 1988.
89. *Star*, 18 October 1988.
90. *Sowetan*, 9 September 1988.
91. *Weekly Mail*, 24 February 1989.
92. *Southscan*, 1 March 1989.

Chapter 8: Resistance to apartheid

1. *Work in Progress*, No.13, July 1980, p.52.
2. *Work in Progress*, No.13, July 1980, p.12.
3. *Focus*, No.68, January/February 1987, p.3.
4. Swilling 1984, p.47.
5. Swilling 1984, pp.62–3.
6. Haysom 1983, pp.1–2.
7. Swilling 1984, p.57; *Survey of Race Relations* 1985, p.196.
8. Surplus People Project 1984, p.68.
9. West 1982, p.478.
10. Surplus People Project 1984, p.135.
11. Unterhalter 1987, pp.91–137; Cole 1986, pp.38–9.
12. *SASPU National*, Vol.2, No.6, August 1981; Vol.3, No.1, February/March 1982.

13. *SASPU National*, Vol.2, No.3, May 1981.
14. *Grassroots*, March 1981, Vol.2, No.1.
15. Harlov 1983, p.15.
16. *Work in Progress*, No.13, July 1980, p.14.
17. *Focus*, No.55, November/December 1984, p.6.
18. *Star*, 22 July 1985.
19. *Focus*, No.59, July/August 1985, p.8.
20. *Focus*, No.59, July/August 1985, p.1.
21. Friedman 1987, p.438.
22. Foster 1982, pp.81–3.
23. *South African Labour Bulletin*, Vol.11, No.1, September 1985, p.102.
24. *South African Labour Bulletin*, Vol.10, No.6, May 1985, pp.23–5.
25. *Grassroots*, October 1980, p.7.
26. Food and Canning Workers Union 1982, p.56.
27. Lewis 1983b, pp.11–18.
28. Njikelana 1984, pp.32–3.
29. *Work in Progress*, No.31, May 1984, p.19.
30. Labour Monitoring Group, 1985a, p.75.
31. Labour Monitoring Group, 1985a, p.83.
32. Labour Monitoring Group, 1985a, p.83.
33. Labour Monitoring Group, 1985a, pp.74, 81.
34. Labour Monitoring Group, 1985a, pp.85, 88.
35. Communiqué of the meeting between COSATU, SACTU and the ANC, 7 March 1986.
36. Naidoo 1986, p.38.
37. Labour Monitoring Group, 1985c, p.108.
38. Labour Monitoring Group, 1985c, pp.87, 104–5.
39. Labour Monitoring Group, 1985c, pp.87, 104–5.
40. Labour Monitoring Group (Natal), 1985d, p.110.
41. *South African Labour Bulletin*, Vol.10, No.7, June 1985, pp.6–9; Labour Monitoring Group (Natal) 1985d, pp.94–101.
42. *IDAF Briefing Paper*, No.20, 1986, p.2.
43. *Focus*, No.61, November/December 1985, pp.1–2.
44. *Star*, 27 September 1985.
45. *IDAF Briefing Paper*, No.20, 1986, p.2.
46. *Weekly Mail*, 9 May 1986.
47. Labour Monitoring Group, 1986a, pp.78–9.
48. Labour Monitoring Group, 1986a, pp.80–1.
49. Labour Monitoring Group, 1986a, pp.83–4.
50. Labour Monitoring Group, 1986a, p.87.

51. Labour Monitoring Group, 1986b, p.108.
52. Labour Monitoring Group, 1986b, pp.95–6.
53. *Focus*, No.66, September/October 1986, p.1.
54. *Focus*, No.71, July/August 1987, p.1.
55. Labour Monitoring Group, 1987, p.52.
56. *Focus*, No.67, November/December 1986, p.3; IDAF 1988, p.3.
57. IDAF 1988, p.3.
58. IDAF 1988, p.3.
59. IDAF 1989, p.23.
60. IDAF 1989, p.23.
61. IDAF 1989, p.24.
62. IDAF 1989, p.24; IDAF 1989, p.15.
63. Middleton 1986, p.7.
64. *Work in Progress*, No.39, October 1985, pp.9–12.
65. *Work in Progress*, No.39, October 1985, pp.28–30.
66. *Work in Progress*, No.39, October 1985, pp.13–14.
67. *Work in Progress*, No.39, October 1985, pp.8–28.
68. Jaffe 1986, p.5.
69. *State of the Nation*, April 1987; *Work in Progress*, No.49, September 1987, p.25.
70. *Star*, 30 June 1987; *Focus*, No.66, September/October 1986, p.3.
71. *Focus*, No.55, November/December 1984, p.1.
72. South Africa (Republic of), 1953.
73. Bennett 1987a, p.76.
74. *Focus*, No.71, July/August 1987, p.1.
75. *Focus*, No.76, May/June 1988.
76. Congress of South African Trade Unions, 1988.
77. *Work in Progress*, No.54, June/July 1988, p.10.
78. As quoted by Van Niekerk 1988, p.165.
79. Bennett 1987b, p.78.
80. Von Holdt 1989, p.22.
81. *Financial Mail*, 18 July 1986.
82. *Work in Progress*, No.54, June/July 1988, p.10.
83. COSATU assistant secretary general as quoted in *South African Labour Bulletin*, Vol.13, Nos 4/5, June/July 1988, p.38.
84. Von Holdt 1988a, p.33.
85. Von Holdt 1988a, p.36.
86. Von Holdt 1988a, p.39.
87. *SA Barometer*, Vol.2, No.11, pp.163–5.
88. Von Holdt 1988b, pp.59–60.
89. Labour Monitoring Group 1985a, p.86.
90. Von Holdt 1988b, p.53.

Bibliography

Newspapers, periodicals and serials

AFRA Report Sheets, Association for Rural Advancement, Pietermaritzburg.
African Labour News, International Confederation of Free Trade Unions, Liberia.
Annual Report on Apartheid, International Labour Organisation, Geneva.
Annual Survey of Race Relations, South African Institute of Race Relations, Johannesburg.
Argus, Cape Town.
Bulletin of Statistics, South Africa (Republic of), Central Statistical Services, Pretoria.
Business Day, Johannesburg.
Cape Times, Cape Town.
Citizen, Johannesburg.
City Press, Johannesburg.
Critical Health, Johannesburg.
Daily Dispatch, East London.
Daily News, Durban.
Debates of Parliament, Cape Town/Pretoria.
Die Burger, Cape Town.
Finance Week, Johannesburg.
Financial Mail, Johannesburg.
Financial Times, London.
Focus on Political Repression in Southern Africa, International Defence and Aid Fund for Southern Africa, London.
FOSATU Worker News, Johannesburg.
Grassroots, Cape Town.
Guardian, London.
IDAF Briefing Papers, International Defence and Aid Fund for Southern Africa, London.
ILO Info, International Labour Organisation, Geneva.
Independent, London.

Indicator, South Africa, Durban.
Learn and Teach, Johannesburg.
Lutheran World Information, Geneva.
Mining News, Johannesburg.
Morning Star, London.
New Era, Cape Town.
New Nation, Johannesburg.
New Statesman, London.
New York Times, New York.
Observer, London.
Phambili Basebenzi, Cape Town.
Quarterly Countdown, South African Institute of Race Relations, Johannesburg.
Rand Daily Mail, Johannesburg.
SA Barometer, Johannesburg.
SALDRU Labour Research Series, Quarterly Bulletin, Monitor of Minimum Wage Measures, Cape Town.
Sash, Black Sash, Johannesburg.
SASPU Focus, South African Students Press Union, Johannesburg.
SASPU National, South African Students Press Union, Johannesburg.
Social Dynamics, University of Cape Town, Cape Town.
Solidarity News Service, Gaberone, Botswana.
South, Cape Town.
South African Catholic Bishops' Conference Dossier, The Commission for Church and Work, Congella, Durban.
South African Journal of Human Rights, Johannesburg.
South African Labour Bulletin, Durban/Johannesburg.
South African Reserve Bank, Annual Economic Report, Johannesburg.
South African Review, ed. South African Research Services, Ravan Press, Johannesburg.
Southscan, London.
Sowetan, Johannesburg.
Special Report of the Director-General on the Application of the Declaration concerning the Policy of Apartheid in South Africa, International Labour Organisation, Geneva.
Star, Johannesburg.
Star Airmail Weekly, Johannesburg.
State of the Nation, Johannesburg.
Summary of World Broadcasts, British Broadcasting Corporation, London.
Sunday Express, Johannesburg.
Sunday Star, Johannesburg.

The Sunday Times, London.
Sunday Tribune, Durban.
Survey of Race Relations, Annual, South African Institute of Race Relations, Johannesburg.
The Times, London.
Voice, Johannesburg.
Waarheid, Amsterdam.
Weekly Mail, Johannesburg.
Work in Progress, Johannesburg.
Workers Unity, London/Lusaka.
Zimbabwe Chronicle, Bulawayo, Zimbabwe.

Books and Articles

Adler, G., 1986, 'The strike at General Motors', *South African Labour Bulletin*, Vol.12, No.1, November/December.

Adler, T., 1979, 'The prevention of occupational diseases and industrial accidents in South African industry', *South African Labour Bulletin*, Vol.4, Nos 9, 10, March.

Adler, T., 1987, 'The extent of shift work in the manufacturing sector in South Africa', *South African Labour Bulletin*, Vol.12, No.8, October.

Barrett, J. *et al* (eds), 1985, Vukani Makhosikazi: South African Women Speak, Catholic Institute for International Relations, London.

Baskin, J., 1982, 'Growth of a new worker organ – the Germiston shop stewards council', *South African Labour Bulletin*, Vol.7, No.8, July.

Beinart, W., 1984, 'Review of the Surplus Peoples Project – forced removals in South Africa', *Journal of Southern African Studies*, Vol.10, No.2, April.

Bekker, S., 1984, 'Levels of living in Ciskei: a quantitative and qualitative analysis', Paper No.277, Second Carnegie Inquiry into Poverty and Development in Southern Africa, Cape Town, 13–19 April 1984.

Bekker, S. and Humphries, R., 1985, *From Control to Confusion: The Changing Role of Administration Boards in South Africa, 1971–83*, Shuter and Shuter in association with the Institute of Social and Economic Research, Pietermaritzburg.

Bell, T., 1986, 'The role of regional policy in South Africa', *Journal of Southern African Studies*, Vol.12, No.2, April.

Benjamin, P., Cheadle, H. and Khosa, M., 'A guide to the Labour Relations Amendment Act, (1981)', *South African Labour Bulletin*, Vol.7, Nos 1, 2.

Bennett, M., 1987a, 'COSATU's two constituencies', *Indicator, South Africa*, Vol.5, No.1, Spring.

Bennett, M., 1987b, 'Maligned and unaligned: labour's old guard after TUCSA', *Indicator, South Africa*, Vol.4, No.3, Summer.

Bernstein, H., 1985, *For Their Triumphs and Their Tears: Women in Apartheid South Africa*, International Defence and Aid Fund for Southern Africa, London.

Bird, A., 1987, 'Metal workers win national maternity benefits', *Work in Progress*, No.47, April.

Black Sash Johannesburg Advice Office, 1980, *Annual Report of the Johannesburg Advice Office, February 1979–January 1980, to Black Sash Conference, 1980*, Johannesburg.

Bonner, Phil, 1983, 'Independent unions since Wiehahn', *South African Labour Bulletin*, Vol.8, No.4, February.

Bot, M., 1988, *Training on Separate Tracks: Segregated Technical Education and Prospects for its Erosion*, South African Institute of Race Relations, Johannesburg.

Brooks, A. and Brickhill, J., 1980, *Whirlwind before the storm*, International Defence and Aid Fund for Southern Africa, London.

Budlender, G., 1985, 'Incorporation and exclusion: recent developments in labour law and influx control', *South African Journal of Human Rights*, Vol.1, Part 1, May.

Budlender, G., 1989, 'Reform in perspective', *Quarterly Countdown*, No.13, Third Quarter.

Budlender, D., Hendrie, D. and Young, G., 1985, *Industrial Council Wage Rates: A Comprehensive Analysis of the Minimum Wage Rates Set by South Africa's Industrial Councils*, South African Labour Development Research Unit, Cape Town.

Bunn, D. and Taylor, J. (eds), 1987, 'From South Africa, new writing, photographs and art', special issue of *Triquarterly Magazine*, North Western University.

Bureau for Economic Research, Co-operation and Development (BENSO), 1983, *Statistical Survey of Black Development, Part II, Independent States, 1982*, Pretoria.

Catholic Institute for International Relations, 1989, *Fruit of the Vine: The Human Cost of South African Wine*, London.

Chisholm, L., 1984, 'Redefining skills: black education in South Africa in the 1980s' in Kallaway, P. (ed.), *Apartheid and Education: The Education of Black South Africans*, Ravan Press, Johannesburg.

Claasens, A., 1979, 'The Riekert Commission and unemployment: the KwaZulu case', *South African Labour Bulletin*, Vol.5, No.4, November.

Cobbett, M., 1986, *The Land Question in South Africa: A Preliminary Assessment*, University of York Centre for Southern African Studies: The Southern African Economy after Apartheid Conference, 29 September–20 October 1986.

Cobbett, W., 1987, 'Onverwacht and the emergence of a regional labour market in South Africa', mimeo.

Cock, J., 1980, *Maids and Madams – A Study in the Politics of Exploitation*, Ravan Press, Johannesburg.

Cole, J., 1986, *Crossroads: From Popular Resistance to Mini-Bantustan*, Western Cape Roots and Realities Conference 16–18 July 1986, Centre for African Studies, University of Cape Town.

Community Resource and Information Centre (CRIC), 1984, *Report: The Trade Union Unity Talks*, Johannesburg.

Community Resource and Information Centre (CRIC), 1985, *Background to the Forthcoming MAWU National Metalworkers' Strike*, Johannesburg.

Congress of South African Trade Unions, 1988, *COSATU Office Bearers' Assessment for 1988*, Congress of South African Trade Unions, Johannesburg.

Cook, A., 1982, 'Akin to slavery: prison labour in South Africa', Fact Paper on Southern Africa No. 11, International Defence and Aid Fund for Southern Africa, London.

Cooper, C., 1983, 'The established trade union movement in South Africa', *South African Review*, No.1, 1983.

Cooper, D., 1988, *Working the land: a review of agriculture in South Africa*, Environmental Development Agency, Johannesburg, p.71.

Copelyn, J., 1982, 'Problems in collective bargaining', *South African Labour Bulletin*, Vol.8, No.1, September 1982.

Corbett, P., 1982, 'Council housing for low-income Indian families in Durban: objectives, strategies and effects', in Smith, D. (ed.), *Living under Apartheid* (London Research Series in Geography 2), George Allen and Unwin, London.

Cornell, C. and Kooy, A., 1981, 'Wiehahn Part 5 and the White Paper', *South African Labour Bulletin*, Vol.7, No.3, November.

Council of Unions of South Africa, 1982, 'Press statement following National Conference held at the end of July 1982', *South African Labour Bulletin*, Vol.8, No.3, December.

Davies, R., O Meara, D. and Dlamini, S., 1984, *The Struggle for South Africa: A Reference Guide to Movements, Organisations and Institutions*, Vol.2, Zed Press, London.

De Clerq, F., 1980, 'The organised labour movement and state legislation – unity or fragmentation?', *South African Labour Bulletin*, Vol.5, Nos 6, 7, March.

De Graaff, J.F., 1988, 'Rural schools: Cause for hope', *Africa Insight*, Vol.18, No.1.

De Klerk, M., 1984a, 'Mechanizing farming: implications for employment, incomes and population distribution', Paper No.27, Second Carnegie Inquiry into Poverty and Development in Southern Africa, Cape Town, 13–19 April 1984.

De Klerk, M., 1984b, 'The incomes of farm workers and their families: a study of maize farms in the Western Transvaal', Paper No. 28, Second Carnegie Inquiry into Poverty and Development in Southern Africa, Cape Town, 13–19 April, 1984.

Diseko, M., 1983, 'An injury to one is an injury to all: South African mining unions', *Sechaba*, African National Congress, London, November.

Duncan, S., 1982, 'Citizenship – the consequences of its loss', *Sash*, Vol.25, No.1, May.

Evans, G., 1982, 'The Leyland strike', *South African Labour Bulletin*, Vol.8, No.2, November.

Farm Labour Project (FLP), 1982, *Submission to the National Manpower Commission on Farm Labour*, Johannesburg.

Federation of South African Trade Unions (FOSATU), 1980, 'The parallel union thrust: memorandum issued by FOSATU on 8 November 1979', *South African Labour Bulletin*, Vol.5, Nos 6 & 7, March.

Federation of South African Trade Unions (FOSATU), 1984a, *Women Workers*, Johannesburg.

Federation of South African Trade Unions (FOSATU), 1984b, *An Introduction to the Federation of South African Trade Unions FOSATU*, Durban.

Federation of South African Trade Unions (FOSATU), 1985, *FOSATU Report, 1984*, Cape Town.

Fine, A., 1987, 'Trends and developments in organised labour', *South African Review*, No.4, 1987.

Food and Canning Workers Union (FCWU), 1982, 'Search for a workable relationship', *South African Labour Bulletin*, Vol.7, No.8, July.

Food and Canning Workers Union (FCWU), 1983, *Annual Report of FCWU and AFCWU by the Secretary General to 43rd Annual National Congress*, August 1983.

Foster, J., 1982, 'The workers' struggle – where does FOSATU stand? Keynote address at FOSATU Congress, April 1982', *South African Labour Bulletin*, Vol.7, No.8, July.

Friedman, S., 1987, *Building Tomorrow Today: African Workers in Trade Unions, 1970–84*, Ravan Press, Johannesburg.

Gandar, M. and Bromberger, N., 1984, 'Economic and demographic functioning of rural households: Mahlabatini District, Kwa Zulu', *Reality*, September.

General and Allied Workers Union (GAWU), 1984, *Report on the Organisational Policy and Practice of the General and Allied Workers Union*, GAWU, Johannesburg.

Golding, M., 1985, 'Mass struggles on the mines', *South African Labour Bulletin*, Vol.10, No.6, May.

Green, P. and Miller, S., 1979, 'The Commission of Enquiry on Occupational Health', *South African Labour Bulletin*, Vol.4, Nos 9, 10, March.

Harlov, J., 1983, *Black Labour Regulations and Black Workers Struggles in South Africa*, Scandinavian Institute for African Studies: Research Report No.68, Uppsala.

Hartford, C., 1985, 'Curfew laws: white by night', *South African Journal of Human Rights*, Vol.1, Part 2, August.

Haysom, N., 1983, *'Ruling with the Whip': A Report on the Violation of Human Rights in The Ciskei*, Centre for Applied Legal Studies, University of the Witwatersrand, Johannesburg.

Haysom, N., 1984, 'The Industrial Court: institutionalising industrial conflict', *South African Review*, No.2, 1984.

Haysom, N. and Thompson, C., 1984, 'Farm labour and the law', Paper No.84, Second Carnegie Inquiry into Poverty and Development in Southern Africa, Cape Town, 13–19 April.

Hepple, A., 1971, *South Africa: Workers under Apartheid*, International Defence and Aid Fund for Southern Africa, London.

Hindson, D., 1984, 'Union unity', *South African Review*, No.2, 1984.

Hindson, D., 1986, 'Urbanisation and influx control', *Work in Progress*, No. 40, February.

Horner, D., 1974, 'Control of movement and employment: registration for employment, labour bureaux and migrant labour', *South African Labour Bulletin*, Vol.1, No.2, May.

Human Awareness Project (HAP), 1986, *An Introduction to Transkei (A Human Awareness Study)*, Johannesburg.

IDAF (International Defence and Aid Fund), 1983, *Apartheid: The Facts*, London.

IDAF (International Defence and Aid Fund), 1988, *Review of 1987: Repression and Resistance in South Africa and Namibia*, London.
IDAF (International Defence and Aid Fund), 1989, *Review of 1988: Repression and Resistance in South Africa and Namibia*, Fact Paper on Southern Africa, No.16, London.
Institute for Planning Research, University of Port Elizabeth, 1986, *The Household Subsistence Level in the Major Urban Centres of the Republic of South Africa*, Port Elizabeth.
International Confederation of Trade Unions (ICFTU), 1985, *Report of the ICFTU Mission to South Africa, 16–30 September 1985*, Geneva.
Jaffe, G. 1984, 'Living with unemployment: Strategies for survival', *Work in Progress*, No.34, October 1984.
Jaffe, J., 1986, 'Creating mass power: beyond the cannon of Mamelodi', *Work in progress*, No.41, April.
Joffe, H., 1986, *Stayaways in Cape Town, 1986*, Western Cape Roots and Realities Conference 16–18 July 1986, Centre for African Studies, University of Cape Town.
Keegan, T., 1983, 'Onslaught on black farmers', *Sash*, Vol.26, No.2, August.
Keenan, J., 1981, 'Migrants awake: the 1980 Johannesburg municipality strike', *South African Labour Bulletin*, Vol.6, No.7, May.
Keenan, J., 1983, 'Trickle up: African income and unemployment', *South African Review*, No.1, 1983.
Keenan, J., 1984, 'Agribusiness and the Bantustans', *South African Review*, No.3, 1984.
Keenan, J., 1988, 'Counter revolution as reform: struggle in the bantustans' in Johnson, S. (ed.), *South Africa: No Turning Back*, Macmillan Press, London.
Kooy, A., Horner, D., Green, P. and Miller, S. 1979, 'The Wiehahn Commission: a summary', SALDRU Working Paper No.24, Cape Town.
Kraak, G., 1981, 'Financing of African Workers' Accommodation in Cape Town', SALDRU Working Paper No.35, Cape Town.
Labour and Community Resources Project, 1989, *Comrade Moss*, Learn and Teach Publications, Johannesburg.
Labour Monitoring Group (LMG), 1985a, 'The November stay-away', *South African Labour Bulletin*, Vol.10, No.6, May.
Labour Monitoring Group (LMG) (Natal), 1985b, 'Monitoring the Raditsela protests', *South African Labour Bulletin*, Vol.10, No.8, July/August.

Labour Monitoring Group (LMG), 1985c, 'Eastern Cape stay-aways', *South African Labour Bulletin* Vol.11, No. 1, September.

Labour Monitoring Group (LMG) (Natal), 1985d, 'Monitoring the Sarmcol struggle', *South African Labour Bulletin*, Vol.11, No.2, October/December.

Labour Monitoring Group (LMG), 1986a, 'May Day stay away, 1986', *South African Labour Bulletin*, Vol.11, No.6, June/July.

Labour Monitoring Group (LMG), 1986b, 'June 16th stayaway', *South African Labour Bulletin*, Vol.11, No.7, August.

Labour Monitoring Group (LMG), 1987, 'Soweto Day, 1987', *South African Labour Bulletin*, Vol.12, No.5, July.

Labour Monitoring Group (LMG), 1988, 'Stayaway Survey June 6–8', *South African Labour Bulletin*, Vol.13, No.6, September.

Labour Research Committee (LRC), 1981, 'State strategy and the Johannesburg municipal strike', *South African Labour Bulletin*, Vol.6, No.7, May.

Lacey, M., 1984, 'Feudalism in the age of computers – an analysis of recruitment strategies, to reserve and allocate labour', *Sash*, Vol.26, No.4, February.

Lambert, R. and Lambert L., 1982, 'Dock worker dispute', *Work in Progress*, No.24, October.

Lambert, R. and Lambert L., 1983, 'State reform and working class resistance, 1982', *South African Review*, No.1, 1983.

Leger, J., 1984, 'Hlobane mining accident', *South African Labour Bulletin*, Vol.9, No.5, March.

Leger, J. and Van Niekerk, P., 1986, 'Organisation on the mines. The NUM phenomenon', *South African Review*, No.3, 1986.

Leger, J., Maller, J. and Myers, J., 1986, 'Trade union initiatives in health and safety', *South African Review*, No.3, 1986.

Lemon, A., 1982, 'Migrant labour and frontier commuters; reorganizing South Africa's black labour supply' in Smith, D. (ed.), *Living under Apartheid* (London Research Series in Geography 2), George Allen and Unwin, London.

Levy, N., 1984, 'Background document on discriminatory labour legislation and practices in South Africa in the field of farm labour', prepared for the ILO Pilot Programme on Equality of Opportunity and Treatment, October, London.

Lewis, D., 1983a, 'Trade Union organisation and economic recession', *South African Labour Bulletin*, Vol.8, No.5, April.

Lewis, D., 1983b, 'General Workers Union and the UDF', *Work in Progress*, No.29, October.

Lodge, T., 1983, *Black Politics in South Africa since 1945*, Longman, Harlow.

Lombard, J., 1983, 'Black urbanisation and structural change in the South African economy – a suggested approach', in Van Vuuren, D., Wiehahn, N.E., Lombard, J.A. and Roodie, N.J. (eds), *Change in South Africa*, Butterworths, Durban.

Luckhardt, K. and Wall, B., 1980, *Organise or Starve, The History of the South African Congress of Trade Unions*, Lawrence and Wishart, London.

Luckhardt, K. and Wall, B., 1981, *Working for Freedom – Black Trade Union Development in South Africa Throughout the 1970's*, World Council of Churches, Geneva.

Lundall, P., Schroeder, I. and Young, G., 1984, *Directory of South African Trade Unions: a Complete Guide to All South Africa's Trade Unions*, South African Labour and Development Research Unit, Cape Town.

McCarthy J. and Swilling M., 1985, 'Transport and political resistance', *South African Review*, No.2, 1985.

McGregor, L., 1980, 'The Fattis and Monis dispute', *South African Labour Bulletin*, Vol.5, No.7, March.

Makanjee, V., 1988, 'Apartheid's satellites: from urban to rural revolt', in *Political Conflict in South Africa, Indicator*, Durban.

Makhoba, M., 1984, *The Sun Shall Rise for the Workers*, Ravan Press, Johannesburg.

Mann, M. and Segal, S., 1985, 'The transport industry: carrying apartheid's burden', *Work in Progress*, No.38, August.

Manzini, M., 1982, 'The Process and Structure of Manpower Development', unpublished MA thesis, University of Amsterdam, Amsterdam.

Marchand, C., 1977, 'A consideration of the legal basis and some practical operations of labour bureaux', *South African Labour Bulletin*, Vol.3, No.9, November.

Mare, G., 1979, 'Relocation and Riekert – attempts at rural and urban stabilization', *South African Labour Bulletin*, Vol.5, No.4, November.

Maree, J., 1978 'The dimensions and causes of unemployment in South Africa', *South African Labour Bulletin*, Vol.4, No.4, July.

Maree, J., 1980, 'The UAW and the 1979 PEBCO strikes', *South African Labour Bulletin*, Vol.6, Nos 2, 3, September.

Maree, J., 1982, 'SAAWU in the East London area: 1979–1981', *South African Labour Bulletin*, Vol.7, Nos 4, 5, February.

Markham, C., 1987a, 'Organising local authority workers', *South African Labour Bulletin*, Vol.12, No.3, May/June.

Markham C., 1987b, 'PWAWU victory at Mondi', *South African Labour Bulletin*, Vol.12, No.3, March April.

Matiko, J., 1987, 'Metal talks and MAWU's national wage campaign', *South African Labour Bulletin*, Vol.12, No.3 March/April.

Matiko, J., 1988, 'Metalworkers prove their strength', *South African Labour Bulletin*, Vol.12, No.6, September.

Metal and Allied Workers Union (MAWU), 1983, *MAWU and the Industrial Council*, MAWU, Durban.

Middleton, J., 1986, 'The consumer boycott: a people's weapon', *Sechaba*, April.

Miller, S., 1982, 'Trade Unions in South Africa 1970–1980, A Directory and Statistics', South African Labour Development Research Unit Working Paper, No.45, Cape Town.

Monamo, R., 1983, *A Study of Pass Laws and Their Implementation in the Johannesburg Commissioner's Court*, Centre for Applied Legal Studies, Johannesburg.

Morris, M., 1986, 'The stevedoring industry and the General Workers Union', *South African Labour Bulletin*, Vol.11, No.5, April/May.

Muller, N., 1984, 'The labour market and poverty in Transkei with special reference to the implications of the changing spatial division of labour', Paper No.43, Second Carnegie Inquiry into Poverty and Development in Southern Africa, University of Cape Town, 13–19 April.

Myers, J. and Steinberg, M., 1983, 'Health and safety organisation: a perspective on the Machinery and Occupational Safety Act', *South African Labour Bulletin*, Vols 8.8, 9.9, September/October 1983.

Myers, J. and Steinberg, M., 1984, 'Health and safety: an emerging issue on the shop floor', *South African Review*, No.2, 1984.

Naidoo, J., 1986, 'The significance of COSATU', *South African Labour Bulletin*, Vol.11, No.5, April–May.

National Union of Mineworkers (NUM), 1985, *A Union Fighting the Miners' Cause: One Union One Industry*, NUM, Johannesburg.

National Union of Mineworkers (NUM), 1986, *A Thousand Ways to Die: The Struggle for Safety in the Gold Mines*, Learn and Teach Publications, Johannesburg.

National Union of South African Students (NUSAS), 1981, *An Injury to One is an Injury to All*, NUSAS, Cape Town.

National Union of South African Students (NUSAS), 1982, *Introduction to Labour Organisation in South Africa*, NUSAS, Cape Town.

Nattrass, J., 1984, 'Rural poverty in Kwazulu', *Reality*, November.

Njikelana, S., 1984, 'Unions and the UDF', *Work in Progress*, No.32, July.

Obery, I., 1986, 'Unusual alliance blocks Kwa-Ndebele independence', *Work in Progress*, No.44, September/October.

Obery, I., 1987a, 'Anti-apartheid bosses are not our friends', *Work in Progress*, No.46, February.

Obery I., 1987b, 'A new road to socialism', *Work in Progress*, No.48, July.

Obery, I., 1988, 'Combining employment and family life', *Work in Progress*, No.55, August/September.

Pallister, D., Stewart, S. and Lepper, I., 1987, *South Africa Inc: The Oppenheimer Empire*, Simon and Schuster, London.

Pillay, D., Budlender, D. and Young, G., 1985, *Wage Determinations in South Africa: An Analysis of the Wage Rates set by the Wage Board*, South African Labour and Development Research Unit, Cape Town.

Pillay, P., 1985, 'Women in employment in South Africa; some important trends and issues', *Social Dynamics*, Vol.11, No.2.

Plaut, M., 1978, 'Report on the Anglo American Corporation gold mines', *South African Labour Bulletin*, Vol.2, No.8, April.

Plaut, M. and Ward, D., 1982, *Black Trade Unions in South Africa*, Bertrand Russell Peace Foundation, Nottingham.

Pretorius, F., Addleson, M. and Tomlinson, R., 1986, 'History of industrial decentralization in South Africa Part II: historical development and impact of the policy', *Development Southern Africa*, Vol.3, No.2, May.

Roodt, M., 1984, 'Capitalist agriculture and bantustan employment patterns: case studies in Bophuthatswana' *South African Review*, No.2, 1984.

Roux, M., 1980, 'Daily events of the wildcat strike', *South African Labour Bulletin*, Vol.6, Nos 2, 3, September.

Sarakinsky, M., and Keenan, J., 1986, 'Unemployment in South Africa', *South African Labour Bulletin*, Vol.12, No.1, November/December.

Savage, M., 1986, 'The imposition of pass laws on the African population in South Africa', *African Affairs*, Vol.85, No.339, April.

Searll, J., 1984, 'The sale of state houses' in Bloch, G. and Kaplan, D. (eds), *South African Research Papers*, Cape Town.

Seedat, A., 1984, *Crippling a Nation: Health in Apartheid South Africa*, International Defence and Aid Fund for Southern Africa, London.

Seleoane, M., 1984, 'Conditions on eight farms in Middelburg: Eastern Transvaal', Paper No.29, Second Carnegie Inquiry into Poverty and Development in Southern Africa, Cape Town, 13–19 April.

Seleoane, M., 1985, 'Nyanga East men's hostel: the condition of migrant workers', Working Paper No.62, South African Labour and Development Research Unit.

Simkins, C., 1981, 'The distribution of the African population of South Africa by age, sex and region type 1960, 1970 and 1980', Working Paper No.32, South African Labour and Development Unit, Cape town.

Simkins, C., 1984, 'What has been happening to income distribution and poverty in the homelands?', Paper No.7, Second Carnegie Inquiry into Poverty and Development in Southern Africa, 13–19 April, Cape Town.

Sitas, A., 1985, 'From grassroots control to democracy: a case study of the impact of trade unionism on migrant workers' cultural formations on the East Rand, *Social Dynamics*, Vol.11, No.1.

Smit, P. and Booysen, J.J., 1981, *Swart Verstedeliking Proses, Patroon en Strategie*, Tafelberg Uitgevers, Pretoria.

Smit, P., Olivier, J.J. and Booysen, J.J., 1982, 'Urbanization in the homelands', in Smith, D. (ed.), *Living under Apartheid*, George Allen and Unwin, London.

South Africa (Republic of), 1953, *Public Safety Act*, Act No.3 of 1953, Government Printer, Pretoria.

South Africa (Republic of), 1978, Riekert P.J. (Chairman), *Report of the Commission of Inquiry into Legislation Affecting the Utilisation of Manpower*, Government Printer, Pretoria.

South Africa (Republic of), 1979, Departments of Labour and of Mines, *Report of the Commission of Inquiry into Labour Legislation Part 1*, Government Printer, Pretoria.

South Africa (Republic of), 1981, Departments of Labour and of Mines, *Report of the Commission of Inquiry into Labour Legislation Part 3*, Government Printer, Pretoria.

South Africa (Republic of), 1982, Department of Manpower (National Manpower Commission), *Report of the National Manpower Commission for the Period 1 January 1981–31 December 1981*, Government Printer, Pretoria.

South Africa (Republic of), 1984, Department of Manpower (National Manpower Commission), *Report of the National Manpower Commission for the Period 1 January 1983–31 December 1983*, Government Printer, Pretoria.

South Africa (Republic of), 1985, Department of Manpower, *Manpower Survey*, Vol.1., No.16, Summary: Occupational Classification, 26 April 1985, Government Printer, Pretoria.

South Africa (Republic of), 1986, Central Statistical Services, *South African Labour Statistics*, Government Printer, Pretoria.

South Africa (Republic of), 1987, Central Statistical Services, *South African Labour Statistics*, Government Printer, Pretoria.

South African Congress of Trade Unions (SACTU), 1980a, *The Year of the Worker, the Year of SACTU*, Memo submitted to the ILO Conference (Geneva), June 1980, SACTU, London.

South African Congress of Trade Unions (SACTU), 1980b, *Life and Labour in Trans-National Enterprises in South Africa*, SACTU, London.

South African Institute of Race Relations (SAIRR), 1986, 'Regional services councils', Background Briefing Paper for a conference at the South African Institute of Race Relations on 19 September 1986, Johannesburg.

Streek, B. and Wickstead, R., 1981, *Render unto Kaiser – a Transkei Dossier*, Ravan Press, Johannesburg.

Surplus People Project (SPP), 1983, 'Forced Removals in South Africa', *The SPP Reports*, Vol.1, Surplus People Project, Cape Town.

Surplus People Project (SPP), 1984, *Western Cape, 'Khayelitsha – New Home – Old Storey'*, Surplus People Project, Western Cape.

Swainson, N., 1989, 'Skills and Sanctions against South Africa, Independent Expert Study on the Evaluation and Impact of Sanctions against South Africa', unpublished manuscript, London.

Sweet, Food and Allied Workers Union (SFAWU), 1985, *Food Workers on the March*, SFAWU, Durban.

Swilling, M., 1984, 'The buses smell of blood – the East London boycott', *South African Labour Bulletin*, Vol.9, No.5, March.

Thompson, C., 1984, 'Black trade unions on the mines', *South African Review*, No.2, 1984.

Transport and General Workers Union (TGWU), 1984, *Some Background Information on TGWU*, TGWU, Johannesburg.

United Nations Organisation (UNO), 1980, *African Women and Apartheid in Labour Matters*, New York.

Unterhalter, E., 1987, *Forced Removal: The Division, Segregation and Control of the People of South Africa*, International Defence and Aid Fund for Southern Africa, London.

Van Heerden, C., 1982, 'Towards a Politics of the Working Class in South Africa', unpublished MA thesis, University of the Witwatersrand, Johannesburg.

Van Niekerk, P., 1984, 'NUM's first legal mine strike', *South African Labour Bulletin*, Vol.10, No.2, October/November.

Van Niekerk, P., 1988, 'The trade union movement in the politics of resistance in South Africa', in Johnson, S. (ed.), *South Africa: No Turning Back*, Macmillan Press, London.

Von Holdt, K., 1988a, 'COSATU Special Congress', *South African Labour Bulletin*, Vol.13, Nos 4, 5, June/July.

Von Holdt, K., 1988b, 'June 1988: three-day stay-away against new labour bill', *South African Labour Bulletin*, Vol.13, No.6, September.

Von Holdt, K. 1989, 'TGWU National Congress – massive growth in membership', *South African Labour Bulletin*, Vol.13, No.6, September.

Webster, E., 1978, 'Background to supply and control of labour in the goldmines' in Webster, E. (ed.), *Essays in Southern African Labour History*, Ravan Press, Johannesburg.

West, M., 1982, 'From pass courts to deportation: changing patterns of influx control in Cape Town', *African Affairs*, Vol.81, No.325, October.

Whiteside, A. and Haysom, N., 1984, 'A separate development: labour legislation in the homelands', *Industrial Law Journal*, Vol.5, Part 4.

Wilson, F., 1984, 'Carnegie Conference overview', Paper No.311, Second Carnegie Inquiry into Poverty and Development in Southern Africa, 13–19 April 1984, Cape Town.

Wilson, F. and Ramphele, M., 1989, *Uprooting Poverty. The South African Challenge: Report for the Second Carnegie Inquiry into Poverty and Development in Southern Africa*, W.W. Norton and Company, London.

Witulski, U., 1986, 'Black commuters in South Africa', *Africa Insight*, Vol.16, No.1.

Yawitch, J., 1981, *Betterment: The Myth of Homeland Agriculture*, South African Institute of Race Relations, Johannesburg.

Zille, H., 1983, 'Deciphering decentralization: an analysis of the government's industrial decentralization strategy', in Cooper, L. and Kaplan, D. (eds), *Reform and Response: Selected Research Papers on Aspects of Contemporary South Africa*, Dept of Economic History, University of Cape Town, Cape Town.

Index

ACTWUSA, 201
Administration Boards, 11, 55, 216
AECI, 166–7, 185, 188
AFCWU, 136, 137–8, 189
African Tobacco Workers Union, 178
Afrikaner nationalist movement, 175
Aggett, Neil, death of, 179, 195, 220
agribusiness, 41–3, 47–8
AGRICOR (Bophuthatswana), 42
agriculture, xxi, xxv, 22–3, 41, 133
   in bantustans, 41–3
   labour supply, 15, 40–1
   modernisation, 22–3, 29–30, 31
   see also farm labour
'Aid Centres', 11
alcohol, 35–6, 55–6
Alexandra, Johannesburg, 210, 239
Alfa Romeo, 150, 165–6
AMWU, formation, 102
ANC (African National Congress), 49, 102, 217, 246–7
   ban on, 182, 249
   COSATU and, 205, 227
   Freedom Charter, 205, 227
   and Inkatha, 249–50
   SACTU alliance with, 181, 197
Anglo American Corporation, 47, 92–3, 101, 102, 106, 107, 151, 153
Anglovaal mining company, 107, 108
Angola, SADF in, 246
apartheid,
   campaigns against, 131, 181, 205, 209
   transition from, xix, 250

apprenticeships, 82
ASEA Cables, 160–1, 168
assembly centres, 15
Association for Rural Advancement (AFRA), 38
Athlone, Cape Town, 196
Autoplastics, 166
AZACTU, 193–4, 198, 202
AZAPO, 193, 225
AZASO, 172

B & S Metals strike, 173
BAMCWU, 105, 193, 205
BAMTWU, 105
Bantu Investment Corporation, 211
bantustans, xxi, xxv, 3, 42, 43, 44–5, 212
   commuters and contract labour in, xxiv, 4, 142, Table 1.2(b)
   employment in, xix, 5, 18, 43–5, 74
   independent, xix, 19, 24–5, *see also* Bophuthatswana; Ciskei; Transkei; Venda
   labour relations in, 65, 125–6
   population, 6, 12, 43
   'self-governing', 125
   see also townships
Barayi, Elijah, 108, 198
BAWU, became SAAWU, 191
BCAWU, 188, 200
'betterment schemes', 42, 43
black consciousness movement, 180, 184, 191, 193–4, 225, 242, 247
Black Management Forum, 245

Index

Black Sash, 171
BLAGWU, 193
Bloemfontein, population, 22
BMW motor company, 150–1
BMWU, 143, 193
Bophuthatswana bantustan, 6, 19, 42, 43
  employment statistics, Table 0.1(b)
  industrial relations, 125–6, 147, 188, 248
Botha, P.W., resignation, 246
Botha, Thozamile, 159
Botswana, labour from, 92
boycotts,
  20th anniversary celebrations, 131, 210, 224
  'Black Christmas', 236
  bus, 62, 126, 131, 191, 210–13, 222
  bus (Mdantsane), 48, 192, 212–13
  consumer, 141, 147, 151, 160, 171–2, 211, 225, 236–9
  election, 57, 131, 210, 218–19, 221, 223, 246
  meat, 218, 222
  potato, 45, 236
  rent, 56, 57, 133, 210, 216–17, 235–6
  school, 48, 49, 131, 133, 138–9, 210, 225–6
  school (Soweto), 217–19
BRICKAWU, 200
BRT-Sarmcol, strike at, 140–1, 228–9, 247
Buthelezi Commission, 42

Cape Housing Action Committee (CAHAC), 216
Cape Town, xx, 128
  Crossroads, 214–15
  popular resistance in, 115, 218
Cape Town Municipal Workers Association, 201–2

Carnegie Inquiry into Poverty (1984), 54
CAWU, 200
CCAWUSA, 161–2, 164, 201, 202, 227
  and COSATU, 197, 198, 244
  influence of, 183, 184
  strikes, 157–8, 190
CGWU (later CWIU), 184
Chamber of Mines, employers' federation, 91, 92–3, 94, 105–6
  and NUM, 106, 107, 109–10
chambers of commerce, 139, 237, 245
chemical industry, 151, 166, 185
Cheseborough Pond, 167
child labour, on farms, 32, 33–4
churches, 38, 230, 245
Ciskei bantustan, 19, 41–2
  employment statistics, 43–4, Table 0.1(b)
  hostility to trade unions, 125–6, 146–7, 192, 194, 223
  Mdantsane bus boycott, 48, 192, 212–13
  Mdantsane township, 6, 48, 51
  Tsweletwsele area, 44, 45
Ciskei National Independence Party (CNIP), 213
Ciskei Transport Corporation (CTC), 212
closed-shop agreements, 78, 79, 82
closer settlements, 29, 43
CNETU, formation of, 181
Colgate Palmolive, strike, 151
colour bar, industrial, 73, 77, 175
Coloured labour preference policy, 6, 12, 17–18, 32, 214
Coloured population, 30, 50, 58, 216, 218
  employment, xx, Table 0.1(a), Table 0.2

parliamentary representation, xvii, 57, 218
and stay-aways, 228, 231
union organisation of, 46–7, 169–70
Commission of Enquiry into Riots in the Mines (1975), 103–4
Commissioners' Courts, 12, 14
community organisations, 48, 216, 231, 236, 248
area committees, 239–40
street committees, 239–40, 248
and trade unions, 171–3, 222–3
see also boycotts; local government; organisations
commuters, 6, 32, 85, 130, 212–13, Table 1.2(b), *see also* boycotts, bus; contract labour
Conciliation Boards, 117–18, 123, 132
Conference for a Democratic Future, 245–7
Congress Alliance, 45, 220
Conservative Party, 238
construction industry unions, 200
contract labour, xxi, 3–5, 12, 18, 103, 163, Table 1.2(b)
foreign workers, 92
housing, 10, 14, 50, 51–3
recruitment of, 4, 16, 91–2
and trade unions, 130, 169, 170
Coronation Brick and Tile, 128
Corporation for Economic Development, 61
COSAS, support for boycott, 172
COSATU, 162, 180, 188, 193, 220, 225, 226–7, 236, 240
affiliates 47, 155, 183, 200, 227, 244, Table 7.1, Appendix
Central Executive Committee, 198, 242
co-operation with NACTU, 167, 204–5, 245

formation, 134, 180, 185, 194–9, 226
influence of, 247–8
May 1988 conference, 243–4
offices attacked, 145, 241
political activity by, xviii, 136, 227, 241–4
and stay-aways, 230–1, 234
UWUSA and, 147–8, 249
see also FOSATU
Crossroads, squatter camp, 214–15
curfews, 10, 14
CUSA, 163, 170, 182, 184, 187–8, 225, 229, 230
affiliates, 105, 136, 186, 188
becomes NACTU, 202
and FOSATU, 194, 196, 197, 198, 204
CWIU, 151, 161, 163–4, 170, 184, 185, 205

Dairy Belle company, strike, 160
Dairy Maid Ice Cream Corporation, 160
de Klerk, F.W., President, 246
deaths,
Germiston, 145
in industry, 87
in mines, 96–7, 98, 99
mining strikes, 103, 105
pesticide, 38–9
of strikers, 145
Department of Co-operation and Development, 12, 20, 34
Department of Education and Training, 39–40
Department of Health, Factory Inspectorate, 88
Department of Manpower, 65, 85, 122, 147, *see also* National Manpower Commission
Development Boards *see* Administration Boards
disinvestment, foreign, 165–6

Index

Dlamini, Chris, 198
dockworkers, 71, 189–90
domestic workers, 53–4, 72, 85, 90, 200
Dunlop Flooring strike, 146
Durban, xx, 55, 58, 128, 186, 230
Durban Housing Action Committee (DHAC), 216
DWA, 85
DWEP, 85

East London, 71, 139, 191–2
East Rand, 24, 216, 235
   strikes, 151–2
   trade unions in, 186–7, 225
East Rand People's Organisation (ERAPO), 225
Eastern Cape, 70–1, 74, 239
   stay-aways, 228, 245
   strikes in, 149–50, 165
   trade unions in, 139, 185–6
Eastern Cape Agricultural Co-operative, 46
EAWTU, 188
economy, decentralisation of, 5–6, 21–3, 74
Edgars clothing chain, strike, 160
education and training, 39–40, 77, 82–3
Empangeni bus boycott, 222
employers,
   and labour relations, 119, 139, 158–9
   and skills shortage, 79, 82–3
employment statistics, xix–xx, Table 0.1(a), Table 0.2
   job losses, Table 3.2
   occupations, Table 3.3
Engineering Industrial Workers' Union, 179
EPSF&AWU (later SFAWU), 184
Erasmus Commission, 88–9, 97

factory occupations, 134, 154, 167–8

farm labour, 30
   assaults and deaths, 37–8
   children, 32, 33–4
   farm schools, 39–40
   labour relations, 29, 34–6, 250
   labour tenancy, 15, 31
   parole system and, 12, 32–3
   'tot' system, 35–6
   wages, 36–7, Table 2.1
   women, xxi, 32, 46
   working conditions, 34, 37, 38–9, 85
Farm Plantation and Allied Workers Union, 45
Fattis and Monis strike, 137–8, 169, 171, 222
FAWU, 46, 47, 147–8, 200, 227
FBWU, 160, 186, 188, 205
FCWU, 136, 137, 160, 179, 184, 198, 200, 222–3
   influence of, 183, 189
FEDCRAW, 160
FEDSAW, 162
Firestone, 165, 193
food sector, 160, 169, 186, 189
Ford Motor Company, 149–50, 159, 192
foreign workers, 15, 19, 78, 83, 92
FOSATU, 132, 169–70, 182, 184–6, 186–7, 220–2, 225
   affiliates, 155, 167, 185
   and consumer boycotts, 238
   and CUSA, 194, 198, 204
   federation proposals, 195–6
   and Industrial Councils, 139, 220
   non-racialism of, 136, 187
   shop-steward committees, 221–2, 225
   and TUCSA, 141–2
   see also COSATU
Foster, Joe (FOSATU), 221
Frame textile company, 141
free trading zone, Kew, 73
funerals, 48–9, 229, 230, 237

GaMojadi farm strike, 46
GAWU (Garment and Allied Workers Union), 201
GAWU (General and Allied Workers Union), 190, 192, 200, 201, 224
GAWU (Glass and Allied Workers Union), 184
Gazanzulu bantustan, 125
GENCOR mining company, 107, 108, 147, 151
General Motors (GM), 149, 166
Germiston, shootings, 145
go-slow actions, 129, 150
Gold Fields mining company, 101, 108, 109
Goodyear Tyre company, 149
government, 158, 179
  and Defiance Campaign, 246
  see also legislation; police; State of Emergency
GWIU, 201
GWU, 136, 137, 168, 183, 184, 195, 198, 222–3
  strikes, 138, 143–4, 163
  see also WPGWU
GWUSA, 193, 195, 200, 202

HARWU, 201
health and safety, 52, 85, 87–90
  on farms, 38–9
  mining, 96–9
health service, strikes, 144
Hoexter Commission, 14
hostels see housing
Household Subsistence Level (HSL), 71
Household Supplemented Living Levels (HSLL), Graph 3.1, Graph 3.2
housing, 10, 21, 23, 35, 51, 54, 58
  for contract workers, 51–3
  costs, 216–17
  for domestic workers, 53–4
  hostels, 10, 12, 52–3, 100–1
  as means of influx control, 10, 21–2
  in mining industry, 100–2
  shortage, 13, 51, 54, 56
  tenure, 6, 56–7, 236, 250
  see also boycotts, rent; squatter camps
hunger strikes, 245

IAWUSA, 194
ICU, 181
'illegal' workers, 12–13, 14, 17, 213
IMF (International Metal Federation), 153, 154, 155
Indian population, 50, 58, 169
  employment, xx, Table 0.1(a), Table 0.2
  parliamentary representation, xvii, 57, 218
  and stay-aways, 230–1
industrial colour bar, 73, 77, 175
Industrial Councils, 65–6, 71, 72, 82, 113, 117, 121, 132, 175, Graph 3.1
  NICISEMI, 151, 152, 153, 154
  union activity against, 148–9, 178, 194, 196
  union weakening of, 151–6
Industrial Court, 116–17, 121–3, 124, 132, 140, 163
industrial law, 113–26, see also legislation (for Acts of Parliament)
industry, general,
  decentralisation policy, 5–6, 14
  development of, xxiv, xxv–xxvi
  general trade unions, 191–3, 196, 223–5
  Riekert Commission and, 16–19
  single trade union organisation, 199
  wages in, 65–6, 191

see also individual industries; labour; trade unions
influx controls, 19–20
　over labour, 3–12
　restructuring of, 13–25
　see also pass laws
Inkatha, 125, 148, 184, 220
　and ANC, 249–50
　and UWUSA, 140, 147–8
international aid and investment, 165–6, 250
International Labour Organisation (ILO), 177
International Metal Workers Federation, 102
international opinion, 115
international trade embargoes, 33
ISCOR, workers' hostels, 53

job reservation, 73, 77–8, 79, 178
　in mining, 93–4, 97
Johannesburg, 53, 115, 145
　municipal workers strike, 15–16, 143, 193

Kangwane bantustan, 125
Kelloggs company, 163, 167
Khayelitsha settlement, 215
Komani, Nonceba, 14
Kromrivier Apple Co-operative strike, 46
KwaNdebele bantustan, 49, 60, 62, 125
KwaZulu bantustan, 5, 42, 44
　and bus boycotts, 211, 222
　industrial relations, 125, 147–8
　KwaMashu township, 6, 51
　Mhlabatini area, 44, 45
　Umlazi township, 6, 51

labour,
　contract *see* contract labour
　controls on, 3–12, 13
　immigrant, 15, 19, 78, 83, 92
　shortage of skilled, 16, 22, 73–4, 77, 78–9
　stratification of workforce, 83–4
　working conditions, 84–7
labour bureaux, 4–5, 15, 17, 31
Labour Party, 184
labour relations,
　and bantustans, 65, 125–6
　reforms, 250
　Riekert Commission, 13
　unfair practices, 122, 124, 163
　workers' challenges, 158–9
　see also trade unions; Wiehahn Commission
labour zoning, 15–16, 21
land,
　dispossession, xxv, 47
　hunger in bantustans, 41–3
　tenure, 30, 42, 250
Langa, Cape Town, 214
　conference, 194, 196
laws *see* industrial law; legislation (for Acts of Parliament)
Lebowa bantustan, 48, 125, 188
legislation, 113–26
　Abolition of Influx Control Act (1986), 23, 24, 52, 215
　Admissions of Persons to the Republic Act (1972), 19–20
　Aliens and Immigration Laws Amendment Act (1984), 20, 25
　Apprenticeship Act (1922), 78
　Bantu Homelands Citizenship Act (1970), 19
　Bantu Labour Regulations (1968), 4, 142
　Bantu Labour Relations Regulation Act (1973), 114
　Bantu Labour Settlement of Disputes Act (1953), 114, 177
　Basic Conditions of Employment Act (1983), 37, 73, 85–6, 121

Black Labour Regulations Act (1911), 34
Black Local Authorities Act (1982), 57
Black (Urban Areas) Consolidation Act (1945), 7–10, 18, 23
Co-operation and Development Act (1983), 18–19
Group Areas Act (1947), 58, 60, 228, 250
Industrial Conciliation Act (1924), 175
Industrial Conciliation Act (1937), 241
Industrial Conciliation Act (1956), 78, 79, 113, 177, 189
Industrial Conciliation Act (1979), 117, 142
Industrial Conciliation Acts (bantustans), 125–6
Industrial Conciliation Amendment Act (1980), 82, 117, 122, 168
Internal Security Act (Ciskei), 147
Intimidation Act (1982), 120, 121
Labour Relations Act (1953), 126, 241
Labour Relations Act (1977) (Transkei), 126
Labour Relations Amendment Act (1981), 117, 120–2, 124–5, 131, 134, 195, 205, 241, 242
Labour Relations Amendment Act (1988), 246
Labour Relations and Wages Act (1981), 72
Land Act (1913), 30, 41, 250
Land Act (1936), 41, 250
Machinery and Occupational Safety Act (1983), 89, 98, 121
Manpower Training Act (1983), 82
Masters and Servants Act, 30

Mines and Works Act (1911), 93
Mines and Works Act (redrafted 1986), 94, 97, 99, 107
Occupational Diseases in Mines and Works Act, 100
Orderly Movement and Settlement of Black Persons Bill (1981), 18
Physical Planning Act (1967), 5
Preservation of Pensions Bill (1981), 164–5
Prevention of Illegal Squatting Act (1951), 23, 24
Prisons Act (1959), 32
Public Safety Act (1953), 241
Regional Service Councils Act (1985), 58
Restoration of SA Citizenship Act (1986), 25
Slums Act (1979), 23
Taxation of Blacks Act (1984), 165
Temporary Removal of Restrictions on Economic Activities Act (1986), 72
Trespass Act, 10–11, 24
Workmen's Compensation Act (1941), 39, 87
Lesotho, labour recruitment, 92
Leyland motor company, 171
liaison committees, 140
local government, 55–7, 58–9, 238
finances, 55–6, 58–9
and housing, 235–6
and trade unions, 142, 143, 144, 193–4
'locals' *see* shop-stewards' councils

MACWUSA, 165, 192–3, 194, 195, 200
Malawi, workers, 15, 95
malnutrition, in bantustans, 45
Mamelodi, 230, 239
Mandela, Nelson, 229

Mangaung, 22
manufacturing industry *see* industry, general
Mavi, Joe, 143
MAWU, 71, 128, 141, 163, 170, 173, 184, 185, 200, 225
   and Industrial Councils, 151–3
   shop-stewards' councils, 186–7, 220
   strikes, 140–1, 167–8
   and UDF, 225, 228
   workers' health, 88–9
   see also NUMSA
May Day, 48, 108, 230–1, 234, 241, Table 8.1
meetings, 102, 138
   funerals, 48–9, 229, 230, 237
metal industry, xxiv, 161
   trade unions in, 151–5, 170, 185
Metro Cash and Carry, 161
MGWUSA (later MWUSA), 190, 193, 202, 224
MICWU, 179, 200
mining industry, xxi, xxiv, xxv, 15, 91–110
   asbestos, 99–100, 193
   housing, 100–2
   and stay-aways, 226, 230, 231, 234
   strikes, 102–5, 147, 174–5
   trade unions in, 105–10, 200
   wages, 63, 92–3, 102
   working conditions, 95–6, 96–9
Ministry of Mineral and Energy Affairs, 94
Mndaweni, James, 205
motor industry, xxiv, 70–1, 140, 161, 165–6
   trade unions in, 149–51, 184, 192–3, 200, 220
Mozambique, labour from, 30, 92
MWASA, 188
MWU (white union), 94
MWUSA, 202

NAAWU, 150–1, 168, 184, 185, 194, 200
   stay-aways, 228
   strikes, 150, 166
   in Uitenhage, 221, 222
   see also NUMSA
NACTU,
   affiliates *see* Appendix
   and COSATU, 136, 167, 204–5, 245
   formation, 180, 193, 202, Table 7.1
   split, 247
Naidoo, Jay, 198
Namibia, 127, 246
Nampak, factory occupation, 167
Natal, 5, 21
   bus boycotts, 115, 210–11, 222
   stay-aways, 228, 230, 231, 245
   strikes, 147, 164
   trade unions in, 183, 185, 220
National African Federated Chamber of Commerce (NAFCOC), 245
National Committee Against Removals, 38
National Education Crisis Committee (NECC), 227, 243, 245
National Federation of Workers, 192
National Housing Commission, 58
National Initiative for Reconciliation, 230
National Institute for Transport and Road Research, 62
National Manpower Commission, 29, 63, 76, 82, 120, *see also* Department of Manpower
National Party, 175, 181
National Training Board, 82
National Transport Commission, 61
National Transport Policy Study, 62

National Union of Furniture and
  Allied Workers, 179
NEHAWU, 201
Newcastle, bus boycotts, 211
NICISEMI, 151, 152, 153, 154
Nieuwenhuizen Commission, 97
night work, 86–7
Northern Transvaal People's
  Congress, 243
NUDAW, 179
NUFW, 188
NUM, 94, 147, 238
  and COSATU, 198, 227
  and CUSA, 188, 198
  growth of, 105, 106–7, 107–10
  and safety conditions, 98, 99
  and stay-aways, 231, 245
  and strikes, 133–4
NUMARWOSA (later NAAWU),
  137, 184
  strikes, 140, 149–50
NUMSA, 154, 155, 200, 227
NUTW, 88, 128, 129, 141, 155,
  168, 184, 186, 201, 243–4

OK Bazaars, 157, 161
Orange Free State, 238
Organisation of African Unity,
  Harare Declaration, 246–7
organisations,
  Defiance Campaign, 245–6
  political campaigns of, 183, 195,
    197, 209, 210
  and rent boycotts, 235
  repression of, 123, 240–2
  and trade unions, 171–3, 197,
    226, 239, 242, 243
  youth, 215, 239, 248
overtime, 86
OVGWU, 47, 144

paper industry, 155–6, 185, 201
Paper, Wood and Allied Union,
  47

parliament,
  Acts of *see* legislation
  tricameral, xvii, 57, 218–19, 246
pass laws, 3–4, 11, 32, 213–15
  popular resistance to, 13–14,
    181, 210, 213
  prosecutions under, 11–12, 14
  see also influx controls
pensions, strikes over, 164–5
Pick 'n Pay supermarkets, 157, 158,
  159, 162
police,
  attacks on strikers, 46, 128, 145,
    149
  bantustan, 48, 49
  and rent protests, 210
  riot, 143, 211
  and squatters, 215
  and striking miners, 103, 109
  and 'third force', 250
  violence by, 145, 149, 218, 219,
    226, 229, 230, 240–1
  see also State of Emergency;
    violence
political organisations *see* ANC;
  organisations; United
  Democratic Front (UDF)
political reforms, xvii–xviii, 218,
  246, 249–50
popular resistance, xvii–xviii, 197,
  209–10, 217–19
  and mining industry, 107, 108
  repression of, 123–4, 217
  in rural areas, 45–7, 48–9
  and trade unions, 115, 119, 131,
    183, 209
  see also boycotts; stay-aways;
    strikes
population,
  in bantustans, 6, 51
  controls, xxvi
  distribution of African, Table 1.1
Port Elizabeth, 192, 194, 196, 228
  consumer boycotts, 237–8

stay-aways in, 231
strikes, 143–4, 149, 159
Port Elizabeth Black Civic Organisation (PEBCO), 159, 216, 228
Port Elizabeth Youth Congress (PEYCO), 228
postal workers, strike, 145
POTWA, 145
poverty, 44–5, 64
PPAWU, 201
prescribed areas, 9–10
President's Council report, 18, 20–1, 23
Pretoria, 21, 140
Pretoria, Witwatersrand and Vaal area (PWV), xix, xxiv, 21, 24, 55
  boycotts, 235, 238
  stay-aways, 226, 229, 230, 234, 245
  trade unions in, 183, 188, 190
prison labour, 12, 32–3, 45
public sector,
  employment, xxiv
  trade unions, 142–6, 201
PUTCO, attacks on buses, 62
PWAWU, 141, 156, 167, 168, 184, 185, 201

Quail Commission, 41–2
Qwaqwa bantustan, 43, 45, 125, 188
  Botshabelo, 22, 45

racial discrimination, 145, 159, 159–61
Raditsela, Andries, death, 229
railways, 61, 134, 142, 143–4, 212
Ramaphosa, Cyril, 199
Rand Mines company, 105, 109
RAWU, 200, 201
redundancy (retrenchment), 162–4
Regional Service Councils, 58–9, 63

rents *see* boycotts, rent; housing
repression *see* police; violence
resettlement camps, 23, 24, 31
retail sector, 157–8, 161, 201
retrenchment agreements, 162–4
Rhikoto, Mehlolo, 14
Riekert Commission, 13, 15, 16–19, 21, 214
rural areas, 9, 29, 229, 243, *see also* farm labour

SAAWU, 71, 137, 190, 191–2, 197, 201, 202
  and Ciskei authorities, 126, 139, 146–7, 212–13, 223–4
SABMAWU, 144–5, 193–4
SABS, 152, 178
SACLA, 176
SACOS, 171, 222
SACTU, 45, 105, 181, 196, 220
  repression of, 127, 182, 189
SACTWU, 201
SACWU, 140, 166–7, 188, 205
SADF (S.A. Defence Force), 47, 49, 236, 246
SADWA, 85, 200
SADWU, 200
SAISWA, 176
SALDRU, 65–6
SAMWU, 105, 202
SARHWU, 145–6, 202
SASOL state company, 170, 185
SAT & LC, split, 177, 181
SATS, 117, 143–4, 145–6
SATV, strikes at, 146
Sebokeng, violence at, 219
SEIFSA, employers' federation, 18, 151, 155
Sentrachem company, 185
service sectors, unions, 182–3
SFAWU, 167, 184, 186, 198
  Simba Quix boycott, 172, 225
  see also FAWU
sharecropping, 30

Sharpeville massacre, 213
shop-stewards' councils, 172,
    186–7, 197, 204, 220, 225, 240
Sigma motor company, 140, 193
Simba Quix strike, 172, 225
sit-in actions, 134, 167
skills shortage, 73–4, 77, 78–9,
    82–3, 94, 115–16
Soshanguve, 22
South African Chloride, 139, 191
South African Communist Party,
    102, 181
South African Council of Churches
    (SACC), 38
South African Indian Council, 131,
    224
South African Women's Legal
    Status Committee, 71
Soweto, 198, 235–6, 239
    uprising (1976–7), 13, 62, 217
Soweto Civic Association (SCA),
    216
Soweto Students' Representative
    Council, 27
squatter camps, 14, 23–4, 55, 210,
    214–15, 249–50
State of Emergency,
    (1960), 47, 182, 213
    (1985), 123, 133, 210, 219, 227
    (1986–7), 108, 123, 124, 133,
        210, 231, 234, 235, 240
    (1988), xviii, 124, 236
stay-aways, 135, 141, 144, 181,
    204–5, 217–19, 227–31, 234,
    Table 8.1
    June, 231, 234, 245, 248, Table
        8.1
    May Day, 48, 108, 230–1, 234,
        241, Table 8.1
    PWV area, 226, 248
strike, right to, 117, 168
strikers,
    arrests of, 123, 138, 195
    casualties, 103, 105, 107, 145

police attacks on, 128, 143, 145,
    149
strikes, 127–9, 129–30, Table 6.1,
    Table 6.2
    against racial discrimination,
        145, 159
    by white workers, 160
    company-wide, 166–7
    and dismissals, 46, 118, 123,
        133, 143, 144, 147, 168
    on farms, 46–7
    for higher wages, 124, 127–8,
        130, 134
    legal, 151, 168
    metal industry, 151–5
    mining industry, 99, 102–5
    motor industry, 71, 149–51
    non-racial unity in, 130
    over pensions, 164–5
    over retrenchments, 128, 163–4
    public sector, 142, 143–6
    and recession, 128, 132, 158
    for recognition, 137–41
    restrictions on, 117–18, 120–1
    sympathy, 124, 160, 165, 166–7
Supreme Court strike ruling, 166–7
Surplus People's Project, 215
Swaziland, labour from, 92

TAWU, 188, 204, 205, 244
taxation, changes in, 165
TEBA, labour recruitment, 91–2
textile industry, 84, 141–2, 155, 201
TGWU, 71, 86, 144, 162, 184,
    198, 200, 202, 204, 205
Tomlinson Commission, 41
townships, 6, 50, 54, 235
    administration of, 55–7, 235
    civic associations, 133
    popular resistance in, 217–19,
        235
    and trade unions, 172–3
    see also bantustans; local
        government; urban areas

Index

Toyota, wage negotiations, 150
trade unions, xviii, 113, 219–27
  attacks on members, 148, 213, 242
  in bantustans, 125–6, 146, 248
  and closed-shops, 141–2, 142–3, 175
  community support for, 172–3, 239–40, 241
  craft (Coloured), 78, 141, 174–6
  cross-union co-operation, 153, 194–7, 204–5, 226–7, 243–4
  'established', 174–80
  factory committees, 128, 138
  general, 191–3, 196, 223–5
  growth of, xvii–xviii, 130, 139, 181–2, 185, 209, 219–20
  independent, 113, 114, 128, 144, 148, 170, 174, 178, 180–3
  and Industrial Councils, 65, 131, 148–9
  and industrial law, 118–19
  mergers, 199–202, Table 7.1
  in mining industry, 105–10
  non-racial, 136, 180, 187–8, 190, 191
  parallel, 106, 178
  political role of, 124, 134–5, 181–2, 192, 195, 198–9, 220, 223, 226–7, 246, 247–8
  public sector, 142–6
  and racial unity, 169–71, 247
  recognition of, 131, 137–41
  registration, 113–14, 116, 117, 118–19, 131, 136–7, 139, 190, 195
  repression of, 114, 127, 129, 135, 183, 191, 197, 240, 241–2
  restrictions lifted, 113–15
  and retrenchment, 162–4
  and Wiehahn Commission, 113, 114–17, 118
  and working conditions, 84–5, 89–90, 98, 158
  see also individual unions (by acronyms); organisations; strikes
trade unions, white, 77, 153, 175–6, 180
  closed-shop, 78, 174–6
  multi-racial, 176–80
training, 77, 82–3
Transkei bantustan, 5, 19, 47
  employment statistics, 43, Table 0.1(b)
  industrial relations, 125–6
transport, 59–61, 61–2
  railways, 61, 134, 142, 143–4, 212
  taxis, 61, 62–3, 211, 245
  see also boycotts, bus; commuters
Transvaal, 40, 71, 238
  strikes, 128, 234
  trade unions in, 184, 185, 190, 192
Transvaal Knitting Council, 155
Triomf chemical company, 140, 160
TUACC, 129
TUCSA, 147, 169–70, 180, 231
  affiliates, 177, 178, 184, 201
  closed-shops, 141–2
  and mixed unions, 176–80
TWIU, 128, 129, 141, 201

UAW, 149, 159, 184, 192
Uitenhage, 54, 149, 220, 231
Uitenhage Black Civic Organisation (UBCO), 220
UMMAWUSA, 200, 225
Unemployed Insurance Fund (UIF), 76–7
unemployment, 73–4, 76–7
  in agriculture, 40–1
  in bantustans, 5, 43–5, 74
  of women, 74, 76
  youth, 76, 228

Union Carbide, 147
Union of Johannesburg Municipal Workers, 143
United Democratic Front (UDF), 215, 240, 242, 245
  and COSATU, 243
  Simba Quix boycott, 172, 225
  and stay-aways, 228–9
  and trade unions, 183, 223, 226
  trade unions affiliated to, 190, 191, 192, 210, 223
  urban areas, controls on, xxvi, 3, 7–10, 12, 17, 21, Table 1.2(a)
  see also townships
urbanisation policy, 20–2, 23
UWUSA, 125, 140, 147–8, 249

Vaal Triangle, 133, 197, 210, 217, 235
Venda bantustan, 19, 49, 125–6, Table 0.1(b)
vigilante activity, 49, 148, 213, 215, 231, 239
violence,
  against councillors, 57
  against strikers, 103, 105, 107, 128, 143, 145, 148, 149, 213
  against workers, 37–8, 160–1
  ANC and Inkatha, 249–50
  Cape Town, 218
  PWV area, 226
  Soweto, 217, 235
  see also police; popular resistance
Volkswagen motor company, 150

Wage Boards, 65, 71, Graph 3.2
wages, 5–6, 63–4, 73, Graph 3.1, Table 3.1, Graph 3.2
  in bantustans, 44–5
  farm workers', 36–7, Table 2.1
  freeze, 135, 153
  low, 71, 127, 190
  minimum, 65, 125, 156–7
  in mining, 63, 92–3, 102
  real earnings, 64, 130, 133
  regional variations, 70–1
  women's, 71–3
  see also strikes
WCACC, 171
WCTA, 171
Welgemoed Commission (1983), 62
Western Cape,
  boycotts in, 131, 211
  Coloured labour preference policy, 6, 12, 17–18, 32
  Coloured population, 30, 32, 33, 169
  labour in, 14, 34, 35
  popular resistance in, 115, 229
  squatter camps, 214
  stay-aways in, 231, 245
  strikes, 46–7, 168
  trade unions in, 141–2, 189
Western Province Garment Workers Union, 201
white population, employment, xix, Table 0.1(a), Table 0.2
Wiehahn Commission, 13, 77
  and job reservation, 79, 82, 94
  and trade unions, 113, 114–17, 178
  and unregistered unions, 119–20
Wilgespruit, trade union conference, 195
Witwatersrand see Pretoria, Witwatersrand and Vaal area (PWV)
women,
  in agriculture, xxi, 32, 46
  domestic workers, 53–4, 72, 85, 90, 200
  and employment, 5, 10, 74, 76, 84, 213
  in industry, xxiv
  maternity leave, 161–2
  residence rights, 14

Index

in services sector, xxiv, 86–7
wage discrimination, 71–3
Woolworths, 157
work-to-rule actions, 129
workforce *see* employment; labour
working hours, 85–7
Workmen's Compensation Commissioner, 87

WPGWU (later GWU), 188, 189–90, 222
WPMAWU, 137, 169–70, 184

youth organisations, 215, 239, 248

Zebedelia Citrus estate, 46
Zimbabwe, labour from, 19, 92